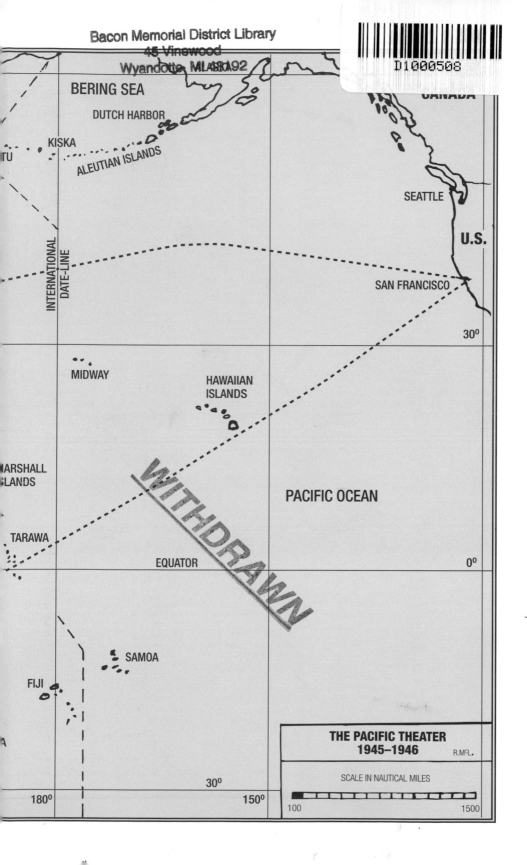

BERING SEA

DUTCH HARBOR

KISKA

ALEUTIAN ISLANDS

ALASKA

CANADA

SEATTLE

U.S.

SAN FRANCISCO

30⁰

INTERNATIONAL DATE-LINE

MIDWAY

HAWAIIAN ISLANDS

MARSHALL ISLANDS

TARAWA

PACIFIC OCEAN

EQUATOR

0⁰

SAMOA

FIJI

THE PACIFIC THEATER
1945–1946

R.McL.

SCALE IN NAUTICAL MILES

100   1500

30⁰

180⁰   150⁰

Boy Soldier

1. THE BOY SOLDIER ARRIVES AT THE FRONT. The cartoonist sees grim humor when fuzzy-cheeked 18-year-old replacements start arriving at the battle-fields to help the grizzled, older veterans. The caption reads: "I guess it's okay. The replacement center says he comes from a long line of infantrymen." From: Bill Mauldin, *Up Front*, (New York: Henry Holt & Co., 1945), P. 126.

Boy Soldier

Coming of Age During World War II

Russell E. McLogan, P.E.

TERRUS PRESS

Published in the United States by Terrus Press, Box 238, Reading, MI 49274

1st Printing 1998
2nd Printing 1999

Some of the names in this book are fictitious.

ISBN 0-9663444-0-5

Library of Congress Cataloging-in-Process Data

McLogan, Russell E., 1926–
    Boy soldier : coming of age during World War II
    Russell E. McLogan.—1st ed.
        p. cm.
    Includes bibliographical references and index.
    Preassigned LCCN: 98-60068
    1. McLogan, Russell E. 2. United States. Army—Biography. 3. World War, 1939–1945—Personal narratives, American. 4. Soldiers—United States—Biography. 5. Purple Heart. I. Title.

D811.M35 1998   940.54′8173
                                                 QBI98-207

Grateful acknowledgement is made to the following for permission to reprint previously published material:

"Ac-cen-tchu-ate the Positive": Lyric excerpt by Johnny Mercer/music by Harold Arlen. Copyright 1944 (Renewed) Harwin Music Co. All rights reserved.
AP/Wide World Photos: Figure no. 60 American soldiers demonstrating on page 323.
Barzun, Jacques and Henry F. Graff: Excerpt from their book *The Modern Researcher: Fourth Edition*, Orlando, Fla.: Harcourt, Brace & Co., copyright 1977.
Corbis-Bettmann L.L.C.: Figures no. 18. President Roosevelt on page 102; 20. Civilian internees on page 110; 46. Army nurse on page 228 and 57. Korean men on page 295.
Fussell, Paul: Excerpts from his book *Thank God for the Atom Bomb and other Essays*, New York: Ballantine Books, copyright 1988.
McGiffert, Robert C.: Excerpts and Figure Nos. 54 & 55 from his article "Surrender on Cebu" in *The American Legion Magazine*, Oct. 1981.
Moskowitz, Faye: Excerpt from an interview in the *Jackson (Mich.) Citizen Patriot*, Nov. 20, 1991.
National Geographic Magazine: Excerpts from "Flying Our Wounded Veterans Home" by Catherine Bell Palmer, September 1945; "Jap Rule in the Hermit Nation" by Willard Price, October 1945; "Your Navy as Peace Insurance" by Admiral Chester W. Nimitz, June 1947; and "With the U.S. Army in Korea" by General John R. Hodge, June 1947.
Sharpe, M.D., George: Excerpts from *Brothers beyond Blood*, Austin, Tex.: Diamond Books, copyright 1989.
Steinberg, Ralph and the Editors of Time-Life Books: Excerpts from their book *WWII:Return to the Philippines*, Alexandria, Va: Time-Life Inc., copyright 1980.
Terkel, Studs: Excerpts from *"The Good War": An Oral History of World War II*, New York: Pantheon Books, copyright 1984.
Underwood, Bill: Excerpt from his article "Freeing Camp Santo Tomas" in *The American Legion Magazine*, March 1995.
Willoughby, Charles A. and John Chamberlain: Map nos. 1, New Guinea and no. 2, The Battle of Leyte Gulf from their book *MacArthur 1941-1951*, New York: McGraw-Hill, copyright 1954.
Wilson, A.N.: Excerpts from his book *Incline our Hearts*, New York: Viking-Penguin Books, copyright 1989. Courtesy of Sterling Lord Literistic, Inc.
Wolff, Tobias: Excerpt from an interview in *Time Magazine*, April 19, 1993.

Dedicated to the men of the 6th Infantry Division, those who went the full 306 days of combat and those who were killed and wounded along the way. Real heroes, they did their best to save our way of living from the totalitarian forces that would have destroyed it. Amazingly, most of the survivors say they would do it again if their country called.

Contents

List of Maps

List of Figures

Preface and Acknowledgements

When I got out of the service, I looked at my 'tour' as routine-not unusual. Then . . . [after a while], I began to see myself and my former buddies as a rare breed. We actually fought . . . we fired rifles . . . we threw hand grenades . . . we were shot at . . . we took artillery . . . we were wounded . . . we were killed . . . we were the people they make movies and write books about. There weren't that many of us in the first place and those that were, that survived, were not great in numbers . . . [We] are a rarity.

—Combat Wounded Veteran[1]

For a long time after World War II, I was busy finishing my education, working, marrying, and raising six children. I enjoyed a full, demanding and satisfying life as life is meant to be lived. My Army experience, which seemed commonplace, was shunted off to distant memory banks and seldom thought about. Like the anonymous veteran, I considered it to be routine. Hadn't most of my generation been called upon to serve their country in this greatest of all wars?

Yes, they were. However, the vast majority had regular jobs in the services that were similar to civilian occupations. Some of them spent their whole time in school learning skills that they never had to use, because the war ended so abruptly. When I was a rifleman, training with thousands of other young men, riding a crowded troopship, cringing in a foxhole while shells landed around me, or cautiously moving down a jungle trail looking for the enemy, I thought combatants were in the majority, not some kind of a "rarity."

The picture of the inequality of sacrifice in the way that Americans fought World War II or, for that matter, all the other wars, emerged only in later life. This developed after talking to many veterans over a long period of time. I eventually learned that the ratio of infantry combat veterans to all the others who served is about one in twenty. Even artillerymen, airmen and navy gunners seldom came close to the enemy they were shooting at.

I am not disparaging anyone who served but did not fight. Certainly all those rear echelon jobs were necessary and the people who had them were dedicated and hard-working patriots. When a veteran tells me that he spent the war as a mail clerk in an Army Post Office, I say that I sure appreciated any mail that got through to me. If he was a cook or a baker, I tell him that the Army generally fed me quite well. I even enjoy a little Spam (once in a while) to this day. If he spent two years at college learning to be a Navy officer or on an Army air base training to fly an airplane and then was declared surplus and discharged a few weeks after the war ended, I say: "That's great! I would have done the same thing if given the chance." If they were medical technicians of any kind, I am grateful for the splendid health care that I received and the medical treatment for the wound and the malaria that I suffered. If they were involved in transportation, I tell them that I certainly am grateful to have been safely carried many thousands of miles on boats, trains, airplanes and trucks.

My actual combat experience was mercifully short so I can't claim to be a hero. The real heroes, at least the ones that I know personally, are the infantrymen of the 6th Infantry Division that I was sent to replace. Many had been fighting for a long time. Besides New Guinea, they fought all over Luzon, from the invasion on January 9, 1945, to the Purple Heart Valley campaign, the Cabaruan Hills, Munoz, the *Shimbu* Line, mopping up in Central Luzon and the campaign in Northern Luzon. The survivors were still at it when hostilities ended on August 15-a remarkable 219 days of continuous combat!

This fighting was done under extraordinary physical hardships, in rain, mud and heat, against an enemy who was seldom more that a few feet away and who fought fanatically until he was killed rather than surrender. More about them later but first let us look at how this book came to be written.

My father, Wendell G. McLogan, served in the Navy in World War I. He was a fireman on the U.S.S. *Huntington*, a troopship that carried the doughboys to France and back. He said he made eight crossings. What was it like for a twenty-year-old youth from Detroit, sailing through German U-boat infested waters in 1918? I do have a letter, written in the spring of 1919 to his sister, my aunt Katherine, when he was at the Brooklyn Navy yard and looking forward to getting out of the service. There are also oral traditions handed down to family members of what he spoke about. We will never really know the details of how he got into the Navy, what he had to eat, how he was trained, what he actually did on the various ships he served on or how he felt about World War I. He died in 1958 without leaving any written records.

Wayne Doty, a disabled veteran of the European Theater, once showed me a hand-written monograph his grandfather had written when he joined a Michigan regiment during the Civil War. It told in homey detail how he enlisted, rode a train to Detroit and learned to drill. He never finished it although he went on to fight in some battles and was wounded. I thought how wonderful it would have been for his children and grandchildren if he had finished it—or if my dad had written something similar.

In 1984, when there was a lot of media attention to the fortieth anniversary of such events as MacArthur's return to liberate the Philippines, it awoke in me an interest in that part of World War II, mostly because I had been there and this was a notable historic event that I had participated in. I decided to write a small volume of memoirs so that my children and grandchildren would have a record of my role.

I vowed to write the complete story from the day I was drafted until the day I was discharged. I would include all kinds of detail—the people I met, the places I went, what we had to eat, how I felt about it, et cetera. The generals—MacArthur, Kreuger and Eichelberger—had all written books but I had not seen very many written by the grunts at the bottom of the chain of command, those who were in the mud and had to do the dirty work.

Although I have a pretty good memory, I soon found out that what you remember needs to be structured on facts. I didn't have many records—my Army discharge, a menu of a Christmas dinner, a few pictures, medals and souvenirs. We were forbidden to keep a diary or journal, lest it fall into the hands of the enemy, and no one had thought any of my letters home worth saving.

Hoping to construct a narrative based on places and dates that would be in my Army records, I wrote to the National Personnel Records Center in St. Louis, Missouri. Under the Freedom of Information Act, these records are supposed to be available to former servicemen. Unfortunately, there was a large fire on July 12, 1973 that destroyed many World War II veteran files and mine were in the area of the worst damage.

I did get a chance to look through the records in my file at the Detroit office of the Department of Veterans Affairs which had copies of my medical records. Other names, dates and places had to be es-

2. THE COLONEL AND THE KID. The author meets his battalion commander after 42 years. Colonel Arndt L. Mueller was big, mean and heroic-looking in my memory. He turns out to be a kindly-looking grandfather, who was very generous in supplying me with information for this book. Photo taken by Terri McLogan at the 6th Infantry Division reunion in Peoria, Illinois, August, 1988.

tablished the hard way, by doing extensive research. I visited the National Archives in Washington, D.C. twice to obtain information on unit histories and combat intelligence reports for the time that I was in combat. I also revisited the Army posts where I was inducted, trained and sent overseas.

Art Tindall, a veteran living in nearby Osseo, Michigan put me in touch with the 6th Infantry Division Association. He had served in one of its artillery battalions. They have yearly reunions which I started attending in 1987 and met some of the veterans of Company K, 63rd Infantry, whom I hadn't seen in almost fifty years. Men like Olin Amidon, Tom Atchley, Eddie Barent, William Harrison, Hubert Hile, Arnold Kretch, Glen Laub, Orville Lewison, Ed Marek, Arndt

Mueller, John Munschauer, Jim Nail, Delmar Price, Wilford Schifsky, Gerry Van Mol, Jim Watters, Joe Wessely and Bob Wit. They have all been very helpful in providing long-forgotten names and events, even allowing me to videotape as they told stories from those heroic days of yore.

The reunions take place at various cities around the United States and involve side trips, business meetings and banquets. At Columbus, Georgia, in 1990, we had a visit to the Little White House in Warm Springs where President Roosevelt died, as well as a visit to Fort Benning, the home of the infantry. These are all worthwhile activities but what the men enjoy most is sitting around and reminiscing about their Army days.

Stories like the time machine gunner Ed Marek shot up the Japanese staff car, a 1940 model Lincoln Zephyr loaded with high ranking officers. Or, the training accident in New Guinea when a rifle grenade blew up and put Joe Wessely in the hospital for the next year and a half. He missed the Philippine Liberation but survived serious wounds to come back to the reunions in later life.

One of the wives remarked to me that she couldn't understand how they could come back, year after year, and listen to the same old stories over and over again. She missed the essential nature of these reunions. It is a chance for men from all over the country—who were brought together as strangers to serve the nation in its hour of need, trained and bonded together, were a team for a long time, endured horrible living conditions, did heroic deeds and then were disbanded and returned to their various homes—it gives them a chance to renew old friendships, relive exciting historical times, remember the dead, laugh at things that are not really funny and purge old ghosts.

The stories actually change from year to year as new men show up and give their points of view and add additional detail. It is quite dramatic when a veteran shows up for his first reunion and the last time anyone saw him was when he was dragged off a hill or carried out of the jungle horribly wounded. It is definitely not boring to the participants.

This book is more than a memoir. It is also a history book. I have incorporated many of the larger historical events: the liberation of the Philippines, the death of President Roosevelt, the dropping of the atomic bomb, the occupation of Korea, the demobilization story, and the trial of General Yamashita, because they shaped my life and affected or caused what happened to me in the Army. I have also included some of the music we listened to, the books that I read, the movies, and the USO shows that we saw and other items of popular culture because they aid in understanding the nature of those times.

So many people helped me to finish this book that I hope I don't leave anyone out of my acknowledgements. Thanks go to my wife Terri, who had to put up with my determination to get this book written when she wanted other things done. She also took pictures and helped with the research. To my daughters: Betsy McLogan Carlisle for editing and suggesting word changes and Mary McLogan Calligan for running numerous copies of chapters.

My earliest attempts at writing memoirs, before I got a word processor, were all typed by Dorothy Wilson. Credit is also due to Eva Martin, Connie Britner, Dr. Janet Kaufman and Michael Joyce, all teachers of writing whose courses I took at Jackson Community College to prepare for writing this book.

I also owe a lot to Linda Peckham who teaches "Writing for Publication" at Lansing Community College. She read the whole manuscript, corrected many errors in punctuation and made many valuable suggestions to improve the readability of the book.

Special thanks are due to Colonel Arndt L. Mueller, U.S.A., Retd. He was the 3rd Battalion commander when I was in the Philippines and Korea and has provided me with extensive information. I have also quoted liberally from his writings. John Munschauer, who arrived as a replacement officer a month before me, has also provided me with material. His written account of the taking of Hill A was used to supplement my narrative. E.R. "Sammy" Simpson, an officer in Service Company in Korea, provided valuable information and pictures.

My thanks to Bob Wit for putting me in touch with Tom Atchley, my platoon leader. Tom was very helpful in providing me with names and events that happened while I served with him. Harry Nagle, a retired federal prosecutor, helped me get a pass into Eglin Air Force Base so that I could do research at the base library while wintering in northwest Florida. He also invited me to reunions of his outfit, the 49th Fighter Group, which saw action in the Philippines. Harry was a ground crew chief and introduced me to P-38 pilots who provided me with data on the war from the air. Jim Gallagher, their communications officer, provided me with information on the comedian, Joe E. Brown, and pictures of the Mexican airplanes.

I am indebted to Wayne McDaniel of the University of Florida Alumni Office for providing me with biographical information on Colonel Everett M. Yon, who was my regimental commander. Also to Jack J. Adrian, Veteran Services Officer at the Detroit office of the

Department of Veteran Services, who provided me with the opportunity to peruse my medical records and to his staff who provided me with copies of the ones I selected.

There were also many anonymous librarians all around the country who helped me look up facts and become familiar with computerized card catalogs and micro-film machines. To name just a few: Mitchell Public Library, Hillsdale, Michigan; Hillsdale College Library; Jackson Public Library, Jackson Michigan; Michigan Historical Library, Lansing, Michigan; Scottsdale Public Library, Scottsdale, Arizona; Lake Forest Public Library, Lake Forrest, Illinois; and the San Francisco Public Library.

I have also been encouraged by numerous friends, relatives and even complete strangers who made complimentary comments or offered helpful suggestions. It is amazing how friendly people are when they find out that you are writing a book!

Studs Terkel, in his introduction to *"The Good War"—An Oral History of World War Two*, quotes an ex-combat soldier:

> "I was in combat for six weeks . . . I remember every hour, every minute, every incident of the whole forty- two days. What was it— forty years ago?" As he remembers aloud, the graying business man is transformed into a nineteen-year-old rifleman . . . "World War II has affected me in many ways ever since. In a short period of time, I had the most tremendous experience of all of life: of fear, of jubilance, of misery, of hope, of comradeship, and of endless excitement. I honestly feel grateful for having been a witness to an event as monumental as anything in history, and in a very small way, a participant."[2]

My sentiments exactly! A good reason to write a book.

Russ McLogan
Hillsdale, Michigan
December 6, 1996

ONE

The Boy
Becomes a Soldier

You're in the Army now, you're not behind the plow.
You'll never get rich, you son-of-a-bitch, you're in the
Army now.
            —Tell Taylor and Ole Olson

I never expected to be in the Army—*especially* as a combat soldier. Nor did I want to be one. My role as a combatant in World War II was determined for me by the inexorable forces of history, the timing of my birth and my genetic inheritance. When I came of age in 1944 to serve my country in its greatest peril, the battle had been joined all over the world. The Army had an acute need for combat soldiers to replace the thousands who were being killed or severely wounded every week in France, Italy and the islands of the South Pacific.

The demand for service troops and technicians—the clerks, cooks, bakers, mechanics, truck drivers, doctors, nurses, lawyers, accountants, postal workers, laborers and every other administrative, technical or service occupation it takes to field a modern Army, Navy, or Air Force at war—had all been fairly well met by this third year of the conflict.

While I had played at being a soldier when I was a little boy, that was only for fun. I also played at being a fireman, a cowboy, a policeman or a priest. When we were very young, I fought with my brother Bob, often and viciously, but I really didn't enjoy fighting. I was usually defending myself against his aggression. He was a year younger

1

but grew faster and soon was bigger than me. There was a lot of sibling rivalry until our mother died when I was eight years old. After we went to live with my paternal grandparents, who didn't tolerate fighting, we seemed to get along better. I would also avoid playground or neighborhood bullies who would try to start a fight.

I had a childhood friend, Bill Sincock, from my class at St. Benedict School and later on in the Boy Scouts who I played with a lot. We built forts and pretended to be soldiers. Adults who didn't know us very well would assume we were brothers because of our similarities.

Aviation was our big interest in our early teen years and we built model airplanes together. Bill followed me to the Henry Ford Trade School where we were getting our high school education when the Japanese attacked Pearl Harbor. There was a rush of patriotism as young men volunteered to help avenge this dastardly attack on our country.

The Ford Trade School was a vocational high school where we alternated shop work and classroom studies. It was also a private school run by the Ford Motor Company and was located in the heart of the vast Rouge plant in Dearborn, Michigan. My job of millwright took me to the air tool repair Department where Bill was working in late December, 1941. I was surprised and skeptical when he told me that he was joining the Marines.

"You can't, you're too young!" I exclaimed. We were both 15 years old, although he would turn 16 in early January.

"I'm going," he declared. "I want to fight those rotten Japs!"

His attitude was typical of a lot of Americans. There were long lines of patriotic young men at the military recruiting offices. Bill made it into the Marines in January and by August I was getting letters from him postmarked "Somewhere in the British Solomon Islands." I never saw him again. He didn't even get a furlough home.

Likewise, parochial school classmates Joe McCollum, Gil and Howard Lubin and Charlie Ford all joined up over the next year or so. The minimum age was 17 with your parents' permission but they faked their age or the recruiting officers were accommodating. I wanted to be an airplane pilot and that required two years of college. I planned to finish my education before I had to serve my country. Besides, the money I earned at the Ford Trade School was a big help to my grandparents. They were struggling to raise six grandchildren on a small pension and the rent from the upstairs flat.

As we approached graduation from high school, most of us in the class of 1944 realized that the war was going to continue for a while. We would all be in it unless we were classified 4-F by the local draft

2

boards, which had been drafting 18-year-old boys since the latter part of 1942. Nobody that I knew wanted to be rejected as physically unfit. That seemed to be a disgrace, although actually, of the 17,955,000 men examined for induction from 1941 through 1945, 35.8 percent (6,420,000) were rejected as physically or mentally unfit.[1] It didn't seem that high at the time, but the generation that grew up during the Great Depression was not a healthy bunch.

The opportunity to get into the Navy or Air Corps, where the "good" or the "safe" jobs were, had to be taken during your seventeenth year because the day that you became 18 years old, you were under the control of your local draft board. In 1944, those draft boards had large monthly quotas to process into the war machine which usually meant *Army*. None of us wanted to become "cannon fodder."

I was torn between the Army Air Corps and the Navy. I dreamed of flying airplanes but my Dad had talked so much about his Navy experience that I had felt drawn to it. My cousin, Dick Farrell, had joined the Navy when he graduated from college in 1942. It seemed a family tradition to favor the Navy over the Army.

However, the Army Air Corps recruiters visited Mr. Ford's school first. Anyone, the announcement said, who was interested in applying for pilot's training could sign up for a test to be given at the school in the spring of 1943. By this time they had dropped the two-years-of-college requirement and were accepting as cadets anyone who was 17 and would soon be graduating from high school.

I passed their test and was sent a notice to go to Selfridge Field, near Mount Clemens, Michigan, for a physical examination. Much to my surprise, I was rejected for defective color perception. I couldn't read some of the numbers on the color charts which were made of little circles of various hues. What looked like a three was really an eight or vice versa.

Shocked and disappointed, I learned that I had inherited from my mother a defective gene that caused color blindness. It occurs when a person lacks certain cone-shaped color sensing cells in the retina of the eyes. "Blindness" is really a misnomer because most men who suffer from it—about one in twelve in the general population—only have the condition to a limited degree. Very few are completely color deficient. I, for instance, never have any trouble with traffic lights and can readily distinguish between the various colors of the spectrum. The problem is with subtle shadings. I never knew that I had this condition until the Air Corps doctors tested me for it.

Defective color perception is rare in women but they routinely pass on the defect to their sons because males have only one X-chromosome. Because the color defect genes are recessive, a woman can inherit defective color vision only if the same defect is carried in both her X-chromosomes, a coincidence that occurs infrequently.[2]

In the fall of 1943, the Navy came to our school to recruit boys for their V-12 College program where you attended the school of your choice while training to become a naval officer. Again I passed their mental tests and was notified to go to downtown Detroit to the Book Building for a physical examination. The Navy doctors quickly discovered my defective color perception and also rejected me.

After this double rebuff, a tremendous blow to my self-esteem, I decided to attend college while waiting to be drafted. If the Army also rejected me, I would be that much farther along with my life and education. Unlike the Vietnam War, there were no college deferments for attending school during World War II.

At the Henry Ford Trade School, if you completed the academic part before you were 18, as I did, they kept you on as a senior student, working in the various shop departments until your birthday and your draft status was finalized. If you passed your physical and were classified 1-A they kept you on until you were called into service, usually only a matter of weeks. However, if you were rejected for military service (4-F), the school found a job for you with the Ford Motor Company, generally in the huge tool and die Building at the Rouge plant in Dearborn. Here you continued your training as a skilled machinist by working and attending the Ford Apprentice School. Senior students at the Trade School were given an immediate raise of 20 cents an hour as an incentive to stay with the school.

Jobs were plentiful and labor scarce when I graduated, so the school authorities were anxious to accommodate me when I told them I had enrolled at the University of Detroit, College of Engineering. Arrangements were made for me to work a partial second shift in the grinding machines department from 5:30 to 11:30 P.M. every night so that I could attend classes during the day.

Our graduation ceremonies were held in the Fordson High School auditorium on Saturday, January 29, 1944. Henry Ford II came to pass out the diplomas and shake each graduate's hand. He had been recently released from his Navy post because the government wanted the Ford Motor Company, which was heavily involved in war production, to continue without problems. The elder Henry Ford was 80 years old and in failing health. Edsel Ford had died the previous May. Henry II, the grandson, appeared quite youthful being only about eight years older than most of us graduating. In his speech, he made

3. THE BOYS OF THE JANUARY, 1944, T-A-1 CLASS, Henry Ford Trade School, pose for a group portrait in the school library. The author is standing at the far right.

some remarks about being on an apprenticeship just like we were. It sounded good, but he was being groomed to head the mighty Ford Motor Company, not learn the tool and die-making trade.

Most of my classmates were soon off to the Navy or the Air Force. Others began long working careers with the Ford Motor Company. I started my college courses the following Monday morning. There were only 27 starting freshmen in the College of Engineering, mostly 4-F's or 17-year-olds like myself. Total enrollment at the University that fall had been 1,800[3] in all its colleges.

Women, who were exempt from the draft, were numerous, about seven hundred on campus, but few in number in the Engineering Building. However, I did have a couple of classes in some of the other buildings. In the chemistry building, we were assigned seats in the lecture arena alphabetically and I found myself seated between two young ladies who had both failed Chem 101 in the fall semester and were repeating it because of parental pressure. The three of us did our laboratory experiments together which was a refreshing change from the all-male atmosphere of the Ford Trade School.

There were also about four hundred soldiers on the campus. They were getting a college education in the Army Specialized Training Program, mostly engineering-oriented, until the Army needed them. This took place during the middle of the semester when they were sent to Camp Polk, Louisiana for assignment to an armored division.[4]

I found the course content and the amount of homework the professors gave out to be a big shock after the relatively easy workload of high school, but I took it all in stride. After the rigid rules and regimentation of the automotive pioneer's industrial school, the freedom and intellectual stimulation of the college campus was refreshing. The University of Detroit is a Jesuit institution and I had priests for four of the five courses that I was taking. They were very learned men and, because of the low enrollment, took a personal interest in all of their students. Father Edward Dowling, S.J., who taught mechanical drawing and was my advisor, was especially helpful.

Some of my classes would begin as early as 8:30 A.M. Grandma would pack a huge combination lunch/supper and off I would go on the Six Mile bus, loaded down with food and books. My last class got out at 4:30 P.M. and I would take two busses to get from the campus at Six Mile and Livernois to the Rouge plant in Dearborn. There I would work my shift, grinding parts for the war effort, until 11:30. Then it was home on another bus and street car, where I fell in bed about 1:00 A.M. Homework had to be done in the free hours between classes or on weekends. I was one busy kid but managed to finish the semester with mostly Bs.

During this time, I applied to the Merchant Marine Academy to become an engineering cadet. I knew that they had the same physical requirements as the Navy but they were also known to give waivers for defective color perception to engineering officers because they served below decks where this would not be a problem. In reply to my application, they sent me to the Grosse Isle Naval Air Station for a special color test. It was done in a darkened room with colored lights. They found that the defect was in the blue/violet area of the color spectrum. Unfortunately, the Merchant Marine Academy had a surplus of applicants that year and my waiver was denied.

In May, when I turned 18, I registered for the draft as required by law. At my physical examination, my defective color perception was noted, but I was assured that it was no bar to getting in the Army. There were jokes in circulation at that time about how the Army took everybody including the blind, deaf, dumb, the armless or the legless and then adapted them to some simple tasks the Army needed done.

Part of the examination was a two or three minute session with a psychiatrist whose main purpose was to determine the sexual orientation of the potential soldiers. He delivered his questions with a kind of man-to-man *bonhomie*, mostly about your interests and social life. Then, leaning forward like a priest hearing confession, he asked confidentially: "Do any screwing?"

I thought that was funny and had to suppress a laugh. I almost said: "Don't I wish!" While I was secure in my male sexuality, was attracted to girls and had severe crushes on several of the prettier classmates at St. Benedict School, I was also extremely shy and hadn't had much experience with members of the fair sex. The few dates that I had had in my young life consisted mostly of taking virtuous young ladies to well- chaperoned school activities.

During World War II, many studies were made of the psycho-sociological profile of men selected to serve in the Armed Forces. I apparently participated in one because I received a letter to appear at the Rackham Building in the cultural center of Detroit on an evening in late July. Attendance was voluntary and other veterans that I have talked to do not remember having this experience.

The sociologist turned out to be a woman from nearby Wayne State University. We chatted for an hour or so about my family, work, school, ambitions, social life and how I felt about being drafted. She asked a lot of penetrating questions on topics I hadn't given much thought to. At the end she said that I should do well in the Army and that, based on my high I.Q. and vocational training, would be assigned to some technical specialty. She also advised me to get my affairs arranged so as to be able to leave home in early September.

A few weeks later I met Dr. Byrnes, the chiropractor, on the corner of Woodward and Six Mile Road. When I told him that I was going into the Army in a couple of weeks, he assured me, "You don't have to worry, the war will be *over* by Christmas!"

A lot of people, like him, were highly optimistic at that time because the Allies had finally opened a second front by landing forces on the Normandy Peninsula on D-Day, June 6, 1944. After some bitter fighting, the Allies had broken out of the beachhead and were racing for Paris. At the time Dr. Byrnes and I were talking, there had also been another landing in southern France and an assassination attempt on Hitler's life by some of his generals.

On the Italian Front, a second beachhead had been established at Anzio in January with the hope of racing on to Rome. Stiff resistance from the Germans and poor planning by the Allies spoiled this scenario, but the Germans finally gave way and the Allies entered the Eternal City on June 4. They now occupied more than half of the Italian peninsula.

Meanwhile, the Russians had driven the Germans back into Poland and were threatening Warsaw. It looked good in Europe, but actually the Allies were a long way from the unconditional surrender they were seeking.

In the Pacific Theater, there was much progress but also a long way to go. By the summer of 1944, the island-hopping campaign had seen the conquest of Guadalcanal, Bougainville, Tarawa, Eniwetok, and Kwajalein, landings made at various places on the huge island of New Guinea and even some American territory—Attu, Kiska, and Guam—recovered. However, most of the Dutch East Indies and all of the Philippines were still in Japanese hands. Given the Japanese propensity to fight to the last man, victory was not in sight there either. Dr. Byrnes turned out to be a poor prophet.

In 1942, Grandma had rented the upstairs flat to the Diamond family. Their son Hugh, who was a classmate of mine at St. Benedict School and also a fellow altar boy and Boy Scout, received his induction notice to report the same day as I did. That was great news! I would have a buddy, a familiar face alongside me as I faced an unknown future.

I don't remember any fear or reluctance to go on my part. There was more a feeling of excitement about leaving home for parts unknown, with thrilling adventures and foreign travel ahead. I hadn't been to very many places in my young life. The draft notice had also said something about greetings from the president (meaning Roosevelt himself) and about being selected by a board composed of your friends and neighbors. It felt good to be picked for an important mission. How naive we are at age eighteen!

In retrospect, it now seems incredible that America would grind up its young boys in such a manner! My own sons seemed so youthful and immature at that age. I am sure that Hugh Diamond and I were similarly as callow that day as we went off to war together. However, at that time, Hitler was reaching down into the ranks of Germany's 14-year-olds to feed his faltering war machine and the Japanese were preparing their youngest for kamikaze suicide missions. In the light of that history, it is a bit more understandable.

So, there were two families weeping on our front porch when we left. Hugh's older brother, Dan, accompanied by his father, drove us downtown to the Michigan Central Depot where our draft notices told us to report. At the railroad station, the two older men gravely shook our hands and wished us well before departing. I was glad none of the women had come along. There had been enough tears on the front porch to last me for a long time.

We boarded a train with a group of other inductees and headed for Chicago. It was warm and sunny, the kind of a mid-September day that favors the Great Lake State. We went into the dining car for supper and watched the mid-Michigan scenery fly by as we ate. I found all this to be very exciting as I had never eaten on a train before.

In Chicago, we marched as a group from the depot to the Hotel Stevens where we were booked for the night, six or eight to a room. When we were told to enjoy our last night of freedom, a lot of the boys went out to find adventures in downtown Chicago. However, Hugh had an older sister Helen, who was a Navy nurse and was stationed there. He telephoned her and we took a cab to the apartment she shared with several other nurses. After eating all her cookies and ice cream, we took a cab back to the hotel and went to bed.

We were awakened early the next morning and fed breakfast at the hotel's coffee shop. Afterwards we marched to the Chicago induction center which was nearby. Most Detroit area men went through the Detroit induction center, but for some reason, probably capacity considerations, we were sent to Chicago. My records show that I was inducted at Chicago, Illinois, although my draft board was in Detroit.

At the center, one of the first things that I noticed, was a crudely lettered chalkboard that read:

	Army	Navy
White	4	1
Colored	15	1

We were moving along in a single column. It parted as we passed the sign, those going into the Army kept moving ahead, while every fifth white male was taken out for service in the Navy. Hughie, standing in front of me, was the lucky fifth man and disappeared into the Navy. It would be two long years before I would see him again.

The processing consisted of repeating the physical examination all over again and some preliminary orientation with a movie about how we were about to enter the greatest Army in the world. Then we were gathered into a group of about 30 for the swearing in ceremony. This involved taking a step forward and swearing an oath of allegiance to the Army of the United States of America.

Much to my surprise, a member of this group was Stanley Zaija, a fellow engineering student at U of D. He had been in the large group on the train and at the hotel but we had not seen each other until the swearing-in ceremony. This was great. I had already been separated from my friend Hugh Diamond, but now I had another comrade with whom to share the unknown future.

We rode the train to Fort Sheridan, located about 25 miles north of Chicago. The fort, named after Civil War General Philip H. Sheridan, had been created through the efforts of leading Chicago industrialists who thought they needed federal troops nearby because of disasters like the Great Chicago Fire of 1871 and the Haymarket Square riots of 1886. By donating the land and enlisting the help of General Sheridan, who had his headquarters there and was active in social affairs, they persuaded Congress to create the fort in 1887.[5]

In 1894, on the occasion of the Pullman Company strike, the Fort's soldiers were called upon to keep order. They moved into Lake Front Park in downtown Chicago and set up their tents. Their presence was enough to deter further incidents of violence. That was the only time that the original purpose of the fort was discharged. Starting with the Spanish-American War, the fort became a troop movement center. Between the wars it was primarily a garrison for infantry, cavalry and artillery units. Newly commissioned Lieutenant George C. Patton served there from 1909 to 1911, his first posting.

During both World Wars, Fort Sheridan served as an induction and midwest training center for men and women entering the Army from Illinois, Wisconsin and Michigan. When the draft was initiated in 1940, the fort became one of four Recruit Reception Centers in the country and was the first to actually receive the new inductees. By the time that I arrived there on September 15, 1944, the Army had also created a Separation Center to out-process some of the thousands it had taken in. Between the Recruit Reception Center and the Separation Center, Fort Sheridan processed approximately a half million men and women into and out of the Army during World War II, including the first soldier separated through the point system.[6]

I remember spending the first five days in quarantine. That meant staying in the barracks all the time except when on official Army business. We were marched as a group to the mess hall for our meals which were served cafeteria style on large stainless steel trays that had pockets for the various food items. I was surprised to be served by German prisoners of war who worked in the kitchens and did other menial jobs at the fort. They looked quite ordinary, although old and foreign looking, not members of a "super race."

That year, Fort Sheridan had assumed administrative control over all prisoners of war camps in Illinois, Wisconsin and Michigan. A total of 15,000 prisoners performed labor on farms, in factories, and on civilian construction projects in the three state area. Some 2,000, mostly from the Afrika Korps, were interned at the fort performing K.P. and maintenance type work. Nine are buried in the post's cemetery, having died while in captivity. The others were all repatriated back to Germany before I got back from overseas.[7]

During this time we were also going through the initial processing that turns a civilian into a soldier. We were measured and given many uniforms, shoes and equipment which smelled new and felt stiff. Everything was an olive drab brown, even the underwear and towels.

We were given intelligence and mechanical aptitude tests. The sergeant administering them admonished us to do as well as we could on these tests because the Army was very much interested in placing us in jobs where our education and abilities could best be utilized. "Selection and placement is a very serious business," he said. "We want to put all the round pegs in the round holes and vice-versa."

We wandered for miles while stark naked, being poked and prodded, given medical shots, filling out forms, and answering numerous questions. At one point in the proceedings, I remember entering a room and being told to stand on a small stool and turn my five-foot-eight-inch tall, 140 pound, skinny body, slowly around while a couple of doctors looked me over. I thought I heard one of them say "Infantry!"

"What did you say?" I asked.

"Keep moving, soldier," was the only reply I received.

The sergeant giving the aptitude tests must not have been coordinated with the doctors. They were looking for low-profile-target specimens for the infantry.

We also got haircuts and assembled for a group picture. It's amazing how soon everybody started looking and talking the same. The rather diverse group that arrived on the train started to be cohesive. We were also taken out to the parade grounds and given some preliminary lessons in close order drill by a large, black drill sergeant in a Smoky-the-Bear hat who didn't seem at all happy with his job. I'd had some experience in marching from my Boy Scout days but others were not so fortunate and felt the sergeant's wrath when they went left after he said to go right.

After the five days of quarantine were over, we were farmed out to various parts of the fort to perform menial labor while awaiting orders for shipment to a basic training camp. The first job I had was at one of the mess halls peeling potatoes. It wasn't too bad. There was a certain camaraderie as we were all new and getting used to the Army's strangeness. Somebody told a joke and that inspired others to tell their favorites. The jokes got dirtier and dirtier as the mountains of potatoes disappeared and the huge aluminum pots filled with bald, white spuds. When the potatoes were all peeled and we thought we were done, the Mess Sergeant spoiled our expectations by bringing out an enormous amount of carrots for us to scrape. After the noon meal we spent hours cleaning dirty cooking pans and getting food ready for the next meal. It seemed like a never-ending job.

The next day I was assigned to work in the Separation Center. Even in those days Fort Sheridan was busy discharging people although they took in a lot more than they let go. I reported to two medical technicians whose part in the separation process was to give the veterans a urine test. My job was to pour the urine from the collection jars into test tubes and add some chemicals. Depending on the color it changed to, this indicated the presence of sugar or albumen. We also checked the specimens for specific gravity. After this information was noted on the records by the technicians, I would then wash the test tubes and receiving jars.

One day a group of WACs came through. This created some excitement, since women soldiers were rare. Their urine tested about the same as the men—none had anything wrong show up in their samples. The whole process seemed useless to me. Nearly all of those we tested, men or women, had healthy urine. The Army must have had other reasons for discharging these soldiers.

4. NEWLY INDUCTED SOLDIERS line up for picture-taking at Fort Sheridan, Illinois, September, 1944. The author is crouched in the front row at the extreme left. Stanley Zajia is in the front row at the extreme right.

The sergeants had been doing this for some time, one for almost two years. "We're piss experts," they would joke. "It's an important contribution to the war effort!" The senior man was from New Jersey and was going home on furlough at the end of the week. He used to burst into song every so often, treating us to renditions of "Don't Get Around Much Anymore" and "I'll Walk Alone," popular songs of the time.

On Friday night there was a USO dance in the gymnasium with a live band and girls from the local communities. Although the soldiers outnumbered the women about 10 to one, I did manage to get in a few dances. A young lady from Lake Forrest asked me how long I had been in the Army. When I admitted that it was just over a week, she expressed surprise because my hair didn't look real short or botched like most of the new recruits' haircuts she had observed. That made me feel good. I was even starting to look like a soldier.

The sergeant in charge of our barracks said that we could sign up for weekend passes so most of us did. Stanley and I decided to go home. Saturday afternoon, we rode the train together to downtown Chicago. When we went to purchase tickets to Detroit, Stan discovered that he had left his wallet back at the barracks. I offered to lend him the money but he insisted on getting it from the Red Cross. He looked up their address in the phone book and we walked over to their office. After a long session with the manager, he emerged with the money.

It was a short visit home as I arrived there very late Saturday night and had to start back Sunday afternoon. I enjoyed telling people that Army life wasn't bad, so far, and showing off my new uniforms. I wore my field jacket home which got a lot of attention. This was a new item of Army apparel—to be worn in the field with fatigues—not with suntans as I was dressed. One of the soldiers on the train told me that I was "out of uniform" and would get in trouble. No one had told me that I couldn't wear it home and the M.P.s at the railroad station didn't bother me. If the Army gave me all those clothes, I figured that I could wear them.

The next day, Stan told me that he had been "bingoed," slang for getting notified that he was alerted to be packed and ready to ship out. He didn't know where he was going. Soon, the rest of us in the barracks found our names on lists pinned to the bulletin board. The Army was thorough. They told us what to wear and what to carry and what was to be shipped through in our barracks bags. However, because of wartime security, not *where* we were going.

A rail spur ran right through the fort so that the thousands of soldiers that were processed there could board the trains inside the grounds without having to be transported to a railroad depot. We chugged out of there early one morning in late September, heading south. When the train stopped, usually in a small town, we would lean out the windows and ask people, often small boys hanging around the depot, where we were. Our route was south through Illinois, then southwesterly through Missouri and then into Oklahoma. We were on that train the better part of two days.

There was a long delay in Tulsa. I remember looking out the train window and seeing a big sign, "Tulsa Welcomes Dewey," with a lot of people standing around waiting for the presidential candidate. The 1944 presidential campaign was in full swing and the Michigan native was making a vain attempt to unseat the ever-popular FDR, who was running for a fourth term.

After awhile, a lieutenant came through the car that I was riding in and made an announcement: "I can tell you now where you are going. We have been detaching several rail cars of soldiers who are going to Fort Sill, Oklahoma, for basic training in the artillery. The rest of us are heading for Camp Hood, Texas. There you will be getting your basic training at the IRTC—Infantry Replacement Training Center."

There were a few groans as we realized that our fates had been sealed, but the lieutenant, who was an infantry officer, said that infantry training was the best you could get and we would all be better men for it no matter where our Army paths led us. As for my friend Stanley Zaija, he was lucky. He took his basic training with the Army Engineers at Fort Belvoir, Virginia, and served out the war as an Army surveyor. It was many years before I saw him again.

TWO

Killer's Kollege

*We must hate with every fiber of our being. We must
lust for battle; our object in life must be to kill; we must
scheme and plan night and day to kill. There need be no
pangs of conscience, for our enemies have lighted the
way to faster, surer, crueler killing. They were past
masters. We must hurry to catch up with them if we are
to survive.*
— Lt. Gen. Leslie J. McNair[1]

You shall not kill.—Exodus 20:13

In March of 1992, I re-visited Camp Hood, Texas. It had been 47
years since I had endured basic training there and I was curious
to see what it was like now. What I saw was nothing like what I remembered.

Driving westward from I-35 at Belton on a modern superhighway,
the Central Texas Expressway, the first thing that I noticed was that
the former village of Killeen was now a four-exit metropolis of 63,500
citizens.[2] My memory was of a crossroads hamlet, just outside the
camp, with hundreds of idle soldiers standing on its few street cor-
ners. We called it "Guadal-Killeen" then because it might just as well
have been that far-off island in the Pacific. There wasn't much there
of interest to us.

The camp, now known as Fort Hood, had grown and prospered
tremendously. I remembered a scene of mud, temporary wood buildings and barbed wire fences, a picture of a concentration camp in a
remote area, about what the Nisei were thrown into at the beginning
of the war. Modern Fort Hood, with its manicured lawns, brick buildings, houses, schools, churches, banks and traffic-filled streets is now

16

the proud home of two historic Army divisions: the 1st Cavalry (MacArthur's pet division), and the 2nd Armored (Hell on Wheels) Division, once commanded by General George C. Patton.

Fort Hood is also the headquarters of the III Mobile Armored Corps, and its 339 square miles is home to more than 39,000 soldiers, 15,000 family members and nearly a billion dollars worth of tactical vehicles. When you add the retirees, survivors, and off-post military family members, it supports a population of 192,125.[3]

On the telephone, the female captain in the Public Affairs Office said that Fort Hood was an "open" military reservation and that I could drive right in and look around. "Be sure and visit our two museums and talk to our curators," she replied in response to my inquiry about historic information.

What I learned was that—unlike Fort Sheridan which came into being during the late nineteenth century so that the "Robber Barons" of Chicago could have their own private army to keep their obstreperous workers in check—Camp Hood was created because the Army needed a large reservation to develop an American response to Hitler's tank warfare in the early 1940s. There were also promoters and politicians most anxious and willing to have a huge Army post located in the central Texas area. It would be economically stimulating after the stagnation of the Great Depression. Mainly responsible was Frank W. Mayborn, publisher of the *Temple Daily Telegram* and owner of radio station KTEM, who promoted the area. Assisting him were Congressman W.R. "Bob" Hoage and Senator Tom Connally.[4]

In 1939, when German tanks and troops swarmed all over Poland starting World War II, the United States Army was woefully inadequate, standing at 190,000 men located at some 130 small, battalion size posts, like Fort Sheridan. We ranked about seventeenth in the world as far as Army strength. This had come about through the disillusionment with things military following World War I, the rise of isolationism and the economic constrictions of the Great Depression.

In 1940, as the German Blitzkreig overran most of Europe, President Roosevelt and most of the members of Congress became aware of the threat we were now facing and the need to increase the size of our Army. We also needed to develop new weapons and tactics. Congress voted to raise the Regular Army to one million men by October 1, 1941 and to two million by January 1, 1942. This could only be accomplished by mobilizing the Reserves and the National Guard and by conscription, the first peacetime draft in the nation's history.

The Army's planning branch was assigned to the task of devising innovative ways of coping with the seemingly invincible German war

17

machine which made use of so many tanks and airplanes. Placed in charge of this unit was Lieutenant Colonel Andrew Bruce, a native of St. Louis, Missouri and combat veteran of World War I. After months of study and several anti-tank conferences over the summer and fall of 1941, a detailed plan was formulated calling for the use of 75mm guns mounted on half-tracks and organized in separate anti-tank battalions. These soldiers were to be trained at a new Tank Destroyer Tactical and Firing Center which, because this new kind of warfare called for vast numbers of men and machines maneuvering over large areas, required a post much bigger than any then in existence. Colonel Bruce was placed in charge of the new program in November, 1941. It was temporarily located at Fort Meade, Maryland.

The Japanese attack on Pearl Harbor and our subsequent declarations of war on all the Axis Powers suddenly made his task very urgent. On December 19, 1941, Bruce, along with a few of his top officers, made a quiet and hurried inspection of several sites that had been recommended. When he and his staff arrived in Temple to make their unannounced and incognito visit to the Killeen and Gatesville area, they were surprised to be met by Frank Mayborn and his Defense Projects Committee. Mayborn had been tipped off by his contacts in Washington.

However, Colonel Bruce liked what he saw on his hosted tour and, after getting the problem of insufficient water solved, gave the necessary recommendation. On January 10, 1942, the Army announced that the new Tank Destroyer Tactical and Firing Center would be located at Killeen, Texas and would require 109,000 acres of land. It would be the largest military post in the United States Army. About 1,800 buildings would be built at a cost of thirty-five million dollars.

The Army wasted no time. Before the farmers and ranchers of Bell and Coryell Counties could realize the full significance of what was happening, government agents were buying their land. By February, the Army had title to 22,000 acres and in March it had another 45,000 under option. When some landowners resisted, the Federal District Court in Waco issued a "take order" that gave the Army the right to move onto the land, even on those parcels not under option at the time. This was done under the Second War Powers Act that Congress had passed on March 27. There would subsequently be 220 trials over the land taken for Camp Hood but the owners were dispossessed immediately and the Army was operating Camp Hood as the trials got underway.[5]

On January 30, Colonel Bruce recommended that the new post be named in honor of Civil War General John Bell Hood, the "Fighting General" who led a Texas brigade in the Confederate Army of Northern Virginia. This was in accordance with an Army policy of making a new post more palatable to the people of the area by naming it for a military figure held in high esteem by the locals. The War Department gave the necessary approval.

The selection of Camp Hood for a name did not appease all the land owners who suddenly had to vacate their homes. John Pace, a 74-year-old rancher, refused to sell. His 2,500-acre Pine Knob Ranch was then condemned, declared unimproved land and taken for one dollar an acre. He was given 30 days to vacate his livestock.[6] Others, on in years like John Pace, had been born there and eked out an existence for their entire lives. Their forefathers, going back to the Civil War, were buried there and they had hoped to pass the land on to their sons and daughters; thus, they were very reluctant to sell.

Because of the haste, some of the residents found soldiers on their front porches and Army trucks in their flower beds even before the government bought their land. Once the deal was signed, the residents had ten days to pack up their belongings and leave. Some saw their barns being burned or smashed by bulldozers as they rode away. Most had to move before they were paid, some waiting as long as a year and a half. Finding new homes and pasture land for their animals was difficult and many lost part of their herds or had to sell them at a loss. At least three suicides are attributed to the sudden disruption of the 470 families that were involved. They are a small part of the millions of victims of World War II.

Actual construction of Camp Hood began on April 7 with 5,000 carpenters and more than 12,000 other laborers erecting frame barracks, office buildings, roads and other infrastructure needed for a major military installation. Also in April, two Tank Destroyer Battalions arrived from Fort Meade and began their training even though there were still civilians living on parts of the new post.

All the work on the first 108,000 acres was completed in eight months and Camp Hood was officially dedicated on September 18, 1942. Further expansion with the construction of North Camp (and the disruption of 200 more families) near Gatesville, took place during the following year. By September 1943, the base consisted of 160,000 acres making it truly one of the largest military installations in the world. It now had 35 firing ranges and 5,630 buildings.

The Tank Destroyer Center accomplished its goals of training men to destroy tanks so well that by the end of 1943 its activities had to be curtailed. In November, General McNair announced that the

Army Ground Forces had reached sufficient strength to be able to attain all the strategic objectives of the war. In short, all that would be needed for final victory would be to train replacements for those *killed or wounded* in the final campaigns.

By early 1944, manpower numbers at the camp shrank as the remaining Tank Destroyer Battalions finished their training and were shipped overseas. Camp Hood was then given a new lease on life when an Infantry Replacement Center was activated at the South Camp on March 10, 1944 and the remaining Tank Destroyer activities were consolidated at the North Camp. Training inductees in infantry skills so that they could replace battle casualties soon became the largest activity of the post. By September 21, 1944, it reached a peak of 31,545 trainees out of a camp population of some 60,000.[7] The need was critical as total American casualties, killed and wounded, were running about 10,000 a week world wide at that time. I arrived for this training shortly afterwards.

When I peeled off the expressway and drove into Fort Hood almost a half-century later, there was no gate, barbed wire fence or M.P.s, as I remembered, but only an open road and a large sign that said: "WELCOME TO FORT HOOD, THE GREAT PLACE." My first view of this "Great Place" had been on a dull grey morning in late September, 1944. It had rained most of the night as we chugged from Tulsa south through Fort Worth and on into central Texas arriving at Camp Hood in the dark. It was just getting light when we were herded off the train. In one direction, there was a vista of slowly rolling, grassy hills, punctuated only occasionally by a lone tree or two.

"*So this is Texas,*" I thought. "*Why, there is nothing here!*" It looked bleak compared to Fort Sheridan which was located in a busy suburban, highly forested setting. In the other direction, however, there were a few white-painted buildings along a road and others farther on.

We were marched to the first building, ordered to strip down to our boots and given another medical examination and some more shots. There was a lot of mud on the bare wood floors of the receiving center. The man in front of me fainted after getting a shot and by the time a medic dragged him across the room and sat him on a chair with his head down between his knees, his bare body was covered with mud. The line kept moving.

Everyone seemed cranky and mean. The doctor administering the shots bent the hypodermic needle on his first attempt to stab it into my skinny arm. Glaring harshly at me, he bellowed: "Now look at what *you* did!" While I shook in my boots, he changed needles, held my arm in a tight squeeze and managed a successful inoculation on the second try.

When I think about my arrival at Camp Hood, I am reminded not only of the Nisei but also of those poor Jewish families who were, at that same time, arriving at Auschwitz, Dachau or Buchenwald, there to be robbed of their possessions and put to work at slave labor or to death in gas chambers. At this American concentration camp, young boys were robbed of their innocence and trained to do the killing necessary to finish the war.

After our initial processing, we were marched to some barracks and told that we were under medical quarantine. This time it was for two weeks. Training began almost immediately. Long days began with reveille at 5:30 A.M., when we stumbled out of our beds and lined up on the street in front of the barracks for a head count, and lasted until taps at 10:00 P.M., when a lot of us were already asleep. The days were filled with hour-long sessions of physical training, close order drill and bayonet practice, interspersed with lectures on military courtesy, Army rules and regulations and the nomenclature and functioning of the M1 rifle. They even had Mess Sergeant James M. Kennedy, a tyrant of the kitchen, talk to us about correct table manners and his ordinances and decrees which had to be strictly obeyed when we were in his territory.

The quarantine meant that we couldn't leave the barracks in those short hours after supper and before lights out or on week- ends. There weren't many places to go to—a crowded P.X. with limited merchandise available, or a post theater where you had to stand in a long line to (maybe) get in to see a movie. According to *Fort Hood: The First Fifty Years*,[8] there were three swimming pools, a nine hole golf course, several tennis courts, a football field, three bowling alleys and baseball and basketball courts available for recreational use when the camp was completed. They must have been well hidden or for the use of the officers only. I didn't get to use them. We would have been too exhausted after a day's training anyway. Even after the quarantine was lifted, we were often restricted to the barracks for some breach of military discipline or other so it got to be a way of life.

I was assigned to Company B, 173rd Infantry Replacement Training Battalion. This unit was comprised of four similar training companies occupying 12 barracks buildings which made up a block. Each company consisted of 240 trainees and a staff of 32. We were housed in two-story wooden buildings that held 80 recruits and some of the staff. We slept in double-decker bunks in huge dormitory rooms of 40 trainees, one room on each floor. The staff had small rooms at the end of the building. On the first floor, there was a latrine consisting of six toilets, one long urinal, six wash bowls and six shower heads to accommodate about 90 men. It took a while to get used to the lack of privacy: I was constipated for the first few days, but I adjusted.

Across the street from the row of barracks were the company mess halls and other service buildings. There were block after block of identical training battalions, all in different stages of a 17-week training cycle. I was there when infantry training was at a peak. Besides the 100 battalions that were trained at the Tank Destroyer Center, 56,313 Infantry Replacements were trained during the first three years of Camp Hood's existence. One study revealed that a little over three percent of all United States military personnel serving in combat had been trained here.[9]

About half the boys in Company B were from Texas. They enjoyed hillbilly music. If they could get Grand Ole Opry on the radio they were content to lay around listening to Roy Acuff belting out those mournful tunes. Some of them had guitars and would play and sing along. Their favorite seemed to be "San Antonio Rose" which, when I hear it occasionally played today, instantly transports me back to those wretched days and nights when we were restricted to the barracks at Camp Hood.

Company B was commanded by a fat captain who wore glasses and said he had been in the Army eight years. He would start us out in the morning marching to the training areas which were some distance from the housing blocks. However, his jeep and driver would soon appear and he would swing aboard and disappear. Most of the actual training was done by the lieutenants and sergeants but the captain did give us a talk once in awhile.

One day, when we were at bayonet practice, he appeared and said that he wasn't satisfied with our performance. "My main purpose in life," he said, "is to change your attitude so that you will want to close with the enemy and kill him with your bare hands!" He kept us overtime, yelling like banshees, running at and stabbing the practice dummies, kicking them viciously to get the knife out after burying it to the hilt and then clubbing it with the rifle butt.

Another of his favorite drills was to make two lines of soldiers face each other and go through the motions of thrusting, parrying and following through with the butt of the rifle to smash your opponent's face or kick him in the chest to get your bayonet out. The drill was to come close to each other without actually doing it so that we would

☆RIFLEMAN☆

The Rifleman belongs to the Infantry, the backbone of Uncle Sam's Army whose main duty is to take enemy territory and hold it. He excels with the rifle and in bayonet fighting using the Springfield, the Garand semi-automatic, or the latest M-1 rifle. The Rifleman knows how to operate anti-tank guns, machine guns, mortars and field pieces. He throws a hand grenade with deadly aim.

At the rifle range the Rifleman learns to shoot straight at both standing and moving targets. If he hits the bull's-eye often enough, he may be awarded a Marksman, Sharpshooter, or Expert medal, any one of which he will wear with pride.

The thorough training and hardening-up course which this fine American soldier undergoes produces an all-around fighting man whose outstanding ability is respected and feared by the enemy.

5. THE RIFLEMAN. Typical of the wartime propaganda that glorified war. This is from a book intended for children. See: George Avison, *Uncle Sam's Army: How it Fights*, (New York: MacMillan, 1944), p. 8

become familiar with hand-to-hand fighting. We were lucky that no one got seriously hurt.

I don't think that the captain had any actual combat experience, but he would repeatedly tell us that after our training we would be sent to Fort Meade, Maryland, or Fort Ord, California, for shipment to a regular outfit that was in combat. We had better pay attention and learn everything well or we would be killed right away. That fate seemed too far away to worry about. We were too miserable and struggling to get through each day without dying of exhaustion.

Many times the captain's jeep would appear as we straggled back to the barracks, late in the afternoon and worn out after a hard days training. "Okay, men," he would bellow, "let's double time the last mile or so!" With that, he would jump out of the jeep and start jogging at the head of the column. We would mutter to ourselves that "Old Fat Ass" was probably fresh from taking a nap and needed some exercise. But we had to humor him. Any laggards were sent to do disciplinary K.P. that evening with the despotic Mess Sergeant Kennedy.

The fat captain was transferred somewhere midway through the training cycle. I hoped it was to a unit in combat where he could close with the enemy and practice what he preached. He was replaced by First Lieutenant Harry L. Troutman. We didn't see much of the new commander. I think he preferred to administer the company from a desk in his office.

The officers always dressed in crisp suntans, shiny boots and helmet liners with their names and ranks painted on the front. They carried swagger sticks which were useful for pointing at charts or diagrams when they were lecturing; or for rapping some trainee on the head if his attention was straying. The NCOs wore fresh fatigues. Their helmet liners also showed their names and ranks and they also looked militarily sharp.

We trainees were a different story. Our helmet liners had our last names stenciled on them but we had no rank. Our uniforms were either the drab fatigues or two sets of blue denim uniforms that we were issued at Camp Hood that made us look like jail inmates. The uniform for the week was posted on the bulletin board on Sunday and we wore the same shirt and pants all week depositing them in the laundry on Saturday. We trainees were a grubby-looking lot by the end of the week.

We also wore the standard Army shoe which came over the ankle and canvas leggings which laced up the sides. The ends of our pants were tucked into the leggings and bloused over. We wore an Army belt to which were attached a first aid kit and a canteen. An M1 rifle had been issued to each of us and we had to memorize its serial number and be able to recite it whenever called upon. They were carried everywhere and weighed about 10 pounds with the bayonet.

If you appeared in fatigues when the uniform for the week was blue, you were punished and made to change. The cadre had a saying: "We can't force you to do anything, but we can sure make you sorry you didn't do what you were told to do." Trainees were forever doing

6. PHOTO OF THE BUDDING RIFLEMAN taken sometime in the fall of 1944 at Camp Hood, Texas. Background is the wooden barracks that was home for over three months.

push-ups, working in the mess hall and the latrine or being restricted to the barracks until they learned unquestioning obedience to all orders, commands and established routines.

The worst thing you could say was, "But I thought . . ." You would be cut off in mid-sentence and told in no uncertain terms that you weren't allowed to think, that the Army did the thinking for you and that your only function in life was to *obey*. It was a lot worse than the rigid rules and discipline of the Henry Ford Trade School, but I had gotten used to taking orders there so I managed to get through basic training with a minimum of punishment.

Company B was divided into four 60-man platoons, arranged alphabetically by our last names. That put me in Sergeant Joe Usic's 3rd Platoon which consisted of men with last names that began with the letters L through P. The platoon was further divided into four squads of 15 men each. I was in the 2nd squad. Early on, they had lined us up by height, making the tallest recruit in the squad first and, in descending order, the shortest man last. Since I was of average height at 5'8", I ended up in the exact center of the 15-man squad. A lanky Texan named Dave McMinn was first in our squad followed by names like McCrea, McCurry and McGraw. Bringing up the rear was a short fellow from Wisconsin named McCoy. These were permanent assignments so every time we formed up to do anything, we assumed these positions.

The Army was good at mixing its soldiers. There I was in Texas with a bunch of complete strangers. The only other man in my company from Michigan was a fellow from Watervliet named Leroy Merschman. I also made friends with a couple of boys from Minnesota, Gene Malecha and Verne Mattson. Gene was off a farm and Verne was from the small town of Mankato. They were both 18 years old and had entered the Army through Fort Snelling, Minnesota. Another was Otto May. He was a Chicagoan and had come down to Texas from Fort Sheridan although I don't remember him being on the train.

The Texans, some of whom were not far from their homes, having grown up in places like Temple and Coperas Cove, were harder to get close to. They talked differently and we had some language differences. "Whut's on for this evenin'?" McCrea would say in the brief moments after lunch and before we started training again. He would be looking at the schedule posted on the bulletin board. "Don't tell me we are going to do this crap in the dark!" a northerner would groan. But McCrea meant, what were we going to do after the noon meal which the Texans called dinner and we called lunch. Dinner had always been the evening meal to me.

Texans also tended to preface their conversations with "You yan-kees" when speaking to all northerners. This surprised me. I had never thought of myself as a yankee. Why, yankees were people from New England or New York and New Jersey. I was a midwesterner, but the Texans lumped us all together and even seemed to want to re-fight the Civil War. I hadn't even been aware that Texas was a partici-pant in what they called the "Great War to Save the Confederacy." I thought I was out west where the history was about settlers and Indi-ans and cowboys and cattle drives.

It was a cultural shock to this northern boy, who had gone to school with blacks and had sat many times at the back of the bus wedged between black and white Ford factory workers, to learn that Texas was part of the deep south and practiced segregation. There were separate drinking fountains and toilets for blacks at bus stations and other public facilities. When we went to town to a movie, we whites had to sit on the main floor. The balcony, where as a teenager in Detroit I had liked to sit, was known as the "loge" and was for col-ored patrons only.

Jackie Robinson, who later would become the first Negro to play baseball in the major leagues, served as morale officer for black troops at Camp Hood shortly before I got there. He found Texas laws to be much more discriminatory than those in Kansas where he had completed Officer's Candidate School at Fort Riley. On July 6, 1944, he refused to move to the back of a commercial bus, even after being ordered to by M.P.s. He was subsequently court-martialed for insub-ordination but the trial judges ruled that he had acted within his rights because the Army had ended segregation on military buses.[10]

The Army had practiced segregation since the founding of our country, putting Negroes in separate all-black units. All other races were put together. Thus, our training company had no blacks, but we did have Hispanics and a native American Indian named Hollis C. Lit-tlecreek from Minnesota. He suffered from the dual handicap of being from the north and being an Indian as well. The Texans gave him a hard time.

Camp Hood was in a part of Texas that was only about 75 years from the days when the Indians and the settlers had wrestled for con-trol of the land. Coryell County was named after an early settler named James Coryell who got into a fierce fight with Indian warriors in 1837 and was killed and scalped. Other settlers were murdered by raiding Comanche and Kiowa Indians who slipped out of their reser-vation north of the Red River and headed south to central Texas to rob, kill and kidnap the white people. It was not until 1875 that the

Army was able to remove this threat. The area then grew dramatically.[11]

So we northerners tended to stick together. We were aliens in a strange land. We told jokes about the Texans that seem kind of mean in retrospect. Some samples that I remember:

1. Northerner: "What's a Texan?" Second Northerner: "That's easy. It's a Mexican on his way to Oklahoma!"
2. Northerner: "Do you know how to make a really small midget?" Second Northerner: "Yeah. You take a big Texan and beat the shit out of him!"

Most of the trainees were boys of 18 and 19 but there were exceptions. Clay Millsap, who was in my platoon, was in his mid-thirties and the father of six children. His draft board in Tennessee must have been desperate to meet their quota. A farm worker, he was exceptionally strong and demonstrated his prowess one time by lifting two 60mm mortars, one in each hand, high above his head. We marveled that a man almost twice our age could endure the rugged training, which he did without much complaining.

Another older man was Louis Gasparas, an alien who was using Army service as a way of getting his U.S. citizenship. He was short, fat and bald and spoke with a thick accent. He seemed to be in trouble with the cadre a lot because he was rather clumsy and didn't always understand their commands fast enough.

Bobbie R. McCurry, who occupied the bunk below me, was also another "older man." He was from deep in the swampland of South Georgia and was illiterate when drafted. He apparently spent his youth hunting and fishing instead of going to school. He said that he and his "pappy" lived too far into the swamp for the truant officer to bother him. When his draft board finally caught up with him, the Army had sent him to school and taught him the rudiments of reading and writing before sending him to Camp Hood for basic training.

I learned this that first weekend when we were restricted to the barracks. He was laboriously writing a letter home. Actually, he was printing it in large block letters and asked me how to spell the word "happy." After I told him how, plus several other simple words, he showed me the books he had used at "goon school" as he called it. They were like the "Dick and Jane" readers used in the primary grades except that the characters were soldiers and the situations military. In spite of his lack of education, McCurry was quite intelligent. He learned many of the things that we were taught in basic training a lot faster than some of the rest of us who were well educated.

McCurry also had a varicocele in one testicle. This is a birth deformity in which the veins of the spermatic cord are enlarged or varicosed. His was quite large. He would often walk around the barracks, naked and holding this massive testicle, all purple and mottled, in one hand, bragging about his sexual prowess and how women were always impressed with the size of his genitalia. Cries of "Cover up that ugly thing!" would only encourage him.

Our platoon sergeant, Joe Usic, was tough. All Army rules and regulations during our drills, but he did smile once in awhile and converse with the trainees when we were on breaks. He had been in the Army for several years and had spent a couple of them on the island of Trinidad, off the coast of Venezuela, which he remembered fondly as a tropical paradise. We were the third group of men he had trained at Camp Hood. Some of the first group had written to him from Italy where they had been sent. He had two assistants, a corporal and a private first class. They seemed to be along for the ride without doing anything really important.

The real power in the company was Technical/Sergeant Homer E. Magrini, who headed the field cadre. He was from Pittsburgh, Pennsylvania and bragged that he was as tough as the steel that his home town was famous for making. Several times he offered to fight any man in the company to prove it. Nobody took him on as far as I can recall. Magrini never smiled. One of his favorite sayings was usually delivered at the end of a hard day's work. After pointing out our shortcomings he would finish with "This company is restricted to the barracks."

Because inspections were on Saturday mornings, we spent Friday nights having a "G.I. party." This was not fun and games, but a thorough cleaning of our quarters and equipment. We donated some money from our fifty dollars a month pay to buy extra cleaning materials, learned how to use them, and worked diligently to make everything spotless. Bunks had to be made up so that a coin would bounce if it was dropped on the tightly wrapped blankets.

At the appointed time on Saturday morning, an officer, accompanied by the NCOs, would enter the room. We recruits would all jump to attention and stand motionless while the inspecting party went from bunk to bunk looking for flaws. If they were checking rifles, we had to go through a little ceremony of opening the bolt and presenting the rifle with arms extended while looking the lieutenant squarely in the eyes. He would suddenly snatch it out of your hands. You had to let go of it at the exact moment he made his move or you were in big trouble from holding on to it or dropping it on the floor.

I could hardly believe my ears the first time the inspecting officer, holding my rifle high to the light, yelled: "You call this rifle clean, soldier? It's filthy! Sergeant, see that this man has extra duty until he learns what a clean rifle is." Then he threw it back at me. I had spent a lot of time cleaning that rifle but the whole process was intended to break you down and turn you into an automaton. Hardly anybody passed their first inspections.

That weekend was spent ignominiously cleaning pots and pans and separating the garbage for the mess sergeant. He had cans for everything: paper, cardboard, glass, tin cans, coffee grounds, bones, grease, peelings, etc. Mix up any of them and you were liable to be stuck on K.P. for a month.

Enormous amounts of food were prepared and eaten in that mess hall. The Army provided about 3,800 calories for each man and there were often second servings available. We sometimes had meat and potatoes at all three meals of the day. One breakfast item that I will always remember was creamed hamburger on toast. It was universally disdained as "shit on a shingle," but most of us gobbled it up and everything else that was available to eat. It seemed like I was always hungry. I burned up all those calories and didn't put on any weight.

I eventually learned to do everything the way the Army wanted so that I could get a weekend pass. This was the reward for perfect performance but there was one more hurdle. Before the First Sergeant would issue the necessary paperwork, he quizzed you on the rules for guard duty. We had to memorize some 13 in all beginning with: "Order Number 1, I will walk my post in a military manner, keeping always on the alert . . . etc., etc.

When I finally qualified for a pass, I took a bus from Killeen to Temple, the nearest big town. So did thousands of other soldiers. The bus lines at that time ran 108 round trips daily.[12] Every seat was filled with some people standing for the entire journey, about 25 miles. In Temple, I went to the USO Club, located in the former YMCA building. It had a dance hall, swimming pool, badminton court, bowling alley and rooms for reading and writing letters. It was also crowded with soldiers.

A dance was held on Saturday night with a live orchestra but you couldn't dance more than a few steps before someone cut in. At midnight, all the girls disappeared. Rather than take the bus back to Camp Hood, I spent the night at the American Legion Post. For fifty cents, they provided a cot and blankets. I slept that night in a big room with many other soldiers. You just couldn't get away from them.

Sunday, after church, I wandered around town for a while but there wasn't much to see. I went back to the USO and wrote letters. They not only provided free writing materials, but if you left the letters with them, also mailed them free, which was nice. We had to be back in the barracks at 6:00 P.M. Sunday so it didn't seem worth all the effort.

I also went to Austin on another weekend pass. There I spent time wandering around the state capitol building absorbing Texas history. I also visited the University of Texas campus. There weren't many students and it made me homesick for the campus of the University of Detroit where I would much rather have been.

That Saturday night, the USO lady had sent me to a private home when I had inquired about sleeping accommodations. She gave me an address and directions and I arrived at a rather large house about 1:00 A.M. after staying at the Saturday night dance until the very end. I had to wake up the lady of the house who rather sleepily showed me to a very comfortable bedroom upstairs. It was great sleeping in a private room without other soldiers. It still amazes me that people would open their homes to complete strangers, but that is how it was back then in wartime Texas and other places in a patriotic America.

On another Sunday, I went looking for David Hans, a fellow Ford Trade School student. I had learned in a letter from classmate Walt Canney that Dave was taking infantry training at Camp Hood. After walking for miles past block after block of identical barracks, I finally located his training battalion. When I found him, he was in the latrine carefully combing his hair. He hadn't changed a bit.

We went to Killeen together and spent a useless afternoon doing nothing, like all the other soldiers wandering around that little town. Dave later served with the 11th Airborne Division in the Philippines and made the jump at Atsugi Airport in Tokyo when the first Americans entered Japan at war's end.

In 1943, Frank Loesser composed a song that has become identified with the branch of the Army in which I served. Some of the words are "What do you do in the infantry? We march! We march! We march!"[13] It's a true song in my experience. We did a tremendous amount of walking and running during our basic training and afterwards. Camp Hood was large and the training sites spread out over miles and miles of the Texas hill country.

One time we got lost. We marched in circles all morning looking for the place we were supposed to go for that morning's training. The cadre was embarrassed by this blunder but we secretly enjoyed their consternation. Our feet hurt from this useless walking from one site to another all morning without a break but we couldn't complain or they would take out their wrath on us.

I was lucky my size 9 1/2-C Army shoe fit me quite well and that I had done a lot of walking when I was growing up because we never had a family car. I also did a lot of hiking in the Boy Scouts. At the Henry Ford Trade School, I was on my feet all day during the work weeks. Some of the other soldiers weren't so fortunate. They got huge blisters on their feet and some were bad enough to require medical attention. If they were really disabled, the medics gave them a release and they got to ride out to some of the training areas until they healed. It was rumored that some of the country boys had never worn shoes before entering the Army.

There is something that gets to you when you are in the Army. When I saw thousand-man battalions form up to shouted commands or marching by in long columns, I got goose pimples. It seemed the epitome of what it means to be a soldier. Often, when we were marching cross-country in two columns, and I could see the men, all looking alike spread out over hill and dale and broken only occasionally by a platoon guidon, it became, in my eyes, a beautiful picture. There is a danger here. You can get to like things military and forget what its real purpose is: to kill and destroy.

With all this marching, we got quite proficient and our maneuvers became more complicated. We would display them at the dress parades that usually took place on Saturday mornings when whole battalions would pass in review for the camp's commanding officers to review.

At the end of a day's training, we usually assembled for mail call. Before the letters were distributed, a sergeant would read the news, the Army's way of keeping the troops apprised of what was going on in the world. It was mostly war news but also briefly reviewed the major sports events or political happenings.

In the fall of 1944, the Allies were bogged down in what became known as "The Rhineland Campaign of 15 Sep 1944—15 Dec 1944." After the marvelous progress made from breaking out of the Normandy beachhead and racing across France in late summer, the Allied advance was halted at the German border by poor weather conditions, difficult terrain, stiffening German resistance and a lack of supplies. We heard about severe fighting in places like the Arnhem area, the Schelde estuary, the Metz and Saar regions, and Aachen, where American troops entered Germany for the first time.

Life Magazine ran pictures of the Germany that the Allies were going into and I thought that I would like to be sent there. The civilization of Beethoven and Goethe looked a lot more interesting than the jungled islands of the Pacific. Besides, some of my mother's ancestors had come from Bavaria and Alsace-Lorraine. Maybe I would meet some distant cousins.

On the Italian front, the Allies drove north from Rome during the fall of 1944 but here too, fierce enemy resistance, bad weather, mountainous terrain and a shortage of replacements halted the offensive south of the Po River plain by late autumn. On the Russian front, our Communist ally had pushed the Germans out of the last parts of Russia, Bulgaria and Rumania during the summer of 1944. In October they battled their way through the Baltic states and then invaded East Prussia, Germany's homeland in the east. In Poland, they stopped short of taking Warsaw so that the Polish rebellion could be put down by the Nazis and the country weakened for a post-war Communist government. In late fall, they also settled in for a long winter.

In the Pacific Theater, the big news was the invasion of the Philippine island of Leyte on October 20. It proved to be a major battle on land, sea and air, lasting until we were almost through our training. The Gods of war weren't hampered by Father Winter in the Pacific, as they were in Europe.

Life went on at home. In baseball, our Detroit Tigers were battling it out with the perennial cellar dwellers, the St. Louis Browns, for the American League pennant. The Browns won it on the last day of the season when they dispatched the New York Yankees and Detroit lost to Washington. In the all-city World Series, the St. Louis Cardinals easily beat the Browns 4 games to 2. In football, Army had its best team in 28 years, trampling Notre Dame 59 to 0 and arch-rival Navy 23 to 7 to tally up an unbeaten, untied record.

Probably the biggest domestic news story was the election of Franklin D. Roosevelt to an unprecedented fourth term. While his popular vote was slightly less than his 1940 victory, his electoral college margin of 432 to 99 reflected his continuing popularity and the unwillingness of the American people to change leadership in the middle of the war. There had been a big debate in Congress that year over how to allow soldiers to vote. Southern legislators were against any liberalizing of voting laws that would allow black soldiers to threaten their hold on political power. A compromise bill was finally enacted giving the individual states the responsibility. Some 4,300,000 servicemen requested ballots in the fall election. At age 18, I was excluded from this program. Old enough to die for my country, too young to participate in the election of its leaders.

Since we were training to be infantrymen, we had to master the many weapons that infantrymen use. First and foremost was the M1 rifle. There were many lectures, demonstrations and practice sessions. On what was called the "thousand inch range," we learned the various firing positions, how to hold the rifle with the sling wrapped around your arm for support, how to adjust the sight for yardage and prevailing winds and how to breathe and squeeze the trigger. The Army does make things complicated! Only after learning all the basics were we allowed to shoot the rifles on the rifle range. I had never fired a real gun before. With all the noise and smoke it was quite exciting.

We spent two whole weeks on that rifle range. The recruits were divided into three groups: coaches, shooters and target operators. I was a coach first. My job was to help one of the trainees remember all we had been taught while he fired his weapon from the prone position, the sitting position, the kneeling position and the standing position. The firing was also done at various distances of 100 to 500 yards from the target. It took all of three days to fire off all the required rounds. We used a huge amount of ammunition and had to pick up all the spent brass casings at the end of the day.

Scores were kept, points being given for how close you got to the bull's-eye and medals eventually awarded. They kept some of the trainees over until they obtained the minimum rating of Marksman. Since I had the benefit of being a coach before I did my firing, I easily mastered the operation and was awarded a Sharpshooters medal. Marching back to the barracks every night, I noticed chirping noises in my ears that sounded like a thousand frogs all croaking at once. The Army didn't provide us with ear protection (or eye protection either) like they use on modern rifle ranges. It's a wonder that we didn't all suffer from permanent hearing loss.

After I finished my own firing, I spent the rest of the days in the pits operating the targets. At the sound of a buzzer, I would raise the target by pulling on a rope. After the shot was made another buzzer signal told me to lower it. I would then examine the target and raise it up again and indicate with various pointers, white for a bull's-eye hit and a black X for a hit in the concentric white rings, where the bullet had gone through.

If the recruit had missed the target completely, I would wave a red cloth which was attached to the end of a stick. Known as "Maggie's Drawers," this was considered to be a disgrace and the unfortunate soldier would get plenty of attention from the officers. At another signal, I would lower the target and repair it with tape so that it would be ready for the next round. There was a lot of waiting time on this job so I brought reading material out with me whenever I was assigned to the targets.

We were also taught to fire the Browning Automatic Rifle or "Bee-Ay-Ar" as it was known. This was a very heavy, semi-automatic weapon dating back to World War I. It had a magazine capacity of 20 rounds and was equipped with a bipod so it could be used as a light machine gun. Every rifle squad had a BAR team with one man to carry the weapon and two men to carry ammunition for it.

The Browning M1919A4 .30 caliber light machine gun was also a standard infantry weapon to be mastered. I enjoyed firing it because every fourth bullet or so was a tracer and you could see its trail as it flew out to the target. Another important weapon was the M2 60mm mortar. We spent many hours, in three man teams, learning to set it up and work the sight on another "thousand inch range" that was set up like a miniature town. However, we got to fire it for real only a few times. It sent a 2.9 pound bomb out about a thousand yards or so with a very satisfactory "ka-chung" when it left the tube and a very loud explosion when it landed.

Since Camp Hood was the home of the Tank Destroyer School, some of our training involved tanks. Early on we had to dig a foxhole and stay in it while a tank drove over us. After being nearly buried alive, we were expected to jump up and throw a dummy grenade at the back of the tank, that being its most vulnerable spot. Most of us were too rattled from the noise and the dirt to throw a hand grenade very accurately.

Later on we had to throw a live grenade while standing on open ground and then hit the dirt before it went off. The idea was to show you that you didn't have to be too far away for the exploding fragments to miss you as they generally went up. It's a good thing they did, as I could never throw a heavy grenade very far.

We also learned to fire a rifle launched anti-tank grenade. This device fit on the end of our M1 rifles. We got to shoot them at an old automobile tire hanging from a metal frame like a child's swing. The kick from the launching of the heavy grenade almost tore my shoulder off. Hardly anyone managed to put it through the tire hole as we were supposed to do.

I did better firing the "Bazooka." A relatively new weapon, first developed in 1942, it got its nickname from the first soldiers who used it. It looked to them like the musical instrument played by a home-spun comic of the day named Bob Burns. An infantry company was issued two of these new weapons and they were primarily meant to be an anti-tank weapon.

Officially known as the M1 rocket launcher, it was a shoulder-fired recoilless weapon which sent a 2.36 inch, 3.4 pound, finned, rocket-propelled projectile out to 500 yards. The smooth-bore rocket tube was 54 inches long and was served by a two-man team, one to load the rocket in the rear of the tube and the other to aim and fire the weapon. Like all recoilless weapons, a mighty back blast accompanied each firing with lots of smoke and dust raised as the electrically fired rocket whooshed out of the tube. I only got to fire it twice but one of my rounds scored a direct hit on an old tank hulk that we were using as a target.

We were also taught to make home-made grenades using explosives, igniters and scrap iron. Another model was known as a "Molotov cocktail." It consisted of an old glass bottle filled with gasoline and stoppered with cotton rags. To use them, the cotton cloth wick was ignited and the bottle thrown at a tank or other target. The bottle broke and the gasoline caught fire as it ran all over the objective. This knowledge was to be used if we found ourselves in a situation where we didn't have regular hand grenades.

Besides training us to be proficient in all these tools of war which were meant to take human lives, the Army also had a program to psychologically prepare the boys for their role as killers. A series of films entitled "Why We Fight"[14] were shown over a seven week period. "Wait until you see those Japs throwing babies up in the air and bayoneting them as they come down," Sgt. Usic told us. "It will really make you mad." Actually, the one hour movies we were treated to once a week were mostly a rest period for a lot of us, rather than a stimulus to do battle. I don't remember seeing the Japanese actually bayoneting the babies. Maybe I slept through that part.

I did find them mildly interesting from a historical perspective as they traced the origins of World War II back to the days of the Nazi beer hall Putsch, the rise of Mussolini and the Japanese takeover of Manchuria in 1932. They went on to show the treachery of Hitler and his conquest of most of Europe as well as the Japanese conquest of Asia and the Pacific Islands.

However, they were crude propaganda. The grainy black and white footage of grinning Japanese soldiers raising their rifles and shouting "*Banzai!*" as they tore down and trampled on the American flag, or the grim faced Nazi soldiers wheeling their tanks and motorcycles through the conquered countries as civilians wept, didn't arouse much emotion from the soldier audience. We had seen a lot of that before in newsreels and Hollywood movies. One thing that was missing was the killing of six million Jews in the gas chambers. We didn't even hear about that until the following year when the war ended in Europe.

Our training also included a lot on the art of patrolling which is a primary infantryman job. It's divided into two kinds depending on the purpose. Reconnaissance patrolling is going behind enemy lines for the purpose of gathering information or intelligence as the Army calls it. The idea is to sneak in, find out the information and get out without being detected. Combat patrols, on the other hand, are those for the express purpose of finding the enemy and destroying him, his weapons, supplies or installations.

One day we saw a movie on a night reconnaissance patrol where some American soldiers were sent into enemy territory to gather intelligence on enemy strength and positions. In one sequence they had to overcome a couple of enemy guards who looked like Germans. The Americans tie and gag the enemy and leave them as they proceed on their mission. After the movie was over, we had a critique in which we discussed the movie and answered questions. The lieutenant leading the discussion insisted that the movie was wrong in one aspect. The soldiers should have slit the throats of the enemy guards after they had been tied and gagged. He expected us to do the same.

Some of us received this instruction with more than a little apprehension. It was one thing to kill an enemy by firing a weapon at some one who was firing back. It was quite another to kill a helpless person in cold blood. After all, most of us had been raised in a Christian faith. Killing helpless people was something the Japanese or Nazis did, not us. That's why we were fighting them; their leaders were an evil menace and they threatened to destroy our way of life and make slaves of us. At age 18, most of us hadn't thought our way through all the moral aspects of the complex problems of war, which is why the Army likes to have young soldiers. The younger, the better.

Our training also included a week of bivouacking with 50 miles of forced marching and some special activities at Killer's Kollege. Sergeant Usic told us that if we survived Killer's Kollege, we would be able to take on any six Marines. He did like to exaggerate! But it proved to be the toughest part of our training. It coincided with the Christmas holiday, which that year was on a Monday. Since half the company was from Texas, only the natives were allowed to have week-end passes. The rest of us were assigned the duties necessary to keep the post running.

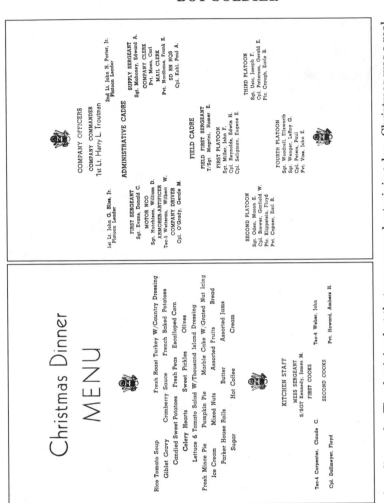

7. CHRISTMAS DINNER MENU. We had a turkey dinner for Thanksgiving but that was a regular training day. Christmas was a real holiday and a memorable feast. Each soldier was given a souvenir menu, partially reproduced here.

I pulled guard duty, which meant I spent the 24 hours from noon on Christmas Eve to noon on Christmas Day in the guardhouse, except when I was walking my post. I remember it as a gloomy Christmas with a lot of cold rain and fog. The only bright spot was the Christmas dinner which is, traditionally, a *feast* in the Army. Sergeant Kennedy and his cooks outdid themselves putting on a lavish turkey dinner with all the trimmings and even printed a souvenir menu. I got off guard duty just in time to partake of this meal which was served at noon on Christmas Day.

By 6:00 P.M. the party was over and the Texans were back. At 20:00 hours (8:00 P.M.), we formed up in the dark and marched off to bivouac fully loaded with our knapsacks, steel helmets, rifles, bayonets, canteens, blankets, pup tents, and since it was cold, overcoats. We marched for miles and miles in the dark, cold foggy night but eventually reached our camping grounds, a patch of woods, sometime in the wee hours of the morning. Here we set up our two-man tents in the dark. I shared mine with Verne Mattson.

It seemed like we had hardly gotten the tent pitched and crawled in and closed our eyes to sleep, when we were awakened for reveille. Our cooks had set up field ranges and we listened to the whisper of artillery shells passing over our heads as we ate breakfast off our mess kits. We were an Army in the field ready for combat, or at least its simulation.

It was not like the camping I had done with the Boy Scouts. After breakfast we marched off to Killer's Kollege. I remember passing under an arch at the entrance to the campus that had grinning devils, surrounded by flames on both sides and the inscription "Welcome to Killer's Kollege" on the overhead. Nice touch! It was like entering Hell.

We spent the next week there during the days and some of the nights. It was here we went through the infiltration course where we had to crawl under barbed wire while live machine gun bullets were fired inches over our heads and explosive charges went off as we crawled around obstacles set in our path. We did this twice, once during the day and again at night. You had to keep from panicking when you got caught on the wire, so that you didn't lift your head too much as you worked to free yourself, and continue dragging yourself and your rifle to the end of the course.

There was also a Nazi village set up where we practiced house-to-house combat, throwing hand grenades through open windows, kicking in doors and spraying the room with gun fire. Another drill was an imitation jungle trail that featured silhouette targets that popped up as we made our way through the woods. We used blanks, which was about like shooting the cap gun I had when I was a little boy. In spite of all the Army's efforts at realism, that is about what we were doing, playing at being soldiers. The real thing would come later and it would be a lot worse.

On New Year's Eve, we marched the long way back to the barracks. It had been exactly ten years since my mother died on another cold, dark New Year's Eve. I thought about her as we made our slow, painful steps, wondering if she would be happy to see her oldest son training to become a combat soldier. Her grandfather, Jacob Blum, had come to America from Bavaria to avoid military service.

When we had left the barracks on Christmas night, we had rolled up the mattresses on our bunks. McGraw was so exhausted when we got back that he immediately lay down on the bare wire springs and went to sleep without even taking his shoes off. Somebody rolled his mattress over him. In the morning, he was still asleep between the mattress and the springs. "We better see if he is still alive!" someone said, as he hadn't responded to reveille. Fortunately, he was still breathing when he was uncovered. A little stiff, maybe, but he had gotten more sleep than those of us who took the time to make up our beds.

Our training came to a sudden halt shortly afterward. The Army decided that it needed replacements so badly that it reduced our training from the planned 17 weeks to 14. The 10-day furlough promised after basic training was also reduced to five days. The reason for all this was the Battle of the Bulge, the name given to the last real counter-offensive Hitler's troops made on the Western Front, beginning on December 16, 1944.

We heard all kinds of bad news during this period, how the *Werhmacht* overran a large part of Luxembourg and Belgium, killing large numbers of Americans, taking numerous prisoners and making a huge bulge in the Allied line. The Germans had hoped to split the Allies and capture Brussels and the port of Antwerp. However, fierce resistance from the Americans at Bastogne forced the Germans to slow down, allowing the Allies to regroup and hold. It took six weeks of hard fighting to regain the lost territory. American casualties were 72,000, making the need for replacements very critical.[15]

We soon found ourselves being processed for the big move. The furlough that we were given was to be a "delay en route," Army jargon that meant we would be allowed to go home for five days while we were traveling to our new post. I had to pay for the portion of the train fare that would take me to Michigan, about $25.00. Considering

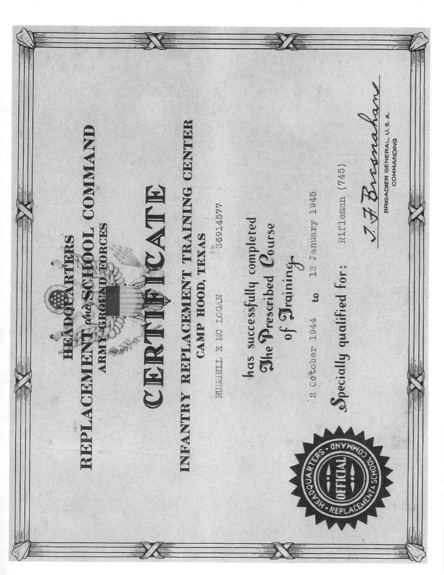

8. RIFLEMAN CERTIFICATE. We didn't have any graduation ceremonies because our training was cut short by the Battle of the Bulge. We did get diplomas attesting to our qualifications. Nobody failed the course that I remember.

all the talk about the Battle of the Bulge and the sudden curtailment of our training, I was sure that we would all be going to Fort Meade, Maryland for shipment to Europe. As usual, I was wrong. The Army, in its infinite wisdom, gave most of us envelopes full of tickets and travel orders that were marked "Fort Ord, California." While I was disappointed not to be going to Europe, California sounded like an exciting place. I had always wanted to go there.

As I turned in those blue denim uniforms, I felt like a hard timer who has suddenly had his prison sentence shortened due to overcrowding. As the train pulled out of Camp Hood and headed north, I certainly didn't shed any tears about leaving or have any fears about what was in the future. Rather, I felt a sense of elation. I had been tested to great extremes and had survived and grown from the experiences. There would be a lot more tests to come in the future.

THREE

Fort Ord and a
Long Voyage

*Though we travel the world over to find the beautiful, we
must carry it with us or we find it not.*
—Ralph Waldo Emerson

One of the few things I liked about being in the Army was the traveling I experienced. I had never been very far from home in all of the first 18 years of my life, yet in the two years that I was a soldier, I was mostly on the move and saw more of the world than many people get to see in their entire lifetime.

It required a long, long, journey to get replacements from the training camps to the far-flung battlefields where they were so desperately needed. Unlike the war in Vietnam, in which soldiers said goodbye to their loved ones and were flown to combat units in a matter of hours, World War II G.I.s made do with much slower modes of transportation—the railroads and ocean-going vessels. Distances to the southwest Pacific battlegrounds were especially lengthy and in my case, it took almost as long to go from Camp Hood, Texas, to the front just outside Manila as it did for the Army to provide training for the job that I was supposed to do.

The long journey began with a train ride in the wrong direction so that we could spend time at home before heading overseas. A troop train took us to Chicago where we split up to take regularly scheduled trains to our various destinations. I had a long layover. To use up the time, I wandered around downtown Chicago, visited the big USO club on Michigan Avenue and did some shopping. I wanted to look my best when I got home so I bought a garrison cap and a pair of brown low shoes. I didn't want to wear those high army shoes after they had been scuffed up by marches all over central Texas, and I had asked Grandma to send me a ration stamp. The clerk at the shoe store said that I should have gotten an authorization paper from the Army instead of wasting a civilian ration stamp but I knew Grandma had plenty. We always wore the same shoes for a long time and generally had them repaired several times before they were finally discarded.

I remember being a vain teenager and wishing that I had some insignia to wear on my dress uniform similar to that worn by other soldiers I had seen. However, as a replacement, I was unattached to any definite organization. All I had to show for my four months of service was the infantry blue piping on my overseas cap, the crossed rifles lapel badge and the Sharpshooter's medal worn on the blouse pocket. They would have to do until I earned some more, which seemed to me to be only a matter of time. I had collected a lot of merit badges and had moved up in rank in the Boy Scouts. I expected to do the same in the Army.

On the train to Detroit, I got into a long conversation with some businessmen who were involved in the production of airplane parts for the war effort. I must have impressed them with my knowledge of aeronautics, the names and performance figures of the various warplanes then in use and the men and machines that made up the history of aviation. These I could rattle off quite readily. "A young man like you should be in the Air Corps," said one. I didn't want to replay that painful part of my past so I only said that the Army needed infantrymen and I was going to do the best I could. He wished me well but his general attitude was, "What a waste!"

I was home about six cold, wintry days in the middle of January. Like most vacations, it flew by. People seemed genuinely happy to see me. Grandma asked many penetrating questions about Army life. When I told Grandpa about my trip to the Texas capitol at Austin, I was surprised to hear that he had been there, before the turn of the century, as a traveling salesman for the Ferry Seed Company, and was quite knowledgeable about the history of Texas. I had only known about his Kentucky territory, which he was working before he retired in 1937. Grandpa, almost 82 years old, was getting physically frail but his mind was still very alert.

Bob, my younger brother, was in his senior year at St. Benedict's and in the middle of another successful basketball season. My older sister, Rosemary, was working at the Maccabees Insurance Company.

The rest of my siblings looked a little older. Life goes on, even when you are not there. They all said that I talked funny. After four months of hearing mostly Texas twang, I could only reply, "Ah cain't he'p it!"

I had filled my barracks bag with cartons of cigarettes at the P.X. in Camp Hood—Chesterfield's for Aunt Margaret and Lucky Strikes for Aunt Katherine. I delivered them when I went to their houses for dinner. They were overjoyed. I had only paid fifty cents a carton for them but they insisted on reimbursing me many times over and told me how scarce they were on the civilian market.

Mrs. Taliday, a widowed lady who lived across the street, called me over and gave me five dollars and a box of candy. This was the same woman who had paid me only twenty-five cents for mowing her lawn a few years earlier. It was quite an unexpected and generous gift.

Everywhere I went I was well received. I hardly ever had to ride the public transportation system, which was free to servicemen. If I stood on a corner, waiting for a bus, strangers driving cars, seeing the uniform, would stop and ask me where I was heading and then offer me a ride. Sometimes they would go out of their way to take me where I was going. My hosts would ask me what outfit I was in and, before I had much chance to reply, would regale me with the military history of their sons, brothers, cousins, et cetera. Everyone was patriotic and supportive of the war effort and wanted to do something for the servicemen they met.

When I visited the campus of the University of Detroit, I was disappointed to find that they were between semesters. The only students who were on campus were the Catholic students who were on their annual retreat at Gesu Church. (Non-Catholics were excused from this religious exercise.) I passed around my new address at Fort Ord and eventually got a few letters but I could see that my former classmates were pulling far ahead of me. They were sophomores already and I didn't even know when I would be coming back to school.

At the Henry Ford Trade School, it was business as usual, although the boys looked younger than I remembered them being when I was there. They had just concluded a "Buy a Bomber" campaign. By pledging $333,523.75 in the Sixth War Loan Drive, students, instructors and other personnel of the Ford Industrial Schools had more than topped the cost of a B-24 Liberator which was then costing the government $250,000.00. Named "School Daze," the airplane was flown off to war after dedication ceremonies at the Willow Run Air Base.[1]

Mr. Stoelting, my former journalism teacher, offered me a ride part way home. We rode the school elevator for the first time in my life (as a student, I had been forbidden to use it), and then walked out to his special disabled parking spot next to the building. When he stopped for gas at a station on Wyoming, he bought me a candy bar and we munched and talked the rest of the ride. He wished me well and assured me that the war would soon be over as he dropped me off at Six Mile Road.

Walt Canney, a classmate from the Ford Trade School, turned 18 in October and was waiting to be drafted. I visited him at his home and his mother gave me a large piece of cantaloupe to eat just before we went downtown to see a movie. At the Fox theater, there was a display of Army weapons. When I rattled off the specifications of the Browning M1919 A4 light machine gun, Walt was impressed. "The Army sure taught you a lot," he exclaimed. "Don't worry," I replied, "the Army will fill your head with all that crap, too." He went through infantry training and was on a boat bound for Guam when the war ended.

I also visited my old Scoutmaster, Henry Cooke. A native of England, he had come to Highland Park in 1930 by way of Scranton, Pennsylvania, where he worked in the coal mines. He founded the troop which was sponsored by St. Benedict Church and was its Scoutmaster for 21 years. When I told him that a lot of the things that I had learned as a Boy Scout, like close order drilling, first aid and map reading, were a big help to me in basic training, he didn't respond very heartily. He had lived through World War I and was troubled by the fact that so many of his former scouts were then in the service. Too many had been killed, severely wounded, or reported missing in action.

I briefly visited my father who was living on the east side of Detroit with my stepmother and two year old half-brother. It was awkward. We didn't have too much in common since he had gotten remarried in 1939 and left us in the care of his mother and father.

Suddenly it seemed my time home was over, and amidst the tears and emotions of leaving and getting to the train station on time, I left my Army blouse hanging in the front closet. I had worn my Army overcoat because of the cold weather and didn't miss it. Grandma found it in time to send it with brother George, who caught up with me at the depot. I also left my dog tags hanging on the bed at home.

The Army did a poor job on the routing. There were better ways to get to Fort Ord than the way I was ticketed. First, they sent me by way of Fort Wayne, Indiana, to Chicago, which must be at least 50 miles longer than on the regular route through Kalamazoo. I was alone, there were no familiar faces from Camp Hood and the train was only partially full.

Changing trains in Chicago was a different story altogether. We boarded late at night with hundreds of people trying to get on. Since they let servicemen on first, I got a seat next to a window. When they let the civilians on, there was a mad dash for the remaining seats. A portly woman came waddling down the aisle and asked if the seat next to me was taken. When I told her it wasn't, she plopped herself in it with a great sigh of relief. There were more passengers than seats on this train and some people had to sit on their suitcases all the way to California. It was a long and uncomfortable ride, as we left Chicago around midnight Tuesday and arrived in Los Angeles the following Saturday morning.

Our Mickey Mouse route took us through southern Illinois and across Missouri to Kansas City the next morning, where we had a layover. I got off the train and walked around the town in front of Union Station. I was already tired of this train and we had barely gotten started. Crossing rural Kansas we stopped at every dinky town along the way. Each one seemed to consist of a general store, a grain elevator and a few houses. A farmer or two, in bib overalls and a straw hat, would get on and ride to the next town which looked just like the town he had just left. We seemed to be going nowhere.

By nightfall we were in Dodge City. This was a bigger and more western-looking town than all those farming communities we had passed through. During the second night we made Pueblo, Colorado and then turned south for New Mexico where we found it snowing. We were in the mountains and followed a route through Albuquerque and Flagstaff. The snow and the pine trees were not what I had expected to see in the southwest.

Life on that crowded train consisted of long days of staring out the windows at the ever-changing scenery, making your way down crowded aisles and standing in long lines to use the few bathroom facilities, or getting off the train every time it stopped for a few minutes of exercise walking around the station. This was followed by long nights of sleeping fitfully in a sitting-up position, awakening with every jerk of the train or when your body screamed for a change of position.

Grandma had packed me a huge bag of fruit, sandwiches and candy bars which sustained me for the first few days. After that I lived on snack foods that I bought at stations or from vendors who came through the train hawking their wares.

My seat mate was a middle-aged woman from Tampa, Florida

who worked in a cigar factory and told me all about the art of cigar making. She was on vacation, had visited relatives in Chicago and was on her way to Los Angeles to do the same. She might get a job there, she said. She had heard that the aircraft factories paid a lot better wages than cigar manufacturers. My fellow traveler spent a lot of time waiting in the dining car line and then would report back on how bad the food, service and prices were.

When we finally arrived at Union Station in downtown Los Angeles on Saturday morning, I learned that I had a 12-hour layover while the railroad officials got up a special troop train to take a bunch of us to Fort Ord. In those pre-freeway days, Los Angeles had an electric street car system that was quite good, so I took a street car about eight miles out to Hollywood, a place that I had always wanted to see. There I looked up a friend of Grandpa's who owned a stamp and coin store on Hollywood Boulevard. When the dealer had visited us several years earlier, he vividly described selling stamps to some major Hollywood stars who were collectors. However, when I found his store, I learned from a clerk that he had sold the business a few months earlier, retired and was living somewhere in the San Fernando Valley.

I had also wanted to visit the Hollywood Canteen, a USO club sponsored by the movie industry's leaders as their answer to the New York theatrical community's Stage Door Canteen. Both had been featured in movies which I had seen. *Hollywood Canteen*, the most recent hit, told the story of a wounded South Pacific veteran named "Slim," played by Robert Hutton, who comes to the Canteen and meets the girl of his dreams, St. Benedict's own Joan Leslie, who plays herself. (Joan Leslie had been in my sister Rosemary's class at St. Benedict School and I had seen her perform in some of the musical programs.)

While Slim and Joan are falling in love and dancing to the music of Jimmy Dorsey, Carmen Cavaliaro, and the Sons of the Pioneers, they are being entertained by the Golden Gate Quartet, the Andrews Sisters, Jack Benny, Joe E. Brown and Roy Rogers. The canteen is just crawling with the likes of Joan Crawford, Betty Davis, Faye Emerson, Janis Paige, Ida Lupino, Eleanor Parker, Barbara Stanwyck, Alexis Smith and Jane Wyman—all big Hollywood stars at that time.

The movie was panned by the *New York Times* as a most distasteful show of Hollywood's sense of its own importance and what it was doing for the boys in the service.[2] It was a smash hit with the public, however, and a lot of servicemen didn't read movie criticism. We thought it was a realistic picture of what we could expect when we visited the canteen.

I remember standing in a long line waiting to get in. There were servicemen there from the Army, Navy, Marines, the Royal Air Force and some of His Majesty's Ships that were then in port. (The latter had the names of their vessels stitched onto their uniforms.) We all expected to dance with real movie stars to famous dance bands, as per the movie. Reality was that the Hollywood Canteen was much like the other USO clubs that I had visited. The Saturday night I was there, the music was provided by an Army Air Corps band, the hostesses were local residents of average looks and they were outnumbered by the servicemen ten to one. I did see Bette Davis, one of the prime movers in setting up the canteen, sitting in a glassed-in office that overlooked the dance floor. She never came down to dance.

I was exhausted when I made my way back to the Union Depot and caught my midnight train to Fort Ord. While I slept soundly, the train made its way up the coast and through the mountains. As we chugged south from Castroville into the Fort Ord spur, I had my first view of the mighty Pacific Ocean. It looked like Lake Huron.

Although it was Sunday, the Army was on duty and we spent the day being processed. It was a much friendlier reception than the one I had encountered at Camp Hood. Same Army, but there were regional differences. Perhaps the bleak landscape, deep south culture and a history of fighting Indians and Yankees made Camp Hood seem such a hostile environment to me. Certainly the gorgeous setting of Fort Ord, between the mountains and the sea, the mild climate and the laid back attitude of the base personnel were easier to take.

"Lost your dogtags?" No problem. New tags were promptly stamped out. A soldier on the train with me, who was a day late, thought he would be thrown in the guardhouse for his tardiness but he was processed through without comment. My papers said that I was to be there by twelve noon on Sunday, January 28, 1945 and we arrived about ten o'clock in the morning. When I got to the barracks to which I was assigned, there were some familiar faces from Camp Hood—Gene Malecha and Otto May. They had come by the northern route in three days, where it had taken me five.

Fort Ord was smaller and better-looking than Camp Hood. There were large areas of green grass and even flowers in bloom around the barracks. Located on the historically rich and scenic Monterey Peninsula, its topography ranged from the rolling plains and the sand dunes of the ocean area to the rugged hills of the inland East Garrison region. It was considered ideal for its mission of training infantry soldiers. Fort Ord was located four miles northeast of the fishing port of Monterey and 14 miles from Salinas, the hub of a rich agricultural valley.

The fort's beginning goes back to World War I.[3] In 1917, needing land for use as a maneuvering area and an artillery range for the llth Cavalry and the 76th Field Artillery, which were then stationed at the Presidio of Monterey (the area's original military installation), the government purchased 15,800 acres from the David Jacks Corporation. The site was named the Gigling Reservation in honor of the pioneering Gigling (or Geigling) family who lived on a bluff overlooking the Salinas River. During the 1920s and 30s the reservation was used for summer maneuvers by the 30th Infantry Regiment from San Francisco.

In 1933, the name was changed to Camp Ord in honor of the distinguished Civil War and local hero, Major General Edward Otho Cresap Ord. Born in Cumberland, Maryland in 1818, Ord had graduated from West Point in 1839 and had seen immediate action in the Seminole War in Florida. During the war with Mexico, he performed garrison duty at Monterey where he was instrumental in mapping the lower part of the new state of California.

He distinguished himself during the Civil War in many battles, was wounded, promoted to Major General, commanded the Army of the James and was present at the surrender of Lee at Appomattox. Following the Civil War, General Ord was sent to the Presidio of San Francisco and assigned the task of ridding the West Coast of hostile Indians. He died in Havana on July 22, 1883.

On August 15, 1940, Fort Ord became a permanent Army installation when the coastal section, known as Camp Clayton, and some other parcels were combined with Camp Ord to form Fort Ord. By 1942 it consisted of 28,514 acres. I spent my time at Fort Ord in the coastal section.

The 7th Infantry Division was the first major unit to occupy the new fort, having been activated in July of 1940 and trained there. It departed for service in the Aleutian Islands in April, 1943, the only unit to leave Fort Ord directly to combat in World War II. Other units which staged and trained there were the 3rd, 27th, 35th and 43rd Infantry Divisions. As many as 50,000 troops were on the installation at one time but the average during World War II was about 35,000. It seemed quite busy to me when I was there in early 1945. At that time its main mission was processing replacements for overseas duty.

One of the first things I heard about when I arrived at Fort Ord was the million-dollar servicemen's club. The club had been planned and construction begun in 1940 by General Joseph W. Stilwell,[4] then commander of the 7th Infantry. Donations from soldiers and WPA grants helped to finance the building, which was completed in September, 1943. The big attraction to the enlisted men was that it was open to all soldiers, not just the officers. This was practically unheard of in other Army posts where a strict caste system prevailed. You could buy a large pitcher of beer for fifty cents there and drink it in very ornate surroundings on a bluff overlooking the Pacific Ocean.

I went there the first evening. After touring the facility, which was magnificent, I went out on the patio and descended to the beach to get my first close look at an ocean. It was a raw, cold night, typical for February in that part of California. As I stood on the shoreline, looking out to sea, the surf crashed noisily in the darkness and the wind blew on shore and pelted me with a cool, misty rain. I wondered how soon it would be before we would be on a boat crossing that angry sea to an unknown destination.

I revisited the Servicemen's Club in September, 1992. It was still impressive in spite of the peeling paint and general deterioration. The rooms were huge and the view of the ocean superb. While modern Fort Ord has newer and nicer NCO and Officer's Clubs, the old one, now known as Stilwell Hall, is still used occasionally. It was the scene of a big rummage sale the weekend before I visited and they were still cleaning up the debris. The club is now cut off from the rest of the base by coastal Highway 1 which was made into a freeway in the 1960s. You can no longer go down to the beach from the clubhouse. Signs forbid it and the bluff is laced with barbed wire. A sentry post on the left side of the patio, looking out to sea, was manned by three soldiers—two young men and a *woman*! They were having a great time, talking and laughing. That's not how I remember guard duty.

As infantry replacements, we were organized into battalions at Fort Ord and subjected to further training or T-days as they were called. We were told that there could be as many as 14 T-days but would, more likely, be less if transportation to the Southwest Pacific Theater became available sooner. They started the day after we arrived and were similar to basic training but didn't seem as harsh as the training we received at Camp Hood. I remember lectures on what to expect on the crowded troopships and on keeping healthy in the tropical climate to which we were being sent. (Rumor had it that since we were issued mosquito netting and light weight clothes, the Army was going to send us to Alaska. This was to fool the enemy.) There were more medical shots and movies on venereal diseases.

We were taken to a swimming pool and told to jump in and swim its length. This was easy for me to do as I had earned both Swimming and Life Saving merit badges when I was a Boy Scout. Anyone who couldn't was held over for swimming lessons. One of these was Gene Malecha. This surprised me. "I thought you farm boys all did a lot of swimming and fishing," I said, when he finally got back to the barracks. "No," he replied wearily, "we didn't have an 'old swimming hole' on our farm in Minnesota. You city boys have more opportunities to learn to swim than we do." It was a struggle for him and a lot of other soldiers who had to learn to swim in a hurry.

We were issued M1 carbines and spent a lot of time in the field learning to handle this new weapon, first on the thousand-inch range and then on a regular rifle range with live ammunition. The M1 Carbine was originally designed to replace the pistol and be more accurate. It was compact, lighter and more cheaply made than the Garand M1 rifle that we were used to. It fired a special round derived from the Winchester .32 caliber commercial cartridge and had a magazine that held 15 rounds. We also went to the beach and in full combat gear practiced amphibious landings on the sand from some landing barges that were berthed there and also spent many hours doing close order drill and calisthenics.

One night we had to go through the infiltration course again. It was dark and raining steadily. We were thoroughly soaked before we even got started as we had to wait a long time. Somebody said they were putting through a large group of officers and they were extremely slow. We finally got our turn to crawl through the mud with the machine guns firing live rounds close to our heads and the explosive charges going off and spraying mud all over as we picked our way through the barbed wire. By the time we got back to the barracks, cleaned off our muddy clothes and equipment, and got to bed, it was after midnight. Then the real excitement began.

I had just fallen asleep when I was rudely awakened by a flashlight burning into my eyes. It was held by a Military Police sergeant who was telling me, in a very harsh voice, to get up and spread all my clothes and personal items out on the bed. Somebody had reported his wallet missing and the M.P.'s were conducting a midnight shakedown search for it. I don't think they ever found the missing wallet— it was probably buried in the mud of the infiltration course, but they kept us up most of the night while they made a futile investigation. The disruption was good practice in being miserable, which is the life of an infantryman.

On Saturday afternoon, we had a dress parade for the commanding general. There were also a few civilians in the stands watching as we passed in review. Even though we replacements had come from training camps all over the country and had been together barely a week, we were already becoming a cohesive unit. A pride in things military was felt again.

Sunday was a free day. Otto said that he knew where he could buy hard liquor and that he was going to get drunk. That didn't appeal to me. Gene said that he was going to stay on base, rest up and write letters. I didn't want to do that either. I was anxious to see some more of California and went with another soldier to Monterey where we wandered around Fisherman's Wharf.

Commercial fishing was at its peak in Monterey in 1945. That was also the year that John Steinbeck's book *Cannery Row* was published, popularizing the place and its colorful characters. The sardine canning factories are now a tourist trap of gift shops, art galleries and restaurants because the fish mysteriously disappeared in the early 1950s. Not much remains of what I saw then.

Eventually tiring of the historical buildings, we went to the movies. My companion then wanted to go to Salinas, some 18 miles away. He had heard that there were more girls and less soldiers there. We rode a bus to get there but his information was wrong. We didn't find any girls in Salinas, only lots of soldiers standing around this one-horse agricultural town which I didn't think was as interesting as Monterey. We ended up eating dinner in a restaurant and going to the movies for the second time that day. The memory of that day comes back as kind of a wasted day to me.

The Army was a pro-smoking environment. The official quartermaster ration was a pack a day per man (or the equivalent in pipe or chewing tobacco) and they were included in combat rations.[5] Some local draft boards presented each departing inductee with a carton, as did some Red Cross volunteers at pier-side when the troopships were being boarded, although I didn't personally experience this. If you smoked up all the free ones and had to buy some more, they were sold rather cheaply at the P.X., usually a nickel a pack. Every time we took a break, the cry went out: "Smoke 'em if you got 'em!" The tedium and perils of wartime service supplied plenty of incentive to smoke and the materials were readily available. It is no wonder that we turned out to be a generation of smokers.

I had tried smoking cigarettes when I was about 12 years old but I hadn't really enjoyed it, especially when I had come home for lunch one day after puffing away in the bushes on a pack I had found on the street. The jelly sandwiches Grandma served tasted burned. I thought

I had lost my sense of taste. However, it was just coincidence because that jelly was homemade and had been scorched. I abandoned my smoking attempts after that. This was reinforced by the strict ban on smoking at the Henry Ford Trade School. Henry Ford didn't smoke and didn't want his workers to either. In those pre-war, pre-union days, getting caught with a pack of cigarettes could cost you your job. The whole Rouge complex was a non-smoking zone.

Gene took pleasure in puffing away on his pipe and I remembered Grandpa enjoying his pipe smoking so I decided to try one. I went to the P.X., bought a pipe and some Model tobacco, (the kind Grandpa used to smoke) and smoked it vigorously for about a half hour while I waited to get in to see a movie at the base theater. It was *National Velvet* with Mickey Rooney and Elizabeth Taylor. I remember it well because about midway through, I felt severely nauseated and just made it to the rest room where I threw up a vile tobacco tasting liquid along with my dinner. That should have discouraged me from smoking but it didn't. I kept trying to smoke that pipe until I learned how to do it slowly, without much swallowing. (No wonder Grandpa always had that spittoon parked next to his chair.) Eventually I switched to cigarettes.

When we straggled in after our ninth T-day, we were informed that we were on alert to be shipped out the next day. We turned in our weapons and packed up our gear for shipment. This was it. We were heading overseas. I don't remember being more than mildly apprehensive. I was young, innocent and unknowing of what I was really getting into. The excitement of travel and the importance of the mission we were on overcame any reluctance.

As we were lined up, preparing to board the train the next morning, the fort's commanding general appeared for inspection. He went down the line, stopping now and then to adjust some soldier's pack or to ask a question. When he was done, he wished us well. He looked like he wanted to go with us.

The train proceeded north about 130 miles to San Francisco where it went right downtown to the Embarcadero. We got off the train, marched across some roadway and tracks and boarded the troopship, carrying most of our gear in a duffel bag slung over our shoulders. We were a small part of the huge movement of one million troops that were sent to the Pacific Theater from January 1942 to August 1945. Over 360,000 of these were sent in the first eight months of 1945 when I went overseas.[6]

We wore helmets and carried gas masks, back packs, tents, blankets, mess kits, entrenching tools, first aid kits and canteens, all the equipment necessary to go into combat except weapons. It was a sunny afternoon, an Army band was playing "Sentimental Journey"[7] and Red Cross ladies were passing out donuts and Cokes, which we consumed while we waited our turn to go up the gangplank. It all seems rather festive in retrospect.

After we got our bunk assignments, a narrow piece of canvas stretched between a steel tubular frame and stacked six high in rows filling a cavernous hold for about five hundred soldiers, we went back topside and watched the loading procedure. Shortly after supper, the engines started, the ropes holding us to the pier were undone and we were underway. It was 6:07 P.M., Friday, February 9, 1945.

That evening, Bay Area residents sitting down to their newspapers would not read about the sailing of the USS *Cape Meares* because of wartime censorship. They would read on page one of the *San Francisco Chronicle* a story about a conference between Roosevelt, Churchill and Stalin to make plans for the post-war period. No location was given but this turned out to be the Yalta Conference, where many concessions were given to Stalin to persuade him to enter the war with Japan and which led to a Communist Eastern Europe and other post-war complications.

On the Western Front the Allies had recaptured the territory lost in the Battle of the Bulge and were poised on the west bank of the Rhine River, the last natural barrier to the heart of Germany. In the Philippines, the battle for the city of Manila raged with the 37th Infantry Division reported crossing the Pasig River which bisects the city. There were photos of gaunt American soldiers being liberated after U.S. Rangers and Filipino guerrillas made a daring raid on the prison camp at Cabanatuan. The Americans had been held prisoners by the Japanese for almost three years.

A story on page two had the Secretary of War, Henry Stimson, reporting that American casualties (killed, wounded, missing and prisoners of war in all theaters) were 676,796 as of the end of 1944.[8] This amounted to the equivalent of 50 combat divisions, he said. Of the wounded, 200,000 had been returned to duty.

Another story concerned a Camp Roberts, California, private named Henry Weber. Although a conscientious objector, the 27-year-old married shipyard foreman had been drafted into the Army anyway. When he refused to drill, he was court-martialed and sentenced to death. This was later commuted to life imprisonment. Supporters were campaigning Congress to investigate his case and Senator Burt Wheeler was promising his support. Weber was quoted by his wife as "willing to do anything I can to get the war over, as long as I do not have to kill people."

Another local soldier, who had been drafted into the Army 22 days after reaching his eighteenth birthday, was reported to be finishing his high school credits while on furlough between basic training and shipment overseas. By special arrangement with his high school principal, he was cramming it all into eight-hour days. "I'm doing it now because I will probably be too old to attend high school when I get back," he said. He must have gotten more furlough than I did.

On page five of the *San Francisco Chronicle*, Frank Sinatra, the heartthrob of teenage girls (and many of their mothers and older sisters), was reported to have completed his second physical examination for military service and sent to Governor's Island for observation. The controversial 29-year-old singer had been previously classified 4-F because of a punctured ear drum. However, since that time Congress had passed a "Work or Fight" bill that required young men to be in uniform or in essential war work and draft boards were reviewing all deferments. After three days of medical exams, Sinatra was declared 2-AF, meaning that his punctured ear drum still disqualified him from the military and that he was exempt from war work because his singing was "necessary for the national health, safety and interest." While his fans breathed a collective sigh of relief, this new classification stirred a national debate over his draft status. Newspapers editorialized "Is Crooning Essential?" and angry letters were written to editors all across the country. He was eventually put back in the 4-F classification.

Part of the resentment against Frank Sinatra was because he had not been overseas to entertain the troops. He finally went to Italy with the Phil Silvers show in June 1945, after hostilities had ended there. He was well received by the G.I.s but started another controversy when he criticized USO personnel as "shoemakers in uniform . . . They didn't know what time it was."[9]

And so it went in the world at large. My world for the next 30 days was confined to the narrow spaces of the troopship as we made our way across the vast Pacific. I watched on deck as we passed under the Golden Gate Bridge and some underwater, anti-submarine nets had to be opened to let us out to sea. It was stirring and I stayed on deck a long time watching the sun set under dark, scudding clouds in the western sky. A cold wind blew and the ship began plowing through some rather high swells as land receded rapidly from our stern. This gave the ship a decided up and down motion.

That didn't bother me while I was on deck and enjoying the stim-

10. CLASS DAY AT THE HENRY FORD TRADE SCHOOL, January, 1944. While American women idolized Frank Sinatra, young men made fun of him. Here, classmate Walt Canney, supported by a coat rack, lip-syncs "Embraceable You" and then collapses. From: The 1943-1944 Henry Ford Trade School Yearbook.

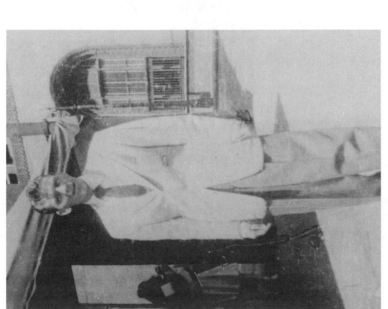

9. FRANK SINATRA in downtown Detroit, circa 1941. The singer was appearing at the Michigan Theater with the Tommy Dorsey band and was rising in popularity with the bobby-soxers. That's my sister, Rosemary, clutching her books in the background. Photo by Grace Muckle.

ulation of my first ocean voyage. The loudspeaker had announced that our destination was Finschhafen, New Guinea, and that it would take 15 days to get there. However, when I finally went below decks, I entered an appalling spectacle of hundreds of seasick soldiers. They had vomited in their helmets, in their bunks, on the stairwells and in the latrines. Everywhere!

Mal de mer, or motion sickness, affects about 80 percent of all people to some degree and it usually strikes fast. We had hardly gotten out to sea when we had a whole boat load of very sick soldiers. Scientists believe that the malady is caused by motion interrupting the delicate relationship that exists between the eyes and the vestibular sensory organs, which are the tiny balancing mechanisms located in the inner ears. A cluster of fine nerve fibers, they sense both position and motion and then relay those messages to the brain. Abnormal motion increases the activity of the tiny fibers. Some individuals are more sensitive to these fibers being stimulated and feel discomfort that can be manifested in malaise, cold sweating, dizziness, nausea and vomiting.[10]

There is a psychological factor too. I was feeling very well when I was on deck watching the sun go down, but when I descended into that fetid hold with my numerous, puking bunk mates, I soon lost it and was as miserable as the rest. For the next three days I was deathly ill, lying in my bunk, watching helmets spilling their contents as they swayed from the bunks they were hung on, often splashing the seasick soldier below. If I had to throw up, I usually made it to the latrine. It was an even worse mess, with the wash basins and urinals stopped up from soldiers vomiting into them because the toilets were all occupied. The long, free standing urinals, mounted in the center of the room, tipped and spilled their noxious mixture on the floor each time the ship tilted slowly from one side to the other. I tried to spend as much time on deck as I could.

Modern cruise ship passengers can get medications to prevent or alleviate the symptoms of motion sickness but we weren't given any. Dry soda crackers were the only thing offered to those who made it to the galley but couldn't eat the regular meals that were being served to the unaffected few. There is an old English sailors' proverb that says that the only cure for seasickness is "to sit on the shady side of an old brick church in the country." Actually, nature provides a cure. In most people, the body acclimates to the new condition that, in nautical terms, is known as "getting your sea legs." It was surprising how quickly most of us returned to normal by the third day out. The Pacific, named because it was generally calm, became an inky blue,

11. CROWDED TROOPSHIP. Typical crowded scene in the hold of a troop-ship showing bunks stacked six high. From: Admiral Chester Nimitz, "Your Navy As Peace Insurance", *The National Geographic Magazine*, June 1946: p. 708. U.S. Navy photo.

placid sea as the sun shone down and cleanup crews were organized to swab down the decks and stairwells and do some basic plumbing and cleaning of the latrines. Most of the passengers were up and about and we settled into the routine of a troopship at sea.

The USS *Cape Meares* was a standard C1B Maritime Commission freighter built in early 1943 by Consolidated Steel Corporation in Wilmington, California.[11] It was then sent to a shipyard in San Francisco where it underwent an extensive conversion to a troopship. The maiden voyage was in October, 1943 to Australia, New Guinea and back to San Francisco. The *Meares* was busy taking soldiers all over the southwest Pacific during 1944. When we sailed out in February 1945, the ship had just spent a month in San Francisco for repairs.

Our ship had a maximum capacity of 1,815 passengers. Most of us were berthed in the three original cargo holds located toward the front of the ship, except that officer passengers had staterooms on the upper decks. The ship was 417 feet 9 inches in overall length and had a beam (width) of 60 feet.[12] While troopships to Europe were generally escorted, because the German navy and air force were a greater threat, convoys were rarer in the Pacific because of the greater distances and the lack of navy ships. They were busy elsewhere with the many island invasions. We were told that our speed of 14 knots was fast enough to outrun a Japanese submarine, so we were all alone on the high seas.

For years I thought I had been on a Navy troopship similar to what my father had served on in World War I. However, research and a former seaman at the National Maritime Museum in San Francisco revealed that the *Cape Meares* was a commercial ship operated during World War II by the Matson Navigation Company and crewed by the Merchant Marine, who are civilians. They did wear uniforms and the ship had guns and a Marine Corps guard detachment which is probably why I thought it was a Navy vessel. Some other troopships were manned by members of the Coast Guard.

Passenger capacity depended on how it was loaded. We had been told at Fort Ord that on some ships we might be assigned to a bunk with another soldier, using it for twelve hours every day and spending the other twelve on deck as he got his chance to sleep. There might also be only two meals a day. Fortunately, the *Cape Meare*'s load was only about 1,500 passengers and we were fed three meals a day.

The passengers were a mixed group. Besides a sizable load of infantry replacements, there were engineers, medics and Air Corps personnel. The latter all boarded ship with .45 automatic pistols in shoulder holsters. The second or third day out, they were taken away from

12. U.S.S. CAPE MEARES, the ship that was our home for thirty days while we cruised the South Pacific, slowly making our way to the battlefronts. U.S. Navy photo.

them, much to their chagrin. A group of paratroopers, fresh from jump school at Fort Benning, Georgia, were distinguishable by their shiny paratrooper's boots, badges and rowdy behavior. They did something to offend the Army transportation officer who was in charge of the passengers, and he put them on permanent K.P. For a while, they would practically throw the food at us, but they calmed down somewhat as they got used to working in the hot and humid ship's galley.

Other soldiers were given jobs of cleaning out the passenger holds and latrines on a regular basis. Some were appointed "troop sweepers" and several times a day the public address system would call them to their task: "Attention all troop sweepers! Now hear this! Turn to. A clean sweep down fore and aft. Sweep all decks. Clean all ladders. Empty all G.I. and butt cans." They would then grab their brooms and dust pans and proceed to sweep the decks which were usually crowded with soldiers. There were no deck chairs so we sat on the deck or the equipment, or stood around leaning on the railings and giving way when they had to sweep under our feet.

I didn't get assigned to any job so I had plenty of free time. This was spent mostly reading, staring out at the ocean or playing cards. Often it was with Otto and Gene who were still with me. They taught me how to play pinochle and a game Gene brought from Minnesota called *Hasenpfeffer*.[13] We would set up our card game near the ship's store so that when it opened up, which wasn't very often, we could be among the first to purchase items from its limited supplies. Cokes were popular, but limited to two small paper cups each and, when the ice ran out, were sold lukewarm or not at all. The ship's crew had first priority and often bought out the day's supply of candy bars. They would then re-sell them to the soldiers at inflated prices.

We often watched the Marines go through an hour of calisthenics every morning. They did this on a small, raised poop deck that was actually a cover for a cargo hold. Stripped to the waist and using rifles, the sweat would pour off their bodies as their sergeant put them through a strenuous workout of running in place with their rifles held high over their heads. They also did a lot of bending exercises. Soldiers would hoot or make comments about the "sea-going bell hops needing to keep in shape to maintain their so-called tough image." But not too loudly. The Marines' job was to maintain order among the passengers and they patrolled the ships decks and holds constantly, always neatly dressed and carrying side arms and billy clubs. They sometimes broke up crap games, if they became too boisterous, as gambling was officially prohibited. Then again, they often seemed oblivious to what the soldiers were doing and just passed on through the congested areas.

One day, I had to answer nature's urgent call very early in the morning. I made my way to the latrine and had just gotten comfortably seated when sirens sounded and bells rang. There was a flurry of activity and then a sailor slammed and locked the doors to the head. I was trapped there, along with several other soldiers, for what seemed like a long time. We worried about whether a Japanese sub had been sighted and we would be torpedoed. It would be an ignominious death to go down to the bottom of the sea in the toilet. Fortunately, we found out later when they unlocked the doors that it was a routine drill that they performed every morning at dawn. At that time, the ship presented a good silhouette target on the horizon against the rising sun. That's when a submarine would likely fire its torpedoes so a general quarters was sounded and the crew locked all the hatches and manned their battle stations until the sun was well up.

Unfortunately, troopships were sometimes attacked. The four worst sinkings were all in European waters: The *Rohna*, sunk off Algeria on November 26, 1943 with a loss of 1,015 lives; the *Leopoldville*, which went down with 764 men off Cherbourg on Christmas Eve, 1944; the *Paul Hamilton*, a Liberty ship headed for Italy and sunk off Algiers with 504 G.I.s and the crew lost on April 20, 1944; and the *Dorchester*, sunk south of Greenland losing 404 on February 3, 1943.[14]

Religious services were held on Sundays in the Troop Officers' Wardroom. It sounds like a closet but, in nautical terms, means a dining room for officer passengers. It had tables and chairs and portholes looking out to sea, whereas we enlisted men went down into a hot and humid hold and lined up cafeteria style for our food. We then ate it on bare tables while sitting on hard benches. I still have a mental picture of attending Mass in the troop officers' wardroom, the only times I was allowed in there. The tables, covered with nice white tablecloths and set for dinner, would be pushed together to one side and we would kneel in the cleared space while the priest would have his altar set up on a table at the other end of the room. My line of sight was a white tablecloth with the priest between the salt and pepper shakers.

Our route took us southwesterly, past Hawaii, and we crossed the International Date Line somewhere east of the Gilbert Islands. When you cross the Date Line going west, you lose a day. If you go to bed on Tuesday, for instance, it is Thursday when you get up. Like Wednesday never happened! I didn't retrieve my lost day of February 1945 until 18 months later when I crossed the 180th meridian going east and had two of the same days in August 1946. I have never been able to fully comprehend this phenomenon although I realize that the earth is divided into 24 time zones and that the day has to start somewhere. As you travel west you gain an hour for every 15 degrees of longitude and when you reach the Date Line you suddenly lose 24 hours because there is a 24 hour difference in time from one side to the other. Sure.

We crossed the equator as we approached the Solomon Islands. There is an old sailors' custom of initiating any crew members who are crossing the equator for the first time. This is done by the veterans who are members of the Ancient Order of Shellbacks. They took their tradition seriously. In spite of the fact that there was a war on and we were in a war zone, the ceremonies proceeded. I don't know who was running the ship while all this was going on, but we kept plowing on through the waters.

About nine o'clock in the morning, with everyone on deck, an announcement was made, there was a musical fanfare, and out of the sea came King Neptune and his court replete with throne, costumes and tridents. They were riding a cargo sling and swung aboard with a crane. The court was set up on the poop deck where the Marines did their morning drill. It was announced to the king and his ugly looking queen, a sailor dressed in drag with a yellow mop for a wig, that there were a number of soft-shelled sailors aboard who needed hardening for the tasks ahead.

What followed was typical of a rough college fraternity hazing. The victims were blindfolded, stripped down to their shorts, dunked in sea water, paddled, forced to eat horrible combinations of sea creatures and had their genitals sprayed with a purple dye. They suffered these indignities for most of the day before the veteran sailors felt that the novice sailors were fit enough to join their ranks. Soldiers were invited to go through the initiation but I don't think they got many takers even though they promised them a large certificate. I stayed a safe distance away, just in case they decided to draft a few passengers by force. The next day, everyone got a wallet-size card, signed by King Neptune, that said we had crossed the equator and were shellbacks so we really didn't need to be initiated. Life aboard ship went back to normal.

So it was more playing cards, reading, staring out to sea and watching the flying fish which were prevalent in these warm southern waters. This species of sharp-nosed fish travels in schools, and when disturbed by our ship, would throw themselves out of the water with a quick lash of their powerful tails and then glide along with the ship, a few feet above the surface of the water, suspended by their wing-like fins. Their flight often covered several hundred feet. Although some of them grow to 18 inches in length, the ones I saw were smaller. They looked like dragonflies from the height of the ship's deck.

Another thing that amazed me was the vastness of the Pacific Ocean. "Water, water, everywhere / Nor any drop to drink." said Coleridge's Ancient Mariner[15] and he was right. The largest and deepest of the earth's bodies of water, the Pacific covers one third of the surface of the earth. It is said that if all the continents were placed in the Pacific, there would still be room for another the size of Asia. Its color varied according to the amount of light and to its depth. Some days, when the tropic sun blazed its hottest, the sea was the darkest, inky blue that I had ever seen. When the light was modified by fleecy clouds, it appeared a paler blue. At other times, when the sky was overcast and the light weak, it turned a sullen blue green. At night, when we churned up the water, it sparkled from phosphorescent microorganisms radiating the colors of the rainbow.

Every morning I checked for land. If I looked out the port side, all I saw was endless sea meeting the sky on the horizon. If I crossed over to the starboard side, the view was the same. Likewise if I went to the front of the ship as it plowed through the interminable waters. Going astern and looking back still showed no sight of land, only a fast disappearing wake that trailed all the way back to San Francisco. After almost two weeks of this endless vista, we finally passed close enough to one of the Solomon Islands to see green land and trees. A great cheer went up on the decks as we were being assured that even the vast Pacific Ocean has limits.

"Water, water, everywhere / Nor any a drop to drink." Potable water was in short supply so the ship took in sea water and used it for flushing toilets and for bathing. It was terrible tasting stuff. I had imagined sea water as being mildly salty but this sea water was potently briny. Ordinary soap wouldn't lather in it. You could purchase a bar of salt water soap from the ship's store but it didn't lather much either. I always felt slimy after a salt water shower. I would fill my canteen with fresh water and use it for brushing my teeth.

The ship's crew published a daily one-sheet, mimeographed newspaper which was passed around and eagerly read by the passengers. It reported the weather and how far we had traveled the previous 24 hours, usually between 320 and 350 miles. It also gave us an update on the progress of the war. The biggest news was the landing of the U.S. Marines on Iwo Jima, February 19.

This small, eight-square-mile volcanic island was considered indispensable to the air war against Japan. If you draw a line on a map between Saipan, in the Mariannas, all the way to Tokyo, it passes just to the right of Iwo Jima about halfway there. B-29s were beginning to bomb Japanese cities on a regular basis but it was a long, harrowing, 3,000 mile round trip without fighter protection. In American hands, the pear-shaped island would provide a point midway where fighter planes, with their limited range, could be based and still escort the bombers into Japan. It would also provide an emergency landing strip for airplanes having mechanical problems, needing refueling or damaged by anti-aircraft fire over Japan. A decision to invade the island was made by the Joint Chiefs of Staff in October and a date set for February 1945.

The Japanese also appreciated the strategic importance of Iwo Jima and had heavily fortified it as part of their outer defense line. It was laced with caves, tunnels, bunkers and pill boxes. It bristled with artillery and mortar emplacements which covered all approaches. They had also constructed two airfields and were busily building a third. Their fighter planes increasingly rose to give battle to the passing B-29s and the island's radar also served to give Tokyo an early warning of an approaching raid.

The Americans bombed Iwo Jima for 72 days in late 1944 and early 1945, but did little damage to the dug-in Japanese defenders. It only drove them deeper underground. On February 16, General Tadamichi Kuribayshi and his 21,000 defenders looked out of their bunkers and observation posts to find their little island fortress ringed by over 900 ships and a quarter of a million U.S. Marines, soldiers, sailors and airmen. Even Secretary of the Navy, James Forestal, was on hand for the epic battle that was to follow.

After three days of intensive naval bombardment, the Marines landed on the morning of February 19 and immediately became mired in the slippery volcanic ash which made forward movement difficult. From the high ground, Japanese defenders poured round after round of mortar and artillery shells on the Marines as they clawed their way forward foot by foot. By nightfall, 30,000 marines had landed but 2,420 were casualties. Most of the attacking Marines hadn't even seen the enemy.

There were few suicidal *banzai* charges in this campaign. General Kuribayshi, a shrewd professional soldier and one of Japan's better generals, husbanded his resources and made the Americans pay dearly for every position taken. On February 23, the fourth day, Mount Suribachi, an inactive volcano which dominated the southwestern stem of the island, was taken and an American flag flown from its 550-foot height. There it could be seen from the landing beaches and a great cheer went up.

Joe Rosenthal, a photographer for the Associated Press, took a picture of the flag raising that became the most famous picture of the war. It won him a Pulitzer Prize, was put on a U.S. postage stamp and inspired the giant bronze monument to the Marine Corps near Arlington Cemetery, Washington, D.C. But that was only the beginning. The marines had to turn northeast and overcome two cross-island defensive lines that straddled the high ridges on the eastern half of the island.

After five weeks of battle, usually with the marines out in the open assaulting the enemy in their deeply entrenched positions, the last ones were killed and the island became American real estate. We paid a horrific price—6,821 killed and almost 20,000 wounded.[16] It was one of the few winning campaigns where we suffered more casualties than our enemy. Only 216 Japanese were taken alive of the estimated garrison of 21,000. It did not include General Kuribayshi who presumably died in his bunker from dynamiting or flame-throwers. His last radio message was on March 24: "ALL OFFICERS AND MEN ON CHICHI JIMI: FAREWELL.[17]

Japanese newspapers cited his gallant defense as an inspiration to all citizens and the Emperor promoted him to full general. The bloody battle for Iwo Jima would also serve as an awful indicator of the terrible cost that we would pay if we invaded the sacred soil of Japan proper.

While this horrendous event was taking place north of us we were sailing the placid waters of the South Pacific. We docked at Finschhafen, New Guinea, on February 24 as predicted, but only stayed there overnight. The loudspeaker announced that our next destination was the Port of Hollandia as we chugged out of the harbor the next day. We headed in a northwesterly direction, hugging the coastline. The mysterious island appeared as luminous, green hills arising out of a misty, azure sea off our port side. It was my fate to be very close to it, yet not see much of it.

Grandma had a distant relative, Jack O'Brien, who supplied her with past issues of *National Geographic* magazine. During the war years, they printed beautifully detailed maps of the Southwest Pacific so their readers could follow the action in those exotic places. She had given the maps to me when I was home on furlough and I had

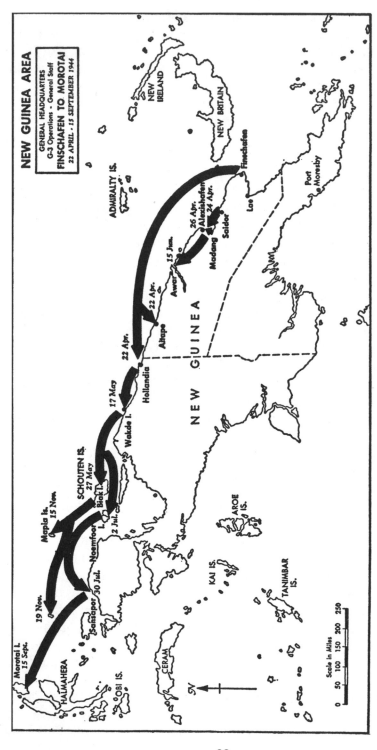

1. NEW GUINEA. Amphibious landings along the north coast of the huge island were made in 1944 as MacArthur's forces by-passed Japanese strongholds and got in position to invade the Philippines. Our troopship followed the route of MacArthur to Hollandia. From: Charles A. Willoughby and John Chamberlain, MacArthur: 1941-1951, (New York: McGraw-Hill, 1954), p. 179.

them with me on board ship. I could follow our route and knew where I was most of the time.

One of them was a detailed map of New Guinea. This huge island, the second largest in the world, is more than 1,500 miles from one end to the other and 430 miles at its widest. Only Greenland is larger. It covers some 312,000 square miles of high mountain ranges, steaming tropical jungles and swamps, much of it then unexplored. In 1938 the population was estimated to be 1,312,013, most of whom were stone-age natives. There was a handful of European settlers, traders, missionaries and government officials, numbering about 3,000.

Portuguese explorers first visited the island in the early sixteenth century. Because the dark-skinned natives resembled the people of West Africa, the Portuguese called the island Nova Guinea or New Guinea[18] and the name stuck. They were followed by the colonists and empire builders. First came the Dutch, who arrived as early as 1660. They claimed the western half of the island as part of the Netherlands East Indies. In the nineteenth century German merchants began colonizing the northern part of the eastern half of New Guinea as well as the Bismarck Archipelago, the Admiralty Islands and the northern Solomon Islands, which they named Kaiser Wilhelmsland. The British,anxious to protect their Australian colony, claimed the lower third of New Guinea, passing it on to the Australians for administration in 1906.

After the defeat of Germany in World War I, the German lands were also ruled by Australia through a League of Nations Mandate and were known as the Territory of New Guinea. The original British/Australian territory is known as Papua. All that is left of Germany's presence are names like Finschhafen or Bismarck Sea.

World War II brought violence and destruction. New Guinea and the nearby Solomon Islands had a prominent position in Japanese strategy as stepping stones for a thrust into Australia and as bases for attacking U.S. convoys to the far east. They invaded New Guinea in March of 1942, seizing Salamaua, Finschhafen and Lae. In July they took Buna. By September, after crossing the Owen Stanley mountains, they got within 35 miles of Port Moresby in Papua. That was to be as far as they would get, as they had to regroup and allow their supply lines to catch up. The Americans and Australians, under the command of General MacArthur, counterattacked. By the end of 1942, Papua-New Guinea was firmly in Allied hands.

In June of 1943, the Allies began a major offensive. By September they had recaptured Salamaua and Lae. Finschhafen was regained by Australian troops in October. During April 1944, MacArthur's forces leapfrogged some 600 miles up the northern coast of New Guinea to capture Hollandia, capital of the Dutch half of the island, and bypassing Japanese strong points along the way. This was followed by landings at Maffin Bay in June and Sansapor in August. MacArthur's brilliant strategy had put him in good position for the invasion of the Philippines.

After two days of hugging the New Guinea coast, we entered the port of Hollandia and tied up at a pier. I couldn't see much. The hills rose steeply out of the water and were covered with palm trees and an occasional corrugated metal roofed building. A dusty road ran along the shore and was clogged with Army and Navy trucks most of the time. MacArthur was rumored to have built a palatial castle on top of one of the hills but we couldn't see it. (He only had his headquarters at Hollandia a short time and had since moved on to the Philippines.)

The cargo hold, where the Marines drilled, was opened up and the crane reached in and pulled out a jeep. Our ship's captain and driver got in and drove off. He returned later in the day with orders to proceed to Leyte in the Philippines. However, we were berthed at that dock for the better part of a week waiting for a convoy to form up for the last leg of our journey. It was a lot hotter than when we were at sea because there wasn't much of a breeze. It was especially hot below decks where the paratroopers were still performing K.P. and not too happy about it. We discharged a few passengers and took on some new ones, mostly technicians, veterans of the New Guinea campaign who were taking their skills up to the Philippines where they were sorely needed.

When we finally got out to sea, we found ourselves in the middle of a huge convoy, not all alone as we had been. There were ships in front of us, ships to the rear, and on both sides of us. The sailors were busy sending signals to the other boats, using flags during the day and lights at night as we followed a zig-zag path through the waters, each ship trying to keep its position. I could see destroyers out in front and along the sides, keeping a wary eye out for Japanese submarines. We recrossed the equator, this time without any fanfare, and proceeded some 1,500 miles in a northwesterly direction to the Philippine Islands.

On March 10, 1945 we laid anchor off the coast of Leyte. Because of the possibility of being attacked by Japanese airplanes, we were told that we would disembark under the cover of darkness and to be all packed up and ready to leave the ship by midnight. At the appointed time, with all our gear—helmets, gas masks, back packs, en-

13. RED BEACH AT LEYTE, OCTOBER, 1944. The beach had been cleaned up when I arrived several months later. I saw little damage except for some broken palm trees. U.S. Army photo.

trenching tools, et cetera—we lined up at the ship's railing and dropped our duffel bags into the Higgins boat bobbing in the water some 30 feet below. We then went over the rail and climbed down the side of the ship hand-over-hand on rope cargo netting.

When we reached the end of the netting, we waited for the signal to drop into the landing craft. Timing was crucial. If we let go too soon or too late, we had been warned, we could land in the water to drown or be crushed between the bobbing landing craft and the mother ship. I closed my eyes, murmured a fervent prayer, and let go when I heard the command. It was a short drop to the boat and I was relieved to be caught by two sailors and told to move on back to the rear of the craft.

A short ride through the tossing waves brought us to shore and we made an amphibious landing through the surf carrying our duffel bags. We spread out on the beach under the shelter of some palm tree and waited for trucks to pick us up. We waited and waited. The sun came up in the east. If the Japanese had any airplanes in the vicinity they would have had a tempting target of about 1,500 soldiers spread out on the beach. It was almost noon when we finally got picked up. I had made it to the war zone.

While there was still some fighting going on in the hills on Leyte— and I would be awarded a battle star on my Asiatic-Pacific Campaign Medal just for being there—I wouldn't be involved in it. Another month of waiting and traveling lay ahead of me.

FOUR

On The Trail Of MacArthur

Stories are precious, indispensable. Everyone must have his history . . . You do not know who you are until you possess the imaginative version of yourself. You almost do not exist without it.

—Lance Morrow[1]

The Philippines! The name itself conjures up visions of exotic tropical islands far, far away—and I was actually there. As a boy I had learned about them in my geography and history classes at St. Benedict School. The nuns taught us that the Spanish explorer, Ferdinand Magellan, on his voyage to circumnavigate the globe, was the first European to visit the islands in 1521. Other Spanish explorers followed and claimed them for Spain, naming them after their King, Philip II. Colonized and ruled by Spain from 1565 to 1898, they were ceded to the United States as part of the peace settlement to end the Spanish American War.

Where the Spanish brought their culture, language and the Catholic religion to the islands, the Americans brought better sanitation and health care, the widespread use of the English language, public schools and a democratic form of government. We had made great efforts to bring the Philippines to self-government and had scheduled complete independence for 1946 when World War II intervened. The Japanese invaded the islands soon after Pearl Harbor and defeated the American forces as part of their conquest of Southeast Asia. They then cynically declared the Philippines an "independent republic" in 1943 but remained as callous oppressors. They hand-picked the new puppet government, controlled the press, curtailed religion and beat and tortured any Filipinos they suspected of subversive activities. Many took to the hills, became guerrilla fighters and awaited America's return.

There was even a Michigan connection to the islands in the person of Frank Murphy. Born in Harbor Beach, Michigan in 1890, Murphy studied law at the University of Michigan and did graduate work in London and Dublin. He was a Captain of Infantry in France during World War I. From 1923 to 1930, he was a judge in Detroit and then served as mayor of the city from 1930 to 1933. President Roosevelt then appointed him as Governor-General of the Philippines. A liberal and a proponent of Philippine self-government, Murphy's tenure was marked by legislation to set a date for their independence. After that, he was in the news regularly as Governor of Michigan, United States Attorney-General and Supreme Court Justice.[2] Since he was Irish and Catholic, the nuns used him as a role model for us to emulate.

I remember Grandpa and I waiting for Murphy to appear at the Michigan State Fair around 1937. We waited and waited at the gate he was supposed to enter as part of the Governor's Day festivities but he never showed while we were waiting. He did have his hands full with all the auto plant sit-down strikes that occurred while he was governor so must have been held up.

Most of the 7,083 islands that make up the Philippine archipelago are small, only 466 being larger than one square mile, and many are unnamed. Leyte is one of the Visayan group, a name given to the central islands located between the largest island, Luzon, to the north and the second largest, Mindanao, to the south. At that time, Leyte had a population of 915,853, mostly Malay-related natives, spread over its 3,090 square miles of plains, low mountain ranges and jungle. The provincial capital, Tacloban, also the main seaport, had a population of about 25,000.[3]

The word "Filipino" in Spanish times meant the same as Creole, i.e., an island native of Spanish descent. The Malay natives were called "Indios" by the Spanish, a term the natives didn't like. After the anti-Spanish revolts and the American occupation of the islands, the natives appropriated the designation "Filipino" for all and it came into general use.[4] Here on Leyte they were mostly simple farmers, living out their lives on small farms where they grew rice, corn and vegetables. The principal export was copra and coconut oil.

My first impression of Leyte was one of warmth, green foliage, monkeys and exotically colored birds. Not a war zone at all. The palm

14. GENERAL DOUGLAS MACARTHUR AND PARTY making his famous return to the Philippines in October, 1944. When his landing barge was grounded by a shoal, he ordered the ramp lowered and waded the rest of the way ashore. It is said that he repeated it several times for the benefit of various news photographers. U.S. Army photo.

tree-lined beach where we went ashore was the same Red Beach where General Douglas MacArthur had waded through the waters on the previous October 20. He came in on the third wave when there were still snipers and fighting was going on. Undaunted, and accompanied by Philippine President Sergio Osmena and Resident Commissioner Carlos Romulo, he made a radio broadcast from portable equipment set up on the sand. In a voice deeply emotional but strong and resonant over the sound of rifle fire in the background, he declared: "People of the Philippines, *I have returned*! By the grace of Almighty God, our forces stand again on Philippine soil—soil consecrated in the blood of our two peoples. At my side is your president, Sergio Osmena . . . with members of his cabinet. The seat of your government is therefore now firmly re-established on Philippine soil . . . Rally to me . . . rise and strike . . . The guidance of divine God points the way . . . ."[5]

As boastful and premature as it was for the head of an invading force that had just barely landed and hadn't secured much of anything, it was pure MacArthur—brave, theatrical and self-centered. He was a man many veterans hated and many others admired. "I hope

75

that you are not going to extol MacArthur, " declared Rudy, my table-mate at a Snowbird's luncheon in Florida when he learned that I was writing a book on the liberation of the Philippines. He was a Marine veteran of the Pacific War and like many who served under Admiral Chester Nimitz, MacArthur's rival for the job of overall Supreme Commander, had a lot of antipathy against the Army Commander. Like him or not, MacArthur was a military prodigy, a mixture of brains, valor and vanity, who was a prime figure in the successful prosecution of the war.

Douglas MacArthur was born in Little Rock, Arkansas on Jan. 26, 1880, the son of a famous general and Civil War hero, Arthur MacArthur. Young Douglas went to West Point where he graduated first in his class in 1903. His first posting was in the Philippines where he helped map the new American territory. During World War I, he was Chief of Staff of the 42nd (Rainbow) Division, was wounded three times, decorated 13 times and cited for bravery seven times. He rose in rank to Brigadier General.

During the 1920s he was Superintendent of West Point, served again in the Philippines and was promoted to Major General. In 1930, he became a four-star General and the youngest Chief of Staff in U.S. history. During his tenure, his record was marred when, on the orders of President Hoover, he drove the veterans of the Bonus Army out of Washington by force. From 1935 to 1941, MacArthur worked as military adviser to the Philippine government as Grand Marshall of the Philippines.

In July of 1941, President Roosevelt named MacArthur commander of all U.S. Army forces in the far east. He took a demotion to Lieutenant General to accept this position, which he was serving when the Japanese attacked. Then followed his losing defense of the Bataan Peninsula and the island fortress of Corregidor against overwhelming Japanese forces. In those bleak early days of the war, America desperately needed a hero and MacArthur filled the bill quite nicely.

The press, helped by MacArthur's self-promotion, published breathless accounts of the "Lion of Luzon" defending Bataan. Honorary degrees were showered on him and so many babies born at that time were named after him that he was named "Father of the Year" for 1942. Some of the adulation was downright silly. *Time* magazine quoted one man as saying, "All the people I know think God comes first and then MacArthur," and another saying, "MacArthur is the greatest General since Sergeant York."[6]

His order to leave his men, a direct order from the President, grew out of a need to placate the Australians who were afraid they would be the next ones invaded by the Japanese. When they threatened to bring home their Army divisions from North Africa to defend the homeland, Churchill persuaded Roosevelt to give the Australians hope by naming MacArthur Supreme Allied Commander of the southwest Pacific and the promise of American troops to defend Australia. MacArthur did not want to leave, preferring to stay with his men to the bitter end. He had even sent his medals and personal papers home when the American governor and the Philippine president were evacuated by submarine. At the urging of General George Marshal, he finally consented.

MacArthur left in four creaky P.T. boats with his wife and small son and a handful of his staff, turning over his command to Major General Jonathan Wainwright on March 11, 1942. After a perilous trip, MacArthur and his party made it to Australia. It was here that he made the famous statement to reporters: "I came through, and I shall return!" Washington asked him to amend his prophecy to, "We shall return!" but MacArthur ignored the request. Much to the new Supreme Commander's dismay, he found there were only 32,000 Allied troops in all of Australia, far fewer than the Army he had left behind on Bataan. He also learned that there was a serious shortage of ships, airplanes and other war materiel. It would be a long time before he could make good on his promise to return.

But return he did, even beating off the Joint Chiefs of Staff's plans to bypass the Philippines and seize Formosa as the base for launching the final assault on Japan. MacArthur, who had planned on invading Mindanao in the fall of 1944, threatened to resign if the Philippines were bypassed. He requested the opportunity to proceed to Washington to personally present his views. This was not granted, but he was requested and finally ordered to attend a meeting with Roosevelt and Admiral Chester Nimitz in Hawaii beginning on July 26, 1944.

The meeting, presided over by Roosevelt, was for the purpose of deciding strategy for the final phases of the war in the Pacific. Nimitz carefully presented the case for Formosa, using charts and statistics, and omitted any moral or political considerations. MacArthur, who didn't bring any visual aids with him, had to rely on his own eloquence. Speaking without notes, he persuaded the President that 1) the United States had a moral obligation to liberate the 17 million Filipinos before assaulting Japan, 2) the Philippines would be a much larger jumping-off base than Formosa, and 3) bypassing the Philippines would be politically disastrous. "American public opinion will condemn you, Mr. President," he stated emphatically, "And it will be justified!"

MacArthur had also declared that abandoning the Philippines earlier in the war had been a major blunder, by implication Roosevelt's. That night, before going to bed, the President had his doctor give him some aspirin declaring: "In all my life, *nobody* has ever talked to me the way MacArthur did!"[7]

On his return from Hawaii, Roosevelt made a radio broadcast in which he simply announced "a complete accord with my old friend MacArthur." This was a clear signal to Americans (and the Japanese as well), that the long-promised return to the Philippines was imminent. The Joint Chiefs, who were not at the Hawaii meeting, still had to be convinced. It took another month of debate before Admiral Ernest King reluctantly agreed. He was finally persuaded that a Philippine invasion demanded fewer troops than an assault on the rugged coast of Formosa. On September 8, 1944, the Joint Chiefs issued a directive setting a December date for landings on Leyte. It was later moved up to October 20 when Admiral William "Bull" Halsey, in his bombing raids, found Japanese defenses in the central Philippines to be weak and recommended an earlier date. The Americans, having taken the Palau Islands and Morotai in September, were in a good position to strike.

Thus, MacArthur returned as the head of a force of over 200,000 men, the 738 ships of the Seventh Fleet (known unofficially as "MacArthur's Navy") and hundreds of airplanes. When Admiral Halsey's Third Fleet (which was under Admiral Nimitz's command, not MacArthur's) of 18 aircraft carriers, 6 battleships, 17 cruisers, 64 destroyers and supporting vessels were added, this was the most powerful naval force yet assembled, even larger than Yamamoto's fleet at the Battle of Midway.[8]

Code named King II, the plan for retaking the Philippines was bold, original and far-reaching. As a result of the decisions made in September, the long-prepared plan to invade Mindanao first had to be scrapped and the timetable advanced by thirty days. There would be greater risk since Leyte was beyond the range of fighter planes based in New Guinea. Air support would depend on carrier based planes until air bases could be built on the island. As developed, the operation was more extensive than the Allied invasions of North Africa and Sicily but smaller than the invasion of Normandy.

The Philippine Islands were crucial to Japan. They were needed to protect the shipping lanes to the Dutch East Indies and southeast Asia, source of Japan's oil supply and other important war materiel.

By the first of October, 1944, the Imperial High Command in Tokyo had concluded that the next American assault would be directed at the Philippines, probably at Leyte. On October 10, Lieutenant General Tomoyuki Yamashita arrived in Manila to take over command of the Japanese 14th Army. This was the unit charged with the defense of all the Philippines.

Flamboyant, on the order of the swashbuckling General George Patton, Yamashita had gained fame for his dramatic capture of Singapore in the early days of the war, but that fame had aroused the jealousy of Premier Hideki Tojo. He had transferred the popular general to a command in bleak Manchuria where he was out of the public eye. However, Tojo had resigned in July, disgraced by all the Japanese losses at Guam, Saipan and in New Guinea.

New commander Yamashita began energetically preparing a hot reception for the returning MacArthur. His confidence that he could drown the Americans in a sea of blood was shared by the Japanese high command. They had also prepared a plan. Code named Sho-Go I (Operation Victory), it called for all the resources that Japan possessed to be pressed into a gigantic effort aimed at preventing the Americans from gaining a foothold in the Philippines. Holding the islands was deemed the "one essential."

Admiral Soemu Toyoda, chief of the Imperial Navy agreed. He was prepared to sacrifice his entire fleet to prevent MacArthur from retaking the Philippines, for without oil, his fleet would be useless. The Japanese were also prepared to sacrifice pilots and airplanes. When the Americans struck, there would be scores of kamikaze suicide pilots waiting to crash their bomb laden Zeros onto the decks of American ships. This was a new and horrifying development in the war, but a logical one from the standpoint of the Japanese military being willing to die for their emperor.

When the battle was finally joined at Leyte and not Mindanao as first expected, Admiral Toyoda came up with a hasty tactical plan to inflict a crushing defeat on both the American navy and General MacArthur's toehold on Leyte. Toyoda's fleet would be divided into three forces. The most powerful, under Vice Admiral Takeo Kurita, would be known as the Center Force. Coming from Singapore, by way of Borneo, they would sail eastward through the middle of the Philippines, transit the San Bernardino Strait and enter Leyte Gulf from the north. At the same time a smaller flotilla, to be known as the Southern Force, would weave through the islands of the middle Philippines and then into Surigao Strait, which empties into southern Leyte Gulf where the Americans were busily landing troops. This

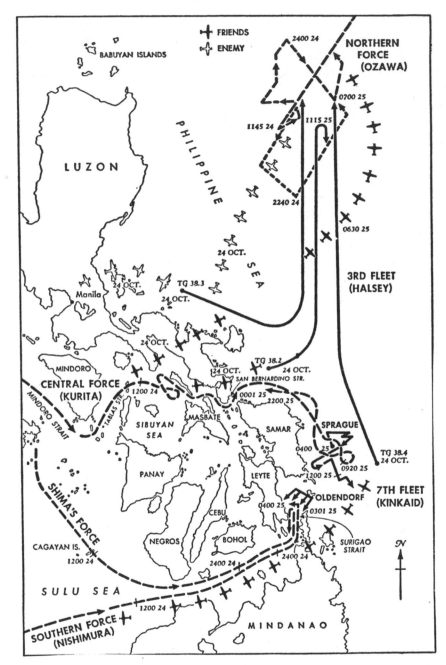

2. THE BATTLE OF LEYTE GULF. Movement of the various fleets in the huge naval engagement is shown on this map. From: Charles A. Willoughby and John Chamberlain, *MacArthur: 1941–1951*, (New York: McGraw-Hill, 1954), p. 179.

fleet, consisting of older, slower warships, was under the command of Vice Admiral Shoji Nishimura and would be augmented by seven cruisers and destroyers that Vice Admiral Kiyohide Shima would bring down from Japan. The two naval forces would converge on MacArthur's beachhead in a classic pincers movement, crushing the American fleet and shelling the beachhead with their large guns.

In the meantime, Admiral Halsey's Third Fleet, which provided a lot of the necessary air support for the beachhead, would be lured away from the Philippines in a northerly direction by dangling a tempting bait. This was the Northern Force under Vice Admiral Jisaburo Ozawa and it consisted of Japan's six remaining aircraft carriers. If Halsey went after them, Kurita's Central Force could sail through narrow San Bernardino Strait unmolested. Execution Day was set for the morning of October 25th.

Kurita's forces assembled at Brunei Bay in North Borneo and sailed on their mission at 8:00 A.M., October 22. Unfortunately for him, he was spotted that night by two American submarines and on the morning of the 23rd they loosed their torpedoes. Badly damaged and out of action was the cruiser *Takeo* and sunk were his flagship, the battleship *Atago* and the cruiser *Maya*. Admiral Kurita was rescued and ordered full steam ahead on his new flagship, the *Yamato*. It was the opening round of the greatest sea battle in history.

Tipped off by the submarine commanders, Halsey sent out air patrols and located the Central and Southern Forces some three hundred miles from Leyte. However, he still hadn't located the Northern Force with its big carriers. On the 24th, there were many air battles as the Japanese used up most of their remaining air power. Pilots from the carrier *Essex* shot down many attacking Japanese warplanes but a glider bomber got through and hit the *Princeton*, one of Halsey's carriers, with a single 500 pound bomb. When the cruiser *Birmingham* moved in close to help take off the wounded, a tremendous explosion on the stricken ship rained down steel debris on the cruiser. On the rescue ship, casualties were 229 killed and 431 wounded. This was in addition to the loss of nearly half of the *Princeton*'s crew. The gutted, still-floating carrier had to be torpedoed by another American ship.

While this was going on, planes from Task Force 38 (a component of Halsey's Third Fleet), were pouncing on the Central Force. They singled out the super-battleship *Murashi* for special attention. Some 20,000 tons heavier than American battleships, she was thought to be unsinkable by the Japanese. Wave after wave of American planes attacked through curtains of flack. After absorbing thirteen torpedoes and seven direct bomb hits, the mighty dreadnought gave a final shudder and plunged to the bottom of the sea. Another lesson in the superiority of air over sea power. The approaching Central Force had no protective air cover.

Late in the afternoon of the 24th, American patrol planes finally located the Northern Force. When Halsey fitted all the pieces of information together, he theorized that they were all heading for a pre-arranged meeting at Leyte Gulf. Scouting planes indicated that the Southern Force was weak and his pilots reported that after the pasting they and the subs had given the Central Force, it was also considerably weakened. Deciding that Kinkaid's largely defensive 7th Fleet could protect the beachhead and wanting to get those big Japanese carriers before they got within range of the beachhead, Halsey gave the order for the full 3rd Fleet to head north at 7:05 P.M. He had swallowed the bait.

At that hour, Admiral Teiji Nishimura's Southern Fleet was about 150 miles from Surigao Strait. Believing that Halsey had San Bernardino Strait blocked off (in the blizzard of coded radio messages that flew back and forth between the fleets, the fact that Halsey was moving his entire fleet north somehow got lost), Admiral Kinkaid rushed almost all of the 7th Fleet's guns and P.T. boats to intercept and destroy Nishimura's oncoming flotilla. Under Rear Admiral Jesse B. Oldendorf, the Americans laid an ambush. Taking advantage of the geography, 40 P.T. boats were deployed to either side of the entrance to Surigao Strait at a point where the Japanese would have to form a column to negotiate the narrow passage.

It was a naval commander's dream: an enemy force moving blindly into a trap. They arrived in the dark of the early morning of October 25. In the ensuing battle (the Americans called it a turkey shoot), Nishimura's Southern Force was virtually destroyed. The Admiral himself was killed when a shell hit the bridge of the battleship *Yamashiro*, on which he was standing. Under his second in command, the Japanese kept coming. Further shells and torpedoes sent the *Yamashiro*, as well as most of the rest of the Southern Fleet, to the bottom of Surigao Strait.

While the Americans were congratulating themselves on this great feat, Admiral Kurita's Central Force, battered but still powerful, steamed under the cover of darkness through San Bernardino Strait and set a course for MacArthur's beachhead. By 7:00 A.M. they came upon Rear Admiral Clifton A. "Ziggy" Sprague's group known as Taffy 3. It consisted of six small escort carriers and six destroyers. This tiny fleet was all that stood in the way of Admiral Kurita's powerful battleships and the American beachhead. It was now the Americans' turn for a suicide mission. They charged into the oncoming flotilla.

Heavily outgunned (five inches against eighteen) and outnumbered, Admiral Sprague's puny force nevertheless fought desperately for the next two and a half hours to keep those powerful Japanese guns from pounding the beachhead. The cost was high. All 12 of Admiral Sprague's fleet were either sunk or badly damaged. It would have been worse if the baby flattops hadn't been converted Liberty ships with thin skins. The armor piercing Japanese shells, meant for use against large fleet carriers with armor protection, mostly went right through Admiral Sprague's carriers without exploding.

While this was going on, Admiral Halsey, far to the north, was launching his first air strike against the Northern Force which he had been chasing. Admiral Ozawa was by now withdrawing north to lure Halsey even farther away from Leyte Gulf. Halsey's airplanes were successful, sinking two carriers and badly damaging two more and their destroyer escorts. Admiral Ozawa had to leave his burning flagship *Zuikaku* and hitch a ride on a destroyer. On the *New Jersey*, Halsey was jubilant and preparing to launch a killing blow against the remainder of the Northern Force when he got a message from his boss, Admiral Nimitz: "Where is Task Force 34? The world wonders."[9] Only then did he realize that the rest of the Navy was under the impression that he had left that part of his fleet to guard the San Bernardino Strait. Task Force 34 had never been formed.

Gnashing his teeth and cussing a blue streak, the "Bull" finally ordered his cruisers and battleships to reverse course and head south at full throttle, but he left three of his fast carrier groups to pursue the Northern Force. In spite of the pounding the Americans gave them, two flattops, two cruisers and six destroyers managed to limp their way back to Japan. Halsey had wanted to get them all.

Meanwhile, back at Leyte Gulf, the battered Taffy 3 group was being assaulted by the first kamikaze suicide planes of the war, as five bomb-laden Zeros suddenly dove out of the clouds. Each one had picked out a target. Fortunately, four of the suicide pilots missed their targets and plunged harmlessly into the waters. The fifth, however, smashed into the flight deck of the already damaged escort carrier *St. Lo*. A mighty explosion followed and the carrier sank within 30 minutes. The new kamikaze program had been successful the first time out. (The name means "divine wind" and is derived from a watershed event in Japanese history in the year 1570 when a Mongol invasion of Japan was thwarted by a typhoon.) This suicidal program was Japan's last hope for winning the war and was used effectively in the remaining campaigns, especially at Okinawa.

A few hours later, Halsey's task force arrived and the tide of battle turned in favor of the Americans. Fearful that Halsey would block the San Bernardino Strait behind him, Kurita retreated, pulling his remaining vessels back through the narrow passage under the cover of darkness. By midnight, the three-day series of naval actions was over.

The Japanese had failed and their navy dealt a crushing blow. Combined losses of their three fleets were four carriers, three battleships, six cruisers, and twelve destroyers all sunk; hundreds of airplanes destroyed and over 10,000 men killed. Many more vessels were seriously damaged. Our Navy paid a huge price too. A light carrier, two escort carriers, and three destroyers were all sunk, 200 airplanes lost and 3,000 sailors and airmen killed.[10] But, the beachhead on Leyte was now secure.

When MacArthur's troops first landed, they had met with only minimal opposition because the Japanese had expected the first blow to come at Mindanao. Thus, they only had one division, the 16th, on Leyte. It was a unit that had been involved in the infamous Bataan Death March. When MacArthur first landed on Leyte, he strolled around the beach battle area and turned over several Japanese corpses to look at their insignia. With a look of satisfaction, he turned to his companion, Carlos Romulo, and said, "Sixteenth Division. They're the ones who did the dirty work on Bataan!"[11]

Yamashita would rather have fought this decisive battle of the Pacific on the rugged terrain of Luzon, some four hundred miles to the northwest of Leyte. He had his best troops and remaining warplanes based there. However, on October 22, he was overruled by his superior, Field Marshal Hisaichi Terauchi, Supreme Commander in the south Pacific, and ordered to fight desperately for every inch of Leyte. Within hours he was loading troopships on Luzon and rushing them to the beleaguered Leyte.

Lieutenant General Sosaku Suzuki, the commander of the 35th Army defending the Central Philippines, had also learned from studying previous American invasions that most beach defenses could not survive the thunderous air and naval bombardments that preceded the troop landings. On Leyte, the majority of the ground fighting took place further inland, in the hills and jungles. By the tenth day, as the Americans reached the Japanese strong points and resistance stiffened, the battle turned into a bloody slugging match.

Typically the ground action boiled down to small groups of American G.I.s trying to root out Japanese soldiers cleverly concealed in

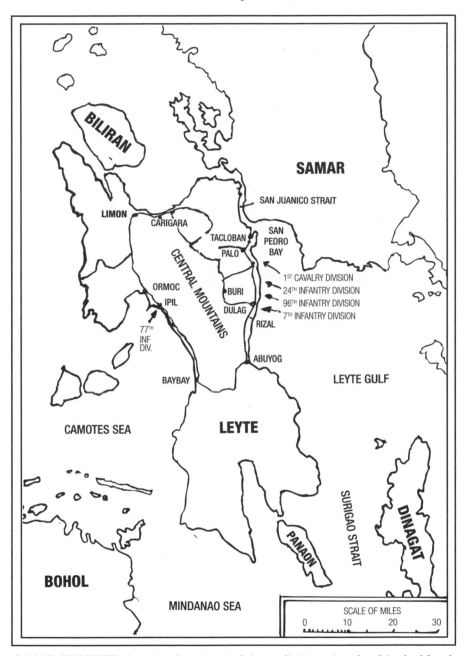

3. MAP OF LEYTE showing the principal Army divisions involved in the bloody campaign to liberate the island. Mopping-up operations, in the northwest part of the island, were still going on when I arrived in March, 1945. Map by the author.

15. COMBAT ON LEYTE. Most of the fighting on Leyte was done in the jungles and mountains under adverse weather conditions. This scene is near Palo and the Replacement Depot where I spent three weeks awaiting assignment to a regular outfit. U.S. Army photo

spider holes and bunkers camouflaged by natural vegetation. It was dangerous, savage work and the casualties piled up. To add to the general misery, rain fell constantly, filling foxholes and making supply trails slippery or impassable. Winds sometimes reached gale force as tropical storms passed over the island.

Over the next two months the battles raged. The American Sixth Army, under the command of Lieutenant General Walter Kreuger, sought to gain control over the whole island, while the ever increasing Japanese fiercely resisted. The American X Corps under Major General Franklin C. Sibert and consisting of the 1st Cavalry Division and the 24th Infantry Division, drove across northern Leyte to Carigara and Limon, then turned south towards Ormoc. Meanwhile, the XXIV Corps under Major General John R. Hodge, made up of the 7th and 96th Infantry Divisions, went south from Dulag to Abuyog and then west over the mountains to Baybay.

The Americans built up five air bases on the island despite the wretched weather conditions. By the middle of November, the influx of U.S. warplanes made it increasingly difficult for Japanese ships to operate in the waters off Leyte to bring in men and supplies.

Yamashita and Fourth Air Army Commander, Lieutenant General Kyoji Tominga, drew up an ambitious scheme for a coordinated air and ground assault on three of the American air bases. Dubbed Operation Wa, it called for heavy aerial bombing of the fields at San Pablo, Buri and Bayug. This was to be followed by crash landings on the runways of the air bases by transport planes holding demolition experts, who would proceed to blow up U.S. warplanes and installations before escaping westward into the hills. Then, about a week later on the night of December 5, two regiments of paratroopers were to land on the air bases at Buri and San Pablo while Japanese troops came down out of the hills and attacked from the west. After capturing the fields and destroying what was left of the American planes and installations, the combined forces were then to advance eastward and capture Dulag.

Unfortunately for the Japanese, Operation Wa went awry right from the start. One of the three transports carrying the demolition experts was shot down by American anti-aircraft fire with the loss of all the men aboard. The other two transports missed their target airfields and crash landed in rear areas. In their haste to get away, the Japanese left most of their demolition charges in the wrecked planes.

When rain squalls temporarily grounded American planes, Yamashita assumed that his demolition squads had been successful and proceeded with the second phase of seizing the air bases. Since the Japanese didn't have enough planes to carry all the paratroopers at once, they were to be dropped in three waves with the planes having to go back to Luzon to bring back other contingents. Bad weather forced a one day postponement. Radio communications were so poor the ground troops didn't get word of the delay. They attacked the airstrip at Buri at dawn on the morning of December 6, as scheduled, and had captured about half of it before the Americans could organize defenses. Many of the rear echelon troops, the cooks, clerks, and mechanics had fled at the first sound of gunfire. Most of our regular infantry troops were in the mountains to the west.

The first wave of Japanese paratroopers dropped from the skies that evening, but only about 60 linked up with the ground troops at Buri. The other 300 drifted down two miles away at the airstrip at San Pablo. At both air bases they blew up airplanes, gasoline tanks and other buildings. Meanwhile, back on Luzon, the second wave took off at 10:00 P.M. but had to return when it ran into turbulent weather. The third wave never got off the ground.

At San Pablo all was confusion as the Americans and the Japanese engaged in lethal fire fights in the darkness. No one could be certain who was who, and many were killed or wounded by friendly bullets. In the morning, Major General Joseph Swing, Commander of the 11th Airborne Infantry Division, which was headquartered there, rounded up a motley crew of cooks, clerks and M.P.s and led them in killing or chasing off the invaders. Many of the Japanese moved over to the nearby Buri strip where they joined their confederates and seized control of the entire facility, but without reinforcements they were doomed. The 187th Glider Infantry Regiment rushed a battalion of infantry to the scene as did a battalion of the newly arrived 38th Infantry Division. Outgunned and outnumbered, the well-dug-in Japanese hung on doggedly until December 10 when one final assault by the Americans recaptured the field. The other Japanese, troops that were to have attacked from the west, got bogged down in the slippery mountain trails, then bumped into other elements of the 11th Airborne Division and never made it to the air base.

Operation Wa was a dismal failure, not only in execution but also in its objective. San Pablo, Buri and Bayug were basically minor air bases not yet up to handling many warplanes. If the main thrust had been against Tacloban air base, home of the 49th Fighter Group and other major air units, a lot more damage to the Americans could have been achieved.

The bloodletting continued. On December 7, the 77th Infantry landed on the west coast of Leyte and then both corps converged on Ormoc, the vital port city and headquarters of the Japanese Army. By Christmas the remaining Japanese forces were completely isolated and without hope of further reinforcement or escape. On December 26, MacArthur optimistically declared, "The Leyte campaign can now be regarded as closed except for minor mopping-up operations."

The phrase "minor mopping-up operations" infuriates the average infantryman who must do the mopping up. It is exhausting and dangerous work without much credit or glory. The Australians were particularly incensed at MacArthur when he was island- hopping to glory and leaving them behind to take care of all the bypassed and dangerous enemies in New Guinea and the Solomon Islands. On Leyte, the Japanese were still an intact force of some 27,000 men under General Suzuki,[12] but reduced to the wild, mountainous northwestern section of the island. (This was far more than the estimated 16,000 who were garrisoned there when MacArthur landed in October.) The Sixth Army under General Walter Kreuger was pulled back to prepare for the invasion of Luzon, and the newly-formed Eighth Army under Lieutenant General Robert L. Eichelberger took over. They were still "mopping up" when I got there in March. When it was really over, about four months after MacArthur's premature announcement, approximately 60,000 Japanese soldiers had died for their emperor versus about 3,500 American G.I.s killed and 12,000 wounded.[13] It was a resounding defeat for the Japanese, but only the opening round in the liberation of the Philippines.

The trucks that finally picked us up on Red Beach took us inland to the 4th Replacement Depot. This was a collection of tents and corrugated metal buildings set up in a grove of palm trees located about three miles south of Tacloban on both sides of the Tacloban-Palo Road. The terrain was low and swampy, consisting of rice paddies and alternating low sandy ridges.

There was no evidence of any battles being fought there. Housing for us replacements was floorless squad tents which were crowded with as many as 20 army cots. We were each assigned to one and told to place our gear on the cot, strip naked and report outside wearing only our boots, rain ponchos and helmet liners. The first order of business was to be a "short arm" inspection.

So there we were, all of the passengers of the *Cape Meares*, standing in long lines in the tropical sun. We slowly made our way to where the medical people were doing the examination. Fifteen hundred "flashers" passing in review. At a command we would lift up our sweaty ponchos with one hand and milk down our penises with the other while the doctors stared intently so that they could be assured that we were free of any venereal disease. I remember a lot of discussion about how could they expect us to be infected after being confined to a troopship for thirty days, but that was the procedure.

Of course, some soldiers were infected. In the Unit Histories that replacement depots submitted to the National Archives, there are many reports by depot surgeons on the rate of venereal disease. They usually blamed any increase on incoming replacements. The doctors also reported that the rate was low among the depot staff, higher among the transient population and very high among Negro troops. One racist doctor stated that "86 percent of the venereal disease occurred among colored troops." They all reported that they were actively enforcing venereal disease control.[14]

Known colloquially as a "repo depo" or "repple depple," the replacement depot was an Army institution which functioned as a clearing house through which soldiers, newly arrived from the States, were sorted out, their health and equipment reviewed and their permanent assignments given. It also acted as a temporary holding area for soldiers who had been released from hospitals or separated from their outfits for other reasons. Sometimes soldiers languished there for months.

Bill Mauldin, in his book *Up Front*, tells about being in a repo depo in Sicily after a bout with pneumonia. His division was only 15 miles away but his promised transportation never came. With two other soldiers from his outfit, who had been waiting three weeks for the same truck, he escaped and made his own way back. Mauldin also tells about another soldier who spent his entire time overseas in a replacement depot without ever being permanently assigned. The man finally went home on rotation. His hometown newspaper called him "a veteran of the Italian Campaign."[15]

The 4th Replacement Depot had been located in the Ahioma District at Milne Bay, New Guinea, before moving to Leyte with the Sixth Army. During the month of March 1945 when I was there, 15,521 enlisted men and 1,175 officers were processed. These figures included Philippine Scouts. Also processed were small numbers of prisoners of war, released civilians of various nationalities, and "British and American evaders, escapers and guerrillas."[16] The records also note there were five air raid alerts and one air raid during March, but I don't remember any.

Replacement depots were organized into replacement battalions and companies. This was for the purpose of continued training of the replacements in physical conditioning, weapons firing, and jungle patrolling. This certainly would have been useful after the month of inactivity aboard the troopship. Also, given the fact that we were subject to going right into combat from there, and had missed three weeks of training because of the Battle of the Bulge, the Army should have been sharpening our skills. However, the 4th Replacement

Depot had no training program that I was aware of. I spent the three weeks I was there doing servile work.

Every day the company bulletin board listed the rosters for the next day's assignments. While hot and laborious, the work was at least somewhat varied. One day I would be assigned to a group at a warehouse where I would spend the day loading and unloading trucks by hand. (I don't remember seeing any lift trucks when I was in the Army. They must have come into general use later.) The Army processed an enormous amount of material goods that came in cardboard or wooden boxes. These had to be unloaded, carried, piled up in stacks or loaded on shelves, stored for a while and then broken down and reloaded on other trucks, all with back-breaking manual labor.

On another day I would be sent to an Army Post Office to sort mail. They were really behind in their work. I remember working on mountainous piles of undelivered packages that rose some twenty feet in height. Stored outside, they were only covered by a canvas tarp for protection against the elements. This was March and a lot of the parcels were Christmas packages from home. With the constant shifting of personnel from the front to hospitals to repo depos and back to their outfits, which were constantly on the move, the postal clerks had a herculean job. Working to a list, we would search through many parcels before we could fill a bag for shipment. Many of the packages were smashed or weathered beyond recognition so would have to be set aside or discarded.

Another day I would be assigned to an engineering battalion which was usually involved in constructing or improving an existing Army installation. It was real grub work, such as digging drainage ditches or pushing a wheelbarrow full of sand or gravel from one place to another. As the war moved on to the other islands, the rear echelon troops were busy building the infrastructure that made their lives so comfortable—theaters, libraries, chapels, and recreational facilities of all kinds.

It was usually hot, sweaty, arduous toil in the tropical sun, so when we got back to the repo depo at the end of the day, we were glad to be able to take showers. These were crude affairs with a tub of water set on top of a wood frame structure. They had multiple shower heads operated by pulling on a rope. The water table where the camp was located was about a foot below the surface of the ground. Dig a hole three feet deep and it would promptly fill up with two feet of water. If the storage tank was empty when you wanted to take a shower, you took a bucket, dipped it in the shallow well next to the shower, climbed a ladder and replenished the tank. If there were several of us we would make up a bucket brigade and fill the tank in short order. We didn't have any hot water but it was so warm and humid anyway that the well water was very refreshing.

The high water table made for a sanitary problem with the latrines. You couldn't use slit trenches or deep latrine holes such as the Army usually dug when in the field. At the 4th Replacement Depot, the toilets were constructed by sinking six fifty-gallon steel drums, with their tops cut off, into the ground to the proper height. Then a removable, six-hole wood toilet seat arrangement was built to span the six sunken drums. Two of these six-hole toilets set back to back and were protected from the elements by an open-sided pyramidal tent.

When the drums filled up with feces and toilet paper, which was usually every day, the wooden seat arrangement would be removed, the drums soaked with gasoline and the waste matter set on fire. It took quite a while for the burning and the cooling down so that the seats could be replaced for the next use. If you had an urgent need, you would have to search out a latrine where they weren't burning up the excrement, although the odor and the smoke were so bad you could tell where they were burning long before you got there. According to the 4th Replacement Depot records, when the barrels got to within one foot of being full of unburnable ash, they were sealed and buried in a landfill.

The movie *Platoon*,[17] which was shot in the Philippines, has many scenes that look familiar to me although it is about an infantry platoon in the Vietnam War. As the beginning title and credits roll, the new replacement gets in trouble with his sergeant and is assigned the task of burning the excrement. Even though this more modern Army had firepower and transportation that we never even dreamed about, they were, apparently, solving their sanitary problem the same as in World War II. Some things never change.

I never had to pull that duty but I did do K.P. and stood guard duty at the replacement depot, when I wasn't loaned out to some labor battalion. I remember an evening guarding a food warehouse. It was just at twilight and Northrup P-61 Black Widow night fighters were out patrolling the skies. The Tacloban air base was close by and they were flying quite low, just over the tops of the palm trees. The sergeant of the guard had admonished me to be especially alert because Japanese stragglers had been known to try and sneak in to steal food. This was the real thing, I thought, as darkness quickly enveloped me and I walked my post, gripping my loaded carbine, nervous and aware.

Nothing happened during my watch, but I remember also being bothered by a letter that I had received that day from a former Trade School classmate, a 4-F who was working at the Ford Motor Company and making lots of money working overtime. He had written optimistically about the war ending soon and how I could look forward to being back on the campus at the University of Detroit, probably in the fall semester. It irritated me because I was rather pessimistic and could not see myself back home for a long time to come. I suppose he was trying to cheer me up but it had the opposite effect.

Even though the local Army Post Offices were behind on their parcel post, letters did get through to us quite rapidly. We were at the replacement depot only a few days when we had our first mail call and it was fairly regular after that. Mail was our only contact home so it was very important to us. If it was irregular, or we didn't get any when there was a mail call, it affected morale and became a frequent subject for complaint. It was reported that the average soldier overseas received fourteen pieces of mail every week in 1943, so the post office was handling a tremendous volume.[18] I don't think that I got that much mail but I was carrying on an extensive correspondence with friends, relatives and former classmates.

One of them was a girl who sat next to me in chemistry class at U of D. Her chatty letters always arrived on blue stationery, in a neat woman's script with the i's and j's dotted with little circles and she used lots of exclamation points. My friend was on the staff of the *Varsity News* and wrote a column called "Fightin' Titans" which gave the news about alumni and former students who were serving their country. She had arranged for me to receive copies so that I could keep up with the activities on campus.

By then the school paper was reporting well over 800 alumni serving as commissioned officers in the Armed Forces of their country. This was quite high for a small school like U of D. One of its more prominent grads was Major General Paul Wurtsmith who was then commanding the 13th Air Force in the Philippines. He had previously served in the 49th Fighter Group. Later on, an air base in Northern Michigan was named after him.[19]

I also received the *St. Benedict Weekly*, our church paper, which was sent to all the boys in service who belonged to the parish. Other soldiers also received their local papers and since we were all hungry for news of any kind about home, we often passed them around and read about each other's local happenings.

The government had a high speed system called V-mail which they encouraged everyone to use. It was free, but in my experience, universally ignored. You had to write your message on a special one page form which was then photographed and the micro-film carried by airplane to the United States where it was reproduced and mailed in the domestic postal system. The single page limited your writing, the reproduction was reduced in size and of poor quality and the speed wasn't that much faster. I sent most of my letters by airmail, paying the extra postage.

Censorship was a source of irritation. It had started as soon as we had left the port of San Francisco. At Fort Ord, we had been lectured on what we could or could not write about when overseas. By the time the officer had finished telling us what we couldn't write about, there didn't seem to be much left that anyone could say to the folks back home. You had to use some ingenuity to get by the censor. My correspondents occasionally reported back that half of my letter had been scissored out, so I wasn't too successful. We had to submit our letters unopened and the actual censorship was done by the local unit officers. This was resented because you couldn't write anything bad about them if they were going to be the first ones to read about it. Officers censored their own mail, which was also resented by the enlisted man.

In the Pacific Theater, five percent of the letters were spot-checked farther up the line and further censored. MacArthur's standing among his troops was established by extracting and collating opinions of him that were found in these letters. It is said that he scrupulously read the monthly reports, which often had unflattering quotes referring to him as a "brass-hatted old bastard," "flannel-mouthed fool," and "egotistical ass," among others.[20] There probably were a lot worse epithets that got censored out at the local level.

We couldn't write where we were specifically, but could write a general address such as "Somewhere at sea" or "Somewhere in the Philippine Islands." No mention of the island of Leyte or local towns was allowed. It was exciting to be in a foreign country, even though you couldn't tell people at home exactly where you were. This was brought home to us a few days after we had arrived when they paid us for the month of February. The money came in the form of a foreign currency, Philippine pesos and centavos at the rate of two pesos for every U.S. dollar. Except for a few Canadian coins, I had never had any foreign money. Now I had a whole pocketful. We also saw an increase in our pay because of the 20 percent allowance that the government provided for soldiers serving outside the continental United States. In the case of privates, like myself and the other replacements, it amounted to a $10.00 raise from $50.00 to $60.00 a month. We certainly weren't getting rich.

Some tried to. With all that strange money in our pockets, there was a sudden increase in the craps and poker games that took place at night. A few of the gamblers were Filipino civilians who worked at the camp. Short, brown skinned and oriental looking, they were usually barefoot and dressed in olive drab army underwear shorts and sleeveless shirts, topped off with a straw hat. The Filipinos could squat for hours as they impassively rolled the dice or quietly placed their bets with a minimum of motion. This was in marked contrast to the Americans who were more physically and vocally involved. They whooped and hollered when they made their point, or groaned loudly when they didn't.

The coconut palm trees that dotted the camp were a source of an alcoholic drink for the Filipinos. Known as "tuba," it was fermented from the juice of the palm tree and was collected in small amounts, much as farmers do in Michigan when they make maple syrup in the spring. Tuba was much harder to get since the sap was collected in containers at the top of these very tall trees. We would watch as a native laboriously shinnied his way up to the very top of the tree, collected his raw material in a bottle he had strapped over his shoulder and slowly made his way down. He then went to the next tree and repeated the process. It seemed like a tough way to make a living.

Besides gambling and watching the tuba juice collector, there were other things to do in the evening. We had movies at the open air camp theater most nights after dark. There were also a couple of boxing matches and a forgettable USO show with a rather untalented comedian. He was always asking for applause, saying that it was an entertainer's "bread and butter." When he got a little applause after a corny joke, he would say "Thanks for the sandwich!"

The best entertainment event while I was on Leyte was when Irving Berlin brought his musical show "This is the Army" to entertain the troops. Because it was a big show using some 350 soldier entertainers, it was performed at a neighboring base which had a bigger outdoor theater. Most of us trudged over to see it.

Basically a rewrite of Berlin's World War I musical "Yip, Yip, Yaphank," the show had been revived to make money for the Army Relief Fund during World War II and had also been made into a movie in 1943.[21] Following the film's release, the touring company continued to perform for live audiences in the States and then headed overseas to combat areas in Europe and the Pacific. By the time it closed in Honolulu in October 1945, it had been seen by over two and a half

16. & 17. TUBA JUICE COLLECTOR. The Filipinos made an alcoholic drink from the sap of the coconut palm trees. It had to be collected from the top as this man is doing. Photos courtesy of Art Petroff.

millon American soldiers and had made over ten million dollars for the Army Relief Fund. For this contribution to the war effort, Irving Berlin was decorated with the Medal of Merit by General George C. Marshall.[22]

I remember it as a lavish vaudeville show with numerous singing, dancing and comedic numbers, all with a patriotic theme. One of the numbers featured the illustrious composer himself, decked out in his World War I doughboy uniform, croaking out the words to his famous song "Oh, How I Hate to Get Up in the Morning." He seemed to me to be quite ancient then (56), but he lived until 1989, passing away at the ripe old age of 101 and mourned as a national hero. In the course of his career he had composed over one thousand songs.

The replacement depot had a loudspeaker system. It was usually tuned to the Armed Forces radio station when not being used for announcements or paging someone. Besides music, it gave us periodic news programs. One item of local news that I remember well, because it was repeated so often, was a shift in driving from the left hand to the right hand side of the road. When the Japanese took control of the Philippines in 1942, they instituted driving on the left side of the road because that is the way they do it in Japan (and in England and some other parts of the world). The civil and military authorities decided to change back to the American system of driving on the right hand side and the changeover had been set for a day in March while I was there. This impending change was announced over and over again. The date finally came and the change was made without the feared terrible accidents probably because most of the traffic was military and Americans are more comfortable with driving on the right hand side, anyway.

None of the roads were paved. They were usually muddy tracks when it rained, but it was surprising how soon they dried up if the sun shone. Then they turned into clouds of dust as the truck traffic stirred them up. We were usually transported to our work details in the back of Army two and a half ton trucks, so often we went out on muddy roads and came back through clouds of dust, or vice versa. It was the "dry" season but it usually rained every day.

The most interesting war news while I was on Leyte was bulletins about the invasions that were taking place in the surrounding islands. MacArthur was determined to recoup all of the Philippine Islands and not bypass large garrisons of troops as he had done in New Guinea and the Solomon Islands. Without authorization from the Joint Chiefs, and while the fighting still raged on Luzon, he ordered Eichelberger's Eighth Army to begin the liberation of all the remaining islands of the archipelago.

MacArthur has since been criticized by many historians. They say the seizure of many of these islands, which had little or no strategic value to the overall defeat of Japan, was especially wasteful since the five infantry divisions being used for this purpose left Kreuger's Sixth Army on Luzon badly depleted. It is also said that MacArthur wanted to hang on to the Seventh Fleet and the 13th Air Force and by keeping them busy supporting his invasions he kept them from being transferred to Nimitz's theater of operations.

The arguments in defense of his decision are more personal and humanitarian. He undoubtedly wanted to be remembered as the liberator of all of the islands and to fully redeem his pledge to the Filipinos that he would return to save them. The Japanese' harsh treatment of civilians and prisoners of war was also a major concern. On Palawan, the Japanese had massacred 140 American and Filipino prisoners, and on Luzon many American prisoners of war had been saved only by quick action. There were genuine fears of more atrocities as the isolated Japanese came closer to final defeat and reacted savagely. The only way to prevent this was to invade and occupy all the islands.

Eichelberger's operations in the south were executed with skill and energy. In all, 14 major and 24 minor amphibious landings were made over a period of 44 days. When I arrived on Leyte it was in full swing. Operations by the 41st Infantry Division on the Zamboangan peninsula of Mindanao were being reported during the middle of March. This was a familiar name to me as we had sung countless choruses of "The Monkeys Have No Tails In Zamboanga" around innumerable Boy Scout campfires. The news of this campaign was soon superseded by bulletins about the 40th Division landing on Panay on March 18, followed by reports of the Americal Division[23] landing on the neighboring island of Cebu. At the end of the month, U.S. forces were invading Negros, the second major island west of us. Although Japanese resistance continued in the remote parts of the islands until the war ended, the airfields, principal towns and most of the roads were in Allied hands by June. Civil government of the Philippine Commonwealth was re-established and life on the islands resumed a semblance of normality. The Philippines did not formally become an independent republic until July 4, 1946, but President Osmena's Commonwealth government enjoyed complete autonomy soon after it returned with MacArthur.

With all that action going on so close by, we wondered how much longer we would be stuck as laborers in the replacement depot. It seemed as though the Army should be moving us on and soon it did. Easter was Sunday, April l that year. Gene Malecha, who was a good Catholic, wanted to make his Easter duty and I had accompanied him to a church where we had made our confessions to a Filipino priest who barely spoke English. We planned to go to Mass together on Easter morning but when I arrived at his tent the next day, he was gone. He had been shipped out to the Americal Division on Cebu. I never did find out what happened to Otto May and the other replacements I had trained with at Camp Hood; they were all gone, too.

A few hours later, I also found my name on a roster to be shipped out and that evening I was boarding a ship in Tacloban harbor. I don't remember the name of the vessel but it was a troopship similar to the *Cape Meares* and we were again packed in the hold six bunks high. My bunkmate was a Negro soldier who didn't say much. Although I didn't get seasick this time because the passage was relatively calm, I felt all alone without any familiar faces around me.

We were in a large convoy that was protected by destroyers and P.T. boats. By this stage of the war, there wasn't too much chance of being bombed by Japanese airplanes but their submarines were still a menace. The passing scenery was gorgeous. Huge green hills rose out of dark blue waters with the colors varying with the time of day and the amount of light and mist. The P.T. boats, usually in bunches, would roar by occasionally, churning up long, whitish wakes as they patrolled the convoy.

The route took us south through the Surigao Strait, where the Seventh Fleet had sunk all those Japanese ships, and into the Bohol Sea with Mindanao off to the port side and the islands of Bohol, Cebu and Negros on the starboard side. Then we entered the Sulu Sea and turned north, passing Panay and Mindoro before entering the South China Sea by way of the Mindoro Strait.

We were still on MacArthur's trail. He had splashed ashore at Lingayen Gulf in January when the Americans had invaded the main island of Luzon. The loudspeaker said our destination was Manila, the "Pearl of the Orient" and the capital city, which was now in American hands. It took about a week to get there because the convoy moved so slowly. We entered the harbor during daylight hours, passing by still-smoldering Corregidor, crossing the bay and anchoring some distance from the shore. Natives, mostly young boys, came out to greet us in small boats, hawking bananas, coconuts and homemade trinkets. If soldiers threw down money, they threw their wares up to the deck. They were also expert swimmers and would dive deep in the murky waters to retrieve coins that were tossed to them.

Manila harbor was littered with sunken ships. Some were over on their sides, others submerged with only their masts or stacks sticking out of the water. Since the docks hadn't been repaired yet, we made another amphibious landing, crawling down the cargo netting draped over the ship's side and dropping into the Higgins boat. It was easier than Leyte because the operation was conducted during the daytime and the waters of Manila harbor were a lot calmer than the swells of Leyte Gulf. One of the Higgins boats filled with water because of a defective landing ramp. It sank before it made shore but all the passengers were rescued. Except for getting soaked and losing some luggage, they were all right. Trucks took us to another replacement depot somewhere on the south side of Manila. I wondered what was in store for me next. It would certainly be exciting, I thought.

FIVE

The Day
The President Died

There is no indispensable man.
    —Franklin D. Roosevelt[1]

Did you ever have a bull or a load of hay fall on you? If
you have, you know how I felt . . . I don't know if you
boys pray, but if you do, please pray God to help me
carry this load.
                                            —Harry S. Truman[2]

It must have been in April 1980 when I was driving to Detroit on a business trip. J.P. McCarthy's[3] voice came out of the radio. He was noting the anniversary of the day that Franklin D. Roosevelt died. I hadn't given it much thought during the intervening 35 years, but people were calling in to the program to tell J.P. where they were and what they had been doing, when they first heard the news. Their stories brought back a flood of personal memories, but something didn't seem right. They kept mentioning the date as Thursday, April 12, 1945, when I definitely remembered that it was *Friday the 13th.*

When I got home, I looked it up in my encyclopedia. It recorded that Roosevelt was in Warm Springs, Georgia, on that fatal day. His health had deteriorated in early 1945 and after returning from the Yalta Conference in February, it worsened. It seems to have been a well-kept secret from the public that he had been diagnosed in January as suffering from congestive heart disease. One indication though, was the fact that when he reported to Congress on his Yalta trip, he

18. PRESIDENT ROOSEVELT GIVING RADIO ADDRESS. In peace and in war, the beloved leader addressed his constituents on many subjects and rallied the nation to support his many programs. UPI/CORBIS-BETTMANN photo.

gave the report seated. He normally always addressed them standing. Pictures of him from those times also show him to be wan and tired-looking.

On March 29, he traveled to the "Little White House" in Georgia to get some very needed rest. At 1:00 Thursday afternoon, April 12, he was sitting before the fireplace doing some paperwork while an artist, Mrs. Elizabeth Schoumatoff, painted his portrait. Suddenly he exclaimed, "I have a terrific headache!" and slumped over. He was carried to his bedroom where he died at 3:55 P.M. of a cerebral hemorrhage. He was 63 years old. The White House in Washington, D.C. announced his death to the world at 5:48 P.M., *Eastern War Time.*[4]

It then dawned on me. That was the explanation. On the other side of the world, in the Philippine Islands, by virtue of Greenwich Mean Time and that damn International Date Line again, it was 7:48 A.M., Friday, April 13, 1945, when the news was first broadcast. That's where I was - in the Army's 5th Replacement Depot, located south of the city of Manila.

James Roosevelt, the President's oldest son, was at that time also in the Philippines. He tells about getting the news on the morning of Friday the 13, soon after it was broadcast. He made an unsuccessful attempt to get to the funeral but was too late, catching up with his mother in New York City as she was on her way from the burial at Hyde Park to Washington to break up housekeeping after all those years at the White House.[5]

I had been near Manila less than a week. The camp was much like the repo depot on Leyte except the soldiers running it hadn't been there long enough to build up some of the infrastructure that made life more pleasant on Leyte. Also, I don't remember being assigned to any work details. I was suffering from a severe head cold and spent most of my time on my army cot reading or watching as my nose dripped on the bare, dirt floor of the tent I shared with a bunch of other replacements.

One of them came back to the tent one day, saying that there were Filipinos selling bananas and souvenirs outside the camp's gate. I went out to see what they had to offer. The bananas were small, about the size of my index finger and green. The souvenirs were crudely made and of little interest to me, but there were several women offering laundry services. I had a lot of dirty clothes, so I went back to my tent and made up a large bundle. I gave them to a Filipino couple who solemnly promised to bring them back the next day all washed and ironed.

That's the last I saw of my clothes. The thieves weren't there the next day, or the next and the other Filipinos denied even knowing them. I had lost about two-thirds of my Army clothes. I couldn't believe I had been so gullible, but the city Filipinos here in the Manila area were a lot more sophisticated than the simple peasants I had met on Leyte and the need for basic items like food and clothing was much greater. It had been only a few weeks since the battles to liberate the city and many had lost everything.

The sergeant in charge of our group woke us up early on that fatal Friday morning and told us to pack up our gear and be ready to ship out by 0800. "Before nightfall, you guys will be in combat!" he predicted. I got a sinking feeling in my stomach—Friday the 13th was going to be a bad day. I was still suffering from my head cold and I hadn't reported the loss of my clothes. Actually, they belonged to the Army and I would have to fill out a statement of charges and pay for them. I could visualize some mean supply sergeant bawling me out for my carelessness, so I just kept putting it off.

The repo depo sergeant's prediction also weighed heavily on my mind. I knew that the front wasn't too far away as there had been a commotion one night and the sergeant had told us it had been caused by some Japanese soldiers who had infiltrated into the area and had been chased off with a lot of gunfire. They had come across Laguna de Bay, a large lake that lay a short distance southeast of the replacement depot.

By midmorning we had loaded onto trucks and were proceeding slowly through the streets of the city. Manila was to the Filipinos what a combination of New York or San Francisco and Washington, D.C. would be to Americans: a major seaport as well as the center of their cultural, social and commercial life. It was also the capital and seat of the commonwealth government and is older than any American city except St. Augustine, Florida.

Founded in 1571 by the first Spanish governor, Miguel Lopez de Legaspi, Manila had grown over the years into a large and beautiful metropolis. Its lovely setting and architectural landmarks earned it the name "Pearl of the Orient" and its pre-war citizens enjoyed a high standard of living, second only to Australia in the Far East. Manila proper covered an area of 15 square miles stretching five-and-a-half miles north and south along the eastern shore of Manila Bay and inland about four miles at its widest point. Greater Manila, which included the suburbs and small towns of Rizal Province made up an area of 110 square miles. The population of the city at the last census (1939) was 623,492, mostly native with about 80,000 Chinese, 5,000 pure Spanish and about 20,000 Americans.[6] This had increased greatly as a result of the war as people flocked in from the rural provinces in search of jobs. Just before the Americans returned in early 1945, the population of the city proper was estimated at over 800,000 and that of Greater Manila at some 1,100,000.

There were 14 districts of unequal size, half on each side of the Pasig River which had its headwaters at Laguna de Bay, ran through the center of the city and emptied into Manila Bay. Three of the more important sections were the Intramuros, or Walled City, located on the south bank of the Pasig River: this was the original Spanish settlement and had many churches, convents, monasteries and public buildings dating back to the colonial times. Tondo, the native and most populous district, which lay north of the Pasig River, had thatch-roofed houses of nipa and bamboo jammed together on narrow streets. Americanized Manila was built on land reclaimed from the bay and stretched south from the Intramuros. Here were broad boulevards with names like Taft and Dewey, and more government buildings, hotels and white residential sections with attractive homes.

When we had first landed and been trucked to the repple depple,

19. LEGISLATIVE BUILDING AFTER THE BATTLE FOR MANILA. The damage from the many hard fought battles was enormous. Photo courtesy of Al Irish.

we hadn't noticed much battle damage. However, as we were traversing Manila from south to north, we saw what the war had wrought. Large parts of the city were utterly destroyed. We passed by row upon row of ordinary houses so completely obliterated that not even their foundations remained. In the better sections, lovely mansions had been dynamited and put to the torch in one of the most senseless orgies ever perpetrated on a helpless people. I was struck by the litter. Thousands of charred automobiles were mixed crazily with the skeletons of sewing machines, barber chairs, stoves and iceboxes.

We passed by the University of the Philippines. Its campus looked like the ruins of ancient Rome. The High Commissioner's Office and other government buildings, clubs, and hotels that were once aristocratic and resplendent were now gutted horrors.

I learned later that all this destruction had been unnecessary. When the Japanese were overrunning Luzon in 1942, General MacArthur declared Manila an "open" city to spare it from destruction and moved his army over to the Bataan Peninsula. The city suffered only minor damage from Japanese air raids until they occupied it on January 2, 1942.

Upon his return in 1945, MacArthur hoped that the Japanese would also keep the city intact. A request was sent through the Swiss government, asking the Japanese to declare Manila an open city. No formal reply was received. The Supreme Commander also put limits on bombs and firepower to be used against targets in the city. It is said that he was anxious to get there and have a big victory parade. He didn't want his moment of glory spoiled by the backdrop of a demolished city.

The Americans didn't expect the Japanese to make any major defense of Manila as military logic was against it. The city lay on a flat plain with little in the way of natural defense terrain and its large civilian population would interfere with troop movement by clogging the roads as refugees. The American plan for retaking it, dubbed Operation Mike II, called for a pincers movement. The 1st Cavalry Division and the 37th Infantry Division would drive down the Central Valley from the north while the 11th Airborne Division, which had landed troops south of Manila Bay on January 31, would attack the city from the south. When they had it encircled, they would move in and take over.

General Yamashita was militarily astute. He did not intend to waste his forces defending an untenable position. Besides, he had already used up too many of his best troops and equipment, against his better judgment, on a useless campaign at Leyte which he had fought on the orders of his superior, Count Terauchi. However, Terauchi had fled to Singapore. The highest ranking navy admirals had also moved to Formosa, leaving Yamashita in charge of all the remaining Japanese forces.[7]

While he would not let the Americans just waltz in, the Japanese Commander-in-Chief planned to hold them up as long as he could with stiff defenses north and south of the city while the remainder of his troops, mostly naval forces, destroyed military installations in the city and moved the remaining troops, supplies and equipment east into the mountains where he had prepared elaborate defenses. There was to be no defense of the city itself. His subordinates were under strict orders to retreat swiftly to the east when they could no longer hold their ground against the Americans. He wanted all the troops and supplies they could gather moved into the mountains where they would be better utilized.

Yamashita had a meeting with his commanders to review the plans and give them their final orders before departing for Baguio, where he would personally direct the larger group in the north. At the meeting, he got a lot of resistance from Rear Admiral Sanji Iwabachi, Commander of the Manila Naval Defense Force, who felt that Manila was a natural fortress and could be defended at great cost to the Americans. His men, he said, would willingly die for the Emperor in a mighty last stand, rather than spend their time destroying the military installations that they had been building up for three years. After much discussion, the operational orders were not changed and Iwabachi reluctantly pledged to follow them.

After the Americans had landed at Lingayan and firmly established their beachhead, MacArthur repeatedly issued orders reminding his field commanders of the urgency of pressing on to liberate Manila. He moved his headquarters even closer to the front than the Sixth Army command post of Lieutenant General Walter Kreuger and spent a lot of time visiting front line troops. He narrowly missed being killed several times, insisting, when told to get down, that the Japanese weren't shooting at him. One time he and his personal physician got lost and wandered behind a Japanese machine gun nest before discreetly withdrawing.[8]

There was even talk about sending the cautious Kreuger home and replacing him with General Richard Sutherland, MacArthur's Chief-of-Staff. However, in spite of MacArthur's petulant reminders that the infantry was displaying a "noticeable lack of drive," advance units had pushed down the Central Valley to within 13 miles of Manila within three weeks of landing on the Lingayan beaches.

On January 30, a company of the 6th Ranger Battalion and 280 Filipino guerrillas went behind the lines near San Jose and rescued nearly 500 starving veterans of the Bataan Death March being held in a prisoner of war camp at Cabanatuan. Inspired by this feat, MacArthur gave the following orders to the 1st Cavalry Division, which had just arrived on Luzon from Leyte and was staging at Guimba, some 70 miles north of Manila: "Go to Manila. Go around the Nips, bounce off the Nips, but get to Manila. Free the internees at Santo Tomas." This was a university in the northern section of Manila which the Japanese had converted into a prison camp for civilians. MacArthur knew some of them personally from his pre-war Manila days.

Brigadier General William Chase, the unit's commander, responded by sending two flying columns of tanks and other vehicles down Highway 5. At speeds of up to 30 miles per hour, they bypassed Japanese strong-points or took the Japanese defenders by surprise and raced across some of the river barriers before the enemy could destroy the bridges. They were helped by Marine Air Groups 24 and 32, whose Corsairs strafed the Japanese defenders ahead of the rapidly advancing column. These were the only Marines units in combat during the entire Philippine campaign.

At Novaliches, only five miles from Manila, they came upon a bridge with the fuses lit and defending Japanese forces lining the south bank. A naval demolition expert attached to the column, Lieutenant Jim Sutton, dashed onto the bridge, zig-zagged through small arms fire and cut through two burning fuses that led to dynamite charges, just in time to keep the bridge from being destroyed. Like a Hollywood movie, but a true story. Unfortunately, the bridge was destroyed by a Japanese raiding party the next night, leading to delays as the main body of the 1st Cavalry Division had to seek other routes into Manila until the engineers put together a temporary bridge. The Army awarded Jim Sutton a Distinguished Service Cross for this feat and a later mine-clearing exploit in Manila. Although a naval officer, Sutton spent almost his entire time overseas attached to Army units. He also earned a Silver Star and two Purple Heart medals. After the war, he served in the U.S. House of Representatives as a congressman from Tennessee.

On the evening of February 3, advanced units of the column burst past guards at the University of Santo Tomas in northern Manila and freed most of the 3,700 Allied men, women and children who had been held prisoner there since 1942. However, some 220 being held in the Education Building were not released until, after tense negotiations, the Americans gave the prisoners' jailers safe passage to the Japanese lines the next day. Freedom came too late for 23 of the internees who died of malnutrition and related diseases during the first two weeks of their liberation.

Among the newsmen accompanying the Cavalrymen was Carl Mydans, photographer for *Life* magazine. He had been a prisoner at Santo Tomas for eight months in 1942 but had been repatriated in a prisoner exchange. He later wrote about the American tank that crashed through the main campus gate: "I remember how astonished I was to see that gate, which had stood so long between me and freedom, fall over like a painted illusion."[9]

In the meantime, the 37th Infantry "Buckeye" Division, which had landed at Lingayan Gulf on January 9 and had to fight some major battles along the way south, entered the northern outskirts of Manila on February 4, only a day after the Cavalrymen. They were met on the outskirts by smiling Filipinos shouting "Veektory" and "Mabuhay,"[10] who led them to a brewery where they slaked their thirst and filled their canteens before moving on. Once inside the city, the Buckeyes quickly seized Bilibid Prison where 1,400 more Americans were being held.

By the evening of February 2, with the outer defenses collapsing, the Americans seizing several strategic bridges before they could be destroyed and about to arrive at Manila's gates at record speed, Admiral Iwabachi decided he didn't have enough time to do the mission he had been ordered to do, which was to destroy military installations and then head for the hills with the supplies and men. Unable to contact Yamashita by radio, he took it upon himself to order a major defense of Manila. Iwabachi had no compassion for the Filipinos living there, either. If it meant destroying a beautiful city and its helpless citizens in order to hurt the Americans, so be it. The epitome of the stubborn officer who acts out of emotional recklessness instead of calm logic, and, no doubt, resenting the fact that Yamashita was in the relative safety of Baguio, leaving him to do the dirty work, Iwabachi decided to do what he had wanted to do in the first place - battle to the death of the last defender.

The die-hard Rear Admiral had plenty of resources. The Americans found themselves confronted by a defending force of some 20,000 Japanese troops. Under his command, besides his Naval Defense Force of 16,000 sailors and technicians, he had about 4,000 soldiers. Most of them did not have combat experience but they were all well equipped with automatic weapons, machine guns and cannons. They were also imbued with the spirit of Bushido and were willing to die for their emperor.

The Manila Naval Defense Force spent the next few days fortifying Manila with barbed wire entanglements and barricades of overturned trucks and street cars. Mines were laid everywhere. Houses and public buildings were utilized since his plans were hastily improvised. His men turned thick-walled buildings into citadels, their entrances sandbagged, the stairways and corridors barricaded and walls ripped open as needed for firing slits for cannons and machine guns. Naval guns were taken from whatever ships were left in the harbor and set up in dug-in positions at strategic intersections. Some of the men continued blowing up military installations but got carried away and also dynamited civilian buildings and private homes, often killing and robbing the owners. The blasts ignited fires and shifting winds soon set many bamboo houses afire.

Between February 5 and 7, the main bodies of the 37th Infantry and 1st Cavalry Divisions poured into the northern parts of the city. On the morning of February 7, MacArthur arrived in Manila and vis-

20. CIVILIAN INTERNEES HELD AT THE UNIVERSITY OF SANTO TOMAS. At the time of their release, the average adult male weighed 112 pounds and the women weighed 100 pounds-an average loss of 27 percent of body weight during their three years of imprisonment. UPI/CORBIS-BETTMANN photo.

ited the freed prisoners. Emaciated veterans stood at attention and raised their scrawny arms in feeble salutes. Weeping civilian women embraced him and many tried to kiss him. Cries of "God bless you, General," or "Thank God you're back" arose as he passed through Santo Tomas University and Bilibid prison. Choked with emotion, the General could only mumble, "I'm a little late, but we finally made it." He is also quoted as saying, "It was wonderful to be a life-saver, not a life-taker."

After returning to his headquarters north of the city, MacArthur issued a typically optimistic communique: "Our forces are rapidly clearing Manila" and predicted that the "complete destruction" of the enemy was "imminent." Churchill and Roosevelt cabled their congratulations but, as usual, MacArthur was much too premature in his claims of victory. After four days of battle within the city, only a small section had been cleared of the enemy. The worst was yet to come.

Dense smoke hampered the Americans as they fought enemy units from street to street, building to building and room to room, the first (and only) such fighting in the Pacific War. Infantrymen found it a lot different than fighting in the jungles or the mountains. American advances were often measured in a few yards or the bloody seizure of a couple of rooms in a fortified building. The Japanese would hold out as long as they could and then the survivors would fall back to other defensive positions. In the meantime the destruction was awful, even with the limits MacArthur had imposed, as the Americans used airplanes, tanks and artillery to reduce the Japanese positions. Napalm and flame-throwers were also used extensively which, while very effective in killing and rooting out the defenders, added to the conflagration.

The Japanese left a trail of murdered and raped Filipino civilians who were unfortunate enough to be trapped behind their lines. The American soldiers were aghast to find men, women and children brutally slashed to ribbons or peppered with bullets. Because the Japanese defenders knew that they were fighting to the death and they wanted to die sexually satisfied, they committed rampant rape against any female, from young children to old women. They then bayoneted or shot their victims. They also looted recklessly, stealing money, jewelry or anything else of value.

In the meantime, the 11th Airborne Division had battled its way up from the south, taking Nichols Field and Fort McKinley after hard fighting. Advance elements linked up with the 1st Cavalry on February 11, completing the planned encirclement of the city. The entrapped Japanese defenders were now doomed to surrender or to battle on to certain death. Most chose the latter.

As the three American divisions slowly closed in, MacArthur became more depressed with each new damage report, either from the fighting or of deliberate destruction by the Japanese defenders. On the evening of February 12, he regretfully issued an order to his field commanders: "I want an all-out attack . . . I don't care if you have to flatten every building inside the city. I want Manila taken; I want it cleared of Japanese and totally occupied. Every minute lost could mean more civilian deaths or injuries."

This order lifted the restrictions on large aerial bombs and heavy artillery. The big guns (155mm) were brought in. The hub of Iwabachi's final defense lay in the old walled Intramuros District, whose thick stone walls, 15 feet high and as wide as 40 feet in some places, held up very well against the American pounding. Intramuros was an enclave two miles long and a mile wide on Manila Bay. It was the most beautiful section of Manila. Iwabachi had 6,000 defenders left by then and had fortified every building. He had also nabbed 5,000 terrified Filipino civilians and held them hostage.

After a lull in the fighting in order for the Americans to bring up supplies and regroup, heavy shelling and bombing of Intramuros began on February 17. Repeated calls upon the Japanese to give up went unanswered, so the Americans attacked from three sides on the morning of February 23. At the end of the day, the fanatical admiral's charred body lay somewhere amid the rubble that was once the Agriculture Building. Some of the Filipino civilians were killed as a result of the bombardment and subsequent fire fights, others were victims of more Japanese savagery and many were rescued.

Among the latter were about 200 women, children, nuns and priests held hostage in Del Monico Church in the northwest corner of the Walled City. Their captors were a motley array of mechanics and clerks led by inept, non-combat officers. When the heaviest bombardment started on the day of the attack, the Japanese scampered away leaving the civilians to bear the brunt of the shelling and to be rescued when the Americans appeared on the scene.

Others were not so fortunate. G.I.s found many civilians bayoneted, raped and shot. In one of the shattered rooms of the Agriculture Building, they found the bodies of more than 50 Filipino men. They had had their hands tied behind their backs, been doused with gasoline and then burned to death. The Japanese had even beheaded several young children.

Mopping up took a while and it was not until March 3 that the last resistance in Intramuros was overcome. Twenty-two dazed Japanese defenders, all that remained of the Manila Naval Defense Force, emerged from the Treasury Building. Among them was Commander Saito Izumuzi, Iwabachi's Chief-of-Staff.

MacArthur never had his parade. Three-quarters of Manila lay in ruins, most of it reduced to rubble. Only Warsaw, of the Allied cities in World War II, suffered more damage. Sixteen thousand Japanese died in their useless defense and only about 2,OOO managed to escape to join their comrades in the Sierra Madre Mountains. The Americans had also captured 8,000 tons of supplies and acres of the Japan-

21. AERIAL VIEW OF MANILA AFTER THE BATTLE. The only city in World War II that sustained more damage was Warsaw. Photo courtesy of Al Irish.

ese equipment that Yamashita wanted moved to the *Shimbu* Line. It had been costly - 1,010 Americans had been killed and 5,565 wounded in the month-long campaign. The unfortunate Filipinos suffered the worst. One hundred thousand of them had died and their beautiful city was demolished.

Dennis Greene, a teen-age prisoner at Santo Tomas, spent the first few weeks of his liberation helping the American Army as it battled to retake Manila. He went out on perimeter patrol and worked as a stretcher-bearer, bringing in the bodies of "dozens and dozens" of U.S. soldiers. "I remember thinking what great-looking American boys these were and how we just piled them up," says Greene who later served in the Korean War.[11]

So, as I passed through this wrecked city on Friday the thirteenth in April 1945, there was an aura of death still lingering. Our truck convoy overtook a Filipino funeral procession with its donkey-drawn hearse followed by black-dressed mourners and a brass band belting out incongruously lively tunes. Another victim of the city's ordeal being laid to rest? Flags on the half-wrecked government buildings still functioning, or at the many American military encampments, stood at half-mast. Somebody important had died which added to the sense of doom and foreboding.

Just before noon, we arrived at the 6th Infantry Division Headquarters, which was located out in the country some distance north and east of the city. It was here, after dismounting from the trucks and standing around waiting, that I heard the news that President Roosevelt had died. Hence, all the flags at half mast. This was turning out to be a very bad day indeed.

Most of us were shocked to hear this news and felt that we had suffered a great loss, so I was surprised to hear some of the negative comments his demise elicited from a few. Voices with deep Southern accents declared that he had given too much to "the Nigrahs" and they were glad to see him dead. Another one who didn't express much sorrow was Douglas MacArthur. The general had never forgiven Roosevelt for the many messages sent to Corregidor during the early days of the war, promising that massive aid was on the way to the beleaguered Army. It never came. "So Roosevelt is dead," the Supreme Commander said to an aide after hearing the news, "Now there's a man who would never tell the truth when a lie would serve just as well."[12]

James Roosevelt, the President's son, also ran into some of this hostility while waiting for his mother in New York the day of the funeral. A cab driver recognized him as he walked along the street and pulled his cab over to offer his condolences and tell the younger Roosevelt how much his father meant to him. His passenger however, resented the delay and yelled obscenities saying, "I hired you to drive me, not to talk about that (foul words deleted) Roosevelt!" Roosevelt writes that he had to restrain the cabby from assaulting his fare and they both ended up in tears as the passenger hastily left.[13]

The voices around me also abused the President's wife. I didn't like to hear this kind of talk. While Eleanor always struck me as being an odd, awkward, humorous public figure (comedians were always imitating her), Roosevelt was right up there next to God. I came from an environment that greatly respected him as a tremendous leader, one who spoke inspiring words and did great deeds. He had said, "The only thing we have to fear is fear itself" as he took office under the crisis conditions of the Great Depression. Also remembered was his calm voice when he spoke over the radio explaining his many programs that addressed the banking crisis, the unemployment and agricultural problems, and old-age assistance through Social Security.

I especially remembered his indignation—"This is a day that will live in infamy!"—as he called for a declaration of war after the Japanese attacked Pearl Harbor. And . . . "This generation [meaning mine] has a rendezvous with destiny!" as he led the free world to the threshold of victory in the most calamitous of all the wars in the history of mankind. Roosevelt had completed his rendezvous with history. I felt mine was just beginning.

Further discussion of Roosevelt's merits was interrupted by an order to assemble to be inspected by Major General Charles E. Hurdis, the 6th Infantry Division Commander. General Hurdis was born in Rhode Island in 1893 and graduated from West Point in 1917,

22. 6TH INFANTRY DIVISION INSIGNIA. The six pointed red star is this Regular Army division's shoulder patch. Its nickname is "The Sight Seeing Sixth" because in World War I it traveled all over France but didn't see much action. Reactivated in 1939 for World War II, its travels dwarfed that of the World War I division and it saw a lot of action in New Guinea and on the Philippine Island of Luzon.

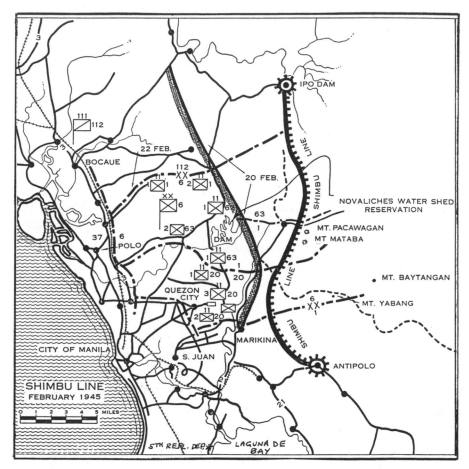

4. MANILA AREA. We traveled by truck from the 5th Replacement Depot at the bottom center of the map, through the devastated city, to the 6th Infantry Division headquarters in the north. From: *The 6th Infantry Division in World War II: 1939—1945*, (Nashville: The Battery Press, 1983), p. 108.

where he was a wrestling champion. He served overseas in World War I in the artillery and won a Silver Star Citation as battery commander. Between the wars he served at various Army posts and as an instructor in military science at Princeton University. Hurdis joined the 6th Division in April 1942 as commander of the four artillery battalions. For gallantry in action at Maffin Bay, New Guinea, he was decorated with the Silver Star Medal. The award was for directing artillery fire from a forward observation post, exposed to direct enemy fire, while the infantry was attacking.[14]

He made a little welcoming speech in which he told us we were getting into a fine outfit with a long military tradition dating back to World War I. It was a regular Army division, consisting of three infantry regiments, the 1st, 20th and 63rd and supporting elements. We would be assigned to one of these units. The division was a veteran of the New Guinea campaign and had fought long and hard since making the landing at Lingayan Gulf in January. General Hurdis also said that he too was kind of a replacement, having been the division commander only a few weeks. He had recently replaced Major General Edwin Patrick, who was killed by a Japanese machine gunner while visiting the front on March 14.

The dead general was a native of Indiana and attended both the Universities of Indiana and Michigan. He was commissioned a 2nd Lieutenant in the Indiana National Guard in 1917 and served overseas with the 14th Machine Gun Battalion, 5th Infantry Division where he was awarded a Silver Star Medal for gallantry in action. Between the wars he attended various service schools and was an instructor at Fort Benning, Georgia. During World War II, he served in the Pacific Theater with the War Plans Section of Admiral Halsey's Staff and as Chief-of-Staff under General Kreuger as the Sixth Army drove up the coast of New Guinea. General Patrick assumed command of the 6th Infantry Division at Sansapor, New Guinea, in September 1944, replacing Major General Franklin C. Sibert, who was promoted to commander of the X Corps. It was while the 6th Division was attacking the *Shimbu* Line near Bayanbayanan, that Patrick, watching the attack from a forward battalion observation post, was mortally wounded by an enemy machine gun burst. Killed with him was 1st Infantry Regimental Commander, Colonel James E. Rees.[15]

I later heard the story about how he came up to the front, spread out his maps and began observing the action through binoculars. General Patrick was a very visible commander. He always wore a special green jumpsuit that could be seen a mile away. The troops referred to him as the "Green Hornet." Two stars on his helmet also made him stand out to his men and the enemy. He made the mistake of visiting the same place two days in a row. A well-hidden Japanese soldier only seventy-five yards away must have been waiting his return. Patrick was one of only three division commanders killed in World War II.[16]

After a lunch of K-rations, we were divided up into smaller groups and again loaded on trucks. I went with the men being assigned to the 63rd Infantry Regiment. At regimental headquarters, closer to the battle front, we were introduced to Colonel Everett M. Yon. Yon was born at Blountstown, Florida on January 13, 1895 and educated in the

23. REGIMENTAL COAT OF ARMS, 63RD INFANTRY. The shield was approved by the War department right after World War I. It is blue and white with a yellow and red sun. The motto on the scroll, added after World War II, is the Tagalog word *mabuhay* meaning "long live." It was used as a victory cry by the men of the 63rd Regiment while fighting with the help of Filipino guerrillas during the Luzon campaign. The crest, consisting of a Malayan tiger at bay, symbolizes General Tomoyuki Yamashita commonly known as the "Tiger of Malaya." When the war ended, the 63rd Infantry was actively driving towards his headquarters in Mountain Province in Northern Luzon.

118

public schools there and at Palmer College Academy in DeFuniak Springs. He attended the University of Florida from 1914 to 1916 where he played football and baseball and was in the ROTC. His National Guard unit was activated in 1916 to fight Pancho Villa on the Mexican border where Yon served as a supply sergeant. A year later, with World War I in progress, he took an examination and was commissioned a Second Lieutenant. The new officer then spent three years in Germany in the Army of Occupation. He returned to the University of Florida in 1923 in the ROTC program and taught military science and also served as the football line coach. He was Director of Athletics from 1926 through 1929. In 1930 he went to the Philippines as Captain of Infantry, returning to the U.S. in 1933. He served in various Army posts in the western states during the thirties and attained the rank of major. Yon was then assigned to ROTC duty at Georgetown University in Washington, D.C. in 1939. When America entered World War II he was promoted to colonel and sent to Guadalcanal with the 93rd Infantry Division, a Negro division with mostly white officers. When that division was disbanded in 1944, Colonel Yon was at-

24. COLONEL EVERETT M. YON. This picture, dated 1944 must have been taken during the preparations for the invasion of Luzon. Yon, in full battle gear is saluting General Walter Krueger, Sixth Army Commander, in the jeep. Photo courtesy of Mrs. Frank E. Yon.

tached to I Corps as liaison officer for the Luzon invasion and made the landing at Lingayan Gulf on January 9, 1945. In late January, he replaced Lieutenant Colonel Harold G. Maison as commander of the 63rd Infantry Regiment when General Patrick shuffled some of his commanders around following the battle for Munoz.[17]

A portly, middle-aged man, I remember Yon wearing wire-rimmed Army glasses and his head seeming too large for the helmet he wore. This gave him an owlish appearance. He stood up in his jeep and we gathered around to listen. The Colonel spoke, in a cultured southern drawl, about his thirty years in the Army and how the 63rd Infantry was the finest outfit that he had ever commanded. He reiterated what General Hurdis had said about this unit's prowess in successfully taking on a tough and tenacious enemy in the jungles of New Guinea and here on the plains and in the mountains of the Philippines.

"May-en," he declared, looking directly at me, "and I call yew may-én even though some of you are hahdly old enough to be called may-en, because you have a may-an's job to do here. Y'all do it way-ll and we will be mighty prow'd of yew and then we cain all go home to our families." I was still 18 years old but looked younger than my age. He probably thought to himself, *My Gawd! Whut kind of chile-soldiers are they sending me to finish this god-dam wahr!* But at that stage of the game, with the enemy well-entrenched in the mountains and his regiment badly depleted by months of combat, he welcomed any kind of soldiers the Army provided.

By this time it was getting on in the afternoon. Colonel Yon looked at his watch. "We bat-ah break up," he said, "the Japs usually drop in a few ra-ounds every afternoon about faw-ur o'clock!" This got everybody moving in a hurry. We were sorted into three smaller groups and loaded on trucks again. It was a short ride for me to the 3rd Battalion Command Post.

Here we met Major Arndt Mueller, the battalion commander. Arndt L. Mueller was born in Minnesota on March 31, 1917 and graduated from South Dakota State University where he played football. He joined the 63rd Infantry in 1941 as a Second Lieutenant and commanded K-Company before being promoted to 3rd Battalion Commander early in the Luzon Campaign when Lieutenant Colonel Rudolph K. Brunsvold was wounded at Cauringan. Mueller subsequently had a long and distinguished military career including service in the Vietnam War. His decorations include the Presidential Unit Citation, a Silver Star and three Bronze Star medals from World War II and a Distinguished Service Cross for extraordinary heroism and another Silver Star and Distinguished Service Medal for his service in Vietnam. He retired as a full colonel in 1972.[18]

Mueller also had us assemble in a group and gave us a welcoming speech which was a lot longer than Colonel Yon's. I kept thinking that the Japanese were going to drop in a few shells and kill us all as we stood there. Major Mueller didn't seem to be worried about it. Standing on a small pile of dirt, he looked mean with his rumpled fatigues, muddy combat boots and a revolver hanging from his belt. He talked mean, too.

"The only thing that makes me happy," he declared emphatically, "is *dead Japs*! It's your job to keep me happy. If you don't, you men are going to have a very miserable time here." He urged us to make maximum use of our weapons, that some new soldiers, he had observed, had been too timid about firing them. "There is plenty of ammunition available," he assured us and we were to "use it up." The sooner we got the job done, the sooner we could all go home. He also said that he better not catch any of us with our helmets off. They were made for our protection and we were required to wear them. Likewise for taking your shirt off in the hot tropical sun. An enemy sniper liked nothing better than a naked body for a target.

"The 3rd Battalion," he continued, "is the finest battalion in the *whole Army*!" We were extremely fortunate to be getting into such an excellent group. We had better make every effort to hold up our end and be worthy of the honor. He then went on to describe a recent battle in which the 3rd Battalion had cracked the *Shimbu* Line northeast of Manila and taken a key position away from the enemy. The battalion had defended it against determined Japanese counterattacks which included hand-to-hand combat. "For this," he said, "the 3rd Battalion has been recommended for a Presidential Unit Citation."[19]

The President is dead, I thought to myself, *how can he give you a Presidential Unit Citation*? I didn't know that at 9:09 A.M. that morning, Manila time, a man named Harry Truman had taken the oath of office. The constitutional power had been transferred; we had a new Commander-in-Chief. But Roosevelt was the only president I had known. His tenure had covered two thirds of my young life. Some twelve years previously, when I was six years old, I had come into the living room of the house on Parker where we were living then, and found my dad listening to the radio. The song "Happy Days" was blaring away. Dad was in a jovial mood and was singing along with the music. He told me to pay attention, that Franklin Delano Roosevelt was being inaugurated as President of the United States and that things were going to get much better. He said that he had voted for him.

After the ceremony, which I really didn't understand, I went into the kitchen where my mother was ironing clothes. "Did you vote for President Roosevelt?" I inquired. "No!" she answered, and definitely not in a jovial mood, "I voted for Hoover." This was my first lesson in our two-party political system and both were represented right in my own home.

My paternal grandparents, who raised me after my mother died when I was eight years old, were Democrats. Grandma, especially, was an enthusiastic supporter of FDR. She listened to all his "fireside chats" and followed his career as he ran for re-election three more times. For most of her life, she had been unable to vote so when, at age 50, she got the franchise by the passage of the nineteenth amendment to the Constitution, she made the most of it.

My reverie was interrupted by Major Mueller. He had finished the glory part of his speech and was barking out orders. The first thing we had to do, he said, was to get rid of our gas masks. We had faithfully carried them with us all the way from Fort Ord, California. They ended up on a large pile of gas masks lying on the ground. We were then to pick out an M1 Rifle from a pile of weapons, clean it thoroughly and take it over to a makeshift rifle range that had been set up with mounds of dirt and paper targets. We were to make sure it functioned well and was zeroed in accurately.

He also said to be sure we got two bandoleers[20] of ammunition, a first-aid kit, an entrenching tool, a poncho and two water canteens. Two water canteens? We had only been issued one. Back at Camp Hood we were often ordered to pour its water out on the ground at the first break in the morning's training. We then spent the rest of the morning with our tongues hanging out from thirst. "Water discipline" they called it. Apparently the Major didn't want us to be thirsty. He was giving us a second canteen.

We got busy. After two months of relative inactivity on trains or aboard ships and in replacement depots, it felt good to finally get ready to do what we had so laboriously trained for - killing the Japanese. This was my first real job after high school and being young and idealistic, I was determined to do it well. My Military Occupational Specialty, according to my service records, was Rifleman-745 (semi-skilled). I had never fired a gun before I entered the service, but I learned to shoot one rather quickly at Camp Hood, earning a Sharp Shooter's Medal. Now it was time to put that skill to work along all the other lessons we had learned at "Killers' Kollege."

By the time we had done our chores and eaten supper, it was getting dark. Mueller had indicated that we would be spending the night at battalion headquarters. We would be assigned to rifle companies in the morning. "Get a good night's rest," he advised, after again admonishing us to keep our helmets on at all times.

It was a warm tropical night. We made our beds on the ground in a sheltered area wrapped in a canvas tent half. It felt good to be finally assigned to a regular outfit, no longer being one of a mass of replacements without any sense of permanence.

I remembered what the sergeant at the repo depo had said. He wasn't a good prophet, I thought. It was past nightfall and we were still in the rear area. I had survived Friday the thirteenth, the day the President died. I felt that I had a good chance to survive other days, too. As Roosevelt said, "The only thing that we have to fear is fear itself." It had been an exhausting day.

Our artillery shells were passing overhead on their way to blasting the Japanese. They made a whispering noise as they passed by. It was a soothing, friendly sound. There wasn't any return fire from the enemy. I soon fell into a deep sleep.

SIX

On The Shimbu Line

*I'm convinced that the infantry is the group in the Army
which gives more and gets less than anybody else. I draw
pictures for and about the dogfaces because I know what
their life is like and I understand their gripes. They
don't get fancy pay, they know their food is the worst in
the Army because you can't whip up lemon pies or even
hot soup at the front, and they know how much of the
burden they bear*

Bill Mauldin[1]

G eneral Tomoyuki Yamashita, the commander of the Japanese
forces in the Philippines, believed that the only realistic approach to the defense of the main island of Luzon was to
fight an extended delaying action, to occupy the American forces as
long as he could, to bleed them as much as possible so that the Allies
would give Japan better peace terms to end a war that he knew was
already lost. Unlike MacArthur's WPO-3 early in the war, Yamashita
didn't intend to defend the beaches, Bataan, or even Manila, although
his control of things in Manila got away from him as we have seen. Instead, his strategy was to withdraw the bulk of his troops to three
mountain strongholds. There he could conduct a prolonged defense
and, at the same time, inflict heavy casualties on the Americans as
they attempted to regain their lost territory.[2] That was the job of the
infantry—to wrest this ground away from a well-entrenched enemy.

Except for the Manila fiasco, Yamashita's plan was generally successful as the bitter fighting continued throughout the winter, spring
and summer of 1945—right on up to the end of the war. When hostilities ended on August 15, his holding action still engaged the full attention of three American infantry divisions and many Filipino

124

troops. He came out of the mountains in September with some 40,000 of his troops still intact.

The strongest and most important of the three positions comprised all of Luzon north and east of Lingayan Gulf where the Americans had landed in January. Yamashita's forces in this sector were

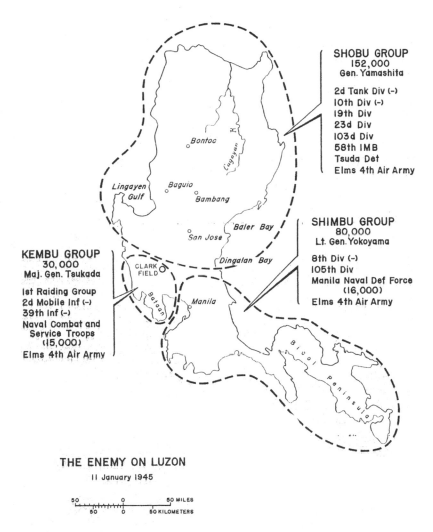

THE ENEMY ON LUZON
II January 1945

5. DEFENSE OF LUZON. General Yamashita's master plan for the Japanese defense of the main island was to use three groups to fight delaying actions and then withdraw to previously prepared mountain strongholds where they could inflict a maximum amount of damage to the attacking Americans. From: Robert Ross Smith, *Triumph in the Philippines*, (Washington, D.C.,: Government Printing Office, 1963), p. 95.

called the *Shobu* Group and were under his direct command. The second and much smaller group, the *Kembu* Group, occupied the mountains to the west of the Central Valley and the important air base, Clark Field. The third command, the *Shimbu* Group, was concentrated in the mountains east of Manila. These forces numbered some 80,000 troops under the command of Lieutenant General Shizu Yokoyama.

It was my fortune to become a member of a combat unit which engaged all three groups during the short time that I was with it, even though the enemy was so widely dispersed. When I joined the 6th Infantry Division on April 13, 1945, the American Army had captured most of the important objectives in their reconquest of the island of Luzon—Clark Field, Manila, Bataan and Corregidor—and the Japanese had been reduced to their three defensible areas, *Shobu*, *Kembu*, and *Shimbu*. My regiment, the 63rd Infantry, was facing the Japanese in the center of the *Shimbu* Line, northeast of Manila in the Mango River area.

On the morning of April 14, we replacements loaded on trucks at 3rd Battalion Headquarters to be taken up to the front line. I had been assigned to Company K. There were about a dozen soldiers in the truck I was riding. Most were 18-year-old boys like myself with one exception. He was an older man in his late twenties, very swarthy looking. With his deep set, gaunt eyes and heavy beard, he reminded me of the characters Willie and Joe in Bill Mauldin's *Up Front* cartoons.

The veteran introduced himself, saying that his name was Dominic Fallo but that everybody called him "Black Cock" because of his dark complexion which extended even to his penis. We received this odd bit of information without much comment because we were too nervous about where the truck was taking us. A Cajun from Louisiana, Fallo had been in the 6th Division almost four years after being drafted in 1941 to serve for only one. Before his year was up, the Japanese had attacked Pearl Harbor and he was stuck for the duration. He said he was returning to duty after being hospitalized for malaria.

Everyone called him by his unusual nickname. When we stopped at checkpoints along the way, grim looking soldiers would look in the back of the truck and, recognizing him, would shout, "Hey, Black Cock, what are you doing with this truckload of replacements? You a nursemaid or something?" or "Hey, Black Cock, the Army must be getting awfully hard up for men to be sending you back to the front with these greenhorns!"

He seemed outwardly more nervous than we were, chattering constantly, his eyes darting about to see what he could out the back of the truck, while we sat in rather glum, apprehensive silence. He had been in combat before and knew what to expect. We replacements were like lambs being led to the slaughter; we didn't really know what we were getting into. We had heard about it, read books about it, seen movies and engaged in simulated training exercises. But—the reality that we were about to experience was beyond our comprehension.

Black Cock questioned the soldiers at the checkpoints and would interpret their answers for us as we moved along to the next one. The third battalion was in a supporting position while the first and second battalions were on the attack. "This is good," he said, "because holding a position is not as dangerous as attacking one." We took whatever comfort we could from those words.

Eventually, we arrived at the base of a very large hill. We were in the area near Mount Mataba (Hill C), which rises about 1,400 feet above sea level and is part of the foothills that ascend to the Sierra Madre range of mountains that lie along the eastern spine of Luzon. The particular hill that was to be our home for the next two weeks was part of the Mataba mountain complex and had been designated "Hill A, B & X" because it had three crests. We dismounted and made our way by foot to near the top. Company K was dug in on the back slope.

I had been placed in the 1st Platoon, which was commanded by Lieutenant Tom Atchley. There weren't any formal introductions but I was told by Sergeant Jesse Wyatt Gibson to find a spot and dig a foxhole. I noticed that Black Cock was already busy digging his. "Make it long enough to sleep in," Sergeant Gibson said. "Y'all might's well be comfortable, we may be heah fo' awhile." He also said to get going right away and dig it deep as the Japanese would likely be sending over some artillery or mortar shells as a way of welcoming us new replacements.

When I asked where the Japanese were, he pointed in the direction of the top of the hill. That seemed awfully close. Actually, they were mostly on the next hill, a large land mass named Mount Pacawagan, across the Mango River. There were also, at that time, a few in the draws and in the Mango River gorge. Some of our companies were engaged in flushing them out. The enemy were labeled "The Kobayashi Force" because they were commanded by Major General Takashi Kobayashi and were roughly equivalent to two regimental combat teams in strength and armament.

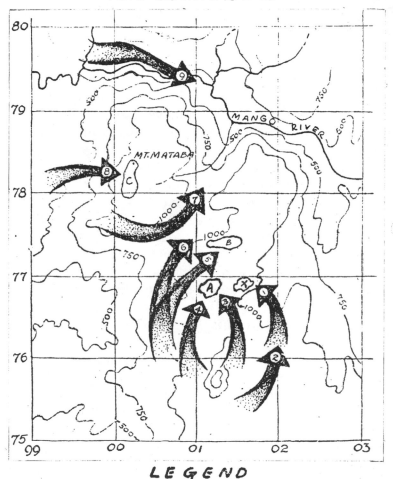

63RD INFANTRY REGIMENT
OPERATIONS IN THE
MT. MATABA AREA
3rd-30th APRIL 1945

LEGEND

1. Co. "G" 6th APRIL
2. Co. "F" 9th APRIL
3. Co. "E" 6th APRIL
4. Co. "K" 8th APRIL
5. Co. "I" 10th APRIL

6. Co. "L" 10th APRIL
7. 1st Bn. CLEANS OUT
   DRAWS 10-17th APRIL
8. Co's "A" & "C" 10th APRIL
9. Co. "G" CLEANS OUT
   MANGO GORGE 20th
   -28th APRIL

6. OPERATIONS IN THE MT. MATABA AREA. We spent several weeks on Hill "A" shown in the center of the map at arrow 4. From: World War II Operations Reports, 6th Infantry Division, File 306, 63rd Inf., National Archives, Washington, D.C.

K-Company was dug in on the back slope of Hill A and had outposts on the side facing the Japanese. We would take turns manning them. There we had a stunning view of the Mango River Gorge with the enemy hidden from view in their caves on Mount Pacawagan. On the reverse slope there wasn't much to see except a line of foxholes and a bunch of grubby-looking soldiers loitering about, although we did have a view of the Marikina Valley and the city of Manila on the far distant horizon.

I went along the hill a short distance, found a spot between two foxholes, got out my entrenching tool and started digging. Before I got very deep into the soft ground, someone yelled "Incoming!" and there was a loud explosion. I flattened myself against the bottom of

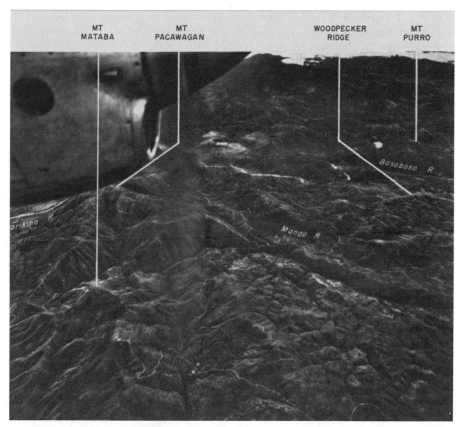

25. AERIAL VIEW OF HILL A, B & X. This picture, taken from the cockpit of a P-38 shows the rugged terrain defended by the Kobayashi Force. Hill A, B & X is in the center of the picture, just below and to the left of where it says "Mango River." From: Robert Ross Smith, *Triumph in the Philippines*, (Washington, D.C.: Government Printing office, 1963), p. 395.

my shallow hole. It didn't seem anywhere near deep enough. The first explosion was followed by about ten more, first a short whistling sound and then a loud bang as the shell exploded. I lay in my slit trench face down with my nose in the damp earth, praying hard. My heart was beating so vigorously that it seemed to shake my whole body.

Before I had been drafted, I had taken to reading the casualty reports which appeared daily in the *Detroit News*. Often they were accompanied by pictures of the deceased. I would look them over very carefully and then assure myself that since none of them looked like me, I would not be killed and appear in the paper someday as they had. I thought about this every time we got shelled. Why this fantasy was so reassuring, I don't know. However, when the shells are landing around you, feelings of invincibility disappear quite rapidly. There was a strong urge to get up out of the hole and run rapidly down the hill, an urge I managed to overcome.

Actually, logic told me that I was fairly safe unless a shell landed right on top of me. I had been through this artillery thing in basic training. After a while the shelling stopped and soldiers got out of their holes and began moving around. No one had been hit but I

26. MTS. PACWAGAN AND MATABA. This picture shows how the mountains rise steeply from the Marikina Valley. The Mango River gorge is in the center with MT. Mataba on the right. Hill A, B & X is beyond the crest of MT. Mataba. From: Robert Ross Smith, *Triumph in the Philippines*, (Washington, D.C.: Government Printing Office, 1963), p. 374.

stayed close to my hole for the rest of that day and many more. It got deeper and more elaborate as time went by.

The older soldiers called the artillery piece that had shelled us "Pistol Pete" and said that the Japanese had it hidden in a cave. They only used it once in a while. It was mounted on rails and they would move it to the mouth of the cave, fire off some rounds and then run it back into the cave before it could be located accurately. Our artillery and airplanes had been unsuccessful in pinpointing its location so that it could be put out of business.

This was not unusual. Colonel Arndt Mueller remembers a time on the *Shimbu* Line when he was plagued with Japanese artillery fire coming from a high ridge. In his memoir, he wrote:

> We felt that the guns had to be concealed in some caves because it was direct fire, not indirect fire. But, if so, the caves were so well camouflaged that we could not locate them. Col. Yon, (who had an extraordinary knowledge of the terrain from his pre-war service as captain of infantry in the Philippines), had the solution. He said that this particular area was known for bats in caves. The bats always flew out of the caves at dusk. All we had to do was to train our field glasses on the ridge at dusk; the bats would tell us where the caves were located. At first I thought this was really a batty story. But, we gave it a try—he was absolutely right. The bats did show us the location of the caves!3

The Army had done its usually efficient job of mixing up its soldiers. There I was with a whole new group of people, none of whom had been in basic training with me or been on board ship crossing the ocean. Even the new replacements that accompanied me up Hill A were strangers, coming from training camps in California and Georgia. However, my new companions were a friendly bunch. There is a foxhole camaraderie. The veterans generally welcomed the new replacements and answered our questions and explained things to us. Other soldiers have told me tales of being resented or ignored when they joined a unit in combat, but I have only memories of being well-received. It was a case of "misery likes company," as the old saying goes. We were there to share it with newcomers and veterans alike.

Company K's men varied from old timers who dated back to the formation of the regiment in 1941 to recent replacements who had been there only a month or so. All were grubby-looking from being too long in the field without baths, shaves, haircuts and changes of clothing. Because the 6th Division had been in almost continuous combat since the landings at Lingayan Gulf on January 9, they expected to be relieved soon and given a period of rest. That sounded good to me. I had just gotten there but I was ready to leave. It would be a while. For me, a long while.

Like soldiers everywhere, they were proud of the outfit they were in. The 6th Division was the best infantry division to be in, the 63rd Infantry the best regiment and the 3rd Battalion, commanded by

27. LIEUTENANT TOM A.E. ATCHLEY. This picture of our 1st Platoon leader was taken after his return to the United States in late 1945. Photo courtesy of Tom A.E. Atchley.

Major Arndt Mueller, who was the former K-Company captain, the fightingest battalion. The men of the lst Platoon thought they had the best platoon leader in Lieutenant Atchley.

"Thomas Alva Edison Atchley!" One soldier would always rattle off whenever he talked about him. It was a familiar sound to me, as the original Edison, the famous inventor, was a Michigan hero who spent his boyhood years in Port Huron, near Detroit. His life had been popularized in the movies of the time: *Young Tom Edison* with Mickey Rooney and *Edison, the Man* with Spencer Tracey. The inventor had also been a special friend of Henry Ford.[4] I had been to the reconstructed Menlo Park Laboratory in Greenfield Village where Edison perfected the incandescent light bulb.

However, his real name is Tom Alvin Edison Atchley, he told me after 50 years, a name that is close to but only inspired by the "genius of Menlo Park." Tom A. E. Atchley came from Dierks, Arkansas, and was working in a lumber mill when his country called him to duty in June, 1941 at age 24. He had joined the 6th Division at Fort Leonard Wood, Missouri, shortly afterwards. Atchley had served it all in K-Company, 63rd Infantry and had worked his way up the ranks and received a battlefield commission shortly before I joined his platoon.

Like most genuine heroes, Tom was a quiet man, not given to boasting. His men respected him because he looked after them and didn't take any unnecessary chances. He had done plenty to boast about. In the Munoz-San Jose Operation, near Abar #2 on February 4, while then a staff sergeant, he had taken over the lst Platoon after the platoon leader and the platoon sergeant were both wounded while attacking a Japanese 47mm gun emplacement. Rallying his men, they were able to destroy the 47mm gun and several machine guns and their crews. For his courage and outstanding leadership, he was awarded the Bronze Star Medal for heroic achievement.[5]

Six weeks later, on the night of March 19 near Montalbon, his platoon was attacked and surrounded by a large force of the enemy. Many of his men were severely wounded. To get relief, Tom had to make his way along a route that was heavily mined. At the risk of his own life, he used a flashlight to find and remove the mines and to signal for reinforcements. As a result of his courageous leadership, the platoon was reinforced and the wounded successfully evacuated. Lieutenant Atchley was awarded a Silver Star Medal for gallantry in action.[6]

There were other heroes. The hill mass we were sitting on had been obtained only after an arduous effort and the loss of many brave men. After cracking the *Shimbu* Line, by capturing Hill 400 (where the 3rd Battalion was recommended for their Presidential Citation), the 63rd was moved to the south in early April and relieved the 20th Infantry in the Hill A, B & X-Mount Mataba area. Before the move, Major Mueller[7] made an advance reconnaissance to see what lay ahead. He observed an attack on Hill A by the 20th Infantry. They struck along the eastern nose and had barely gotten to the end when they were hit by a deadly concentration of 150mm mortars and suffered many casualties. (The Japanese 150mm mortar shell was heavier than our 155mm howitzer and packed more explosive power.) That was the end of that attack. Mueller could see that he and his men had an exceedingly difficult task ahead of them. He later wrote:

> A, B, & X was a fortress. Each hill was large enough to accommodate a company size unit. It made a perfect battalion defensive position. But visual observation revealed little of the individual Jap positions. The entire area was a moonscape having been pounded bare of vegetation by artillery and mortar fire . . . I suspected that the entire area was honeycombed with a tunnel system connecting firing positions . . . heavy bombardment would not be very effective.[8]

From April 4 to the 7, the 2nd Battalion tried to capture the objectives with Company E attacking Hill A and Company G, Hill X. Intense machine gun, knee mortar, small arms and the big 150mm mortars again stopped the Americans and they were forced to withdraw. On the 8th, it was the 3rd Battalion's turn to attack. While Company I attempted to crash through the saddle between A and B to seize X, Company K attacked Hill A. The Japanese positions were all up high, at or near the top. Their tactic was to allow the Americans to advance to near the top and then to subject them to a withering barrage of close range small arms and knee mortar fire. When I-Company reached the saddle, all movement halted as the troops were pinned down by vicious and accurate machine gun fire. Company K suffered a similar fate and both withdrew. Among the casualties was First Lieutenant Paul Strain commanding I-Company, whose right arm was badly shattered.

Mueller decided that before he ordered another attack, he needed to determine the exact location of the Japanese defensive positions. To bait the enemy into revealing themselves and their pattern of defensive fire, he laid on artillery fire, along with the infantry company's mortar fire, delivered time on target at dusk. The idea was to make them think that the Americans were attacking under the cover of darkness. It worked like a charm, the Japanese reacted with flares and their mortar fires and machine gun flickers could be plotted.

Colonel Yon, Commander of the 63rd Infantry, was under extreme pressure to take Hill A. This came not only from the division commander, Major General Hurdis, but also from the assistant division commander, a brigadier general in charge of infantry operations, who, Mueller writes, was "a pompous, stubby fat officer with a very unpleasant personality."[9] And not too much practical combat experience. While the Americans were busily plotting the Japanese positions, Mueller got an order from Colonel Yon to attack Hill A immediately. This was highly unusual. Yon normally gave Mueller objectives and let him work out the methods of achieving them. They had an informal working arrangement, the younger Mueller calling the elderly colonel "Dad" and Yon referring to Mueller by his nickname, "Dutch".

In his memoirs, Mueller writes that he always found Colonel Yon to be deeply concerned about the welfare of his soldiers:

> One time, after a fierce battle . . . he ordered me to report to regimental headquarters in the early evening. Upon arrival I found that he had arranged for a nice hot meal in his quarters with me and the regimental surgeon as guests. Dr. Goldberg[10] . . . had concocted a beverage of medical alcohol, brown sugar and water. "Here," said Colonel Yon, "is some shell shock medicine." Needless to say, I enjoyed the drink and the meal.[11]

Mueller protested the order to attack Hill A, pointing out that it was suicidal to attack now that they had the enemy fully alerted and they were throwing everything they had at us. But Colonel Yon was adamant. The order came from division and it was a direct order to Mueller. K-Company had a defensive line of foxholes at the base of Hill A so the order was passed on to them and they made a futile attack. Among the casualties were two Platoon Leaders, Lieutenant Robert Wit and Lieutenant Lyle C. Krough. Wit had been wounded at Montalbon on February 24 and had just returned from the hospital. Both were old timers and had recently received battle field commissions to Second Lieutenant for their leadership qualities.

Another casualty was Staff Sergeant Glen Laub of Belleville, Pennsylvania. In a letter to me[12] he recalled the experience:

"Advancing up the hill under cover of darkness, we could see the enemy moving about and talking. . . . all of a sudden we were hit with mortar fire. Bob [Wit] said 'both my legs are gone!' and I crawled to him and pulled him into a shell hole. I told him his legs were OK and I called the medics. The medic found Bob had been hit in the buttocks. He [medic] asked me if I was OK. I said, 'I have a burning on the right thigh and right arm pit.' The medic dressed the wounds and they took us back to our starting point."[13]

With the failure of this attack, Mueller writes, he was depressed but didn't have time to cry over the past. Regiment was now planning a coordinated attack by all battalions to take Hill A, B & X and Mount Mataba all at once. Artillery was to concentrate its shelling on the newly plotted Japanese positions with the help of Cannon Company and the heavy weapons companies' 81mm mortars. The Army Air Corps would lay down a smoke screen with B-25s assisted by the Chemical Warfare Section 4.2 mortars. The smoke would hide the attacking infantrymen. This operation would also see the first use of the proximity fuse[14] in the South Pacific. Extra ammunition was issued to all units. It was going to be one huge operation!

All was in readiness for the attack on April 10, which was the next day, when the Battalion Commanders received word to report to Division Headquarters for a meeting to brief the top brass on their plans. Included among them was General Walter Kreuger, commander of the Sixth Army. Mueller writes that after he briefed the generals on his portion of the overall plan, which was to seize Hill X and then A, his plan was severely criticized by the pompous Brigadier General who had ordered the ill-fated night attack on Hill A. However, Mueller was supported by General Hurdis and at the end of the meeting General Kreuger shook his hand and said: "God bless you, son, and God Bless your soldiers."[15] Mueller was elated! He had received the confidence of General Kreuger, MacArthur's primary Army commander and an old soldier with much combat experience dating back to World War I.

When his jeep took him back to the Battalion CP and he looked up at the next day's objective, he could hardly believe his eyes. There were soldiers moving around on the top of Hill A and they weren't the enemy. (Unlike the restless Americans, the Japanese usually remained hidden.) They were his troops! In his absence, Captain Richard Fleming, K-Company commander and Major Bob Wells, 3rd Battalion executive officer, had devised a plan to take Hill A by using two Cannon Company mounted 105s to hammer the top of the hill, keeping the Japanese down, while a small force of infantry made their way up the slope. It had worked.

Lieutenant John Munschauer, of Ithaca, New York, who led the platoon up the hill later wrote:

> We moved in the night to the very base of Hill A. There we sat hunched over our rifles waiting for dawn, waiting in limbo between life and the unknown, waiting to the signal to move up the hill. The first sign of dawn was strangely beautiful, strangely peaceful.[16]
> It made him think of Shakespeare's *Henry V:*

> Now entertain conjecture of time
> When creeping murmur and the poring dark
> Fills the wide vessel of the universe.
> From camp to camp, through the foul womb of night,
> The hum of either army stilly sounds,
> That the fixed sentinels almost receive
> The secret whispers of each other's watch.
> Fire answers fire, and through their paly flames
> Each battle sees the others umbered face.[17]

> We captured the hill without the loss of a man. We dug in. Then it came. It descended towards us with a weird scream something like a sheet ripping. Its explosion sent dirt flying. The Japs were hitting us with a huge mortar (the 150mm's) .... After every explosion one of the men would exclaim: "Dearie me! Gracious me oh my! Bless my soul! or My goodness!" (Others, I'm sure, expressed themselves much more foully.)
> We survived the mortar fire without the loss of a man. Then we began to lose them. Snapping sounds like the crack of a whip cracked by my ear every time I stuck my head out of my hole [sniper fire] .... Yet, it was my job to ... check on the men and the defenses ... I zigged, I zagged, I ran, I stopped, I bobbed. I wasn't going to let a Jap get a bead on me. A blond kid, one of the new soldiers, was sitting beside his foxhole, not in it. I yelled at him to get down. He said, "Aw, Lieutenant, don't worry, when your number is up, your number ...." A small hole in the middle of his forehead oozed blood as he slumped over. Before the night was out we lost two more youngsters that had come in the evening before for their first combat."[18]

With Hill A in American hands, the other crests were soon reduced when the major attack was made on April 10, and the 63rd was in control when I arrived on the 14. It had cost 27 men killed and 127 wounded, an expensive piece of real estate. Exact casualty figures are hard to come by. The Unit History is big on estimating large numbers of Japanese killed and generally underplays American losses. I took the Regimental Casualty Report for the month of April 1945 (National Archives File 306 Inf 63) and counted names. Since it lists the regimental casualties by name, rank and serial number as well as the date and place, it was easy to determine who was killed, wounded or injured at that time and place. The figures do not include the 20th Infantry losses in their unsuccessful attempts before the 63rd took over the task.

I had just missed the excitement of taking the hill but I still remember vividly the ensuing weeks when we just sat there and held this precious ground. My memories are deeply engraved, enhanced by sensory perceptions, and at times the sights, the sounds, the feelings can be experienced again and again:

Our artillery shells make a pleasant sound: kind of like the rustle of leaves as they pass overhead and like distant thunder when they land on the Japanese in the hills across the Mango River. Incoming is a different story. A loud whistling noise that increases in intensity and ends in the loudest bang I have ever heard. I press against the saving earth and feel my heartbeats shake my whole body. Terror is a physical thing. . . .

I peer out into the darkness, straining to see or hear anything that indicates the enemy is abroad tonight. They may be trying to sneak up and retake this hill. Behind us, from the thousand foot altitude of Hill A, the myriad lights of distant Manila gleam in the night like stars. It's hard to believe that people are going about their business in the shattered "Pearl of the Orient" while we sit in our foxholes and worry about the Japanese on the next hill, or are they closer. . . .

During the day, the flies are numerous and pesky, crawling over everything and swarming in black clouds when disturbed. I lie in my foxhole smoking cigarettes and lose count as I swat and kill them. Must be in the hundreds. I know their source: dead bodies. A carabao[19] was killed near the bottom of the hill where we go for supplies or an occasional hot meal. The stench of decaying flesh is overpowering. It wrenches your stomach if you breathe too deeply as you pass by. A mass of maggots feed on the rotten carcass. By sheer numbers, their chewing makes a buzzing sound as the putrid carrion slowly disappears. Soon, all that will be left are bones. From death comes new life. One dead carabao equals a million new flies. . . .

Time passes. It's Sunday and we are notified that Catholic Mass will be held at the bottom of the hill. I go. It is a welcome relief from the boredom and excitement at the top of the hill. The familiar ritual soothes, helps me forget the insanity of war. I remember going to Mass every day at St. Benedict School. The church is full of children, packed into the pews by classes, interspersed with black-robed nuns. I am in the fifth grade again. Charlie Ford, my first altar boy partner, gives me the elbow—hard! I hit him back. Sister Rosemary sees just me, makes me sit next to her for the remainder of the service. I am in disgrace for "acting up in church." I think of Charlie because a recent letter from home reminds me he is dead now—killed in a training accident while learning to be a turret gunner in a Navy torpedo bomber.[20] My generation is not even safe in the United States. . . .

The priest, Captain Ralph Dietz, Assistant Regimental Chaplain sets up his altar on the hood of a jeep. His muddy combat boots stick out incongruously from the bottom of his silky, bro-

28. A SCENE FROM THE 1ST INFANTRY REGIMENT in the hills northeast of Manila. We lived like this for a couple of weeks on Hill A, B & X except I remember that we were spread out better and our foxholes were more military. From: Tom Fallen and Ray Fallen, *The First Infantry Regiment in World War II*, (Chicago: Adams Press, 1990), p. 63. Tom Fallen had a Baby Brownie camera with him and took this picture.

caded vestments. He speaks of Christ's sufferings and how we can share in them by offering up our own misery for the reparation of sins. The congregation is intensely reverent, kneeling in the dirt, some with rosaries clutched in their grimy hands, others wearing them like good luck charms around their necks. Others have their heads buried in their arms supported by their rifles or hold their helmets reverently to their hearts. We are praying for deliverance, physical salvation. "Lord, from the depths of our souls, we cry unto thee. Get us out of here!. . . .

We get a beer ration, three cans per man. I'm only 18, too young to be drinking beer, let alone to be here in combat. I don't care for beer anyway. My father is an alcoholic and my grand-mother speaks often about the evils that alcohol brings. I drink one can. It's warm and sour tasting. I am offered money for the other two so I sell them to an older soldier for a peso a can. He really appreciates it. With five cans, he might blot out the horrors of war for a brief time. I blot out the war by thinking how nice it would be to take the Woodward streetcar to the river where the Boblo[21] boats are docked and the Vernor's Company has its plant. Now there's a drink—sweet and tangy ginger ale! Aged four years in wood! I think Pepsi Cola would taste real good too. Especially with potato chips! The world's first singing commercial comes into my head. "Pepsi Cola hits the spot, twelve full ounces, that's a lot. Twice as much for a nickel too, Pepsi Cola is the drink for you!" All the Army gives its soldiers is beer. . . .

I think about the last time I went to Boblo—the only boat rides I had before the big boats brought me to this green hell. It's the day of the annual Ford Trade School picnic. I have a date with Jean Card. She is 15 and cute and not there when I arrive at her house. I endure small talk with her hostile older brother while waiting for her to finish a baby-sitting job. We are late and miss the 4:00 P.M. boat. She apologizes profusely but I really don't mind. We walk, hand in hand, around downtown Detroit and then catch the 6:00 boat. We eat her picnic lunch—dainty little triangular sand-wiches, oranges already peeled and parted, and homemade cook-ies—as we glide down river. Even the Great Lakes Steel Corp. and the Wyandotte Chemical Works look good as the sun sets behind their belching smokestacks. We catch up with the guys on the is-land and return on the last boat, close-dancing on the moonlit deck. Why do we young have to fight in miserable wars when there are so many more pleasant things we could be doing? I've lost my youth before it really got going. . . .

The long days and nights on the *Shimbu* Line passed one after another. We developed a regular routine. Breakfast was at the bottom of the hill, lunch was C rations at the top of the hill, supper was often again at the bottom of the hill where the company cooks served up a hot meal. We sat in the dirt and ate with one hand constantly waving away the many flies who wanted to share. During the day, we took turns manning the outposts facing the Japanese. Otherwise we lay in our foxholes doing nothing. In between, we often had moments of intense excitement when Pistol Pete would drop a few shells on us.

When it got dark, the flies disappeared and the mosquitos came out—annoying, buzzing bearers of the malaria parasite. We stood guard duty, two hours on and four off, sleeping in our foxholes in teams of six so that we always had another soldier on duty with us. They were long two hour periods and we would pass around an Army watch, staring at the illuminated dial and marveling at how slowly time passed.

On one of my first turns at night guard duty, the quiet night was suddenly rent by a wailing sound: "Fuck you, fuck you!" I clicked the safety on my rifle and slid a little farther down into my hole, the hair beginning to stand up on the back of my neck, my eyes straining to see anything. Was this the signal for a fanatical banzai attack? The older soldier with me put his hand on my rifle. "Relax, son," he whispered, "it's only a fuck-you lizard." The gecko[22] does it again. "Fuck you, fuck you, awk, awk, awk!" I wondered where he learned that? Is he really calling for a mate like the other soldiers insist or is he raging at us for destroying his habitat with our terrible machines of war? Maybe he was imitating the speech of the soldiers dug into the side of the hill.

We received mail occasionally and a daily mimeographed newspaper, *The Sightseer*, published by the 6th Division, was passed around. It consisted of one legal size sheet printed on both sides and reported mostly war news and sports. While I was there *The Sightseer* reported the funeral of President Roosevelt, the American Army link-up with the Russians at the River Elbe, and the discovery of thousands of bodies in German concentration camps as the Allies liberated Belsen and Buchenwald. Mussolini and his mistress, caught by Italian partisans, were hung from a lamp post, and the war in Europe wound down as Berlin fell. In the Pacific, the battle for Okinawa continued against fierce Japanese resistance. Ernie Pyle, the G.Is "Boswell" was killed on Ie Jima by Japanese machine gun fire, and the American Army made gains at various locations in the Philippines.

On the domestic scene, representatives from the United Nations met in San Francisco to organize a new world order for the post-war era, the Detroit Tigers got off to a slow start in the American League pennant race and Senator Happy Chandler was named the new high commissioner for major league baseball.

I had slipped a couple of Armed Forces Editions in my fatigues when I left the replacement depot. These were pocket size books, great classics or other popular works printed especially for soldiers and sailors. One that I had with me was *The Turn of the Screw* by Henry James. My American Lit teacher, Mr. Whitman, had given the high school class a list of ten books he recommended we should read before we went to college and I had been working my way down the list. He had said that this psychological horror story would scare the pants off us but reading it in the situation I was in, with violent death possible at any moment, made the diabolical tale of two little children in league with the devil seem pretty tame stuff. I haven't read much by Henry James since.

I had been on Hill A about a week when Sergeant Gibson, a good old boy from Longdale, Alabama, came around. "Whut's yore name?" he asked. After I told him and he checked a list he had in his hand, he asked: "Whar yew be'n?"

"Right here." I wondered why he asked that. I certainly hadn't gone anywhere, unless told to do so.

Turning to a man with him, he declared: "Ah've had this man fo' a week and I ain't seen him since the day he arrived! Yew be'n hiding from me and the Japs purty good!"

They both laughed. He then asked me when I would be 19 years old and marked it down on the paper. There was a rumor that 18-year-old soldiers were going to be pulled out of combat because of parental pressure on Congress but nothing ever came of it. The Army desperately needed replacements and resisted taking any it already had out of combat. Most of us were within a month or two of our nineteenth birthdays anyway.

Another visitor around that time was Colonel Yon. It was a surprise to see the regimental commander come puffing up the hill. He stopped at my foxhole and asked how I was doing in his cultured drawl: "Son, ah yew gettin' enough to eat?"

"Yes, sir!" I answered, resisting the urge to stand up and salute. It might attract the attention of a Japanese sniper.

"Are yew needin' anythin'?"

"I sure could use a bath."

He laughed and turned to his aide, "Mahk thet down. If these men are heah much longer, we are going to have to beeld them some showers!"

142

They certainly would have been welcome. Sanitary facilities were non-existent. We urinated and defecated on the open ground and buried our excrement because of the flies. Water was in short supply. We drank most of it. When we went down the hill for meals we carried empty five-gallon water cans with us and exchanged them for full cans to be carried back up the hill. We could wash our hands and faces with a little water from our canteens but that was the extent of any personal hygiene. The old timers said that once in a while they sent the dirtiest soldiers back for baths and a rest for a few days but I didn't observe any of that while I was on Hill A. We were too short of men.

On the outposts, we were supposed to keep a sharp watch for any sign of Japanese activity. We would raise up, scan the Mango River valley and Mount Pacawagan some distance away, and then duck down. We were cautioned not to expose ourselves too long or we might draw enemy fire. We had a field telephone to call back to the other side of the hill if we saw any suspicious activity. The outposts were all connected to the same telephone line with the wire laid on top of the ground.

One day when I was on duty, there was an excited voice on the phone. A soldier from one of the other outposts was reporting the sighting of several Japanese.

29. THE BOMBING OF MT. PACAWAGAN that I saw was like this picture. The bombs were not very effective and the infantrymen had a tough time rooting out the Japanese from their caves. U.S. Army Air Corps photo.

"What are they doing?" the voice at the other end asked. He must have been an officer.

"Taking a bath in the river. Shall I shoot them?"

"You can give it a try but they are probably too far away. I scanned the valley and the hills very carefully. This was exciting. Maybe I would get my first glimpse of the enemy. Even the dead ones had been buried by the time I had arrived. I couldn't see anyone. After a while, the voice on the telephone said, "I emptied a clip [eight shots] at them and they didn't even notice. You're right, it's too far away for an M1!"

After Colonel Yon's visit there was increased activity on our hill. The engineers, dodging shells, cut the road up closer to the top with bulldozers. M-Company brought up their 81mm mortars and .50 caliber heavy machine guns. Cannon Company brought up several M7s. These were the 105mm guns mounted on tracked vehicles that were used to help take Hill A. A tremendous number of shells were hauled up and stacked in neat piles around the mortars and cannons. We began to worry about Pistol Pete making a direct hit on a pile of shells and blowing off the whole top of the hill. He had been relatively inactive for the past few days.

The ammo piles didn't remain long. Early the next morning they started to shoot them at the enemy. We were supporting the men of the 145th Infantry, who were attacking Mount Pacawagan. When I was on outpost duty that morning, I had a ringside view of the action. This was total war. Shells were landing on the mountainside like rain. Silvery Lockheed P-38 Lightnings were making strafing runs at the objective. I found this to be particularly exciting as the P-38 was one of my favorite airplanes. I had made several models of it but these were the first real Lightnings that I had ever seen. They were followed by North American B-25 Mitchell bombers who laid down napalm bombs on the targets. Soon the whole mountain was enveloped in smoke. It looked great from my vantage point on Hill A.

But there was a darker side. Under that smoke and too far away to see were infantrymen doing their terrible jobs, killing and being killed. An article in *Yank* magazine[23] describes the action on the mountain itself:

> . . . units of the 145th were sent in for what turned out to be the toughest of Fox Company's many scraps. Attached to the 6th Division, they went into the Wawa Dam sector on April 17th, and were assigned a sector on Mt. Pacawagan . . . Fox Company was on the mountain for a month. It went in with 128 men and came out with

41. Jap 155's did most of it. According to T/Sgt. Frank J. Ward of Benton Harbor, Michigan, one of the old-timers, Mt. Pacawagan was worse than New Georgia, Bougainville, and Manila combined. "You never heard of Mt. Pacawagan, did you?" Sgt. Ward is likely to ask you a little bitterly. "I guess no one has. While we were up there, the war in Europe ended. I imagine people at home were too busy celebrating that to read about places with names like Mt. Pacawagan."

It was hell for the Japanese too, with all the shells and napalm landing around them and setting fire to everything. They often came out of their caves bleeding from the ears from all the concussions. Dazed and confused but still fighting, many were shot in their tracks because very few of them would surrender. If they didn't come out, the Americans dynamited the entrances and left them to suffocate or starve to death.

Back on the other side of Hill A, after my outpost duty was over, I watched the canons and mortars still in action. The huge pile of shells was almost gone. An M7 mount that had been shelling the Japanese all morning moved to the very top of the hill and, sitting right on the skyline, began firing point blank at the enemy. Now this was something that we had been constantly warned not to do. "Stay off the skyline or you are a dead man!" the old-timers would say. When we went to the outposts, we went the long way around the hill instead of over the top to avoid making a target for the enemy.

Apparently the M7 was too tempting a target for Pistol Pete. Almost immediately, he fired a shell which landed to the right and rear of the vehicle. Close, but no one was hurt. The driver, realizing the danger he was in, put the vehicle in reverse and backed very rapidly down off the skyline. It was none too soon as the next shell landed exactly where he had been parked. The sudden motion of backing down hill had caught the gunner off balance and he tumbled out, just missing getting run over by the vehicle or blown up by the Japanese shell. He was slightly hurt, the only casualty on Hill A that day.

Now that the Americans had at least a good foothold on Mount Pacawagan, we no longer had to defend Hill A. We eagerly awaited a new assignment. It wasn't long in coming. Towards the end of April we packed up our few possessions, slung our rifles over our shoulders and filed down the hill for the last time. We loaded on trucks and moved to a place called Balaria Filters in the Novaliches area and bivouacked at a water treatment plant. Our mission was to guard

30. M7 105MM HOWITZER MOTOR CARRIAGE. Our Cannon Company used these very effectively in the hills northeast of Manila. U.S. Army photo.

the water treatment plant and patrol the area for infiltrating Japanese.

Morale soared, everybody seemed happy and friendly. We had cots to sleep on and plenty of water for showers, our first in over two weeks. Word was passed that if we needed any equipment, see the supply sergeant. I was completely out of clean fatigues because most of my field uniforms had been stolen at the replacement depot in Manila. When I told my sad story to Staff Sergeant Hubert C. Hile of Newton, Texas, he merely smiled and asked what sizes I needed. After he located three sets and gave them to me, I waited for the paper work.

"Need anything else?" he asked. "No," I answered. "Don't I have to sign a Statement of Charges for these?

"I wouldn't worry about it. We don't have a lot of time for paperwork here," he said, much to my relief.

The water treatment plant was part of the system that provided drinking water to the city of Manila. It was quite an interesting place. I remember talking to the Filipino workers who were very friendly. When I told them that I had been an engineering student at the University of Detroit, they showed me some of the tests they performed on the water to insure that it was potable. They were proud of their technology and eager to share it with anyone interested in it.

We had our cots in one of the buildings. When I passed a group of soldiers playing cards, one of them asked: "Hey kid, can you play pinochle?"

"Sure," I answered. I had learned to play on the troopship.

"You can be Dick's partner," one said as I sat down to play. Dick was different from the rest of the players. He looked cleaner and his fatigues were pressed. He talked with authority and played his cards aggressively. We easily beat our opponents. I later found out that Dick was Captain Richard Fleming, K Company's commanding officer. I don't remember seeing him up on Hill A or being introduced before.

First Platoon Sergeant Harvey Shaw, who was one of the card players, told me that I would now be one of the two platoon runners. Our forty man platoon, when fully manned, consisted of three twelve-man rifle squads, the platoon sergeant, the assistant platoon sergeant (Jessie Gibson) and the two runners. In addition, we had our Platoon Leader Lieutenant Tom Atchley and a medic from the regimental medical detachment named Melvin Horne, another one of the card players. We moved from the water treatment plant and set up camp nearby so I was now sharing a tent with the platoon leadership, the other runner and the medic.

The duties of the platoon runners were to take messages back and forth between the platoons and company headquarters and to carry the radios. The walkie-talkie wasn't bad but the model 300, which strapped on your back like a knapsack, was quite heavy. Neither one had very good reception.

The Unit History says that we did extensive patrolling in the Divisional rear areas during this time. I remember a couple that I went on. The first was a long patrol with me carrying the 300 radio. After an hour or so we stopped to rest and relieve ourselves. Black Cock found a dead Japanese soldier lying by the side of the road, partially concealed by the bushes. Actually, it was only half of a dead body, the lower half. From the belt up he was completely missing. He showed it to anyone who would look at it, lifting up a foot and letting it fall back to the ground.

After we got going again, he sidled up to me and declared: "Hey kid, now you've seen your first dead Jap!" As if it were some major event of my life.

"Hardly," I replied, "That was only half a Jap! The least important half at that."

"I think it's the best part because it contains his prick, his sexual powers!"

"What about his brain and his soul?"

"Don't know much about souls."

Well, I thought I knew about souls. The previous April, when I had been studying engineering at the University of Detroit, a good Jesuit institution, I had taken Father Edward O'Connor's class in Christian doctrine. He taught that man differs from all the other living creatures on this earth because his animating force was a rational soul. The soul is God's image in man and by virtue of this spiritual principle, man has intelligence, emotion, free will, imagination and the ability to love and create. The soul was lodged in the upper part of his body, in his brain.

I tried to explain that to Black Cock but he wasn't buying it. Another soldier offered the opinion that the Japanese didn't have souls, to which Black Cock readily agreed. We were interrupted by the patrol leader who yelled out:

"God damn it, Black Cock, get your ass back to the end of the column where you belong and keep you eyes peeled for Japs! And you, McLogan, cut the philosophy crap, you're just confusing him. Dead Japs can't hurt you. It's the live ones that we are looking for. The rest of you guys spread out, you're too goddam close together."

So, chastened for our unmilitary conduct, we continued the patrol in relative silence. It was uneventful. We reached our objective and radioed company headquarters. They directed us back by another route so we didn't pass by the corpse on our return. I've often thought of that dead half-soldier, somebody's son or husband, ignominiously left to rot by the side of a road, in a foreign land far from home, the top half probably blasted to tiny pieces by an artillery shell. What a metaphor of the stupidity of war, the waste and destruction of a man endowed by his creator with a soul and capable of greatness. And he was only one among millions! I fervently hoped for a better fate than that.

I also went on a night patrol around this time. This was something that didn't happen very often. Although the Japanese did a lot of moving around at night, we Americans generally stayed in our defensive positions. The patrol leader was a sergeant who was known to be very calm under fire. He was going over a map with Lieutenant Atchley when the rest of us reported for duty. I had been exposed to training films on night patrolling at Camp Hood. When we started out I asked, "Aren't we going to take off our helmets and blacken our faces and hands?" The sergeant laughed and said: "Hell no, kid, this isn't Hollywood! Just be sure you have plenty of ammo and hand grenades."

So, fully loaded, we took off rather noisily for a night patrol, I thought. Our mission was to make contact with another battalion and return, reporting anything of military value that we might see along the way. We even had a password to use when we met any other American units along the way and had to identify ourselves. Somewhere along the route, we passed through a field of watermelons. The sergeant called a halt to our march, found a ripe one, cut up slices with his machete and passed them around to everyone. He certainly was calm! I was definitely not hungry and ready to jump out of my skin from worrying about the enemy and there he was enjoying a midnight picnic!

May 1 was payday and we new replacements had been told that because of our experience on Hill A, we were being promoted to Private First Class and awarded the Combat Infantryman Badge. The Army Air Corps gave its flying personnel 50 percent additional flight pay and sometimes rotated them home after they had completed as few as 25 combat missions. The Air Forces also gave out three-fourths of all the medals issued by the War Department while the Army Ground Forces did little for its soldiers. The poor infantryman was stuck in his dangerous job for the duration—without any additional pay or special recognition.

Finally, in late 1943, the War Department created the Combat Infantryman Badge to be worn above the left breast pocket, in the same position as the wings of an airman. It was a long rectangular badge with a miniature silver rifle mounted on an infantry blue field with a silver border and a silver wreath. The badge was to be awarded to

31. THE COMBAT INFANTRYMAN BADGE is a miniature silver rifle mounted on an infantry blue field with a silver border. The field is three inches long and a half inch wide with an oval wreath in the background. The badge is worn above the left breast pocket in the same position as the wings of an airman.

those "whose conduct in combat was exemplary or whose combat action occurs in a major operation." It also increased the recipient's pay by $10.00 a month. Combat medics were not eligible because they were non-combatants. This created a new sense of inequity among front line troops, since the aid men shared the dogfaces' danger and misery. Toward the end of World War II, the Combat Medic Badge was created with similar regulations and benefits.

The award and promotion meant an increase in pay from $60.00 to $74.80 a month. Corporal Gerald E. Van Mol of Kansas City, Kansas, was the K-Company clerk. When he was not taking care of the paper work, he was assigned to the weapons platoon. He has since told me that the brass always insisted that the soldiers be paid on time so this led to many harrowing episodes as he delivered the money to the men in combat. There were also stories of men in other companies getting killed as they lined up in a pay line and the Japanese shelled these targets of opportunity.

We were paid in Philippine pesos which had an exchange rate of two pesos for one dollar. When I counted my money, I found it to be true. We were now certified combat soldiers[24] and I hadn't even fired my rifle or seen a live enemy!

HISTORICAL ADDENDUM

Most general histories of World War II give only abbreviated accounts of the liberation of the Philippines and end with the battle of Manila. This is probably because the battle for Okinawa is considered more important and occurred in the same time frame as the latter part of the campaign on Luzon, in which I was involved. The interested reader has to go to more specialized works. A good source is the Time-Life Books series on World War II. In the volume entitled *Return to the Philippines*,[25] an extensive description of the campaign after Manila's fall is given in Chapter Six—"Yamashita's Last Stand." The authors declare that the Army's toughest job on Luzon was the destruction of the *Shobu* group to the north, "but the smaller group, known as the *Shimbu* (for martial spirit) presented a more immediate threat. Its forward line lay less than 15 miles east of Manila, close enough for a Japanese counterattack or a long range artillery barrage on the capital. More important, the *Shimbu* forces, which controlled vital dams and aqueducts, had cut off much of Manila's water supply, leaving the capital vulnerable to epidemics. To eliminate these dangers, [General] Kreuger, on February 15th ordered an offensive to capture the dams and push back the *Shimbu* forces."

The book goes on to say that the operation was misguided and prolonged by two U.S. intelligence failures. One was underestimating the strength of the *Shimbu* group and the other was attacking the wrong dam.

Japanese units held a line 30 miles long on the western slope of the Sierra Madre at the edge of the central plain of Luzon. Because Sixth Army intelligence estimated that the *Shimbu* numbered about 20,000 men, Kreuger sent only two divisions against what turned out to be a very formidable force. The *Shimbu* group actually started out with a force of 80,000 men and had been reduced to about 50,000 after the battle for the city of Manila. But these were the better troops. Attacking their well-fortified positions were the 1st Cavalry Division on the right flank and the 6th Infantry Division to the north, the left flank.

There were two major dams in the river valleys behind the Japanese lines, the Ipo Dam on the Angat River and the Wawa Dam on the Marikina River. Intelligence officers, misled by out-of-date information, believed that pipelines still connected Wawa Dam to the city and thus considered it to be an essential target. Kreuger decided to capture it first. That was the main thrust of the 6th Division efforts from February through the early part of April.

Return to the Philippines says "By March 22nd, a month after the campaign had begun, the Americans had penetrated only a few miles into the Sierra Madre and the Japanese still controlled the Wawa Dam. By then the 43rd Infantry Division had replaced the weary 1st

Cavalry on the *Shimbu* front and General Hall's XI Corps had taken over command of the campaign to capture the dam."[26]

The reason for the slow progress was that the Japanese had spent months preparing these mountain defenses. They consisted of deep caves in the hillsides with man-made tunnels leading from a main shaft to numerous exits on the slopes. The Japanese fought with rifles, machine guns and mortars from the mouths of these tunnels and when attacked would move back into the main shaft and reappear at another tunnel exit. American aerial bombs and artillery shells barely damaged the tunnel entrances.

In addition to cave defenses, the Japanese had plenty of artillery including 75mm and 105mm pieces as well as the infamous 150mm mortars and some big naval guns and rockets. They used them to full effect and with the steep mountain terrain helping them, they managed to slow the American advance to a crawl.

It wasn't until April 22, two months after the first effort to seize Wawa had begun, that MacArthur notified Kreuger that the Ipo Dam was "the preferred objective" and that its capture would solve Manila's water shortage. It seemed that his G-2 people had finally checked with the Manila City engineers and found out that the Wawa Dam on the Marikina River had been abandoned as a supplier to the capital back in 1938!

The 43rd Division was immediately transferred from its position south of the Wawa Dam and dispatched to launch a new attack on the Ipo Dam which was 12 miles north of the Wawa. Then *Return to the Philippines* says, "The shift of emphasis left the battered 6th Division alone in the struggle to eliminate the Japanese force around the Wawa Dam. It was not until the 30th of April that the weary division was taken from the line and replaced by the 38th Division. In the two months and ten days since the attack on the *Shimbu* had begun, the 6th Division had lost 335 men killed and 1000 wounded, and three times as many as that had been evacuated from the front lines with injuries, illnesses, and combat fatigue."[27]

The official Army history confirms this, saying, "When relieved by the 38th Division, the 6th Division was in poor shape. Morale was down, men and officers alike were tired and worn, and all units were sadly understrength, especially in combat effectives . . . The Sixth Army's twin millstones of the Luzon Campaign—lack of combat replacements and lack of strength to effect timely rotation of units—had weighed heavily on the division."[28]

Reading that some 50 years later, it seems different from what I remembered. While I can't speak for the rest of the division, I thought that the men of Company K, 63rd Infantry, 6th Division, came off the *Shimbu* Line in good shape. After showers, clean clothes and a good night's rest, we were out patrolling and doing our infantry thing. Morale seemed to be high, at least as seen through my youthful eyes. I was in the company of *heroes*!

SEVEN

In Kembu Country

. . . who will testify, who will accurately describe our lives if we do not do it ourselves? . . . When I put my thoughts down on paper, the memories come flooding back.

—Faye Moskowitz[1]

During the first few days of May 1945, there seemed to be some confusion about where Company K, 63rd Infantry was supposed to be. We had come off the *Shimbu* Line in late April and had bivouacked at a water treatment plant in the Novaliches Watershed area. There we had done patrolling in the 6th Division rear areas, moving our base frequently. By the first of May, the rest of the regiment, less the 3rd Battalion, was en route to new assignments, while we were left behind, still moving around.[2]

For instance, I remember that we got up early one morning in the first week of May and took down the pyramidal squad tents in which we were living. They were carefully rolled up and put on trucks, along with all our other gear. We then moved to another location, still in the area north-east of Manila and still seemingly without firm orders. We then set up camp, which meant a lot of manual labor unloading and erecting tents in the hot tropical sun. By noon we were about set up and looking forward to lunch and perhaps a siesta, when Lieutenant Atchley announced that we were in the wrong place. So, with a lot of groaning and cursing, we took the tents down for the second time that day, packed all the gear back on the trucks and moved again. Needless to say, by the time we had set them up again in the right location, the day was nearly over, and we had worked strenuously and continuously all day long for no specific purpose.

154

The 1st Battalion had some of its elements assigned to garrison duties on the tip of the Bataan Peninsula and Corregidor. They also guarded Highway 3 and the railroad between San Fernando and Manila. The 2nd Battalion was given the task of mopping up around Mount Natib in the center of the Bataan Peninsula and then went to Camp Patrick near Tarlac for a much deserved rest. We were all supposed to have a period of light duty after the long days of continuous heavy combat that began with the landing on Lingayan Beach on January 9 and continued, almost uninterrupted, through the months of January, February, March and April.

Colonel Arndt Mueller comments on this period in a letter he wrote to me: "When the division moved out of the *Shimbu* Line to be replaced by the 38th Division we, the 3rd Bn., were left behind as a rapid reaction reserve in case that the 38th needed us. I understood that the 38th had requested that an experienced battalion be left for a time. We were chosen because we had fought in the entire 6th Div. zone from north to south and thus had the most complete knowledge of the terrain in the zone of action."[3]

Eventually we did get our orders to move to the hills west of Clark Field and so we had a day-long ride in trucks over mostly gravel roads and pontoon bridges up the Central Valley. A highlight of the trip was when we crossed one of the many rivers and passed by some native women who were bathing in the water. They were naked and didn't try to cover themselves as we slowly made our way across the flimsy, temporary bridge. In fact, some of them smiled, waved and made a show of washing their breasts. We had to playfully restrain Black Cock or he would have jumped off the back of the truck and joined them.

The official 6th Division history does give the impression that the following six weeks was a "rest period" and I suppose it was for some of the Division's units. My own memory indicates a rather busy time. This was reinforced by Colonel Mueller who made the following comments:

> Your story reminded me that we were quite active in the Clark Field area. Some other 3rd Bn comrades have also reminded me. My mission was quite simply stated, "Defend Clark Field from attack." What the hell! I said to myself. *How can I defend that mess of territory with my poor, little understrength, beat up battalion?* So, I had a conference with Gen. Ennis "The Menace" Whitehead, the Air Force Commanding General . . . My proposal was this:

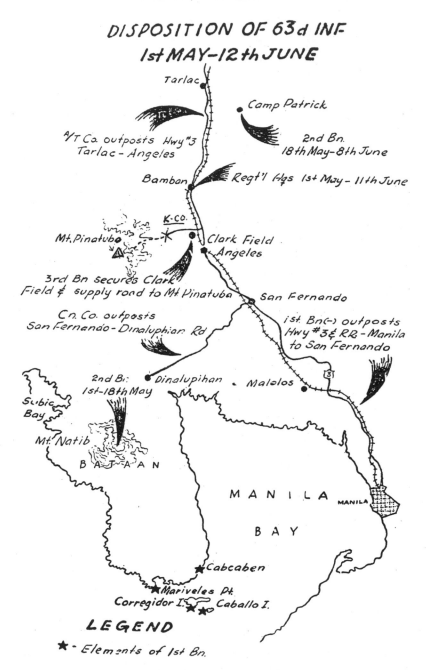

DISPOSITION OF 63d INF
1st MAY-12th JUNE

Tarlac

Camp Patrick

A/T Co. outposts Hwy #3
Tarlac-Angeles

2nd Bn.
18th May-8th June

Bamban

Regt'l Hqs 1st May-11th June

K·CO.

Mt. Pinatubo

Clark Field
Angeles

3rd Bn secures Clark
Field & supply road to Mt. Pinatuba

San Fernando

Cn. Co. outposts
San Fernando-Dinaluphian Rd

1st Bn(-) outposts
Hwy #3 & R.R.-Manila
to San Fernando

3

2nd Bn.
1st-18th May

Dinalupihan

Malolos

Subic
Bay

Mt. Natib

B A T A A N

M A N I L A

MANILA

B A Y

Cabcaben

Mariveles Pt.
Corregidor I.   Caballo I.

LEGEND

★ - Elements of 1st Bn.

7. DISPOSITION OF THE 63RD INFANTRY: 1ST MAY-12TH JUNE. Six weeks of light duty was spent in this area west of Clark Field. From: World War II Operations Reports, 6th Infantry Division, File 306, 63rd Inf., National Archives, Washington, D.C.

1. For me and my officers to organize his ground units—anti-aircraft artillery and base service units into a coordinated local defense organization.
2. To organize a ground defense warning communications network.
3. For us to do the long range patrolling while the local defense forces did the local security patrolling.
4. We would have on alert a quick reaction force to attack any Jap incursion, but the Air Force would have to furnish trucks because we didn't have any for this purpose. Gen. Whitehead agreed and told his Chief of Staff to get word out to all his units to cooperate with us.

. . . In implementing my proposal to the Gen., I charged Lt. [Hinton] Elmore of I Co. with the responsibility of coordinating all of the Air Base units and the communications warning system . . . He did a great job . . . By assigning him the job, I freed my staff to deal with the problems of rehabilitating the battalion, establishing patrol bases for long range patrolling, the reaction force, and integration of replacements into our tactical system.[4]

Most of the island campaigns of the Pacific War were intense but relatively short-lived. The Luzon campaign was different. It was lengthy and drawn out, comparable to the Italian campaign in Europe. When the 6th Division was taken off the *Shimbu* Line at the end of April, the division's public relations section put out a souvenir hand-out sheet that detailed the Sightseer's exploits on Luzon and claimed a record for 112 continuous days of combat in the Pacific Theater. I sent mine home to my dad, but he told me later that when he received it, it was so badly cut up by the military censors it wasn't worth saving.[5]

The official unit history of the 63rd Infantry Regiment has only the following to say about the next six weeks of our lives:

Fort Stotsenburg - Mt. Pinatubo 1 May–12 June [1945]. The 3rd Bn. assumed responsibility for this area. Patrols reconnoitered for routes of advance to Mt. Pinatubo. Clark Field was guarded by the battalion and supply routes to Mt. Pinatubo were secured. On the 20th of May, the Bn. assumed responsibility for securing the bridges between San Fernando and Dinaluphihan. Units not actually engaged in patrolling or guarding bridges, engaged in a training program.[6]

The regiment's historian missed a lot of detail. We did do all of the above but I, personally, remember a lot more. Many events bubble up

32. SOUVENIR SHEET. When the 6th Infantry Division came off the *Shimbu* Line, the division's public relations section had this one page souvenir sheet printed and distributed to all the troops. This copy courtesy of Arthur Tindall.

from the depths of where they are stored. The area to which we went was *Kembu* country, that is, the territory defended by the *Kembu* Group, the smallest of the three defensive forces set up in General Yamashita's master plan for the war on Luzon.[7]

The *Kembu* originally numbered some 30,000 troops under the command of Major General Rikichi Tsukada. About half of these were naval personnel under Admiral Ushie Sugimoto. Their main purpose was to deny to the Americans the use of Clark Field for as long as possible, threaten the right flank of Allied units moving down the Central Valley and, when forced back from Clark Field, execute harassing operations from rugged Zambales Province which is located west of the air base.

Even in those days, Clark Field was a vast complex of pre-war and Japanese-constructed runways, taxiways, dispersal areas, hangers, repair shops, recreational facilities, barracks and houses. I remember passing by row after row of officer's houses, each with a jeep parked on the driveway. The Air Corps had it a lot better than the Infantry.

There were, in all, 15 separate landing strips at the base. Three of these lay on the east side of Highway 3 surrounded by farm land, principally rice paddies that were empty in January and February (the dry season), when the major battles took place. The other strips lay on the western side of Highway 3 in an open area about four miles wide, east to west. In the western section of this airfield region lay Fort Stotsenburg, the pre-war home of various Philippine Scout units. West of the fort, the land rose sharply in bare grassy hills to a height of 1,000 feet only a half mile from the fort's main gate. From this high ground the Japanese had set up their artillery, mortars and machine guns so that they could lay lethal fire down upon the base and keep the Americans from using it.

As usual, American intelligence officers underestimated the strength of the Japanese defenders, thinking that they would number perhaps 4,000 to 8,000 on, or near, Clark Field. They also believed that most of them were service personnel who would offer only minor delaying action. Considering its actual total strength of 30,000, the *Kembu* Group was a serious force, although it was not heavily armed. It was lacking in big artillery and had no air support but did have many other types of fairly good automatic weapons which they had obtained by modifying anti-aircraft guns for ground support use and by salvaging machine guns and cannon from damaged airplanes at the base. These were moved to high ground and emplaced in caves and pillboxes along three eastward facing defense lines which

159

stretched north to south for almost ten miles in the hills west and north of Clark Field. A mini *Shimbu* Line!

During the last week in January, as the Sixth Army had pushed down the Central Valley, constantly urged on by MacArthur to get to Manila, they also had had to take care of this threat to their right flank and to take Clark Field, a major objective. It was to be an important air base in the continuing war against Japan. Two divisions, the 37th Infantry and the 40th Infantry were involved in battles here as the Japanese fought a yard by yard defensive action. They had sown numerous mines all over the air base which slowed down the American tanks. The Japanese had tanks too, which they used for repeated counterattacks while their infantry kept up a withering fire from the rubble of bombed-out installations and hidden positions between the advancing units. U.S. casualties were heavy. However, after about a week of rugged combat, the superior American firepower prevailed and the base was taken.

The Japanese, who had lost over 2,000 of their best troops, then began pulling back into their hill positions. The 129th Infantry Regiment of the 37th Division, heading west from Clark Field, took Fort Stotsenburg, then started up the steep slopes of a 1,000 foot hill that the soldiers called "Top of the World." There gun batteries were still shelling Clark Field. Soon fierce fighting was going on in such close quarters that, according to *Triumph In the Philippines*, "the defenders and the attackers almost reached the point of engaging in games of catch with hand grenades."[8] By the end of January, the Americans prevailed and Top of the World was in their hands.

While the 37th Division returned to its drive towards Manila, the 40th Division, which had taken the town of Banban and the hills north of Clark Field, continued to press the *Kembu*. In three weeks of savage fighting during February, they cleared out the remaining hill positions that threatened the air field. By February 20, it was deemed secure. The *Kembu* Group had defended its ground expertly, inflicting nearly 1,500 casualties on the Americans but had lost around 10,000 men killed. The 20,000 troops remaining under General Tsukada were hardly in good shape but they would have to be rooted out by mopping up operations that would go on until the end of the war.

The 43rd Division relieved the 40th Division in March and the 38th Division carried on the campaign in April. As late as 22 April, during the course of the 38th Division's mopping up, Private first class William H. Thomas, Company B, 149th Infantry, was posthumously awarded a Medal of Honor for helping his platoon seize a strong

Japanese position in the area. When we arrived there in early May to relieve the 38th, remnants of the *Kembu* were still lurking in the untracked, ill-explored wilderness of the central Zambales range. They were an unknown but still potential threat to the air base. We also didn't know that General Tsukada had given up any further controlled resistance at the end of April and had ordered his surviving forces to disperse and continue as guerrillas if possible. Some of them fled north in an attempt to rejoin Yamashita.[9]

K-Company set up its command post in an uninhabited valley surrounded by steep hills. A dirt road ran through the glen heading westerly from the air base into the mountains. At each end of this rather flat basin, which was about a mile long and a third of a mile wide, a machine gun emplacement was set up. Here the road ran through a narrow gorge alongside the Sacobia River, a stream which flowed easterly through the valley.

However, we in the 1st Platoon had a special mission. We bivouacked on top of a hill overlooking the valley where Company K

33. KEMBU DEFENSE AREA. We spent a couple of weeks on top of a hill like this overlooking Clark Field and the Central Valley. From: Robert Ross Smith, *Triumph in the Philippines*, (Washington, D.C.: Government Printing Office, 1963), p. 178.

had its headquarters. We had a magnificent view of the Cabusilian Mountains to the west which included the mysterious Mount Pinatubo, about 10 miles away on the far distant horizon. To the east was the broad Central Valley with Clark Field. We could also see Mount Arayat, which was quite striking as it sets all by itself in the middle of the Central Valley and rises spectacularly some 3,000 feet above the valley floor. Pilots have told me since that they used it as a marker to find Clark Field.

We didn't have much to do except take turns manning outposts and watching the scenery. It would rain every afternoon. In fact, you could almost set your watch by it, it was so regular. The heat would build up, dark clouds would assemble and then would roll through the Central Valley and up the hill giving us a brief drenching and then disappear in the direction of Mount Pinatubo as the sun came out and rainbows sparkled in the distance. For a boy who grew up in the flat, grimy industrial city of Detroit, the Philippine scenery was absolutely spectacular. It was no wonder that the men of the 37th Division called one of these hills Top of the World. It sure felt like it.

We were also supposed to keep in shape and do some training, so, every morning, Sergeant Gibson would put us through an hour or so of calisthenics and close order drill. The hill was steep, so when we marched up the slope, we were strung out and when we marched down hill, we were bumping into each other. Not very military but we were following orders. When we tried marching around the hill, it was also awkward. It was a common joke that only "ridge runners" from Appalachia or the Ozarks could march well on a hill. That was because one of their legs was shorter than the other from growing up in steep hill country.

It was here on May 9 that we heard the news that the war had ended in Europe. There was no celebration, only quiet discussion of how we would now have some help in finishing off the Japanese. Since the beginning of the war, the "Europe First" policy of the Allies had made soldiers in the Pacific Theater feel like second-class citizens. Now with the Nazis defeated, we could expect to have the first priority, the best weapons and more troops. However, it would be months before any troops or equipment could be moved halfway around the world from Europe to the Pacific Islands. We would have to tough it out in the meantime.

It was also on this hill that I noted my nineteenth birthday. There was no celebration for that occasion either—no presents, birthday cake, candles or even birthday cards. Our mail hadn't caught up with our latest moves.

One day there was some excitement when we were visited by a pair of Negritos. They are a race of dark-skinned Pygmies (Negrito means small Negro in Spanish), who were the original inhabitants of Luzon. Subsequent waves of lighter-skinned Malays and Chinese peoples moved in and the Negritos retreated into the more remote mountainous areas such as the Zambales. These were a primitive people who lived by hunting, using bows and arrows or stone axes, and by food gathering. They wore little in the way of clothing. In this case, however, the man had on a makeshift uniform consisting of a dark blue naval cap, blue jacket and Army pants and boots, all of which were too big for him. He was very short and carried a rifle that was bigger than he was. He looked like a 10-year-old kid who had gotten into the attic and was playing dress-up with the family heirlooms.

A woman accompanied him. She was half a head taller and was naked from the waist up. Both were coal black which was sharply different from the brown skin of the average Filipino. These were the first Negritos that I had ever seen.

The sentry on outpost duty, who spotted them trudging up the hill towards our camp, had sounded the alarm, so we all ran over to see what was up. The Negrito male spoke English and said that he was on his way back up to the mountains to hunt the Japanese. He produced a document, signed by a major in the U.S. Army, that attested to his being loyal to the American cause and his having been helpful as a guerrilla fighter. He was to be extended every courtesy.

During the Japanese occupation and subsequent liberation, the Army had encouraged "irregulars" such as this Negrito. Lieutenant Atchley examined his papers and said to give them some water and rations. After they rested awhile they took off in the direction of Mount Pinatubo. We never saw them again. It was a strange encounter, this midget black hunter with his half-naked woman living in the jungle between two foreign nations making war in his homeland. I have often wondered just how successful his hunting was.

One day Sergeant Shaw asked me if I wanted to go down to Clark Field to see a movie. Apparently I was the only one in the 1st Platoon to sign up to go. It meant returning late at night and the older soldiers felt safer staying put. They had enough excitement after all their days of combat, but I was bored and looked forward to a chance to do something besides reading and playing cards, which was all we could do for recreation.

In the early evening, a jeep came up the hill from company headquarters to pick me up. I squeezed into the back seat next to several other soldiers from other platoons whom I didn't know. We took off on a wild, bumpy ride down the hill. The driver knew some off-road short-cuts and the four-wheel-drive jeep could go anywhere, but there were several times when I thought that I was going to be tossed out of the jeep or it was going to roll over.

The movie was being shown at an outdoor movie theater at Clark Field with a very large crowd of servicemen. Seeing that we were infantrymen—we wore our helmets and combat boots and carried our rifles—some of the airmen made room for us on the rude benches near the front. They recognized that they had it a lot better than the average dogface and often gave up their seats to accommodate the few infantrymen that they encountered.[10]

The movie was *Gaslight*,[11] a popular flick that year in which Charles Boyer spends most of the time trying to convince the beautiful Ingrid Bergman that she is crazy. It seemed far-fetched from the realities of the life that we were living but I enjoyed the welcome diversion. Afterwards, the jeep driver drove around the darkened streets of Angeles, a town just south of the base. When I asked where he was going, one of the other soldiers laughed and said, "He thinks he knows where we can get laid!"

I hadn't expected this. About the time that I was pondering my options, we pulled up in front of a large house. There were many soldiers milling around outside. We pushed our way through the crowd and found many more soldiers standing or sitting around inside. While our driver negotiated with the hostess, the rest of us stood about staring. I, for one, had never been in a whorehouse before. The hostess, the only female in sight, was a young Filipino girl with bronze skin, long black hair and a mouthful of gold teeth that glittered when she smiled. I found her strangely fascinating and repugnant at the same time. After a few moments, our driver looked at his watch and motioned for us to leave. He had to get the jeep back to company headquarters by 11:00 and we didn't have time to wait for all the soldiers who were ahead of us. Business was booming.

It was just as well. I wasn't ready for sex on such a short notice. In fact, I was relieved to get out of there with my virtue intact. In the eight months that I had been in the Army, I had been subjected to numerous lectures and films on the dangers of contracting venereal disease and was pretty well intimidated by all of it.

There was a lot of talk, on the way back, about how the prostitutes were accommodating the Japanese until only recently. One story that often made the rounds, then and since, concerned how, as the Americans would take a Philippine town, the Japanese would run

34. THE CARABAO WAS THE BEAST OF BURDEN IN THE PHILIPPINES. In this scene near Clark Field, the animal is pulling a typical cart used for hauling. Note bar and restaurant in background. Photo courtesy of Al Irish.

out the back door of the local brothel while the Americans entered the front. The whores wouldn't even have to get out of bed or change position to service their new customers. A little far-fetched, but then some war stories are like that.

I never got to go see a movie at Clark Field again. When word got around about the other attractions down the hill, some of the older men were suddenly interested in going to the "movies." Since the number allowed to go was very limited, they exercised their seniority. They brought back tales of a prostitute who was missing an arm and part of a leg, but was still quite agile in the performance of her services. Another unfortunate casualty of the war making the best of it.

I did get to see one USO show while in the area. Joe E. Brown, the movie comedian, entertained the troops of the 6th Infantry Division sometime in May. The popular comic was born July 28, 1892 in Holgate, Ohio, the fourth of seven children of a house painter. Brown started in the circus as an acrobat at age nine, playing county fairs in the summer and attending school in the winter. His education ended

35. JOE E. BROWN entertaining the men of the 49th Fighter Group at Lingayan, Luzon June 1, 1945. The rough stage and lack of costumes and props is the way I remember him entertaining the troops of the 6th Infantry Division around this time. Photo by James P. Gallagher.

after the eighth grade when he went into vaudeville full time in 1906. From there he progressed to comedy and then musical comedy on the stage. While playing in Los Angeles in 1926, he was offered a movie contract. Some of his more notable films were, *The Circus Clown* (1934), *Alibi Ike* (1935), and *Shut My Big Mouth* (1942). A devoted family man, who neither drank nor smoked, he married Katherine McGraw in 1915. They raised four children, one of whom was killed in World War II.

Joe E. Brown was one of the first Hollywood actors to entertain the troops overseas. He started doing it in Alaska in 1941 and kept it up all through the war. For his efforts, he was the second civilian to receive a Bronze Star Medal. The first was Ernie Pyle.[12]

Arndt Mueller remembers that Brown spent a few days with the 63rd Infantry at Colonel Yon's headquarters. The comedian pinned his silver oak leaves on his uniform in a brief ceremony when Mueller was promoted from Major to Lieutenant Colonel. Sergeant Ervin Rose of Springfield, Missouri, remembers that, although Joe E. Brown was ailing at the time from a cold or the flu, he still performed many times for the troops on makeshift, outdoor stages in the field. The only thing he couldn't do was sing.

I remember that he only had one other performer with him who was the fall guy for his many jokes. His show consisted of his standard routine of juggling, dancing and imitating a baseball player. He was famous for his big mouth and could contort his face into many different expressions.

Apparently, because he entertained front line troops, Brown got to do a lot of things that other entertainers didn't. General Robert S. Beightler, 37th Infantry Division Commander, said that "Joe . . . had more personal courage than any other entertainer from the U.S." He invited the comedian to help capture the town of Bambang while he was visiting near there in early June. He put Joe in the lead tank. When the Japanese defenders broke out into the open, Brown shot two of them with an M1 carbine. He is quoted as saying, "One went down at 70 yards and another at 100 yards. The boys said I got both of them and they gave me a Jap flag one was carrying." He added that he had previously fired 75, 105 and 155mm artillery and also a .50 caliber machine gun, but this was the first time he had fired a carbine at close range.[13]

We were awakened one night by some loud screaming. When I got out of bed and went outside the tent, I saw, under the beam of Sergeant Shaw's flashlight, one of the older soldiers holding his stomach and writhing in pain on the ground. He had come back from Angeles with a bottle of whiskey and had indulged in too much of it. An ambulance was called and he was taken to the hospital to have his stomach pumped out.

The next morning, Sergeant Shaw was showing everybody the bottle. On the label was printed "Flying Red Horse" with a picture of the red winged horse that the Socony Mobil Oil Company used as a trademark. I had seen it many times when I grew up in Detroit.

"Are you sure it isn't gasoline?" I asked since I had never seen a whiskey bottle with an oil company emblem on it. He opened the bottle and sniffed the contents.

"No," he replied, "it's whiskey all right, although it's piss-poor quality. I sure wouldn't drink it."

Then followed a learned discussion about the making of whiskey. Some of the platoon members had grown up in the south where the making of moonshine whiskey was a fine art. They knew all about the distilling process and spoke of the dangers of not preparing it properly or drinking it before it was aged. They predicted that the stricken soldier would either die or go blind. I never saw him again so I can't report on how he fared.

Melvin Horne, the aid man assigned to our platoon from the 6th Medical Battalion, mixed his supply of medical alcohol with fruit juices and shared it occasionally with other soldiers. That, and an occasional beer ration, were about the only drinking that I experienced during my service in combat. Stories that front-line troops were drunk most the time is not what I observed. We were actually a very sober lot, mostly because we had little access to alcohol.

The visits to Angeles came to a halt after a while. I heard that some racist soldiers took offense when they saw Negro soldiers ahead of them in the waiting crowd at the brothel. They came back and hurled a hand grenade into the waiting room and severely injured several soldiers. We were a segregated Army in those days and there were strong forces bent on keeping it that way. Visits to Clark Field were even more limited and the town of Angeles was declared off-limits to infantry troops.

Tragedy struck the 1st Platoon while we were camped on that hill overlooking Clark Field. One day, as I was playing cards with Tom Atchley, Harvey Shaw and Melvin Horne, we heard a rifle shot. We all dropped our cards and ran in the direction from which it had come, one of our other tents. Just then one of the men appeared, a look of panic on his face.

"Dick's been shot!" he cried. He meant Private First Class Paul C. Dick of Bellefontaine, Ohio, who was an acting squad leader until the regular sergeant got back from the hospital. "Doc" Horne ran back to our tent to get his medical kit while I followed Lieutenant Atchley and Sergeant Shaw into the squad tent. Dick was lying on his back on the ground between two army cots. He was barely conscious with a pained look on his face. The other soldiers were standing around, stunned into inaction by what had happened.

We moved the cots so Doc could have some room to work. Lieutenant Atchley went to call an ambulance while Shaw and I assisted the aid man. Working rapidly, he cut open the wounded man's shirt sleeve and started him on blood plasma. Then he opened his clothing in front, exposing the wound. It didn't look too bad. There was a small hole in his abdomen, just to the right of his navel. Doc wiped off the blood, sprinkled sulpha powder on the wound and then applied a compress. However, a large pool of blood was forming under the stricken soldier.

"We've got to turn you over, Paul," said Doc, motioning for Shaw and me to help him. At his signal, we rotated him over onto his stomach. He groaned and appeared to lose consciousness. When Horne removed the blood soaked clothing from the back, it revealed a much larger hole just to the right of his spine. It was raw, ugly and bleeding profusely. I felt sick to my stomach and went out of the tent for some fresh air.

The other soldiers were all talking about how it happened. As acting squad leader, Dick had them cleaning their rifles for an inspection. He was a serious young man and wanted to keep his squad up and ready for action. He kept his own weapon in good working order and encouraged them to do the same. When hit, he was standing in the aisle between two cots, running a cleaning rod through the barrel of his rifle. Another soldier, sitting on the cot with his rifle cradled in his lap, pulled out his trigger housing and the rifle discharged. At such close range, the bullet passed right through Dick.

The soldier who accidently shot Dick should have emptied his rifle before he started to clean it - that was a fundamental safety rule that we had been taught and he had violated. We never saw him again. He was transferred out of the unit immediately. It is said that he went to one of the divisions up north where the fighting was quite heavy.

The ambulance soon appeared and took Dick to the hospital where he died about a week later. It was very gloomy for a while. The older men couldn't get over the fact that Dick had survived all those battles only to be killed in a freakish accident. It showed how tenuous our lives were, even when we weren't in direct contact with the enemy.

It was a perilous occupation, being an infantryman, and all the hazard was not from the enemy. With all those dangerous weapons about all the time, soldiers would get careless or start playing around. I know of several other instances where soldiers either shot themselves or other soldiers in their company. During this period, we lost another man in the 1st Platoon who shot himself in the foot.

On another occasion, later on, a young replacement seemed to be always pointing his rifle at me. It made me nervous, so I told him to point it in another direction. "Don't worry," he said, "it isn't loaded." To prove it he pulled the bolt back to show me that it wasn't loaded and out popped a bullet. He had taken the clip out but had forgotten to empty the chamber. "Damn," he cried, "I was sure this gun was empty!" In the history of gun accidents, it's always the gun that we think is unloaded that does the damage.

Hand grenades were especially dangerous. One of the worst accidents occurred in another company when we came off the *Shimbu* Line. As they were loading on trucks, the pin on a hand grenade, which one of the soldiers had hung on his suspenders, came loose and the grenade exploded, killing or wounding several other soldiers in the truck. The pin on World War II hand grenades was a simple, split cotter key, the ends spread to hold it in place. They were hard to pull because the bent ends had to straighten to pull through the hole. To make them easier to pull and thus more responsive in combat, we would flatten the bent ends somewhat. We would often do this to three or four grenades and spread them around our foxholes so we could be ready to lob them in a hurry at any Japanese intruders. In the morning, if we hadn't used them, we would re-spread the cotter key or it would be very unsafe hanging from our belt or suspenders. If the cotter key was bent and rebent several times, the metal would fatigue and break off making them very unsafe. It's a wonder more of us weren't killed by our own hand grenades.

Bored soldiers would sometimes unscrew the igniter on a fragmentation grenade and pour out the explosive powder on the ground. They would then reassemble it and pull the pin and toss it at other soldiers as a joke, just to get their reaction. It only made a popping sound like a cap gun and didn't explode.

With the ending of the war in Europe, the Army had announced the implementation of a point system to rotate soldiers home, based on length of service and combat awards. You were given one point for each month that you were in service and another point for each month that you were overseas. Another five points were added for each battle star as well as each medal. If you had children, they were worth six points apiece. Each soldier got a piece of paper that totaled up their score.

Some of the older veterans, who had scores as high as a hundred or more, felt that they were on the verge of going home. It made the death of Private First Class Dick all the more poignant. They remembered how he had spoken of all they had endured together and had hoped that the worst was behind them. I don't remember anyone actually being rotated home. Some high-point men did get non-combat jobs but most were soon back dodging bullets. My slip of paper said I had 18 points, nine for being in the Army nine months, four more for months overseas and five points for a battle star. I knew that I wasn't going home soon.

Shortly after Dick was killed, it was decided that Company K no longer had to maintain an outpost on top of the hill. We struck our tents and moved down into the valley and rejoined the company. There it was more like a permanent camp. We spent a lot of time chopping down bamboo and small trees with machetes and using them to improve our housing. The old-timers were pretty good at it since they had moved many times in their trek across the Pacific, with camps in Hawaii, New Guinea and the Philippines. Lashing the logs together they framed the tent to give it a more permanent and military look. They also showed us how to build a structure over our cots so we could store our gear off the ground. It also made a handy place to hang our mosquito netting.

It was still very primitive camping. Latrines were slit trenches with a roll of toilet paper hanging from a nearby tree and a shovel conveniently planted in the ground for you to cover your latest deposit. There were usually several soldiers straddling it so you seldom got any privacy. We had no showers and water was in short supply. Sometimes we bathed when it rained. Usually though, we made do with two helmets full of water, one to lather up with and one to rinse off. That was known as a "whore's bath."

I remember the food being good. Our company cooks used their field kitchens to prepare three large meals a day. We had no dining facilities, so we usually squatted on the ground and ate from our mess kits which we picked up at the beginning of the mess line. Afterwards, we scraped off the garbage and washed and rinsed them ourselves and turned them in for the next meal.

During our stay in this area, the local Negritos extended their food gathering to our company garbage dump. They ate the scraps that we well-fed Americans couldn't or wouldn't eat. Whole families would be seen foraging in our garbage, much to our chagrin. They also liked tobacco. When we got in a ration of free cigarettes, which was quite often, we gave them the less popular brands like Raleighs and kept the Camels or Lucky Strikes for ourselves. We would then watch them smoke, especially the women. They liked to put the lighted end in their mouths when they took a drag. It was said that they got a bigger kick from the nicotine that way. Black Cock liked to tease them by taking out his denture. They would run like frightened children when he approached them with his teeth in his hand.

We got in some new replacements. They were lucky that they joined the company during this period as they were able to get integrated into the group and get acquainted with the other soldiers before they had to face the perils of combat. I have always thought it was a poor system to bring replacements right off the boat into a combat situation. Too many were killed before they could become effective and the older men really didn't trust a new replacement until they got to know him. That took time and shared experiences.

It was also about this time that a soldier returned from the hospital and reclaimed his job as platoon runner. He had been severely burned with a phosphorus grenade and had not been expected to return to duty. Except for some scars on his chest and neck, he seemed to be fit but the older men marveled at his return.

I was then put into the first of our three rifle squads and assigned to the job of first scout. A rifle squad consisted of 12 men. In combat formation, the first scout headed the line, followed by the second scout. They often traded places because the first scout position is the most dangerous and nerve-racking. Then followed the squad leader and the Browning automatic rifle team. This was the squad's heavy weapon. It could fire 20 bullets in rapid succession like a machine gun. The team consisted of the B.A.R. man and two riflemen who also carried extra ammunition. Bringing up the rear were the assistant squad leader and four more riflemen. Since we were hardly ever up to full strength because of casualties or sickness this part of the squad was usually undermanned.

We had some more training while we were camped in this valley. Captain Fleming led the training program and we were taught some new maneuvers that we hadn't learned at Camp Hood. The first and second scouts were designated the A Team, the B.A.R. man and his two assistants were the B team and the rear riflemen the C team. The captain had us practice the maneuvers over and over again, in morning training sessions, much like a football coach drills his team in football plays. Adding to the excitement, we used live ammunition. It helped to develop a sense of teamwork, integrating the new men in with the older ones.

We also took turns manning the machine guns set up at each end of the valley. This usually meant spending the night with several other soldiers in a sandbagged fortification and taking turns looking down the barrel of a machine gun waiting for something to happen. In the dark, with the moon and the clouds alternating shadows on the rocky pass through the gorge, it was easy to imagine that a whole regiment of *Kembu* soldiers were massing for a *banzai* attack.

Almost every night one of our trigger-happy sentries would fire the machine gun, usually at shadows or noises. One morning, though, there was a dead Japanese soldier lying in the roadway.[14] We all went out to look at him when we heard about it. He looked kind of sad, lying on his back, staring skyward with unseeing eyes, his pockets all pulled out of his uniform where he had been searched for identification papers and souvenirs. Later that morning, First Sergeant Theodore Terpstra of Grand Rapids, Michigan, the highest ranking non-com in K-Company, came around to our tent. He was looking for the soldier who had done the shooting.

"Which one of you killed that Jap?" he demanded.

A young replacement answered, "Right here, Sarge. You going to give me a medal?"

"Hell no!" was Terpstra's reply. "I want that Jap buried. He's stinking up the place. You shot him, you bury him."

Terpstra was a big, imposing man. When he issued orders, they were obeyed. The older veterans also tell me that he was Regular Army, about 50 years old at the time and the father of six children. Several of us jumped up and went out to help our comrade. The Japanese soldier was still lying in the road, his blood congealed and flies crawling all over him. He would rot quite rapidly in the hot sun and soon become a mass of maggots. We dragged him over to the side of the road and dug a long shallow slit trench beside him. Then we rolled him over into the hole and covered him with dirt. We debated whether to put a rude cross at the grave site to mark it, but decided that he probably was not a Christian, so we left it unmarked. We were quite unemotional about the whole process. It didn't seem like this was a human that we were burying, more like an animal.

This was the usual practice. In contrast, dead Americans' bodies were collected, sometimes with herculean effort and danger, and then taken to cemeteries for burial with ceremony. There are some 13,000 Americans buried in military cemeteries in Manila, most of whom lost their lives in World War II during the fall of the Philippines and its subsequent liberation.

Disposition of dead Japanese was a lot more casual. They were usually buried in unmarked graves where they fell. If there were a lot of them, a bulldozer would scrape a large hole and then push the bodies into a mass grave and cover them up. Sometimes we would see a sign that said: "40 dead Japs buried here." Japan lost upwards of 400,000 of her sons in the Philippines so there are a lot of unmarked graves all over the islands.[15]

Manning the machine gun emplacement during the day wasn't as scary, but we had a problem with souvenir hunters. These were usually Air Corps personnel who would drive out from Clark Field in their jeeps to forage in the countryside. They were looking for sabers, pistols and other implements of war which they expected to find all over the grassy hills where the *Kembu* had put up such a battle. When they stopped at our checkpoint, we tried to deter them from going any further but they were hard to dissuade. Most of them were captains and lieutenants and if they insisted on going into the area where the Japanese were, we lowly privates couldn't stop them. Rank has its privileges.

The S-2 Periodic Report for 18 May 1945, says that "3 Japs were killed NW of K Co. C P . . . at 1100 by 3 Air Corps men. Later investigation of area disclosed bodies partially buried indicating more Japs in area . . . ." This didn't seem to discourage the souvenir hunters: more of them came out.[16]

One day when I was on duty, a young Air Corps lieutenant, accompanied by a pretty Army nurse, went through our checkpoint even though we warned him about the possibility of Japanese soldiers in the area west of us. After they were out of sight, there were a lot of lascivious remarks made about what kind of a souvenir the young Lieutenant was going to bring back. Black Cock described an imaginary scenario wherein the looie and his female companion reach a peak of amatory bliss about the time a Japanese soldier crawls under the jeep and blows them all to kingdom come. We all had a good laugh! I think he was a bit disappointed when the pair returned safely about an hour later.

On another occasion, out of the west appeared a Japanese soldier. He was carrying a white flag on a stick with one hand and a holstered pistol in the other. He was quickly surrounded and ordered to drop the pistol. After he was searched for explosives, he was taken to company headquarters. We had to be very careful because surrendering Japanese were known to commit *hari-kari* and try to take an American or two with them. This one appeared to be some kind of an officer, probably a pilot flying out of Clark Field who had fled into the hills and gotten tired of hiding out. It was rare for them to surrender and Army intelligence was glad to get any prisoners who might help them determine how strong the remaining *Kembu* might be.[17]

We also went out into the area west of us on patrols. The first time that I went, it was with a group made up of members of the 1st Platoon with Harvey Shaw as patrol leader. Trucks took us out into the hills and then left us to patrol on foot. After we had gone a short distance through a thick forest, Harvey ordered a halt and a defensive perimeter was set up. He then got out a deck of cards and we soon had a game of hearts going. Except for some lookouts, everybody else was resting or playing cards.

We had played for some time when there was a sudden burst of machine gun fire over our heads. Everyone grabbed his rifle and hit the ground, expecting an attack. Fortunately, no one had been hit and, after a few more bursts there were no more. The elusive *Kembu* decided not to attack. We took it as a warning not to go any further and made an orderly withdrawal back to our pick-up point.

The next time I went out on patrol, there was a man from Regimental G-2 with us. As we traveled by truck, deep into the hills, we

36. ON PATROL. This is typical of some of the terrain we patrolled in the mountains west of Clark Field. There was plenty of cover for the Japanese to hide in. U.S. Army photo.

175

came upon a Filipino settlement. It consisted of a few bamboo-thatched houses in the woods with about 30 or 40 natives living there. The man from G-2 ordered the trucks to stop and told us to get out and search the village for enemy soldiers. The Filipino women started to scream loudly and their children took it up as we poked around, rifles at the ready. The G-2 man and the patrol leader questioned the headman, rather harshly I thought, but didn't get any information on Japanese activities in the area. Normally, we received a friendly welcome when we met Filipinos. This time we must have scared the hell out of them when we suddenly invaded their village. I was glad to get back on the truck and leave with the terrorized screaming still echoing in my ears.

We proceeded farther into the mountains and came upon a party of 10 Filipino men. We got out of the trucks and searched them. One of them had a map and a Japanese hand grenade. The man from G-2 was sure that they were a band of "Pro-Japs" - Filipinos who aided the Japanese cause. We took them prisoner and then we all squeezed back into the trucks for the ride back to headquarters, the Filipinos docile and resigned to their fate, the American soldiers happy to be

37. BRINGING IN THE PRISONERS. This is a picture of 20th Infantry soldiers bringing in a load of prisoners. It is exactly like the way I remember bringing in a load of suspected pro-Japanese Filipinos that we picked up on a patrol into the Zambales Mountains near Clark Field in May of 1945. Photo courtesy of Art Petroff.

done patrolling for the day and the man from G-2 sure that he had brought in a prize. I never did find out what happened to our prisoners but I suspect that they were innocent natives out foraging for scrap metal or whatever else they could find.

The last patrol that I went out on turned to be an extended one. It came about when a Filipino civilian wandered into the K-Company CP on May 23. He said that he had been forced into service with the Japanese army on the day of the American invasion at Lingayan, had escaped from a group of 300 of them living in the vicinity of Mount Pinatubo and it had taken him five days to make his way to our camp. He provided a lot of detail on the enemy so it was decided to send out a three-day combat patrol.[18]

Sergeant Jim Nail of Springfield, Missouri, was the patrol leader. He was the 3rd Platoon sergeant and came around one day looking for volunteers to fill out the patrol which was mostly 3rd Platoon men. Another replacement and I signed up as we were bored and looking for some excitement. It would be a change from our regular routine and we didn't think there was much danger. After all, the previous patrols had been relatively uneventful. Nobody mentioned that we were going out to look for 300 of the enemy.

Army trucks took us deep into the Zambales, this time somewhere in the vicinity of Mount Pinatubo. At the time, we didn't know that Mount Pinatubo was an active volcano. It had been dormant since 1380 A.D. and wasn't even included in the worldwide registry of volcanoes maintained by the Smithsonian Institution until 1981. In 1991 it suddenly erupted in a series of explosions that shot plumes of steam and ash as high as 20 miles into the sky. Debris and ash rained down on the surrounding villages and buried Clark Field, making it unusable. It was later abandoned by the U.S. Also, 330 people were killed and 126,000 Filipinos made homeless. The eruption lofted 20 million tons of sulfur dioxide into the upper atmosphere, which has since dispersed around the globe forming a sun shield that temporarily erased a century's worth of global warming.[19]

But in 1945 we established an operating base there and did some patrolling on foot in small groups. It was difficult, rugged terrain with dense foliage. One of the patrols captured a Japanese soldier who was quite emaciated. The next day we patrolled on foot along a rough roadway that was little more than a trail. One of the soldiers was Harvey Roy, a full-blooded Indian from Minnesota. He was reputed to have extrasensory powers that could smell an enemy soldier a mile away. The older veterans also told about how, when they were in New Guinea, Roy kept an officer he didn't like pinned down in his foxhole by shooting at him every time he tried to get out to answer an order to report back to company headquarters. The hoodwinked lieutenant thought it was a Japanese sniper that was firing at him.

I was right behind Harvey when he made a sudden movement off the trail into the bushes. I hadn't seen anything unusual. He emerged just as suddenly, dragging a Japanese soldier by his shirt collar. The surprised enemy was soon lying on his back in the middle of the roadway with about six rifles pointing at him while the rest of the patrol warily searched the immediate area. He apparently was alone or his companions had slipped away. Strangely, his pants were down around his knees. He might have been in the act of relieving himself when Harvey swooped down on him but other soldiers told me of instances they experienced catching or shooting Japanese soldiers with their pants down. They thought it had something to do with a belief that they would have enhanced sexual powers in the next life if they died for their emperor with their genitals exposed.

A search of his gear turned up no weapons but he was loaded down with sewing equipment. A collection of scissors was found in a cloth roll and he had a large quantity of needles, spools of thread and buttons. He was short and chubby and hadn't missed too many meals like some of the other prisoners we had taken. It was theorized that he must have been a tailor for some high ranking officers. Headquarters was radioed and they said that they would pick him up when they brought our supper out.

In the meantime, the patrolling was to be continued. I was assigned to a small group that would stay and guard the prisoner while the larger group would continue to patrol the area farther west. "Don't shoot that son of a bitch," we were admonished. "G-2 considers him a valuable prize." Some of the other soldiers would have done away with him without any compunction but I had no intention of killing an unarmed, obviously non-combatant soldier whom I found to be quite exotic. This was the closest I had gotten to a live Japanese soldier and I was curious about these strange people who had made war on us. They had disrupted my youth so that I was forced to become a soldier in my teen years instead of whiling away my time at school, sports, trying to make out with girls or other teen age activities.

When lunch time came, we dug into our C-rations and decided that he might like a can of the chicken and rice. We offered it to him with a spoon. Bowing obsequiously, which he did quite often, he accepted the can of rice but declined the spoon. Picking up two twigs, he peeled the bark back about an inch from the ends and, using them as chopsticks, devoured the rice and chicken.

We probably shouldn't have fed him. Art Petroff of Minnesota City, Minnesota, who served in the 20th Infantry, told me at a reunion of the 6th Infantry that he fed a starving prisoner and that the unlucky fellow died on the way back to headquarters. The shock of a lot of rich food was too much for his emaciated body. Medically, starvation causes multiple physiologic and metabolic dysfunctions in the body. Refeeding should be done only under carefully controlled medical supervision or death can be hastened by the very food that can save the starving person.

It was a long afternoon as we sat around guarding the prisoner and waiting for the truck that was to pick him up. We attempted through sign language and pictures on the ground to communicate with him. He did a lot of jabbering in Japanese but we didn't learn much except that he seemed to be a tailor in civilian life, had a wife and children and came from somewhere on the big island of Honshu. At one point, he looked at me, then pointed to his nose and then to his crotch and made some motions with his hands to indicate size. I didn't get the meaning of it right away but the others did and were laughing.

"What he is trying to tell you, Russ," said one of my companions, "is that since you have such a big nose, you must have a big prick!" I didn't think that was very funny. However, it seems to be a common belief in the Orient, where most of the people have small noses, that occidentals, who have bigger noses, must also have bigger sexual equipment. I have never found any physiological basis for the connection.

The truck finally came out with our supper and took our prisoner away. The afternoon patrol had also captured a Japanese soldier, this one quite emaciated from hunger and disease. The high command was always glad to get prisoners, even half-dead ones, as they were a source of information about the strength of the enemy. This patrol had been quite successful. We weren't done though, because we were scheduled to spend another night out there in the heart of *Kembu* country.

The patrol leader selected some high ground and we dug in for the night, taking turns watching for the enemy. I was awakened several times during the night by some furry animals that would scurry away when I rolled over or changed position. I never saw them enough to identify them but several soldiers insisted that they were the biggest rats that they had ever seen. They were attracted to our warm bodies and would creep up under our blankets or shelter halves and snuggle up to ward off the cold.

We patrolled extensively the next day but didn't encounter anything. By then all the Japanese for miles around must have known we were there and kept out of our way.

During World War II, the U.S. Armed Forces Institute was set up to provide servicemen with an opportunity to continue their education through correspondence courses. I had first heard about it when I was at Fort Ord. Figuring that I would have plenty of time to study on the troopship, I filled out an application to take a course in Solid Geometry and sent it in with the $2.00 fee. I never heard from them until I got to the replacement depot on Leyte. Then they returned my money saying that I had to be assigned to a regular unit in order to qualify to take a course. After I joined the 6th Division, I became eligible so I re-applied during this period but didn't receive the course materials until near the end of our stay. The mail had to go all the way to the University of Wisconsin in Madison and back so it took quite a while.

We were well-supplied with books while we were here, especially the Armed Forces editions of the great classics. I remember wading through Herman Melville's *Moby Dick*. This I did lying on a cot on long, hot, humid afternoons when I was not on duty. I was still making my way through a long list of the great works of literature that would make me a truly educated person. While reading I would munch on tropical chocolate bars. These were Army issue D rations supposedly for emergency use as they were fortified with vitamins. There were always plenty of them around because a lot of soldiers wouldn't eat them. It was like eating chocolate flavored chalk. No matter how hot it got they didn't melt. I found they weren't too bad if you washed them down with a lot of water.

The Red Cross came out to our camp once in a while. It was usually a woman in a jeep with a couple of soldiers for protection. She would bring lukewarm, uncarbonated Coca Cola and donuts to give us. They weren't very good. The real treat was to see and talk to a white woman for a change. She had the fairest complexion! It was a refreshing reminder of the real world back home that we hoped to return to some day.

Near the end of our stay, we were notified that the top brass was coming for a visit. Several days were spent getting the camp in good military condition for their inspection. We even had to shave, which I wasn't used to doing very often in my teen years. At the appointed time they came around to each tent to look us over and spoke briefly to some of the older men whom they recognized.

After the inspection, the whole company was assembled by platoons in a cleared area for an awards ceremony. General Hurdis presented Silver Star medals to Lieutenant Colonel Mueller, Captain Fleming and Lieutenant Atchley. Several enlisted men were also given Bronze Star medals. Later on, there was a lot of griping by some of the older men about the awarding of Silver Stars to the officers and only Bronze Stars to the enlisted men. The veterans also seemed to know deserving individuals who had not received any recognition. It was more important now that the medals earned points for rotation.

I learned much later that there would have been a lot fewer medals if it hadn't been for Colonel Yon. When Yon took command of the 63rd, hardly any of the enlisted men had gotten medals for their heroic deeds because the system required company commanders to write up the citations and they were too busy on the field of battle or not skilled enough in the literary arts to get them approved. Deploring this, Colonel Yon organized a team of awards writers in the regimental personnel section and a form was devised. After that, the

38. AWARDS CEREMONY. Captain Richard Fleming, Commanding Officer, Co. K, 63rd Infantry, receives the Silver Star Medal from Major General Charles E. Hurdis. To Fleming's right is Colonel Arndt Mueller and to his left is Sergeant Rufus Bryant who also received Silver Stars. Copied from the 63rd Infantry Regiment Unit History, National Archives, Washington, D.C.

company commanders only had to fill out the basic facts. Yon's writers then expanded the deed in the flowery language needed to pass muster at the reviewing level.[20]

What the gripers didn't realize at the time was that there would soon be ample opportunities for everyone to earn more medals.

CHAPTER EIGHT

Up Against The Shobu

I am sick and tired of war. Its glory is all moonshine. It is only those who have never fired a shot or heard the shrieks and groans of the wounded, who cry aloud for blood, more vengeance, more desolation. War is hell!
—William T. Sherman[1]

War is the supreme test of man, in which he rises to heights never approached in any other activity.
—George S. Patton[2]

By the middle of June 1945, the Pacific War was rapidly moving into its final phases, although the average combat soldier didn't know that. On the ground, die-hard Japanese soldiers were, as always, still putting up a stiff resistance in many places throughout the Pacific Theater. Sudden death or horrible mutilation was a very real possibility for those of us still engaged with the enemy. It seemed like it would go on *forever.*

In Europe, the fighting had been over for a month. Although some combat continued in Czechoslovakia after the surrender date of May 8, all hostilities had ceased by May 12 and peace was restored to the continent. By early June, the four Allies had divided and occupied all of Germany and Austria and the movement of some troops to the Pacific, by way of the United States, had begun.

It was announced that the First Army, under the command of General Courtney Hodges, would be the first ground troops redeployed to the Pacific Theater from Europe. They would keep enough veteran units and personnel to maintain their combat ability. The gaps would be filled up with new soldiers and those who hadn't seen any combat. The general himself was back in his native Georgia, enjoying a hero's welcome as these plans were being implemented.[3]

Happy G.I.s began arriving home from Europe by ship and by plane carrying barracks bags and Nazi war souvenirs. They whooped and shouted and some knelt to kiss the U.S. soil. The fortunate few would have enough points for discharge; the rest, after 30-day furloughs and some retraining, would be heading for the Pacific. The draft went on with men over 30 now exempt and 18-year-olds continuing to be inducted as fast as they became available.

Time Magazine reported that the U.S. was in a curious transition period between partial peace and war.[4] While the price of scrap steel was going down because of war orders being cut, there were still serious shortages of sugar, meat and other foods. Cigarettes, on the other hand, were becoming plentiful and whiskey production was about to be resumed. Soon A-card holders would get more gasoline and plans were being made for the resumption of automobile production along with other civilian goods. Anti-Nazi movies became a drug on the market, but daily, and for some time to come, new European casualty lists would appear in the papers and the fatality telegrams would continue to arrive at family doorsteps. U.S. casualties in World War II had recently passed the million mark.

The Pacific War was vividly brought home to the Americans by the reporting of the first civilian casualties from the Japanese balloon offensive. This was a program whereby the Japanese sent bomb-laden balloons against the western part of the U.S. and Canada. Launched in Japan, they were blown to the U.S. by 125mph jet stream winds, kept aloft by an ingeniously clever system of jettisoning sand bags. It took about 80 to 120 hours to reach the target area where they dropped incendiary bombs, much to the surprise of western loggers and ranchers. They did no real damage until the Reverend Archie Mitchell and his family found one on a fishing vacation in Oregon's Lake County. When one of his children tugged on it, the bomb exploded, killing Mrs. Mitchell and all five of the children. The Japanese claimed that the balloons would soon have "death defying" pilots.[5]

According to the latest *Fortune* Survey, an overwhelming majority of the American people surveyed (80 percent), declared they would not settle for the withdrawal of Japanese forces from the lands they had overrun.[6] Like their government leaders, average citizens stood for unconditional surrender and the occupation of the Japanese homelands. While the Germans had surrendered in huge numbers—

as many as a million men at a time—during the declining days of the war in Europe, nobody expected the Japanese Army to collapse. They would, instead, have to be rooted out slowly and painfully with many U.S. casualties.

This was already the case in the bloody Okinawa campaign which ended in June. The closer the Americans got to the Japanese homeland, the greater the fanatical resistance on the part of the enemy and the higher the price we paid. It was similar to what we had come up against on the *Shimbu* Line—heavy fortifications with numerous caves and tunnels used as shelter against ineffective American bombing and shelling. Costly infantry assaults were the only effective means of dislodging the defenders and gaining territory. The stiffness of their resistance on Okinawa is reflected in the timetable of this campaign.[7]

The Tenth Army landed on Okinawa April 1, the day that I left Leyte to sail to Luzon. Japanese resistance to the beach landings was almost non-existent. They had learned to avoid defending beaches because of the heavy bombardment that preceded the American landings. By April 4, the Army and the Marines had cut across the narrow island. As of April 22, they had driven north and conquered the entire northern two-thirds of the island. However, from April 4 to May 26, the U.S. forces in southern Okinawa advanced only four miles against well-fortified positions and bitter resistance. It then took from May 26 to June 21 to complete the last ten miles to the southernmost tip of the island where General Mitsuru Ushijima, the Japanese commander, committed *hari-kiri* rather than surrender. He did this in full view of the advancing Americans on a small ledge overlooking the ocean where he had no more territory left to defend. Ironically, the Americans had also lost their top commander, Lieutenant General Simon Bolivar Buckner, when he was killed by Japanese artillery a few days earlier on June 18.

Typical of the vicious fighting was the battle at the ancient citadel of Shuri, where the Ryukyu kings had lived before the Japanese had taken over. *Time* reported that an American battleship scored 25 direct hits on the castle but the big shells bounced off like "rubber balls."[8] Whoever controlled 300-foot Sugar Loaf Hill controlled the western approach to Shuri Castle as well as the eastern flank of Naha, Okinawa's capital city. Nine times the Marine 6th Division assaulted Sugar Loaf before it was secure. They were blown off four times and withdrew because of the intensity of the Japanese counterattacks the other times. At one stage of the battle, they got 50 Marines to the top who were then ordered to hold the position that night at any cost. By dawn, 46 of them had been killed or wounded by Japanese counterattacks. Then, the last four were hit by a Japanese white phosphorus shell, burning three of them to death. The last badly-burned survivor crawled down to an aid station and the Marines had to start all over again.

It wasn't always that hard. You just had to have the right man. The 96th Infantry Division had Private First Class Clarence Craft of Santa Anna, California, eight months in the Army and brand new to combat. The Army had been stymied for ten days trying to take Hen Hill, a 450-foot crag just northeast of Shuri, because the Japanese could rake the flanks of any unit attempting to move around the hill. Two battalions had taken turns charging up the steep slope and had been repulsed with heavy casualties every time.

Then, as one of the battalions, its ranks refilled with green replacements, made another assault, it was again pinned down by heavy fire. This time though, Clarence Craft kept going, throwing hand grenades at every enemy he saw. Unbelievably, he reached the top unscathed and stood against the skyline directing the troops below. Two other replacements crawled up to the top to give him covering fire. Others formed a chain to pass him more grenades. Craft moved along the crest, hurling grenades into the Japanese foxholes and trenches as they popped up to fire at him. When they tried to charge him with bayonets and spears, he shot them with his Ml rifle. The whole fight took about 15 minutes. When it was over, he had fired 32 bullets from his Ml and hurled 48 hand grenades and a satchel charge. When the rest of the unit reached the top, they counted 58 dead Japanese, three knee mortars, two heavy machine guns, one light machine gun, 80 rifles and hundreds of grenades. Craft's mother was quoted as saying, "He's the most accurate thrower I ever saw. Why, I've seen that boy kill fish in a stream throwing rocks at them."[9]

The battle for Okinawa also saw the full use of the *kamikaze* suicide policy. The strategy of the Japanese was to drive the American fleet away so that our land forces would be cut off from their source of supply and then destroyed as they futilely attacked the impregnable defensive lines the Japanese had set up on the high grounds. Between April 6 and June 10, the *kamikaze* corps mounted 10 mass attacks of 50 to 300 suicide aircraft against the fleet lying offshore, about 1,900 individual kamikaze missions in all.

The American Navy suffered its heaviest toll of the war, even worse than the pounding they took at Pearl Harbor—38 ships were sunk, of which 14 were destroyers and 17 were LSTs. Numerous others were badly damaged. Over 5,000 sailors lost their lives including 39 percent of the crew of Admiral Spruance's flagship, the new aircraft carrier, *Bunker Hill.* The *kamikazes* were difficult to repel, but in the end, the overwhelming numbers of the fleet proved to be too much for the fanatical Japanese and the Americans prevailed. Okinawa became a base for the next phase of the war—the invasion of the Japanese homelands.

The cost of taking Okinawa had been enormous. We Americans suffered over 49,000 casualties, of which 12,000 had been fatalities— Army 4,000, Navy 5,000 and Marines 3,000, approximately. The Japanese lost 117,000, of whom only 7,400 were captured; the rest died for their emperor. Also, somewhere between 70,000 and 160,000 Okinawan civilians lost their lives.[10] This was out of a total population of 450,000 at the time.

The American policy of victory through air power was having great results over Japan—if you could believe its proponents. General Henry A. "Hap" Arnold, the commander of the Army Air Corps, visited Guam looking for parking spaces for some of the 12,000 combat aircraft he was planning on moving to the Pacific Theater from Europe. The proud Hap Arnold told newsmen that the Air Corps would deliver bombs to Japan at the rate of two million tons a year. "We are going to do the same thing to Japan . . . that we did to . . . Germany. Japan will be a terrible place to live in."[11]

For some Japanese, it already was. B-29s had been attacking Tokyo for about a year by then. General Curtis LeMay, commander of the 20th Air Force, whose Superforts operated out of the Marianas, reported that 51.3 square miles of the capital city was burned or bombed to ashes and that four and a half million people were homeless.[12] Other major cities were in equally bad shape as the numbers and intensity of the raids had been stepped up tremendously in the previous three months. "Yokohama is gone," LeMay said, "Nagoya is no longer a worthwhile target. Kobe is gone. Soon we'll be striking smaller cities in the 100,000-population class . . . It is just a matter of time before we get everything of value in Japan."[13]

The ground war continued. There were many isolated skirmishes on numerous islands as the mopping-up continued in the southern Philippines. Major battles were still being fought on Mindanao, the second largest of the archipelago's islands.[14] Driving overland from two directions, the Americans reached Davao, the island's capital and last major Philippine city still in Japanese hands. When it fell on May 4, MacArthur immediately announced victory in Mindanao. Tactically he was correct because the 24th Infantry Division held the port of

Davao and the adjoining coastline and could bring in supplies and re-inforcements. However, the Japanese 100th Division was far from de-feated. They had abandoned their beach defenses and established a formidable defense in the hills northwest of the city. It consisted of nine infantry battalions strung out in a fortified line, 25 miles long, running roughly parallel to the coast and about two miles inland. The Japanese defenders were well-supplied with artillery, rockets and mortars.

It took five weeks of bitter fighting for the infantrymen to over-come the Japanese in the Davao hills. On June 10 the last organized resistance in this area ended. General Eichelberger informed MacArthur that operations were concluded everywhere on Mindanao on June 30, but the mopping up continued at various locations until the end of the war. In fact the Americans made an amphibious land-ing at Sarangani Bay on July 12 and Gen. Tomochika didn't surrender his surviving troops until September 12. And so it went, the top brass optimistically announcing the end of campaigns while the lowly in-fantryman, who didn't always get this news, had to fight on against a very determined and entrenched enemy.

On the *Shimbu* Line, the 43rd Division had been transferred from its positions south of the Wawa Dam late in April to begin a campaign to seize the Ipo Dam.[15] This was now the preferred objective to re-lieve Manila's water shortage. With the support of a Philippine guer-rilla regiment, the three regiments of the 43rd made a four-prong at-tack against the Japanese defending the area around the dam. The assault, which began on May 7, caught the Japanese off balance. Gen-eral Yokoyama was, at the time, trying to mount a counterattack in the Wawa Dam area, and had moved a battalion of Ipo defenders south.

Weakened by this move, the Japanese fell back. By the evening of May 7th, one American regiment was within two miles of the dam in one direction while Filipino guerrillas had reached it from the other. By May 11 a third regiment had reached the new main Japanese de-fense line. Torrential rains hampered the American advance for awhile but when the weather cleared, the Fifth Air Force mounted the biggest air raid of the campaign against the *Shimbu* positions. These huge air raids were followed by more infantry attacks. Realiz-ing that they could no longer hold Ipo Dam, the Japanese retreated further east into the Sierra Madre. They left so quickly that they failed to set off the demolition charges that they had prepared to destroy the dam. On the morning of May 17, the dam was in American hands and Manila's water crisis was ended.

In the Wawa Dam area, where the 38th Division took over from the 6th at the end of April, it took four weeks of grinding combat before the Japanese loosed their grip on the Wawa on May 27. The men of A-Company, 149th Infantry, fought their way through the last narrow gorge leading to the dam, its 500 foot walls honeycombed with Jap caves. With their supporting tanks stalled in the rocky terrain, those in charge decided to try a bazooka. They called up replacement Private First Class Charles R. Oliver, who the previous year was a Wortham, Texas high school student, and made him the lead man.[16]

Oliver noticed that the sight on the bazooka was broken and a runner was sent back to battalion headquarters to fetch a replacement. But the attack couldn't wait. With two scouts on his flanks to protect him, Charlie Oliver and his bazooka loader moved forward, the rest of the company trailing cautiously behind. They rounded a bend, started up a concrete path and saw a pair of 20mm enemy cannons aimed down the trail. Charlie got them both with a squirrel hunter's "bark" shot, hitting the rock wall beside the guns and splattering them with shell and rock fragments. Next he blasted open the heavy steel doors of a Japanese tunnel and set off a store of enemy ammunition.

Moving closer to the dam, Charlie fired again and again at enemy targets, hitting them all. Sighting four Japanese huts half hidden by boulders on a hill across the river, he fired four rounds and demolished four huts. At the end he spoiled his record. He fired twice at a cave on the opposite cliff and missed both times. That brought his score down to 28 hits out of 30 shots. When he reached the dam, Private First Class Oliver said that the next time he wanted a bazooka with a *good* sight on it.

By May 28, General Yokoyama realized that with Ipo gone he could not hold Wawa either and he ordered the remnants of his *Shimbu* group to retreat deep into the mountains to the east, where they were contained until the end of the war.

As of the middle of June the only large Japanese force left on the island of Luzon was the *Shobu* Group in the north. (*Shobu* is a Japanese word that celebrates the military art.) This was the largest of the three groups defending Luzon and was under the personal direction of Supreme Commander Yamashita. He had started out with a *Shobu* force that numbered 152,000 troops, but by late February was down to about 140,000 following the initial battles that occurred after the landings at Lingayan and as the Americans drove across the Central Valley and then down the valley to Manila.[17] The real test would be when they assaulted him in his well-prepared northern defenses.

The wily general had started as early as November to prepare a triangular defense with the three main points being Bontoc, Baguio and Bambang in the rugged Cordillero and Caraballo mountain ranges. They were built and manned to withstand a long, large-scale assault. He also had the fertile Cagayan Valley behind his defenses. That could feed his troops for months. Yamashita's plan received some help from MacArthur. By transferring the equivalent of three infantry divisions from the Sixth to the Eighth Army for operations in the Southern Philippines, MacArthur left Kreuger short-handed for the job of eliminating the *Shobu* early. Each day's delay allowed Yamashita to improve and strengthen his defenses.

In late February 1945, General Innis Swift's I Corps, consisting of the 25th, 32nd and 33rd Infantry Divisions and Filipino guerrillas, about 70,000 men in all, began a three-pronged attack against the *Shobu* in their mountainous redoubt that spanned the width of Luzon from Damortis to San Jose to Baler Bay. Military historians have criticized this campaign saying that MacArthur should have made an amphibious landing on the open north coast and then driven south down the broad Cagayan Valley, cutting off the Japanese food supply and hitting their stronghold from the rear. But the troops and ships necessary to do this were busy in the southern islands at MacArthur's direction, so the American soldiers on Luzon had to do it the hard way—a grinding series of battles fought over mountains that were even steeper and more rugged than those east of Manila.

To the west, the 33rd Division fought its way for the next six weeks up Highway 11 towards Baguio, the Philippine summer capital and the headquarters for Yamashita at that time. The men of the 33rd exhausted themselves in the rugged terrain against formidable defenses and in April they got help from one regiment of the 37th Division which was moved north from the Manila area. Baguio finally fell on April 26, but 10,000 Japanese soldiers escaped as Yamashita moved his headquarters to Kiangan. Baguio was an important link in his mountain defense chain and its loss hurt him but, as planned, he had tied up the U.S. forces for 10 weeks and they had suffered many casualties in getting there.

In the middle of the *Shobu* defense line, the 32nd Infantry Division (originally Michigan and Wisconsin National Guard units who were also veterans of the New Guinea and Leyte campaigns), attacked along the Villa Verde Trail. This was even harder going. Villa Verde was really only an ancient footpath over craggy, waterless heights. Its twists and turns were often three to five times longer than a straight line between two points. It was mountain and tropical warfare at its worst as the three regiments of the "Red Arrow" Division alternated, one resting while two struggled against the well-dug-in Japanese defenders on the high ground guarding the trail. This went on for three months. Not until May 28 did they push through to Highway 5 beyond Salacsac Pass. It had been costly work—825 Americans were killed and 2,160 wounded, while the Japanese could count 5,750 dead of the 8,750 that they had committed to the defense of the trail.[18] Many of the Japanese wounded were still fighting on despite horrible injuries, such as the loss of a limb or eye. Lack of hospital facilities kept them at the front.

To the east, the 25th Infantry Division drove up Highway 5, the main road north. At first it was fairly easy and they occupied Digdig on March 5. Their goal was to seize Balete Pass, a 3,000 foot saddle that was the gateway to the Cagayan Valley. By March 10 they were within five miles of the pass. However, the Japanese had made extensive preparations to hold it. The surrounding high peaks were honeycombed with their artillery caves. That and other pillboxes and fortifications slowed the advance so that what followed was two months of bitter fighting to cover the last five miles. There were heavy losses on both sides.

39. AERIAL VIEW OF BALETE PASS, a 3,000 foot saddle that was the gateway to the Cagayan Valley. It took the 25th Infantry Division two months of bitter fighting to seize the five mile approach to it. We passed through here in June, shortly afterwards. Photo courtesy of Art Petroff.

Yamashita visited Balete after evacuating Baguio and decided that he had sacrificed enough troops holding it—9,000 out of the original 12,000. He ordered a withdrawal north. By May 13 Balete Pass was in American hands and on May 29 the 25th Division made contact with the 32nd near Santa Fe. The campaign for the gateway to the Cagayan Valley was over. Between them, the 32nd and the 25th lost 1,510 killed and 4,250 wounded.[19] They were both taken out of combat and the 37th Division took over the drive to the flatlands of the valley itself, starting on May 31. These events would affect our lives. The period of light duty that the 63rd Infantry was experiencing in the hills west of Clark Field would soon come to an abrupt ending.

Colonel Arndt Mueller, our battalion commander, made a career of the Army. In a letter[20] he tells about meeting a K-Company veteran many years later, when he recognized the six-pointed red star on the right shoulder of his uniform, which indicated previous service with the division. After talking for a while, the man, a Lieutenant Colonel who had also made a service career, said that the thing that bothered him the most about when he served with K-Company as a replacement on Luzon was that nobody ever told him where he was, where he was going or what they were supposed to be doing.

In his book, *The Men of the Terrible Green Cross*,[21] Herb Fowle, a replacement who served with the 4th Infantry Division in Europe, writes of several instances in combat when his officers came around and told the men the situation they were in, where they were and also the big picture of what was happening in their theater of war. Orientation is what that is called and I think it was an official Army policy.

However, my experience, like that of the soldier that Mueller met in later years, was that the policy was never carried down to the lowest ranks. Nobody ever told me anything—where we were or the significance of what we were doing in relation to the big picture of the Pacific War. I found out afterwards, most of it years later, by doing extensive research.

The move north in June is a classic example. One day we received the word to break our camp near Clark Field, so we spent a day taking down tents, packing away all our gear and generally policing the area in which we had spent most of the last six weeks. Nobody told us where we were going but the guesses were that it wouldn't be good.

We still had our cots so we slept on them that night in the open field of our former campground. I remember that it rained hard that night so we got soaked. Early the next morning we loaded on trucks and began what turned out to be a very long ride over mostly rough roads—past those long rows of houses at Clark Field with the jeeps parked out in front and all the buildings and infrastructure that make the rear echelon soldier's life so much more pleasant than an infantryman's—north through the agricultural Central Valley with its many farms, rice paddies and Filipino villages, and finally an ascent up the tortuous mountain roads of the Caraballo Range. We only stopped occasionally to relieve ourselves by the side of the road or to eat a hasty meal of K-rations. The mood of the soldiers in the slow-moving, constantly bouncing Army two-and-a-half ton trucks grew more somber as, late in the afternoon, we passed blasted-out pill boxes and other evidence of recent fighting. We were going through Balete Pass.

As the crow flies, our destination, Bagabag, was only about 110 miles from the Clark Field area that we had left early in the morning. However it took all day to get there and it was dark when we dismounted from the trucks and set up camp, sleeping again on our Army cots on the open ground. If I had known that we were so close to the enemy, I would certainly have dug a foxhole. I remember that we were up early on the morning of June 14, eating a rather decent breakfast that our company cooks had prepared on their field ranges. It would be our last good meal for a while.

There was evidence of war here in Bagabag, although the town had been taken without much of a battle. Near where we were eating was a burned-out house, its square perimeter outlined in ashes on the ground. Within its boundaries lay an incinerated body, lying on its back with blackened, hollow eye sockets staring blankly at the sky, its white, unburned teeth grinning grotesquely. Whether it was a dead Japanese soldier or some unfortunate Filipino civilian couldn't readily be determined. The stench was horrid. One whiff and I almost lost my breakfast.

We didn't have much time to sightsee. Bandoleers of ammo and hand grenades were being passed out and there was some confusion as we milled about wondering what we were going to do next. Somebody apparently knew. After a while, we were ordered to get on trucks and we rode out of town, northwest along Highway 4 a few miles. There we dismounted and were ordered to load our rifles. Panic struck me. I discovered that I had left my two bandoleers of ammo lying on the ground where we were waiting to board the trucks. They were heavy and I didn't wear them across my shoulders any more than I had to. I quickly borrowed several clips from my buddies and loaded up.

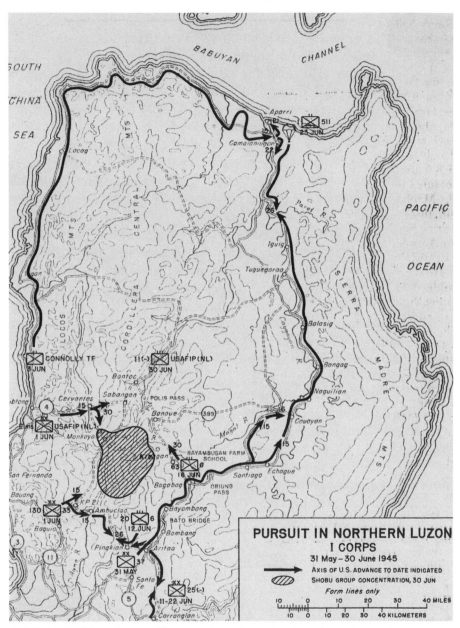

8. MAP SHOWING YAMASHITA'S LAST STAND in Northern Luzon. He was determined to fight on until the last Japanese soldier died. From: Robert Ross Smith, *Triumph in the Philippines*, (Washington, D.C.,: Government Printing Office, 1963), p. 565.

According to the unit history, we (the 3rd Battalion) "established a bridgehead across the LAMUT RIVER 2000 yards Southeast of PAYAWAN. One reinforced reconnaissance platoon [from I Company], left to move up HIGHWAY #4 to contact the enemy."[22] Where I was, we didn't contact any enemies. What I remember is going cautiously across a small foot bridge that spanned a river about the size of the Rouge River in Detroit. We then spread out in both directions along the river bank on the far side. Artillery shells (ours), were passing overhead and we just waited and waited. All day we waited.

We were back in combat. Although I don't remember being given any orientation, it had all been previously programmed. I have this picture in my mind of be-ribboned officers sitting around a table in a room full of maps, debating the merits of various alternatives, deciding the fates of thousands of men and then issuing crisp orders. Must be nice. A lot better than being one of the pawns down in the mud doing the dirty work.

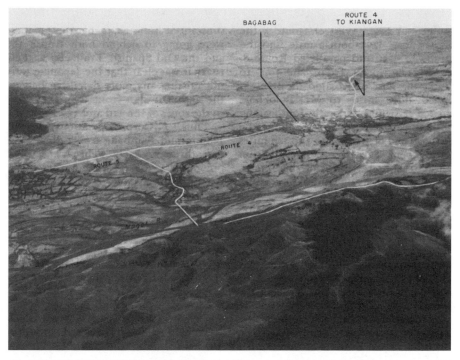

40. AERIAL VIEW OF THE BAGABAG AREA and the junction of Routes 4 and 5. Highway 4 to Kiangan is in the upper right hand corner. From: Robert Ross Smith, *Triumph in the Philippines*, (Washington, D.C.: Government Printing Office, 1963), p. 464.

According to *Triumph in the Philippines*, General Kreuger's Sixth Army planners estimated that, since "the *Shobu* Group had employed the bulk of its strength as well as its best troops in the defense of Baguio, the Villa Verde Trail and Route 5 to Santa Fe, prompt exploitation of the breakthrough to Santa Fe would lead to a quick and complete collapse of all organized Japanese resistance in Northern Luzon."[23] Wishful thinking! Plans for the pursuit of the Japanese required some quick redeployments.

The 32nd Division would move off the Villa Verde Trail beginning June 1 and, after a short rest, would relieve the 33rd Division at Baguio. The rest of the 37th Division would move north from Manila, relieve the 25th Division by passing through them along Route 5, lead the drive straight up Route 5 from Santa Fe through Bambang to Bagabag, and then swing east through Oriung Pass into the Cagayan Valley. On June 15 they would be followed by the 6th Division. After the 37th had passed through Bagabag, the 6th would strike northwest up Route 4 into the deep Cordillera Central. The 6th Division was to also strike southwest from Bambang along the road leading to Pingkian. The 6th's 63rd Infantry Regiment would handle the first assignment while the 20th Infantry Regiment would take on the second. The 1st Infantry Regiment would be held in reserve and then moved north at the end of June.

The plans were approved and orders issued. Men and machines began the trek northward. Moving rapidly against light resistance, the 37th "Buckeye" Division, with the 129th Inf. Regiment in the lead, reached Bambang before Yamashita could ready any strong resistance south of the town as he had planned.

The town fell to the Buckeyes on June 6. Without stopping to rest, the 145th Regiment took the lead and continued the drive north on Highway 5 and captured the strategic juncture with Highway 4 near Bagabag on June 8. The next day Bagabag was in their hands. The 148th Infantry, the last of the 37th's three regiments, then came up to take responsibility for Bagabag and the important road junction while the rest of the division continued northeast on Highway 5 to Oriung Pass and the Cagayan Valley. We arrived at Bagabag two days earlier than planned when we relieved the 129th Infantry in the area late on June 13 and began our campaign up Highway 4 the next day. That accounts for what I thought was a very sudden move without any orientation of the troops.

Late in the afternoon of the 14th, the first platoon was ordered out of the bridgehead we had established across the Lamut River. We recrossed the foot bridge and reboarded some trucks that took us to a landing strip near Bagabag. Our job for the night was to guard the L-5 Piper Cub observation planes that belonged to an artillery unit that was supporting our drive. The tarmac was hard, made out of some kind of paving stones. Cots were brought out so we could sleep under the wings of the airplanes. It rained quite hard; the wings of a small airplane don't provide any shelter at all during a rainstorm.

We had a man in our platoon who had recently rejoined the company from the hospital. Some of the older men had mockingly nick-named him "Combat" because he had managed to avoid a lot of it by getting sick every time they got near the enemy. Combat Smith (not his real name), kept waking me up during his turn at guard duty, saying that he heard noises. I finally had to sit up with him for the rest of his turn because he was so jittery. No Japanese came to destroy the airplanes that night. Except for getting rain-soaked and bitten by ravenous mosquitos when we had to relieve ourselves, it was a relatively quiet night.

The next day we were again slogging up Highway 4.[24] This was really not a highway as one would ordinarily visualize a highway. It was a gravel, two lane path cut into hills with lots of steep grades and endless curves. On both sides were bamboo thickets, various kinds of other tropical vegetation and an occasional grassy meadow. A lot of napalm had been used by the Air Corps so there were many burned-out spots that helped visibility. The road led deep into the steep rugged mountains of the Cordillero Central and sparsely populated, partially unexplored Mountain Province. There weren't many houses, civilians or other signs of civilization.

Some 25 miles ahead of us was the regimental objective, the small mining town of Kiangan. There General Yamashita had set up, in June, the 14th Area Army—*Shobu* Group headquarters. Surrender was not on his agenda. His mid-June plans called for his remaining units to start withdrawing slowly toward a new perimeter, see map #8. When this last-stand perimeter collapsed, all remaining forces would hole up in the barren Asin Valley between Toccucan and Kiangkiangan, there to fight to the last man.[25] Since most of his units had sufficient ammunition for machine guns, mortars and small arms, he felt that he could still hold out for a long time and keep a large force of the Americans tied down and bleeding as he had done in the past.

My memory of the next week is disoriented and fragmented but following the day-by-day unit history, weaving in what I remember and other facts I gleaned from the Regimental S-2 and S-3 Periodic Reports, gives some semblance of order to the confusion. For this period the history says:

14–15 June . . . A patrol up HIGHWAY #4 engaged in a firefight with an estimated company of Japs. 21 of the enemy were killed by small arms fire and another 17 by artillery and mortar fire. Company K pushed on through positions of Company I, with their objective the PAYAWAN REST HOUSE.[26]

What that means is that after being relieved of guarding scattered installations on Highway 4 by B Company, we regrouped as a company and moved forward through I Company positions to take the lead. Enemy positions were dispersed. There didn't seem to be a main line of resistance, only occasional small groups of soldiers who were there to fight delaying actions to slow us down while Yamashita prepared his last-stand positions. I was struck by the huge number of abandoned trucks and carabao carts strewn along the road. They had been hit by Air Corps planes who regularly strafed the highway. There were quite a few dead bodies and abandoned supplies, like boxes of new rifles still covered with grease.

Late in the afternoon, Sergeant Harvey Shaw sent Combat Smith and me to take out a Japanese soldier who was firing at us from a pillbox a short distance from the road. I understood the plan was for the rest of the platoon to cover us with rifle fire while we crawled up close and threw a hand grenade through the narrow firing slots in the pillbox. We were only about halfway there when Combat suddenly stood up and started firing his rifle at the target, so I did the same. There was an unexpected, muffled explosion inside the pillbox and Combat headed back to where Shaw and the others were. When I got there Shaw was patting him on the back and saying, "Hey guys, Combat finally got himself a Jap!" But Combat was shaking like a leaf, saying that he was sick and couldn't go on. He left, walking south on the road in the direction from which we had come. I never saw him again.

While we were waiting by the side of the road, a lieutenant came along. He looked like death warmed over. He said that he was quite sick and asked if there was an aid station close by. Harvey told him there should be one back a little ways down the road. After he left, Harvey swore and said, "If this keeps up, we won't have anybody left." But most of us hung in there.

Even though we were scared much of the time, we felt that we had to stay and do what had to be done. It was the way we were brought up and what we had been trained for. As little boys we used to dare each other to do mildly dangerous things and we usually did them because we didn't want to be considered chicken. Even though it was extremely dangerous here, I didn't want anybody to sarcasti-

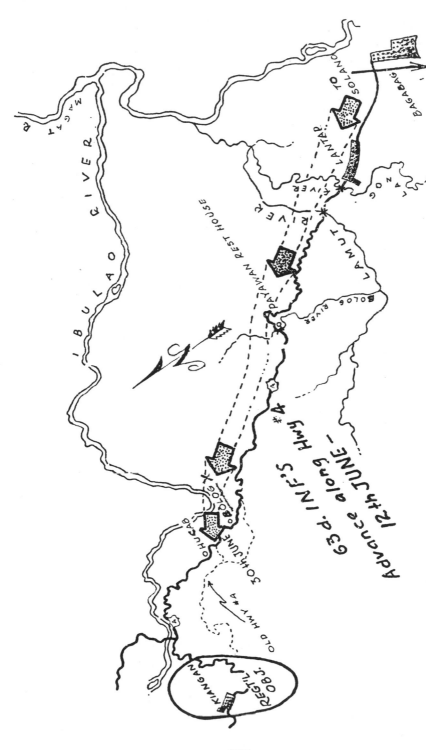

9. ADVANCE ALONG HIGHWAY 4. The campaign from Bagabag to Kiangan took 30 days of hard fighting. From: "Kiangan Operation", *Unit History-63rd Infantry Regiment*, File 306 Inf (63)).3. National Archives, Washington, D.C.

cally call me "Combat." There was also the feeling of togetherness. We depended on each other to stay together and keep going. There was a safety in numbers. Unless you were wounded or severely sick, you were betraying your comrades if you left without a good reason.

It was also immensely exciting. Like Patton said, it was the supreme test of a man. We would survive one firefight or mortar attack and then expect to survive the next one. Morale was high even though living conditions were horrible and instant death quite possible. We were on a great patriotic mission to rid the world of an evil scourge and we were being successful at it. The Japanese, while not beaten, were weakened and on the run. We were the pursuers, which is a lot better than being the pursued.

The point system made things different from the way they were when we were in combat in April. For the first time in the Pacific War there was a definite system for rotating long- service, high-point men home for discharge. Naturally, there was some reluctance on the part of those with high scores to engage in the more hazardous duties. The burden was often shifted to the newer men who were given the opportunity to earn more points.

We were short-handed right from the beginning. I don't remember having Black Cock or Jesse Gibson with us. They might have been assigned to less hazardous duty because they were very high point men but Lieutenant Atchley reports that they were all there.

In the 1st Platoon, the burden seemed to have fallen on Sergeant Shaw. Instead of operating in squads, per our recent training, we were operating as a platoon, assembling in assorted groups to meet whatever situation presented itself.

15–16 June . . . Company K pushed up HIGHWAY #4 to reach a point 900 yards south of PAYAWAN REST HOUSE, in spite of intense enemy machine gun and small arms fire. A Jap counterattack during the night was repulsed.

While one platoon advanced along the highway, the others would patrol on either side. This was tough work moving through dense vegetation, mostly bamboo thickets that provided good hiding places for the enemy. Firefights, although isolated and sporadic, were sudden, vicious and at extremely close range. You hardly knew what was going on 50 feet away from you. There would be a sudden burst of enemy fire and we would hit the ground and answer with fire in the direction from which we were being fired upon. We often withdrew a short distance and called for mortar or machine guns to help us out.

41. TYPICAL SCENE ALONG HIGHWAY 4 north of Bagabag as the 63rd Infantry drives north in June, 1945. From: *The 6th Infantry Division in World War II: 1939–1945*, (Nashville: The Battery Press, 1947), p. 130.

The end result was usually some dead enemy and only an occasional casualty on our side. While the enemy body counts in the operations reports may have been exaggerated somewhat, it definitely was a lop-sided war.

On this day, K-Company had its first fatality. Staff Sergeant Edward J. Konon of Omaha, Nebraska[27] was shot between the eyes by a Japanese soldier. When the word of his death passed through the ranks it was especially chilling. It made us realize again how tenuous was our life expectancy. The soldiers thought it was worse because Konon had been through so much before and now, with only a few points separating him from being rotated, he had been killed. But the Japanese didn't know about our point system. They killed anybody they could, whether he was an old veteran or a fresh replacement.

The Japanese have since been identified as remnants of the 105th Division, a regular infantry unit. There were also other service outfits helping them. They had been given arms and turned into ill-trained combat units. A probationary officer captured at this time identified one of these as the Sukegawa Independent Infantry Company. It was made up of officer candidates such as himself and discharged patients from various hospitals who were from various Japanese units. This company was provided with small arms and machine guns and then divided into small groups called Penetrative Detachments. Their mission called for "persistence until death."[28]

16–17 June. . .Company L pushed through Company K and occupied the PAYAWAN REST HOUSE area. 48 Japs were killed in the advance and about 50 were found dead in the hospital area. At the close of the period, Company L was temporarily halted by enemy heavy machine gun and small arms fire. Company I was moving forward.

When Company L came forward to take the lead on the morning of the 17th, we were dug into the side of two hills astride the highway. They spread out on both sides and we shared our foxholes for a while as the artillery softened up the area ahead where they were going. The young L-Company replacement who shared my foxhole didn't say much. Instead, he pulled out a small Bible and started reading it. Since he didn't seem to want to talk to me, I went over to the next group of foxholes to chat with a K-Company man. Much to my surprise, there was a duplicate of the Bible-reading soldier in that group. He was also fervently reading the Bible. It turned out that they were twin brothers.

It was very unusual to have twin brothers together, especially at the front. Early in the war, the five sons of Mr. and Mrs. Thomas Sullivan of Waterloo, Iowa, were lost when the light cruiser, *Juneau*, was sunk by a Japanese submarine in the naval battle near Guadalcanal. As a result, the Navy issued regulations forbidding close relatives from serving on the same ship. The Army had a similar policy but these two had somehow managed to stay together.

While we were waiting for L-Company to move on, one of its soldiers went out in the woods ahead of the line of foxholes, dropped his pants and squatted to relieve himself. While he was in that position, a Japanese sniper shot him in the leg. When he let out a scream, several of our soldiers reflexively started firing in the direction of his screams. When they finally dragged him out, the poor fellow was wounded in both legs, once by the Japanese and once by his fellow Americans.

17–18 June . . . On the night of the 17th, Companies I and L were astride HIGHWAY #4 about 2500 yards Northwest of PAYAWAN

REST HOUSE. During the night, Company I was attacked by the enemy, who used machine guns and knee mortars. In the morning, 16 Japs were counted dead. During the day, as Company I advanced, they killed another 64 Japs. On the 18th, Company L pushed forward against scattered enemy resistance.

When we were not in the lead, we were guarding new bridges that the engineers hastily built and the enemy just as hastily tried to destroy. We also did patrolling in the rear areas. On one of our patrols we came upon a camera setting on a tree stump. Before anyone could reach this enticing souvenir, the patrol leader yelled out a warning not to touch it. He then demolished it with several rifle shots. "It could be a booby trap or in a sniper's line of fire," he said as he directed us to give it a wide berth as we proceeded on through the jungle.

We also carried supplies to the forward elements. I remember carrying ammo that was so heavy I thought my arms would drop off before we got it to where it was needed. My skinny, 140 pound body wasn't up to carrying loads up to half my weight. Another time, when I was carrying a five-gallon can of water across an open area, we were fired upon. I made a record dash to cover on the other side of the field, the 50-pound can bouncing and digging into my shoulder as I ran. Most of the others had dropped their loads but I didn't want to go back and retrieve mine if I didn't have to.

It was also very hot and humid during the day. Our shirts turned white from the salt as we sweated profusely from the exertion. We used up the water in our two canteens quite often and hardly ever needed to urinate. If there were no five gallon cans of fresh water available to refill them, we used the water in the ditches or small streams we came across, purifying it with halazone tablets that we carried in our first aid kits. This was done in spite of the dead Japanese bodies that might be lying in the water nearby. "Adds a little tang!" we would grimly joke.

18–19 June . . . The 3d Bn continued the attack against scattered pockets of resistance. A convoy to the forward positions was ambushed by a number of Japs. One 1 1/2 ton truck was knocked out by enemy machine gun fire and by a satchel charge. 3 Japs were killed in the attack. Company L was attacked during the night by the enemy, who used   mortars. Infiltrating parties of Japs continued to harass our troops. Mortar fire fell intermittently on Companies L and K. On the 19th, Company I pushed off to the right flank of Company L. At the close of the period, Companies I and L were in contact on the high ground in the vicinity 3000 yards Southeast of BOLOG.

At the end of the day, we established a defense perimeter by digging a line of foxholes, usually on high ground. They were shallow and long enough to sleep in, with our feet facing outward to where the enemy was likely to be. We slept with our rifles beside us, loaded and ready for instant use. Also hand grenades were primed and strategically placed around our foxhole so we could use them in a hurry if we had to.

We replacements generally stuck together in groups of four. We took turns at guard duty of two hours on, four hours off, all night long. These were scary, lonely hours staring out at the dark jungle which was seldom quiet, although the noises were usually insects, animals, birds or the rustling of the wind. The normal noises would be punctuated occasionally by rifle and machine gun fire, or the explosion of a hand grenade, as jittery soldiers thought they heard an enemy on the prowl. Sometimes they were hearing the enemy, who did move around and attack us at night occasionally but, more often than not, our men were hearing only normal jungle sounds and wasting ammunition.

I usually fell into a deep sleep after an exhausting day of heavy physical and emotional exertion. I found that I could sleep rather comfortably in my foxhole by lying on my back, covered by my shelter half and with my head cradled in my helmet. Unfortunately, this caused me to snore quite loudly, much to the nervous apprehension of some of my companions who would wake me up, claiming that I was drawing the enemy to our position and that I should sleep on my side. I would try this for a while but other positions weren't comfortable. I would soon return to sleeping on my back and the cycle would be repeated. One night all the members of our quartet slept through the night because the first man fell asleep on his turn and didn't wake up the second man. It gave us all an eerie feeling because, besides risking death from the Japanese, sleeping on guard duty is a serious breech of military discipline. We didn't tell anybody else about it.

19–20 June . . . The 3d Bn continued to advance. On the 20th, Companies K and L were pushing toward the high ground East of the highway. K Company was on the right flank.

Every day we made a little progress in our drive up the highway. One day, when it was our turn to lead, our platoon was assigned to escort an armored car that belonged to the 6th Cavalry Reconnaissance Battalion, who were sometimes spearheading our forward drive. The cavalrymen were very nervous because the Japanese were known to favor them as a target for a suicide mission. An enemy soldier hidden by the side of the road, carrying a satchel or pole charge, would suddenly rush to the vehicle, dive underneath and set off the charge, blowing up himself as well as the armored car. We had to form a ring of infantrymen, completely encircling the armored car, before they would even proceed. It was very uncomfortable walking along beside the armored car, rifles at the ready watching out for suicidal Japanese because the cavalrymen kept spraying the countryside with their 50 caliber machine guns only inches over the top of our heads as they jounced along at a snail's pace. The noise was deafening.

They finally ran low on ammunition and decided to return to the rear area where they safely spent their nights. Turning around on the narrow roadway was difficult but they finally made it and then took off at a high rate of speed. We were ordered to return to where the rest of K-Company was digging in for the night. I was at the head of the column as first scout when there suddenly were a lot of explosions and gunfire ahead, but out of sight around a bend in the road. I stopped. The second scout came up and said he would take the lead. The patrol leader motioned us to keep going.

As we edged our way around the bend we saw that the company, which was bivouacked in an open area by the side of the road, was under a mortar attack and was returning fire in the direction from which it came, wooded hills to the east of the meadow. When we came charging into the meadow, the Japanese, seeing that the company was being reinforced, broke off the attack and receded into the woods.

In the movie *Platoon*, which is about the war in Vietnam, the action was shot in the Philippines, so the scenery is familiar to me. However, when the patrol comes upon an enemy, all hell breaks loose as all the soldiers have automatic weapons. It's a tremendous display of firepower. In our war, where we didn't have many automatic weapons, it generally was only the exchange of a few isolated rifle shots that made up a skirmish until automatic weapons or mortars could be brought up.

On one of the patrols I was on, the patrol leader handed me a Thompson sub-machine gun[29] and said he would carry my rifle since I was to be the first scout. I had never fired a Thompson before and was hoping that I would get a chance to use it but that patrol proved uneventful. We should have had more of them. While highly inaccurate at longer range, they were ideal for the short distance, sudden encounters with the enemy that we were having. I believe there were only two tommy-guns in the whole company.

According to the Regimental casualty report for the month of June 1945, it had so far cost us 5 men killed, 23 wounded and 4 injured.[30] The Japanese had lost 487 killed and 49 captured.[31] Of the prisoners, 22 were listed as Formosans who were civilians used by the Japanese as laborers. There was also a civilian family of four which consisted of an elderly Japanese man, a woman and two young children. The high body count included 167 "found dead". This means that they were probably killed by our airplanes or artillery shells. About 50 were found dead in a hospital near Payawan Rest Home. It is believed that they were severely wounded Japanese soldiers, unable to be moved who were killed by their own people to prevent them from being captured. One of these wounded was not dead and had killed Staff Sergeant Konon by rising up in his bed and shooting Konon between the eyes as he came upon him.

That's a lot of dead enemy soldiers. I have been asked, usually by the younger generation, how I could justify my participation in such a blood bath. My answer is that I certainly didn't volunteer to be there. I was drafted by the civil authority of my government, trained by its Army to fight in the war and ordered to the front. At age 19, I hadn't developed much independent thinking and the idea of questioning my role hadn't even entered my mind. I had spent my young life doing what I was told to do.

Later on, I would study Catholic philosophy and learn that war presents a thinking Christian with a moral dilemma: whether to participate in its horrors by obeying lawful civil authority when he and his fellow citizens are threatened with destruction by an enemy, or to follow the Christian ethic to do no man any harm. He must follow his conscience, which is a judgment to be made based on knowledge of the particulars of the war he is needed by his country to participate in.[32]

The earliest Christians, following Jesus' teaching of nonviolence, were conscientious objectors. Their refusal to serve in the Roman armies resulted in their executions and the new sect being harshly persecuted. However, despite this the new religion grew and by the fourth century even the Roman rulers had embraced Christianity. St. Augustine was the first Christian bishop and theologian to argue in favor of limited military action. His argument was based on the principles of the "just war" that had been previously enunciated in the writings of Plato, Aristotle and Cicero. Augustine wrote that war may be waged by Christians, but only as a necessity and only to preserve peace. This was in answer to the barbarian invasions of the time that threatened to destroy Roman and now Christian civilization.

In the Middle Ages, the just-war doctrine was further refined by Thomas Aquinas. He listed three elements to be satisfied for a war to be considered just: The combat must be waged by a competent government authority, the cause must be just, such as self-defense or the conquest of evil, and there must be a "right intention" to promote good.

Later Catholic thinkers added notions that war should be a "last resort," after all efforts for peace have been tried, that it should have a probability of success, that anticipated good results must outweigh the suffering and damage that it would cause, and that the combatants must discriminate to protect non-combatants. By those standards, World War II, because of the rampant evils of Nazism and Japanese Imperialism and the fact that we were attacked first, was generally considered to be a just war. Studs Terkel even called it *"The Good War"*,[33] an ironic way of titling a book about such a horrifying event.

Since the majority of Christians who served in World War II were non-combatants anyway—doing civilian type jobs in uniform—most didn't have to wrestle much with their consciences. Selective Service regulations did make specific allowances for conscientious objectors who were allowed to serve in non-combat roles or alternative work. There were a few. Movie actor Lew Ayres was one who declared his moral objections to the war but did serve honorably as a medic in the South Pacific. His unpopular stand cost him. He was never able to make many movies afterwards.

Local draft boards during World War II were made up mostly of veterans of World War I and they generally talked young men out of using the provisions for conscientious objection. They were particularly hostile to Jehovah's Witnesses because of their belief that each one was a minister in his faith and entitled to a deferment. When they drafted them anyway, many refused to take the oath of induction and ended up in jail. Of the 14,000 men imprisoned for resisting the draft during World War II, 4,000 were Jehovah's Witnesses.[34]

But most of us went willingly. We hadn't thought much about the moral issues and didn't really know what we were getting into. When you get down to the situation that we were in, it was too late to do any moralizing. It was kill or be killed. That is another horror of war—that it depends on young and innocent boy soldiers to do the dirty work. The younger, the better.

Thus, in our minds, we were morally justified warriors doing what we had to do to protect our country's freedoms from the barbarians who would take them away. Even though I lacked the philosophic background at the time, I had no doubts that what we were doing was necessary. Time hasn't changed that any. War should be avoided if possible, but if it becomes necessary, then it should be fought all out to win.

At the end of this first week of the campaign, we had driven about 15 miles into Japanese-held territory, to a point just southeast of Bolog. It had been seven long days and nights experiencing the horrible sensations that war is: fear, uncertainty, sweat, dirt, mud, smoke, loud noises, blood, shock, anger, darkness, terror, screams, devastation, fire, stench, quick deaths, slow deaths, ghastly wounds, rotting corpses, hard work, fatigue, endless waiting, rain, heat, thirst, confusion, and immense waste. Somehow I had survived and was still in fairly good shape.

However, we were still a long way from Kiangan and the worst was yet to come as the opposition stiffened. The longevity of a first scout in that kind of warfare is extremely short. It would soon be all over for me.

NINE

The Million
Dollar Wound

Our attempts to recover . . . the past and what really hap-
pened are doomed at the outset to failure because it is we
ourselves who are doing the investigation . . . We move
on. We become someone else.

—A.N. Wilson[1]

The Regimental history continues:

20–21 June . . . Companies K and L continued the attack up HIGH-
WAY #4. They encountered some machine gun and knee mortar fire
during the advance. About 34 Japs were killed during the period.
Company K advanced to a point about 1000 yards east of BOLOG.
Leading elements were slowed up by increasing machine gun fire
which was covering all approaches to the objective.[2]

I remember the night of June 20–21 somewhat more dramatically.
It was another night of terror and misery, terror because the Japanese
had been a lot more active, probing our lines and trying to kill us with
bayonets tied to bamboo poles. It seemed odd because we had seen
abandoned rifles, still in their packing cases, along Highway 4. But
then again, if they fired a rifle, the muzzle flash would give away their
position and they would be dodging hand grenades and small arms
fire from the Americans. One of them had been shot and lay just outside the perimeter screaming "Hirohito!" intermittently and for a long

42. TYPICAL COMBAT SCENE IN NORTHERN LUZON. This is the way we dug in every night. U.S. Army Photo.

time. It took a lot of gunfire and grenades in the darkened direction of his cries to finish him off.

Misery because it had rained heavily and our holes had filled with water. Someone had suggested putting brush and twigs at the bottom of the hole to provide space between our bodies and the mud but the volume of rainwater made this impractical. The brush matted down into the mud and soon we were thoroughly wet as the water cascaded down the sides of the hole. Sleep was difficult but not impossible for very tired bodies. I remember dozing off and waking up several times to the wounded enemy's cries. I thought I had dreamed it but the others verified hearing him. There was evidence of a body being dragged off into the jungle a few feet from our foxholes.

When the rain stopped and the early morning sun came up, the Japanese had faded back into the jungle. We emerged from our foxholes, wrung out our clothes, cleaned our rifles and prepared for another day of war. It was our turn to pursue the enemy in their hiding places until late in the afternoon. Hopefully, we would advance, push them back and gain more territory before we dug in for the night. It was the first day of summer although we didn't note it at the time. It was always summer in the Philippine Islands. The S-3 Periodic Report for the day states that it was "warm with scattered rain clouds, visibility fair." About the same as many of the other days had been since we started on this campaign.

I was wringing out my socks preparing to put on my wet combat boots when Platoon Sergeant Harvey Shaw came up and said, "McLogan, get a move on, you have to go on breakfast patrol." That meant that I had to go with about a dozen other soldiers through the jungle to the highway to pick up the food that the company cooks had prepared. They brought it by truck as close as they dared up the highway to the forward elements.

It must have been a mile or so to the highway, over steep hills, across small streams, around dense bamboo forests and through other vegetation. When we got to the highway we were pleasantly surprised to find that a Filipino carrying party was there. The Army had organized and was paying civilian volunteers to carry out the breakfast as well as fresh water and ammunition. They were the first I had seen since we had moved north. This meant that we would not have to do the hard work of carrying the provisions and could concentrate on looking out for the enemy who might attack the carrying party and turn our breakfast into their breakfast. Luckily, we didn't see any sign of them so the return to the forward position was uneventful.

We had eaten mostly C-rations so far in the campaign. But this breakfast consisted of toasted fried egg sandwiches, two for each man, and coffee. Fried eggs were a new item in our diet. For most of the war the only eggs that the G.I.s ate were powdered eggs, which, no matter how they were prepared, turned out to be a gooey, unappetizing, yellow substance. But technology, always spurred on by the military, had developed, late in the war, a way to package and keep the eggs fresh on the long journey to the tropical war zone. Fresh eggs were a welcome change from the powdered ones but our cooks hadn't mastered the art of cooking fresh eggs. I remember these particular eggs were rubbery from overcooking and the toast was somewhat burnt. Still, they were better than C-rations.

I was still eating mine when Sergeant Shaw said, "Let's go, McLogan, the captain says to get this show on the road!" We had been waiting for the 4.2 and 81mm mortars to finish their salvos before getting the signal to move forward.

Still chewing on the last of my fried egg sandwich, I got in position on the trail leading into Japanese territory. I was in the lead position first scout. Behind me was the second scout, another 19-year-old boy, then Sergeant Shaw, who was acting as squad leader since we were short of leaders. After him came Paul, the 19-year-old B.A.R.-

man and the rest of the platoon. We had done this so many times that it was beginning to seem routine.

It was about 9:00 in the morning when I was given the command to move out. I started down the trail very slowly and quietly. The path was framed by trees that were tall and leafy, not tropical but rather like a Michigan forest with many bushes growing on both sides of the narrow path. It was silent except for some soldiers moving through the woods, downhill and to my left. The captain was apparently sending two columns out. I remember being annoyed that the other column didn't proceed with a little less noise. Stealth was important. The idea was to get the enemy before he got you. It didn't help to let him know you were coming.

I must have gone only about fifty yards down the trail when, moving slowly around a bend in the path, I came upon a Japanese machine gun. It was pointed in my direction and was less than ten feet in front of me. The Japanese soldier manning the gun apparently hadn't seen or heard me coming or he certainly would have shot me as soon as I came into view. I think he had been dozing off. He looked up in surprise just as I spotted him and fired my Ml rifle from the hip. This was an instance where that tommy-gun would have been advantageous. I missed him with my single shot. Not daring to try for another, I turned quickly around to my left and bumped into the second scout. We both went down.

43. JAPANESE HEAVY MACHINE GUN, shown here being used by Filipino guerrillas, is like the one that wounded me. Known as a Type 92 (1932) HV MG, it fired 7.7 mm (.303 caliber) rounds at 450 rounds per minute. U.S. Army photo.

The Japanese machine gunner was wide awake now and spraying the area with deadly bursts of bullets. The second scout and I were pinned down on one side of the trail which ran along the crest of a hill, a "hogback" as some of the soldiers called it. Harvey Shaw and the rest of the platoon were on the other side of the ridge and further to the rear.

"What have we got?" Sergeant Shaw asked across the hill.

"Machine gun, a heavy," I replied. He took this news with a look of despair. He always looked like he carried the weight of the world on his shoulders.

"How many Japs?"

"I only saw one but there are probably lots more."

After a consultation, he called over to us: "Come back to where we are. We are going to hit them with some mortars."

The second scout went first, running diagonally over the crest of the hill and down the trail to the other side and to the rear. He made it safely. Sergeant Shaw made a motion for me to come. I had wrenched my leg in my sudden turn and jump for cover. It still hurt so I must have been a little slow when I made my dash to the rear. Just as I went over the crest of the hill, I felt something hot pass through my lower right leg. I hit the ground on the other side of the trail and rolled to where Shaw and the others were.

This is crazy, I thought, feeling surprise more than anything else. I had always expected that other soldiers would get shot but certainly not me! My right pant leg was turning red from the gushing blood as Shaw and Corporal Melvin "Doc" Horne, the medic assigned to our platoon, pulled me down the hill to a safer spot. Horne quickly cut my pant leg off, applied a tourniquet and bound up the wound. He was about to give me blood plasma when Captain Fleming came up.

"Move him back further," he ordered, "so our mortars will have more room." Then, turning to me, he said, "You're lucky, soldier, getting hit in the leg like that. You have a million dollar wound!"

A million dollar wound was an injury that was serious enough to get you on a boat headed for home but wasn't so bad that you were crippled for life. It was a common topic of conversation among front-line troops. Nobody wanted to get wounded but if they did, they wanted it to be just bad enough to get sent home. Stories were also told about soldiers shooting themselves, usually in the foot or arm, in order to get out of combat. Or laying in their foxholes with their leg up in the air, hoping that the enemy would do it for them. It happened elsewhere in the war but I never saw any of my fellow soldiers deliberately hurting themselves. They only talked about it.

Self-inflicted wounds were prevalent in the European Theater, where it was a serious problem in France during the summer of 1944, but also tended to appear wherever a major offensive was planned. Of approximately 300 cases investigated at the 4th Convalescent Hospital, only 15 were sent on to court-martials. The general attitude was that the men should be given the opportunity to return to combat and vindicate themselves.[3]

In the Philippines, there were a number of self-inflicted wounds in the 32nd Division. By the time the men of the Red Arrow reached Santa Fe, after battling the Japanese defenders for two long, arduous months, many soldiers were suffering from combat fatigue and battle neuroses. Morale plummeted. A number of frontline veterans, hoping to be rotated back to the U.S. under the newly announced point system, deliberately wounded themselves.[4]

My leg was beginning to throb with pain. The bullet had entered the calf of my right leg about eight inches below the back of the knee, passed between the fibula and the tibia and exited out the front of the leg tearing out a rather large hole. Doc gave me a shot of morphine as well as whole blood. The record also shows a "Sulfa Crystal Dressing & Sulfa Tab. 8,"[5] although I don't remember it.

When he was finished with his medical ministrations, six Filipinos from the breakfast carrying party were assigned to haul me out of the jungle on a litter.

"Just a minute," said Horne, as we prepared to leave. He tied a tag, that he had been writing on, to my big toe. "If you lose this, tell the medical officer that you have had a pint of plasma, a pint of whole blood, and a shot of morphine." He repeated it to make sure that I understood.

The six Filipinos picked up the stretcher and we took off through the jungle along the same trail that we had traversed to get our breakfast. It was tough going for the little Filipinos. Their impassive faces glistened with beads of sweat as they struggled to keep the litter level as we traveled up and down steep hills, or forded streams and pushed through dense vegetation. At times the two at one end of the stretcher would have their end high over their heads while the two at the other end would be holding their end below their knees. The two in the middle would be scrambling somewhere in between.

They wore the common Filipino dress: straw or felt hats, cotton short-sleeve shirts, boxer shorts. They were barefoot. My carriers spoke little, only an occasional grunt or a comment in Tagalog that I didn't understand. They seemed to know what they were doing and

44. FILIPINO CIVILIAN CARRYING PARTY. Although short in stature, the men were strong and a great help carrying heavy ammunition and supplies to the forward elements. They also helped evacuate the wounded. From: The *6th Infantry Division in World War II: 1939–1945*, (Nashville: The Battery Press, 1947), p. 136.

had probably done it many times. I still marvel that they would do such hard and dangerous work. I don't think they were paid much.

We were accompanied by three soldiers, one leading the way and two bringing up the rear. I suddenly felt apprehensive that we would run into some Japanese and my litter bearers would drop me and run away. I felt vulnerable because I had no rifle to defend myself. Sergeant Shaw had told me to leave it where Doc had treated me, saying that I would not be needing it anymore. That rifle had been my powerful, constant companion for over two months. I had known her innermost parts and how she functioned. I had kept her clean and well oiled so she wouldn't fail me when I needed her. My very life had depended on her. Now we were separated and I felt the need and the loss.

The apprehension didn't last long as the morphine took effect and I soon felt giddy. *This isn't so bad*, I thought, *I am on the first leg of a long journey home. No more war for me. Maybe I will be back at school for the fall semester.*

We eventually reached Highway 4 where we found an ambulance waiting for us. The 6th Medical Battalion, Clearing Company C, was providing this service. It was dangerous work. Ambulances had to travel with armed escort because of Japanese infiltrations along the narrow, heavily wooded road and their disregard for some of the civilized conventions of war. The red cross on a field of white, painted on the side of the ambulance, made a nice target to zero in on. If a few non-combatants were shot in the process, that would help the Japanese cause by making it more costly for the Americans to continue the war.

According to the 6th Medical Battalion's unit history, on June 22 (the next day), the Japanese attacked a C-Company ambulance as it was bringing wounded back from the forward elements. The ambulance sustained six machine gun bullet holes in its doors, spare tire and body but only the assistant driver, Private First Class Wilbur L. Rardin, was slightly wounded.[6] After that the Americans started bringing back the wounded in 6th Cavalry Reconnaissance half-tracks until they got past the ambush points. They were then transferred to ambulances for the rest of the journey. On July 11, another ambulance was shot up and a driver wounded.

Fortunately for me, my ambulance wasn't shot up. I thanked my unknown Filipino carriers and said good-bye to the soldiers from my company who had guarded our way through the jungle as they slid me into the back of the ambulance. A medical corpsman rode in the back with me. As we drove down the highway, he examined my bandaged leg and read the tag attached to my toe.

"That's not so bad," he commented, "we see a *lot worse* every day." I don't know if he was unimpressed with my wound or if he was trying to make me feel better. It seemed serious to me.

It was a rough ride but we eventually arrived at the 6th Medical Battalion Clearing Station Hospital, otherwise known as a Battalion Aid Station. It was a portable hospital consisting of a few tents set up in a meadow along the side of the road.[7]

The function of a portable hospital in World War II was similar to what you saw in the TV program *M*A*S*H*.[8] That was to provide the wounded with their first real medical treatment after the first aid they get in the field. The hospital was located as close to the front as possible and sometimes was shelled or attacked by the enemy. Unlike *M*A*S*H* though, the wounded arrived by ambulance or truck since medical helicopters were still in the experimental stage at that time.

I was carried in and set on the operating table. An orderly then cut off all my clothes with a scissors and I was soon stripped to my undershorts. He emptied my pockets and put my personal things in an envelope and set it on the table. An officer came in. He had captain's bars on one collar and a cross on the other. He examined my dog tags. "I am Captain Luther Swygert, the Protestant chaplain," he said. "I see by your dog tags that you are Catholic. While I am not of your denomination, I am available for any spiritual help that you might need."

"Where's the Catholic Chaplain?" I asked.

"Captain Dietz is off to Solano on business today."

"Well, I guess I will be okay without him."

He looked disappointed as he left. I really didn't feel the need for spiritual help. Anyway, I had been raised in a strict Catholic family and didn't want any heretical Protestant prayers said over me. Ecumenism is something I learned about much later in life.

A doctor came in and examined my leg. He said that he was going to put me under anesthesia in order to work on the wound. An orderly injected a solution into my left arm and told me to count to ten. "Slower," he directed as I reached seven. "Eight," I continued, ". . . nine. . . ."

21–22 June . . . The lst Bn continued guarding the supply route to the forward elements. At the close of the period, Company A was moving to the vicinity of the PAYAWAN REST HOUSE. *Friendly planes, strafing in front of our troops, caused some eight casualties among our men.* As the convoy carrying the wounded men started to leave Battalion CP, the Japs attacked the CP. At the same time, positions of Company C and of the guerrilla forces were hit. Two reinforced platoons of Company I aided in repulsing the attack.[9]

The next thing that I remember, it was dark and I was lying on a stretcher on the floor of what turned out to be the 91st Field Hospital. It was located in Bayombang about 20 miles from where I had been wounded. There were many wounded people lying all around me in the corridor. There seemed to be a lot of confusion and muffled voices as ambulances kept pulling up to the open doorway. The medics were bringing in more casualties and doing their triage. This is a system of assigning priorities for medical treatment to battlefield casualties based on urgency, nature of the wounds, chances for survival, etc.

I lay there a long time listening to the moaning. My leg hurt. Finally, two orderlies came and picked me up and carried me into a classroom that had been converted into a hospital ward. I was put into bed and given another shot of morphine. . . .

The next morning, when I awoke, I recognized the soldier in the next bed. One of the newer replacements in my platoon, he had one arm completely encased in a huge plaster cast.

"What happened to you?" I asked.

"Got hit by a .50 caliber machine gun bullet from an American airplane," he replied. "You were lucky. After you were carried off, we ran into some pretty stiff resistance. A squadron of P-47s came in to strafe the Jap positions. The dumb bastards started their strafing runs too soon and shot us up instead of the Japs!"

"That must have been scary!"

His eyes were bright and his child-like face brimmed with excitement as he continued. "It was really weird. First the leaves and branches started falling off the trees, then bullets were hitting all around us. Then we could hear the racket of the machine guns and the roar of the plane's engines! My arm went numb and when I looked, it was mangled and bleeding."

"Man! That's tough, but better that than being killed. How many others got hit?"

"A bunch. Probably ten or more Americans. Lots of Filipinos too. A carrying party had just arrived and they were hit bad. There was blood and guts all over the hill!"

That would explain the commotion in the corridor the previous night. I thought that I had heard moaning in Tagalog. I wondered if the stalwart Filipino civilians who had carried me out of the jungle to safety had been killed or wounded. There is no way of knowing. The operations reports I examined only list American military casualties.

My cohort also told me about how the airplanes had returned for another run at the target and one of the K-Company men had waved a marker in a futile attempt to get their attention but had been cut down as they again started shooting too soon.

Casualties from friendly fire were more common than generally reported. Artillery rounds that landed short among friendly troops were perhaps the most common mistake of this type, but attacks on Americans by American aircraft in Europe were so frequent that the G.I.s dubbed the U.S. Ninth Air Force "the American Luftwaffe." The most spectacular disaster occurred in a massive air strike against German positions in the Saint-Lo area on July 24–25, 1944. American bombing errors resulted in over 800 American casualties of which 131 were killed. Among the dead was Army Ground Forces Commander

Lieutenant General Leslie J. McNair who had come over from Washington to get a first hand view of combat.[10]

In the Philippines, Sixth Army records show many instances of bombing and strafing of friendly troops by the Air Corps, although they are rarely mentioned in Air Corps histories. Most incidences are attributable to pilot errors in target identification. In February, after our sister regiment, the lst Infantry was strafed at San Jose by Fifth Air Force B-25s (one killed, seven wounded), General Kreuger sent Lieutenant General George C. Kenney, Commander of the Allied Air Forces a blistering message: "I must insist that you stop the bombing and strafing of our ground forces . . . These repeated occurrences are causing . . . a loss of confidence in air support and are adversely affecting morale." He had previously informed General Kenney that the situation had developed when the Fifth Air Force had taken over air support responsibility from Allied Naval Forces' CVE-based planes. Air-ground liaison and control systems improved as the campaign progressed but there were occasional lapses as per the K-Company incident in June.[11]

Lieutenant Tom Atchley, in a letter to me,[12] writes that he remembers the strafing incident

> . . . as if it were yesterday . . . All of a sudden here came three fighter planes, they made a circle around us tilting their wings, I suppose, so they could tell where we were. Anyway, I told Captain Fleming that they were going to strafe or bomb us . . . maybe both. He said: "No, I don't think so." I said: "Wait and see." . . .
>
> "They made another big circle, turned and came one behind the other, the lead plane nose down. They made three runs over us, shooting fifty-caliber machine guns . . . about 12 or 18 of our men got wounded. Several bullets hit the edge of my foxhole, if I had been standing, I would have been hit. I can't recall all who got hurt, but I do remember a fellow by the name of Fuller,[13] out of the weapons platoon who got his leg cut off . . . by the fifty caliber bullets. He was pretty close to where I was, so I went to him first . . . in a few minutes the first aid people were there with stretchers. He got on the stretcher by his own power, reached over . . . picked up his leg . . . laid it beside him, looked up at me and said, "This is it for me!" He didn't shed a tear or complain in any way."

Many years later, when this incident was brought up at a reunion of the 6th Infantry Division, some of the survivors of Company K thought that the airplanes were from the Navy.[14] They weren't, because the Fifth Air Force had taken over ground support operations

45. P-47 THUNDERBOLT from the 201st Mexican Fighter Squadron. Note the American markings on the fuselage and Mexican markings on the rudder. It is like the airplanes that strafed K-Company on June 21, 1945. Photo courtesy of James P. Gallagher.

soon after the landings and most of the Navy airplanes had moved on to the Okinawa invasion of April 1st.

However, right from the start, at the hospital in Bayombang, I heard rumors that the pilots of the airplanes were Mexican and that there was a language problem that caused the mishap. In researching this I found only circumstantial evidence that the pilots could have been Mexican. There was a 201st Mexican Fighter Squadron which arrived in Manila during May of 1945.

> "They saw action in the Philippines where the Mexican airmen in U.S. Thunderbolts (P-47s) bombed and strafed enemy troops. The squadron was received back in Mexico after the defeat of Japan as conquering heroes with celebrations in the National Stadium at Mexico City and decorations of service in the Far East."[15]

To integrate them into the war effort, they were assigned to the American 58th Fighter Group as a fourth squadron at Clark Field. In *The Story of the 58th Fighter Group*, Anthony Kupferer relates various pilot's remembrances of the Mexicans. There was resentment because the foreigners were given the best equipment and there were fears that the language barrier would spell trouble.[16] Several of the Mexican pilots were killed getting indoctrinated to the P-47. On June 4 they began going on the 58th's missions.[17]

On June 16 the 58th was ordered to move to Okinawa. All the squadrons, except the 201st Mexican, became inoperational as they packed up to leave. The missions of the 201st continued through June 25 under control of the 58th, and then they started flying on their own. William G. Tudor of Dallas Texas, wrote a doctoral thesis on the 201st Mexican Fighter Squadron. He sent me some of the Operations Reports for the day in question. They show the pilots flying missions far from Bolog. However, there were a number of their mission reports missing and he doubts that records exist anywhere else.

Tudor says some of the 201st's missions weren't recorded because they were "special missions," even citing one where a Mexican pilot was shot down and killed without any 58th Group record of this operation or some of the others.[18] He doubts that the Mexicans were involved in this mishap and also believes that the markings on their planes would have clearly distinguished them from the American P-47s.

However, my experience is that the infantryman's grapevine was usually accurate. In the same letter, Lieutenant Atchley writes, "Those three planes were flown by Mexican pilots. They were just supposed to be on a recon patrol. They weren't supposed to do any shooting or bombing. We didn't have any way of contacting them."[19]

Third Battalion Commander Arndt Mueller verified the lack of communication but couldn't confirm that the planes were flown by Mexican pilots. He also remembers the incident vividly, as that was the day he not only survived the blowing up of a bridge he was crossing, but it was also the day he thought he was going to lose his whole battalion. Besides the Air Corps helping the Japanese, he was also faced with an attack on his Command Post. He describes the events in a letter that he had written and a diagram made sometime earlier.[20]

Dear J. H.:

Glad to hear that life is a little better for you. I have enclosed a diagram of a battle during which one mortar of your old platoon saved the 3rd Battalion . . . When L Co. reached the bend in the road at Red 2, all hell broke loose. Jap suicide squads with dynamite charges on the end of long poles blew up the two 6th Recon. armored cars. Some L Co. heroes rescued the cavalrymen in those cars. I think they were all wounded or dead. One hero, Charlie Tis-

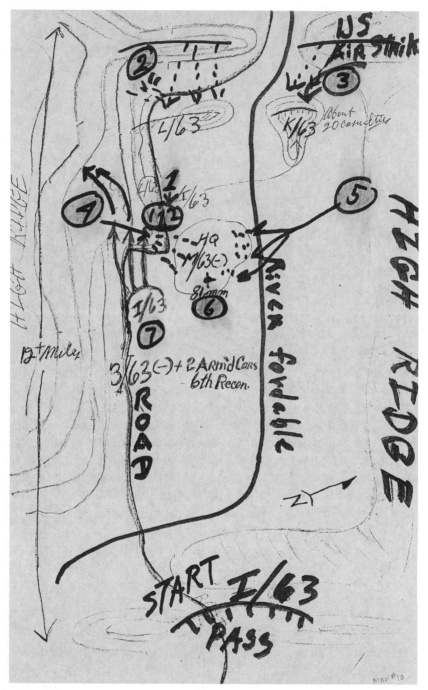

10. ATTACK ON THE 3RD BATTALION C.P. and the strafing of Company "K" is shown in this sketch by Colonel Arndt Mueller, battalion commander at that time.

222

dale, was carrying a cavalryman slung over his shoulder when a Jap officer popped up to try to cut Charlie down with his saber. Of course, some alert L Co. riflemen sent him to glory for his emperor.

We were now receiving heavy fire from the Jap positions on the high ridge above the road. So L Co. took up defensive positions; K Co. was digging in on the hill that they had just taken. About this time, late in the afternoon, two U.S. fighter planes began circling overhead. They were on armed reconnaissance and we had no communications with them. And the rules of engagement said that no aircraft was to strike short of the bomb line unless the ground forces called for it.

[The pilots] took a good look at L Co. and the burning and smoking armored cars. I got a funny feeling that something was going to go wrong. So I called Fleming of K Co. and told him that I had no commo with the fighters and that I was afraid that they had decided that we were the friendlies and that K Co. were the enemy. I suggested that he shoot flares, take off shirts to wave at the planes in hopes that they would recognize them as U.S.

But those two (pilots) had their minds made up. They dove down on poor K Co. It was an awful sight. Each fighter had six or eight machine guns in the wings. K Co. suffered about 20 casualties as far as I can recall. This all happened at Red 3. (See diagram)

Obviously there are some discrepancies here in the number of airplanes, who was flying them, Mexican or otherwise, and how many casualties they inflicted. But then, this is typical of the confusion that surrounds the events of a war as reported by various participants. This incident is not mentioned in the official history of the 6th Division,[21] although it is briefly mentioned in the unit history of the 63rd Infantry Regiment, as I have quoted, and in the daily operations reports. The most accurate count of K-Company's casualties, from the records that I have examined is one killed, seven wounded and four injured.[22] I could not find records on the number of Filipino civilians killed or wounded.

To get some idea of how they operated their ground support missions, I talked to P-38 pilots of the 49th Fighter Group at their reunion in Dayton, Ohio in August, 1993. They had done a lot of enemy strafing in the Philippines. As to the number of planes, they said they normally sent out a minimum of four. Two planes were considered an element and two elements made up a flight. It would be unlikely that the number sent out was two or three because a formation of four afforded them mutual protection from enemy aircraft. They could look after each other as they flew their missions.

The pilots were briefed on the mission before they took off by intelligence officers who had aerial photographs and maps of the target area. They also had radio contact with an Air Corps observer who was with the ground troops and could direct their efforts on the scene. Sometimes the pilots themselves would volunteer to do this, either on the ground with the infantry, or in Piper Cub observation planes which flew slowly and gave them added visibility by flying at altitudes of a thousand feet or more. They were also aided in locating their targets by flares and colored smoke set out by the ground forces.

Since their dive speed, when they were strafing, was in the neighborhood of 350 miles per hour, things happened pretty fast and, depending upon the height they were shooting from, even slight errors in the angle of attack were multiplied in the area of the ground being sprayed with bullets. They also told me that they couldn't rely on their tracers for accuracy since the total bullet pattern from their multiple guns was too widely dispersed. Some said they had heard rumors that they had hit Americans but thought that these instances were rare and that no one had actually been killed.

The main speaker at their reunion banquet was a retired Air Force major-general, also a veteran of the Philippine Campaign. When I broached the subject to him, he said that incidents like that happened because ". . . all you infantrymen were color-blind and always set out the wrong color flares . . . If you hadn't been color-blind, you would have been in the Air Force." He said this jokingly but in my case it hit home. While I never had the job of setting out flares or colored smoke, if I hadn't had defective color perception, I would definitely have been somewhere else.

While all the strafing was going on, I was en route to the rear area or at the aid station. However, that was not the end of the excitement for that day, as Colonel Mueller continues in his letter:

Then, as if planned, the Japs began firing on both K & L Companies. And at the same time, Japs on the high ground above the double bend at Red 4 and the Japs in the bamboo thickets at Red 5, began intense fire on the Battalion Headquarters and M Co.(-) which was one machine gun platoon and the mortar platoon. A double envelopment!!! Great, just great!!

With only two rifle companies, no artillery support, and out of communications with I Co. which, as far as I knew was still at the pass miles behind us and out of reach. I ran back to join the Hq.- M group and found that everybody, machine guns, mortars and all were pinned down by the Jap fire from above us on the left at Red 4 and advancing Japs coming through the bamboo from Red 5. It looked like this was curtains for us. There was no way that either L or K could help us because they had their hands full.

Then a remarkable event occurred. One 81 mortar at Red Six, manned by three or four soldiers, began to lob mortar shells, with no increments, and no sights -just holding the mortar almost straight up. Those shells slowly climbed almost straight up, lazily flipped over and came straight down. I recall Finnerty,[23] who was Battalion S3, yelling, "My God!! They are going to hit us."

But they landed on the Japs in the bamboo thickets on the right. This quieted them down so that the machine gunners could get their heads up and start rapid fire on the Japs. Next . . . I Co. commander (Tarpey,[24] if I remember correctly) came in on the radio net!! He said that they had been released from duty at the pass; that they were hearing heavy fire up ahead and wanted to know if we were in trouble. He said it sounded as though they were a mile or less from the firing. I told him that we were indeed in deep trouble, that I Co. was to come up the road on the double to attack the high ground at the first bend he saw which is where the Japs were who were shooting at us. Tarpey made it in record time from Red 7 to Red 4. I Co. hit the Japs and caught them looking only our way. The next thing we knew, I Co. was up on the high ground at Red 4, whooping and hollering and chasing the Japs who were scrambling for their lives.

Now we got out K Co. and other casualties. I sent Bob Wells back with the few trucks we had, loaded with casualties, machine gunners riding shotgun. They got back to the medics OK and Wells loaded up with ammo and came back. We were almost out of ammo. Some riflemen only had one clip left. I don't remember when Wells got back. It was probably in the morning. During the night we got shelled by the Japs and, of course, it rained. So, we were thoroughly miserable, but alive thanks to those mortarmen of M Co. who fired that mortar almost straight up.

Aren't you proud of them? You bet!!!

Keep the faith,

Arndt L. Mueller

The reason that the Japanese had gotten so close to the Battalion CP was that we were being helped by Filipino guerrilla units, the 2nd Provisional Battalion of the Pangasinan Regiment and an outfit called the Mapandan Company which was attached to the 3rd Battalion. Their main duties were to guard bridges in the rear area and help keep open the supply lines to the forward elements. They were lightly armed and suffering from malaria.[25] According to the S-3 Operations

Report, the Japanese attack on the 3rd Battalion Command Post was coordinated with an attack on the guerrilla positions guarding the highway. The friendly guerrillas sustained 7 killed and 17 wounded as the enemy overran them on the hill overlooking the battalion CP. The medics really had their hands full that night.

At the end of the period, the battered 3rd Battalion was making preparations to revert to regimental reserve. The lst Battalion would take the lead. After a rest and an infusion of new replacements, the men of K-Company and the rest of the 3rd Battalion would soon be back in the fray. It would go on like that for another seven long and bloody weeks—until the war ended in August. They had to do it without my help.

At the 91st Field Hospital the next morning, life was more normal for me. This hospital unit had been activated at Camp Ellis, Illinois, on October 30, 1944 and had landed in Manila about the same time that I did, April 8, 1945. After some duty at Fort Stotsenberg, they moved to Bayombang on June 11 to support the 6th Division's combat activities. Their first quarterly report says that they were set up in four buildings of frame construction, one of which was a provincial hospital where most of the patients were lodged although some had to be kept in tents. They found the buildings to be in poor condition and suffering from battle damage but within 24 hours of arrival they had to set up and take care of severe battle casualties at the rate of 50 or 60 a day. Most arrived within three hours after injury. In the first 19 days the surgical unit handled 740 admissions, one of which was me.[26]

They seemed pretty well organized on June 22. After breakfast, which I devoured ravenously because I hadn't eaten anything since the previous morning when we had the egg sandwiches, a young Filipino girl came to my bed and asked me, rather shyly, if I wanted a bath and a shampoo.

"That sounds great," I said. I hadn't had a bath in about two weeks and must have reeked. She did a good job of cleaning me up, taking care not to disturb my bandaged leg. However, when she started tugging on my undershorts, which were the only thing I had on, I said that I would take over and finished the job under the sheets. She then took away my shorts and gave me some pajamas to wear. One leg had been cut short to accommodate my wounded leg.

In the afternoon, a nurse came by and said that I was being evacuated by air. They needed to make room for more casualties and I was considered fit enough to make the trip. That was fine with me. Soon I was being carried out the door on a litter and put in an ambulance with three other wounded soldiers. The medics who were doing the carrying and loading were from the 604th Medical Clearing Company. They bitched about the heat and argued over who was doing the most work. I'd have traded jobs with them any day; being a rifleman was no fun either.

It was a 12 mile trip to the airstrip at Bagabag where there were several C-47s waiting. This was the military version of the Douglas DC-3 commercial airliner. The airplanes were painted a camouflage green and brown and were emblazoned with lettering declaring them to be "Jungle Skippers". I later identified them to be planes from the 317th Troop Carrier Group. Instead of seats, like the commercial version, these airplanes were fitted with straps and metal hardware to hold the stretchers, four high on each side of the aisle, 24 in all. The equipment could be folded away and the airplane used to carry cargo or paratroopers. That way the plane had dual usage: it could carry men or supplies into a battle zone and then be changed over to evacuate casualties for the trip back to home base. Because they carried war material at least part of the time, they could not be painted white with large Red Cross insignia as hospital ships were. This was in accordance with the Geneva Convention.[27] It also meant we were more likely to be shot at.

Two litter bearers hoisted me up into the airplane and two more strapped me into place along the wall of the fuselage. I was in the second tier from the bottom. Below me was a soldier who was heavily sedated and strapped to his stretcher so that he couldn't move. He mumbled incoherently and drooled at the mouth. Minds were shattered in this war as well as bodies. One difference was that a shattered mind didn't earn a Purple Heart Medal.

The plane crew included a flight nurse. The mass evacuation of the wounded by air was an innovation of World War II and created the need for this type of nurse. The first class of flight nurses graduated from Bowman Field, Kentucky in 1943[28] so the program was still fairly new. Our nurse was an "older" woman of about 30 years, blonde and in well-filled suntans. She went around and checked each patient as they were brought aboard and strapped in. When they were all aboard she asked: "Is anyone here from Detroit?"

"I am," I answered, apparently the only one from the Motor City.

"Good, I'll be around to talk to you later."

After we were airborne she came up to me and told me about herself. Every once in awhile she would reach down and wipe the saliva off the psychoneurotic soldier's chin without a break in the conversation. He got quite loud at times, but she ignored his mutterings.

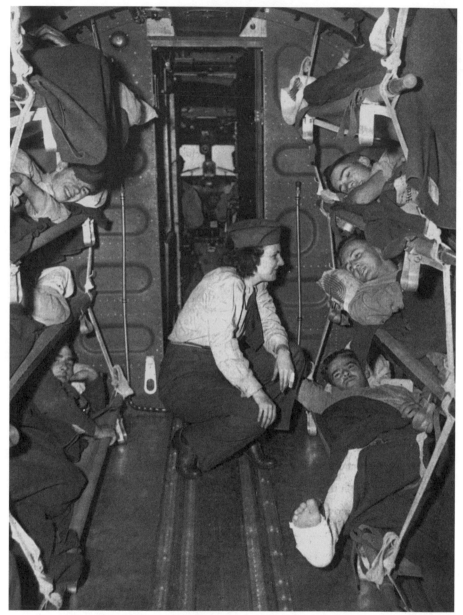

46. ARMY NURSE AND WOUNDED SOLDIERS. I had three rides on C-47's as shown in this picture. From Catherine Bell Palmer, "Flying Our Wounded Veterans Home," *The National Geographic Magazine*, Sept. 1945: p. 378. Used with permission of Corbis-Bettmann, L.L.C.

The nurse told me that she had grown up on the east side of Detroit and had taken her nurse's training at Harper Hospital. When the war came along she enlisted in the Army Nurse Corps and had taken the flight nurse training so that she could get overseas and see some of the world. She had seen plenty of the South Pacific and was now anxious to get back to Detroit. She talked about various bars that she and her nurse friends habituated in the Detroit area. "Had I been to such and such bar?" She apparently had been to plenty.

I had a hard time keeping up my end of the conversation because my social life, previous to being drafted, consisted of high school dances after basketball games in the St. Benedict gym, or Saturday night record hops at the Y.W.C.A. in Highland Park. I was not familiar with many bars.

In fact, the only instances when I had spent much time in a bar had been when I was a small boy and my father occasionally took me with him. He would order a shot of whiskey and a beer for himself and I would have a Vernor's ginger ale. He would reorder several times. I remembered bars as smelling of stale beer and tobacco smoke, of dull adult conversation and of us sitting for interminable hours listening to Detroit Tiger baseball games. To top it off, Dad usually got bawled out when we got home and I somehow shared in his guilt.

The flight nurse, however, was quite enthusiastic about bars and longed for the day when she could get back to the Detroit bar scene. She finally realized that we didn't have much in common except our birth place and moved down the aisle to talk to an older soldier for the rest of the flight. The soldier below me was now sleeping peacefully, his troubled mind temporarily at rest. He reminded me of Combat Smith, but it wasn't him.

I was wide awake. This was my very first airplane ride. We were way up in the clouds. The wind and the vibration made it exciting. I found out that if I stretched my head the right way, I could see out one of the little round windows on the side of the fuselage. The emerald green mountains of Northern Luzon passed slowly under the wing. They looked so cool, pretty and peaceful from 9,000 feet. I knew better. They were hot and humid and wretched people were killing each other down there. I was glad to say goodbye to all that. I was going home.

At least I thought I was . . . .

TEN

Life in Army Hospitals

*If you survive something traumatic, you are never the
same again. If you survive two traumatic things, you
take a quantum leap in your spiritual self.*
            —Phoebe Snow[1]

"Rosales" is what the Detroit nurse had answered when I
asked her where the airplane from Bagabag was taking
us. Soon we were in a descent over another airstrip similar to the one we had taken off from in Bagabag. Rosales lies on a flat
agricultural plain along the Agno River and was of strategic importance because of a bridge across the river to Villasis along Route 3.
Twenty-two miles to the west is Lingayan Gulf where MacArthur and
a cast of thousands, including the 6th Infantry Division, had returned
in January. Before the towns could be taken, strong Japanese defenses in the Cabaruan Hills had to be overcome. These were a series
of 200 foot hills lying west of the Rosales-Villasis area.

Our sister regiments, the 1st and 20th Regiments, were involved
in fierce fighting in these hills where 1,400 well-dug-in Japanese were
killed before the towns were taken with almost no resistance. However, 80 Sightseers were killed and almost 200 wounded getting
there.[2]

I was taken by ambulance to the 7th Evacuation Hospital which
was set up in an Industrial Arts School in Villasis. The classrooms
were surrounded with a covered walkway and there was no glass in
the windows making it a very open construction. When the wind blew
in the right direction, it helped to cool the rooms bringing a measure
of relief from the humid heat. The classroom that I was put in had
about a dozen hospital beds—the white tubular frame kind. I luxuri-

ated in the clean white sheets and the soft mattress. It was so much better than sleeping in a muddy foxhole, or on an Army cot, as I had been doing for so long.

The 7th Evacuation Hospital had been organized during July 1940 by the New York Post Graduate Hospital, and activated on January 22, 1942 at Fort Dix, New Jersey. They moved overseas on April 7 that year. Their unit history doesn't detail what they did or where they were located the rest of 1942 or 1943 but the annual report for 1944 showed them operating as a 750 bed hospital in the Fiji Islands for the first month of the year.[3]

They moved to Guadalcanal on March 4 where they staged for the "Forearm Operation (Kavieng)". When this operation was cancelled they remained on staging status until October 30. The colonel writing the reports tell about how, for the entire period ". . . 150 men from our detachment worked on cargo docks for Service Command, a most unsatisfactory way of employing highly trained hospital men." Medical Officers (doctors) were used to supervise the work. As a result, morale plunged and people started putting in for rotation back to the United States. They had been overseas since the early part of the war and were eligible. At the end of the year, however, they were assigned to the M1 Operation, the invasion of Luzon, and all rotation orders cancelled.

Happy to be doing what they were supposed to be doing after 33 months, the first echelon landed at Lingayan on January 10, 1945 and set up a 300 bed hospital which was soon taking care of casualties from the XIV Corps. They closed this hospital on February 6 and moved to Villasis. There they set up a 1000 bed hospital which was still operating when I arrived in June.[4]

In the morning, a doctor, a nurse, and a male medical technician made the rounds, examining and treating each patient in turn. When they came to my bed, the medic unwrapped the bandage on my leg. Taking a forceps from the nurse, the doctor pulled a two-foot-long piece of bloody gauze out of the hole in the front of my leg. The pain soared immediately to a high intensity. I had to grip the sides of the bed tightly to keep from leaping out.

"What did that to you, soldier?" the doctor asked matter-of-factly.

"Jap machine gun," I barely managed to answer.

"You sure you didn't get in front of one of ours?" he continued as he twisted my leg to look at the small hole on the back side. This caused new spasms of pain. "It looks big for a Jap MG."

"I saw it. It was a heavy, not a woodpecker," I groaned.

He muttered something to the nurse that I didn't catch. She bent down, put her nose to the wound and sniffed tentatively.

"It's okay," she pronounced. They then proceeded, in reverse order, to pack the wound with a medicated gauze strip—instant rise in pain again—and to rebandage the leg. The doctor wrote out some orders and the group passed on to the next bed. Later on when the nurse was back I asked her what the sniffing of the wound was all about. She replied that it was a good way to check for gangrene, that my wound was clean. Then she added, rather unexpectedly: "That son of a bitch is always telling me that he has a cold. He's the doctor. He should be doing the sniffing!"

In his book, *WWII: A Chronicle of Soldiering*, James Jones, a veteran of the Pacific War, writes that our psychic memory is constantly at work winnowing out the bad and the unpleasant from our remembered experience and leaving only the good and pleasant parts. Thus, old soldiers can recall with affection moments of terror from 30 years previous, and tell others that it really wasn't so bad. Because of this, the hardest thing for us to do is recreate events as they really were. This is especially true of pain. He writes, "Physiologically we are so constructed that it is impossible for us to remember pain. We can remember the experience of having had pain but we cannot recall the pain itself."[5]

Maybe so, but for me the remembered experience is uncomfortable. When I think about the dentist's drill long enough, my tooth begins to feel achy. If I remember the time I had bursitis in my arm and the sadistic physical therapist was twisting it to loosen the adhesions, the sub-deltoid bursa begins to phantomly ache. And certainly, when I recall those moments in the hospital at Villasis I remember excruciating pain. My leg remembers the shattered muscles, the severed nerve endings, the missing flesh, the violation of wholeness done by the speeding bullet. It signals its psychic memory and it pains me to think about it. Part of the sharpness of the pain was because they had discontinued the morphine injections saying that I shouldn't become dependent on them.

I didn't stay long at the 7th Evacuation Hospital. While their second quarter report says that they were geared to keep patients for treatment up to 60 or 90 days, depending on the tactical situation, I was on my way again on June 26. Soon I was being carried out on a stretcher and put in one of those boxy Army ambulances for a ride out to the airport. This time my destination was the island of Leyte.

On board the C-47 was a group of paratroopers from the 511th Airborne Infantry Regiment of the 11th Airborne Division. It had been big news the previous few days about an air assault on Aparri, a town in the northernmost part of Luzon. These troopers had been casualties in the operation.

After a short flight down the Central Valley we landed at Neilson Field, Manila. Here, for some reason, mechanical problems probably, we were unloaded and taken to a hospital at the airfield. Actually, it was a large quonset hut made into a hospital. All afternoon and evening we could hear the roar of airplane engines as aircraft of all sorts took off and landed. The commerce of war made this a busy airport.

Occupying beds on both sides of me were the paratroopers who regaled me with tales of their exploits. It must have been Army policy to put leg injuries together—both had broken legs. According to the paratroopers, the Aparri operation had been an unnecessary disaster. It was one of those Army operations that, once begun, aren't changed when common sense tells you that new conditions require it should be changed or rescinded.

According to the official Army history,[6] General Kreuger had considered it necessary to stage an airborne operation into the northern Cagayan Valley to clinch the success of the 37th Infantry Division's drive up the valley from the south. He hoped to trap a large group of Japanese fleeing up the valley towards Aparri. At the same time, the Connolly Task Force was driving on Aparri from the west along Highway 3 which followed the coastline. The Connolly Task Force was named after its commander, Major Robert V. Connolly of the 123rd Infantry Regiment, 33rd Division. It consisted of various units under I Corps command.[7]

Another group, the 2nd Battalion, 11th Infantry, USAFIL(NL), a Filipino guerrilla unit under the command of Colonel Russell W. Volkmann, would join them as they neared Aparri. Colonel Volkmann, a U.S. Army regular, had taken to the hills upon the fall of the Philippines in 1942 and had organized guerrilla operations against the Japanese. After the Americans returned, his forces were taken under the control of the Sixth Army and were known as USA FIP (NL), that is, United States Armed Forces in the Philippines, Northern Luzon. At the time of the Aparri operation, they totaled about 18,000 men.[8]

As things turned out, the combined force of Americans and Filipinos took Aparri on June 21, two days before the paratroopers were scheduled to begin their assault. Despite the success of the reinforced Connolly Task Force, Kreuger did not change his mind about the desirability and necessity for the air drop. Instead, he concluded that the "seizure of Aparri . . . indicated clearly that the time had come for mounting the airborne troops to block the enemy's retreat in the Cagayan Valley." It is not clear just what retreat Kreuger expected to block. Actually, the general trend of Japanese movement had been southward for weeks.

At any rate, an airborne force totaling about 1,030 men took off from Batangas in southern Luzon in 54 C-47s, 14 C-46s and 7 gliders. (This was the first use of gliders in the Southwest Pacific.) When the 'troopers landed on their drop zone, the Camalaniugan airstrip near Aparri, they were greeted on the ground by men of the Connolly Task Force and the Filipino llth Infantry who had filled shell holes and driven carabaos off the airstrip to ease their landing. They had wanted to erect signs saying "Welcome to Aparri—The llth Infantry" but Colonel Volkmann wouldn't let them.

Unfortunately, the wind was blowing between 20 to 25 miles per hour; 15 miles per hour is considered the maximum safe speed for an operation of this kind. As a result of these high winds, many paratroopers were blown away from the target airstrip into adjoining rice paddies. Jump casualties were 2 killed and 70 injured, a high rate of 7 percent.[9] And not a shot had been fired.

My hospital mates were among the jump casualties. They told me about landing in rice paddies and not being able to roll as they landed. A firm terrain was required to be able to do this when they hit the ground with full field equipment, including weapons and ammunition. Instead, when their feet struck the soft mud of the rice paddies, they stuck in place, and inertia caused the rest of their bodies to keep moving, snapping one or both legs.

According to their testimony, they had had a long ride in a C-47 from Batangas to Aparri, made their jump, broken their legs and were then put back on the same C-47s which had landed on the airstrip when it was found to be safe. I could find nothing to substantiate their coming back on the same planes. It is possible because the C-47s were designed to be changed over. However, it would take time and materials to change over a C-47 from one that had equipment used to transport paratroopers to one that could transport wounded soldiers. Plus you need a nurse and medical supplies. It is more likely that hospital planes accompanied the assault or were sent up shortly afterwards. They look the same from the outside.

Once down, the rest of the battalion started south to link up with the 37th Division. The Americans saw only a few Japanese stragglers on their way south and on June 26 met men of the 37th Division near the Paret River, 35 miles south of the Camalaniugan airstrip. The airborne operation had proved both useless and unnecessary.

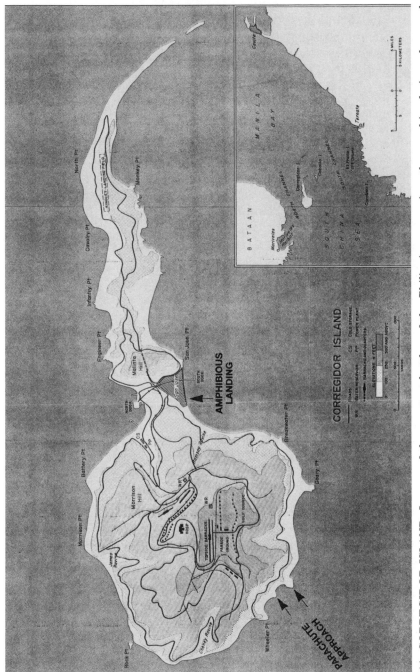

11. CORREGIDOR ISLAND. In one of the greatest battles of the Philippine campaign, the combined air and ground forces re-took the famous island. From: Robert Ross Smith, *Triumph in the Philippines*, (Washington, D.C.,: Government Printing Office, 1963).

My paratrooper buddies thought that the operation was due to MacArthur's insatiable need for publicity. A vertical assault, with the sky full of parachuting soldiers, makes good newspaper copy and he did want to try out those gliders. The official history only says that Kreuger—who was responsible and gave the order—may have been ". . . motivated by a desire to clean up Northern Luzon before the Eighth Army took control of operations, an event scheduled for 1 July."[10] In retrospect, it doesn't seem to be a very good reason for young men to die or be seriously hurt.

Another operation they told me about was the recapture of Corregidor, the island fortress that guarded the entrance to Manila Bay and was a symbol of American resistance during the early days of World War II. Corregidor is a tadpole shaped island that lies in the middle of the entrance to Manila Bay, its head looking out to sea, its tail pointing back at the city. It is a small island, one and a half miles wide at the head and three and a half miles long. I had sailed past it when I arrived in Manila in early April. It was still smoking.

The assault plan[11] called for a parachute regiment to drop onto a parade ground and golf course located on Topside, the highest part of the island. This was a fairly level spot about 400 to 500 feet above sea level. Located in the middle of the tadpole's head, it was surrounded on three sides by steep slopes down to the water's edge.

Concurrent with the air drop, there would be an amphibious landing by the 34th Infantry Regiment at the point where the head of the tadpole joins the tail. Known as Bottomside, its sandy beaches provided a good landing for an amphibious assault. However, they would be subjected to intense shelling from the high ground to the west. To minimize expected casualties during the shore to shore attack, the 34th Infantry troops would make their landing two hours after the paratroopers started jumping. By that time, planners expected, the parachutists would be able to provide fire support for the amphibious assault, while Japanese attention would be largely diverted to the attacking paratroopers on Topside.

It was a tricky proposition to try to land paratroopers on such a small target. Planners had to correlate factors of wind direction and velocity, the speed and flight direction of the C-47s, the optimum height for the planes during the drop, the time it would take to reach the ground, and the drift of the 'troopers during descent. Each C-47 would not be over the dropping grounds for more than six seconds so each plane would have to make two or three passes, dropping six or eight soldiers each time.

My paratrooper friends (who were not participants in the opera-

47. PARATROOPERS LANDING ON CORREGIDOR. The island was small and the winds were strong so many landed on the cliffs or in the water but the operation was successful. U.S. Army Photo.

tion but seemed to know all about it) said it was another disaster, that most of those jumping missed the parade ground and landed in the water or met an untimely end on the steep slopes. Some were rescued by PT boats which were assisting in the naval bombardment that preceded the amphibious landing. *Triumph In The Philippines*, however, considers it to be a successful operation when viewed in its overall complexity and execution.

Surprise was complete. Enough paratroopers landed to seize control of Topside and support the amphibious landing. One unexpected blessing from the scattered drop of the paratroopers was that some 25 of them landed near an observation post where Captain Akira Itagaki, the garrison commander, was observing the American amphibious forces assembling. In the ensuing skirmish, he and seven other Japanese officers were killed. Thus, from the very beginning of the battle, the Japanese had lost their top leaders. No longer capable of coordinated defensive efforts, each group would fight on its own from isolated and widely separated strong points.

The 'troopers were right in some respects. Of the men in the first lift, 25 percent had been injured, and many others had failed to land on Topside. Lowering the altitude for the second pass reduced the casualties for that phase but, overall, of the 2,050 who made the jump, 280 were injured, a very high rate of 14 percent. Jump operations were then canceled and the rest of the regiment came ashore by landing craft.

Corregidor turned out to be a bloody campaign. Planners expected it to be defended by about 850 Japanese. As it turned out, there were over 5,000 troops defending the small island. They fought almost to the last man—only 20 prisoners were taken. American casualties were 1,005, of whom 210 were killed and 5 missing. On March 2, two weeks after the paratroopers started their descent, the island was considered secured. General MacArthur returned to the island he had left three years previously and a simple flag-raising ceremony was held. After accepting the fortress from Colonel George M. Jones, the commander of the 503rd Regimental Combat Team, he said, "Hoist the colors to its peak and let no enemy ever haul them down."[12] Elements of my division garrisoned the island in early May, after we were taken off the *Shimbu* Line.

I never saw the paratroopers again. The next morning I was put on a plane bound for Leyte. After about a three hour flight, we landed at the Tacloban airport and I was taken by ambulance to the 133rd General Hospital which was located on Highway Number 1, about a mile south of Palo. It was not far from the beach where I had made the nighttime amphibious landing in March. I felt that I was getting closer to home in time and in distance. I had retraced over 500 miles of my long journey from Camp Hood to the battlefronts.

Searching through the incomplete documents filed at the National Archives as a Unit History for this hospital[13] provided me with a lot of information that was not evident when I was a patient there. The 133rd General Hospital was organized at Camp Gordon, Georgia and was shipped overseas in the fall of 1944. They arrived at Leyte by LSTs, 24 November 1944, and began building a semi-permanent hospital right away but were hampered by mud, rain, blackouts, native families living within the hospital area and by repeatedly having to move equipment in order to clear space for building the various components that comprised the hospital complex. The battle for the island of Leyte was still raging.

After much heroic work, for which they subsequently received the prized Meritorious Service Unit plaque and a commendation from General Eichelberger, they were prepared to admit 400 patients only six hours after unloading the last L.S.T. on December 1. By Christmas they had admitted 816 patients and increased their capacity to 1,500 beds.

By the end of March, the hospital complex had 23 surgical and medical wards fully completed and in operation. Three of the wards were psychiatric units. Bed capacity had risen to 1,850 and 6,351 patients had been admitted in the first quarter of the year. Of these,

1,324 had been battle casualties, the rest diseases and injuries. The hospital staff consisted of 550 enlisted men, 70 officers and 85 nurses, so it was a big operation. The officers were housed on an island in a swampy area connected to the rest of the hospital by a 100 foot bridge that was constructed by the Army engineers. The nurses and other female personnel were also quartered there but were surrounded by barbed wire and patrolled by 24-hour armed guards. They were being helped by 69 female Filipino civilians who worked as nurse's aids and 170 males who were limited to outside construction type work. There is also a gratuitous remark, by the chauvinistic medical officer making the first quarterly report, about the value of the Filipinos' contribution: "It is estimated that three Filipino man-days are about equal to one U.S. Army soldier man-day."[14] This he attributes to the "high rate of helminthine infestation" that is, intestinal worms.

There was no quarterly report for the months of April through June in the files I researched but the July—September report says that the bed capacity had risen to 2,650 and the hospital census was 2,125 on July 1, 1945.[15] Of the 6,841 patients treated from July 1 through September 30, 5,361 had diseases, 837 injuries and only 283 were battle casualties.[16] The patients were mostly U.S. Army personnel but 898 were a mixture of Merchant Marine, U.S. Navy, U.S. civilians, foreign armed personnel and Filipino Army, guerrillas, and civilians.

What I remember of the 133rd General Hospital is that it was a collection of tents and temporary corrugated sheet metal buildings, all an Army olive drab color. It occupied a swampy area typical of that part of Leyte where the water table was only a few feet below the ground surface. In fact, it looked much like the replacement depot where I had been in March and also like many of the other Army encampments on the island. Leyte was a very busy place and crowded with units building up for the final phase of the war, the invasion of Japan.

The ward that I was taken to was a long tent with a wood frame and a wooden plank floor. There were beds on both sides of a long aisle with the nurses' station in the middle. It probably housed some 72 or more patients most of whom, at least near me, were battle casualties. The sides of the tent were rolled up about four feet on both sides to allow air to circulate. The next tent/ward was only a few feet away with a drainage ditch in between. When it rained, I could watch the water drip down into the mud and be thankful that I didn't have to sleep in it. I was still reveling in soft mattresses and clean sheets.

When I arrived, I was put in bed and immediately surrounded by several nurses who took my vital signs and, after asking numerous questions, told me that the doctor would be around later. They all left but one who proceeded to give me a bath.

"You're quite clean," she declared. "You ought to see the condition some of the patients are in when they arrive here. They're absolutely filthy!"

"Well," I answered, "this is the fourth bath I've had in as many days. I am not used to being so clean." It was also the fifth Army hospital I had been to in less than a week and each one had been determined to clean me up before sending me on. I felt like a U.P.S. package arriving fresh and clean in spite of all the shipping and handling I had received.

The doctor turned out to be a captain in the Marine Corps. This was unusual because the liberation of the Philippines was essentially an Army operation. Why he was assigned to an Army hospital, I never did find out. He might have been new and needing experience treating battle casualties. The Marines didn't have any campaigns going at that time.

The Marine doctor went through the same routine of unwrapping the wound, pulling out the long piece of bloody gauze, and sniffing the wound. I knew what was coming by this time so I struggled to appear nonchalant. He wasn't at all communicative, treating me as if I were an inanimate object. He must not have liked the smell of the wound and the fact that I was running a slight temperature. I learned from the nurse that he had put me on a program of ten days of penicillin.

Penicillin was very new then. Although it had been discovered in 1928, it was never fully developed until World War II. In 1945, the year its discoverer, Sir Alexander Fleming, got his Nobel Prize, it was still relatively unknown. In basic training we were taught that sulpha drugs were the latest medical advance. We carried first aid kits into battle that contained sulpha powders that we were supposed to use on wounds. When I asked the nurse, who came back with a big needle-full of penicillin and injected it into my arm, why they didn't just sprinkle sulpha powder on my wound, she answered that that kind of treatment was obsolete. The new medicine was much more effective because it worked from the inside, destroying bacteria in the blood. Unfortunately, the treatment at that time was an injection every three hours, or eight times a day. In ten days that meant 80 shots. My skinny frame soon ran out of places to put it. I had lost weight in combat and tipped the scales at 130 pounds.

It was especially annoying at night when the nurse came to my bedside, announced in a loud voice, "Time for your medicine!" and then threw back the mosquito netting. She would then proceed to jab my already sore arm, leg or backside. An opportunistic mosquito would sometimes maneuver his way in while this was going on so then I would be wide awake, hurting all over, and trying to get rid of an unwelcome invader. Three hours later, about the time I got back to sleep, this scenario would be repeated.

The treatment was effective. The wound didn't get gangrene and the bloody piece of gauze the doctor pulled out when they changed the dressing got smaller and smaller. The head nurse got me a pair of crutches so I could get out of bed and hobble to the latrine, which was in another tent. After about a week she said I could try going to the mess hall for my meals. This was a large building about 300 yards from the ward. Here the enlisted staff and the patients ate their meals in common, cafeteria style. Encouraging the patients to be ambulatory helped relieve the nurses' workload, but I liked it because, even though it was hard work getting there on crutches, the food was more varied and tasted better than that brought around to the wards.

Early in my stay at the 133rd General Hospital, I was visited by the Catholic chaplain. He offered to hear my confession. However, as far as sin was concerned, I felt theologically inculpable because I had no free will. The Army told me what to do and when to do it. The Army had a strange God—Mars, the God of War. Miss Mass on Sundays? There were no Sundays or Holy Days in combat. The last Mass I had attended was the one at the bottom of Hill A in April. We hadn't seen a Catholic chaplain since. Ditto for eating meat on Fridays. We ate C-rations or anything else the Army fed us. Keep His name holy? The Army communicated in the foulest and most profane language that I had ever heard. Honor your father and mother? The Army was your father and mother and you better do everything they told you. Failure to obey orders meant immediate and harsh punishment. "Thou shalt not kill" was turned into a virtue. The only good Jap was a dead Jap. The sooner we killed them all, the sooner we could go home. Sexual sins were generally well received in confession, but two months in the jungle precluded much of that although some of the nurses were beginning to look interesting. Nothing in my catechism classes had prepared me for what I had just been through. The priest was understanding and didn't push it. He gave me absolution and said he would bring me Communion on Thursdays and Sundays when he made his rounds.

The Jewish chaplain often visited the soldier across the aisle from

241

me, bringing him candy and books and other gifts. The red-haired 19-year-old, who was from Chicago and didn't look Jewish, was embarrassed by the attention he was getting. He volunteered one day that he was not really Jewish, that he followed the religion of his Christian mother, but, because of his last name, his dog tags had been stamped with a "J." He didn't want to disappoint the Jewish chaplain because he had so few patients to whom he ministered.

I told him about Paul, the B.A.R. man in my squad. He was a devout Greek Orthodox whose dog tags were stamped "C" when he told the soldier making the dog tags that Greek Orthodox was not Protestant. He told him he wasn't Catholic either but he couldn't get it changed because they didn't have a category letter for Greek Orthodox. "That's close enough! Move on, soldier," was what he had been told.

Around this time I was awarded my Purple Heart Medal. The award was originally established by order of General George Washington in 1782 for recognizing meritorious action or service in the Revolutionary War. It fell into disuse over the following years but was re-instituted in 1932, the two hundredth anniversary of Washington's birth, for the Army and in 1942 for the Marines. It is now awarded to all service personnel who are wounded or killed in combat operations. To qualify, the wound must necessitate treatment by a medical officer.

An officer and an enlisted man came down the aisle, stopping at each bed where a man was to get the award. It was a simple ceremony. The captain read from the official Army order my name, rank and serial number, the branch of service I served in and the place in Northern Luzon where I was wounded. Then taking a boxed medal from the stack of medals that the enlisted man was carrying, he handed one to me as he shook my hand. It is a beautiful medal with George Washington's bust in gold set against the enameled purple heart-shaped background, surrounded by gold edging. On the obverse side was the legend, "For Military Merit."

I had seen newsreel shots of General George Patton awarding the medal to soldiers wounded in Sicily. The medal was attached to a long ribbon that he draped over the recipient's neck. He liked to visit the "honorably wounded" but didn't think much of the other casualties of war. He got in serious trouble for slapping a soldier who was suffering from exhaustion and had been put in a ward with battle casualties.

The Army had improved the packaging of the medal by the time I got mine. It came in a nice purple box and included a campaign ribbon for wearing on the dress uniform and a lapel pin to be worn on a civilian suit. The other patients told me that the lapel pin would be good for getting free drinks in a bar, but I was only 19 years old and couldn't legally get in a bar.

The Military Order of the Purple Heart, when it communicates with its members or the general public, likes to quote George Washington on its masthead as follows: ". . . and let it be known that he who wears The Order of the Purple Heart, has given of his blood in the defense of his homeland and shall forever be revered by his fellow countrymen . . . ."

I wore my lapel pin briefly after the war but it never got me any reverence or free drinks either. Sometimes it would generate a negative reaction. Smart alecs would say, "What did you do, cut yourself on a C-ration can?" By the time I got home people wanted to forget the war. It was further devalued when my sister Rosemary, after returning from a vacation in Canada, told me that the Canadian Army didn't award medals to their soldiers wounded in battle and thought it was odd that the Americans did. I put the medal away and forgot about it for a long time.

Shortly after the award ceremony the Red Cross lady came around. She said she could send my medal home for me so I gave it to her. I didn't see it again for more than a year. She also asked me if I had written home about being wounded. I said that I had. "Good," she declared. "When a soldier gets wounded, the War Department delays thirty days before notifying the next of kin. It's best if your letter gets there before the War Department's telegram."

The Red Cross had supplied me with writing materials at the hospital in Rosales. They had also supplied me with toilet articles and reading material. In all my Army service, I always found the Red Cross to be very helpful and generous so I was surprised to hear some of the complaints other soldiers had about the Red Cross selling products or services such as coffee, doughnuts, meals and lodging.

Ann Landers first discussed this problem in a newspaper column printed in 1976. Her response to disgruntled "G.I. Joe of Long Ago" was that this practice was dictated by Secretary of War Henry J. Stimson because all English and Australian soldiers had to pay for off-base food and lodging in their servicemen's clubs. The British High Command made an official request to the U.S. government that all American servicemen also be required to pay for whatever they received in service clubs, just like their Allies had to. The Red Cross was opposed to this practice and protested vehemently but had to go along with it when commanded to by Secretary of War Stimson in order to satisfy our ally.[17] I don't think it was adhered to very well in the Pacific Theater of Operations because I certainly don't remember paying the Red Cross for anything that they provided me.

As time passed, there were a few changes to the patient roster. Some were "boarded," which meant that they were sent home on an airplane or a hospital ship. We had movies at an outdoor movie theater, to which I hobbled on my crutches. Music was played on the public address system while we sat on hard benches waiting for the darkness necessary to show the film. Billboard listed the most popular songs for the month of June, 1945, as follows:

1. "Sentimental Journey"
2. "Bell Bottom Trousers"
3. "There! I've Said It Again"
4. "Dream"
5. "You Belong To My Heart"

However, in the hospital on Leyte, the most requested number was "Flying Home,"[18] a jazz instrumental by Lionel Hampton. It was a raucous, swinging piece without lyrics, not emotional and romantic like "Sentimental Journey" which was also occasionally requested. These numbers were usually dedicated to a severely wounded soldier who was being transferred to a military hospital near his home, although occasionally it was dedicated to a staff member who had been in the Army since the beginning of the war and had accumulated enough points to be eligible to go home. We all longed to go flying home too, but we would gladly have settled for a slow boat ride.

One of the patients "boarded" soon after I arrived had been hit by a rifle bullet in the right hip. The bullet had ripped through his intestines and then furrowed the head of his penis before burying itself in his left leg. He claimed to now have a built in "French tickler." Everyone was envious of him going home, but wished him well as he was carried out of the ward to begin his long journey home.

His bed was then filled by a sergeant in his late thirties who had had a heart attack. The nurses put up an oxygen tent around the bed and there was an atmosphere of crisis for a few days with a nurse on duty around the clock and lot of tip-toeing and whispering. After the crisis passed, the tent came down and the doctor prescribed a shot of whiskey several times a day for the stricken soldier. The nurse would bring the liquor in a shot glass on a small tray down the long aisle. Soldiers on both sides would groan, clasp their chests, and claim they were having heart attacks and needed that medicine. The nurse had to stand by the heart patient's bedside until he had consumed the whiskey, which he did very slowly, either from a distaste for alcohol or, more likely, to savor each drop and tantalize his fellow soldiers who had their tongues hanging out.

One of the nurses who had to bring the whiskey was a short, dark haired, Italian woman from Boston. She had an extreme Boston accent. One of the patients was always kidding her about it and asking her to repeat phrases like "Park the car in the garage" which came out "Pahk the cah in the gahrage." She soon tired of this game. Most of the nurses worked hard and put up with the kidding and verbal double-entendres calmly enough. It was not the kind of a job that I would want, taking care of a bunch of wounded soldiers who tended to be cranky or boisterous.

However, they had an advantage. They were officers and we patients were enlisted men. Instead of the starchy white uniforms and nurses caps that you would expect in a hospital, they wore khaki shirts and pants and their badges of rank, 1st or 2nd lieutenant's bars. The head nurse was a captain. They delivered their services in an authoritative manner, a constant reminder of the Army's caste system, so there wasn't much fraternization going on between the patients and the staff.

The hospital Information and Education Section published a daily newspaper. Entitled *The Stethoscope*, it was a four-page mimeographed publication that was passed around the ward to keep us up to date with what was happening in the world. The war news was mostly about MacArthur. On June 28, he announced that Luzon could be considered liberated, as the juncture of the two columns, the 11th Airborne Division and the 37th Infantry Division in the Cagayan valley, had split the Japanese into three groups. All that was left, as usual, was "mopping up."

On July 1, he announced that Bolog, where my regiment was fighting, had been taken. On July 2, Australian troops, with MacArthur on hand, landed at Balikpapan on the east coast of Borneo. The comment from the patients at the 133rd General Hospital was that "Mac and a bunch of photographers were getting their feet wet again." They also had a saying that went, "Stick with Mac and you will never get back!"

On July 5 MacArthur announced that "the entire Philippine Islands are now liberated and the Philippine campaigns can be regarded as virtually closed." The general then added, "Minor mountain actions may continue." "Minor" indeed! On July 12, my regiment slugged its way into Kiangan, the recent headquarters of General Yamashita which culminated the 30-day drive up Highway 4 against stiff Japanese resistance. It wasn't the end of the fighting though. There would be more beyond Kiangan. The official Army history says, "Instead of mopping up, the 6th Division soon found itself involved in mountain fighting as rough as that experienced at any time or at any place throughout the Luzon Campaign."[19]

Fighting tenaciously in the defense of the mountain approaches to Kiangan, the Japanese had employed a complicated network of defensive positions, well disposed and advantageously situated on commanding ground, to effect a strong zone of fire against the attacking Americans. Individual automatic weapons teams and artillery positions were the most difficult to assault as they were suicide defense positions. Holes were dug six to ten feet deep with a tunnel at the bottom offering protection from our artillery and mortar barrages. They had to be taken one by one with savage hand-to-hand combat.

The enemy also used fanatical infiltration tactics to counterattack under the concealment of darkness. Our supply trains were ambushed by teams carrying satchel charges as well as automatic weapons. Bamboo thickets along the road offered excellent hiding places for these groups. Supply was also hindered by the weather and the poor condition of Highway 4. No more than a gravel road cut in the side of steep mountains, it had been bombed extensively by the American air forces and what they didn't destroy, the Japanese did in order to slow the American advance. Unusually heavy rains also made rebuilding the road difficult. Not much had been changed by MacArthur's proclamations.

For its work, the 63rd Infantry received several citations and, afterwards, commemorated the event by celebrating July 12 as its Regimental Day. If I hadn't been wounded on the eighth day of the campaign, I might have gone the whole distance like some of my comrades did. Or been killed trying!

Every day there were reports of five or six hundred B-29 Superfortresses bombing Japan from Saipan. On July 10 they were joined by 1000 carrier aircraft from Admiral "Bull" Halsey's Third Fleet. By this time, he could sail virtually unopposed up and down the Japanese coastline. P-51 Mustangs from Okinawa, now a secure base, also joined in the attack. The Japanese homeland was under severe assault from the skies and the coastal waters, but most people were of the opinion that an invasion was still necessary to end the war. The Japanese had over four million men in uniform and were busily arming and training their civilian population to meet the expected invasion.

In Europe, American and British troops were getting ready to move into their negotiated sectors of occupied Berlin but were having trouble getting the Russians to vacate the area. The Army announced that 340,000 soldiers had been returned from Europe to the continental United States between May 20 and June 30. High point men were to be discharged; the others would be sent on to the Pacific Theater to help fight the Japanese.

On July 7, the War Department announced that 102 soldiers had been executed during the war, all but one for murder or rape. The exception was a man who had deserted twice. It was later learned that he was Private Anton Slovic from Detroit, the only U.S. soldier who was shot for desertion in World War II. The Navy, Marine Corps and the Coast Guard had reported no executions of its personnel.

On July 14, the Supreme Headquarters, Allied Expeditionary Forces was closed down and General Eisenhower left for Antwerp to meet with President Truman who was arriving in Europe to attend the Potsdam Conference. The Army announced that it was modifying its non-fraternization policy in occupied Germany. American soldiers could now talk to Germans on the streets and in other public places. Previously they were subject to severe punishment for doing this.

Some of the domestic news was a little more pleasant. Ford Motor Company reported that the first civilian passenger car since February 1942 had rolled off the assembly line in Dearborn on July 3. "The new 1946 model has many style changes and war- developed improvements," said company spokesmen, but in reality the cars were pretty much the same as those built before the war.

On July 10 President Truman signed a 20 percent pay raise for postal workers, their first general raise since 1925. The President was also changing the cabinet he had inherited when Roosevelt died. James Byrnes became Secretary of State, succeeding Edward R. Stettinius, who was to be the American representative to the United Nations Organization that was forming in San Francisco. Henry Morganthau retired as Secretary of the Treasury and was succeeded by Henry Vinson.[20]

The hospital paper also printed the local news, such as which doctors or nurses were arriving or departing, and how many cases were handled. A big feature which ran for several days was a romance between a doctor and a nurse. Somehow they had gotten permission from the Army to get married. (Probably because they were both officers; I never knew of any enlisted men who got that privilege.) The ceremony was performed by one of the hospital chaplains and the paper reported it in considerable detail—what the bride wore and who the attendants were. A honeymoon hut had been constructed by an engineering battalion on the officers' island and the newlyweds had been granted three days leave to enjoy their nuptial bliss before returning to their jobs. Even in wartime, love conquers all for some people.

This event started me fantasizing about a girl that I had been attracted to in my senior year in high school and still had strong feelings for. I had known her from when we were both in St. Benedict grade school. She had blossomed into a 17-year-old beauty, the Madonna of the Christmas pageant that year. I would see her at the dances that were held in the St. Benedict gym after the Friday night basketball games. My brother Bob was one of the players and the team did quite well that year reaching the all-city finals in the Catholic league.

I decided that I would ask her to the Henry Ford Trade School senior prom. It was going to be the big social event of the school year, a formal dinner/dance at the Hotel Statler in downtown Detroit in early February, a week after we graduated. Henry Ford II would be there with his wife, Anne McDonnell Ford, a prominent Eastern socialite. Henry II had visited the school and had accepted the invitation extended by our class president.

My sister Rosemary kept warning me that time was running out, that girls needed lots of time to get ready for a big social event like a formal dance and that I had better get on with the asking. Rosemary also had a girl friend she thought would be a suitable escort for me, but I wasn't interested in her choice. I preferred to follow my own agenda.

It didn't seem like such a big deal to me. After all, I had gone to the previous class's senior prom in June. My friend, Walt Canney, had suggested that we ask a couple of girls we had met at the Saturday night dances at the "Y." They were friends and lived across the street from each other in Redford.

Everything went smoothly. I borrowed a white dinner jacket, the six of us squeezed into Bob Woolsey's father's Buick and we enjoyed a lovely summer night of dancing and strolling around the grounds of the hotel located on the shores of the Detroit River.

Another time, when Eddie Greiner and I were without escorts for a Trade School dance and time had run out, he suggested we go to the "Y." pick up a couple of girls and transfer to the Trade School dance, which was being held at the Masonic Temple downtown. It worked out but, as part of the deal, we had to take the girls home. They lived in the then far-out suburb of Berkeley and we had to ride on public transportation which didn't operate very often in the wee hours of Sunday morning. Ironically, a picture of us with our two "dates" showed up in the school yearbook, which I didn't even get to see until after I got out of the Army three years later.

In the case of the senior prom, things didn't go smoothly. My friends had their dates lined up early. (Not the same ones as the previous dances. We all seemed to want to try different girls for every event.) As time ran out, the pressure got higher. I had missed several good opportunities to ask her to the prom when we would dance together occasionally. I just couldn't form the words. Adolescent boy-girl relationships are so awkward, especially when they are one-sided. She was only vaguely aware of my feelings.

My intended worked part time at the catalog desk at Sears in Highland Park. I went there on a Saturday afternoon, a week before the big event, determined to pop the question or die trying. It was scary, almost as harrowing as going down a jungle trail looking for the enemy. I stopped off at the catalog desk and said hello a couple of times and then circled the store many times. She was always busy on the phone or waiting on customers. Every time it started to look promising, the phone would ring or another customer would walk up to the desk and need attention. When I finally got the opportunity and managed to express my desire, she said, "I am sorry, but I couldn't possibly get a formal dress in time for the dance." Time had run out on me.

It wasn't too many months later, after we had both graduated from our respective high schools, that I was drafted and she went away to nursing school in Kalamazoo. First loves, especially if they are unrequited, die hard. During my Army period I passed through Kalamazoo several times on the train. I would be reminded of her when the train stopped at the station in Kalamazoo and attractive young ladies would get on and pass out sandwiches to the soldiers. They were wrapped in wax paper on which was imprinted "From the gals in Kalamazoo" and the words to the song, "I've Got a Gal in Kalamazoo."[21] It would have been nice to have a girl in Kalamazoo but after my big rejection, I hadn't pursued the relationship. Going to college and working the afternoon shift had precluded any further attendance at the basketball games.

When the doctor and the nurse got married in the hospital on Leyte, I remembered my former schoolmate, still in Kalamazoo, and thought it would be great if the Army sent me to Percy Jones Hospital, in nearby Battle Creek, which at that time was treating a lot of wounded Michigan soldiers. My friend could visit me and, like Lieutenant Henry and the nurse, Catherine, in Hemmingway's *A Farewell to Arms*, we could be in love and forget all about the war. Such a lovely dream!

This fantasy kept me going for awhile but, alas, it wasn't to be. The head nurse informed me one day that I was being transferred to a convalescent hospital. I would need some clothes and some shoes. What sizes did I take? I had lived in pajamas and slippers since the medics had cut off all of my clothes in the battalion aid station some three weeks earlier. Reality set in. My million dollar wound had suddenly devalued to zero. I was on my way back to duty, *not home*!

I learned, much later, that from the beginning of the war in December 1941, only a small percentage of wounded soldiers had made it back from the Pacific war zone. Only a relatively few met the stringent qualifications set up by the Army. The official policy was to send home only those litter patients requiring hospitalization for 90 days or more, patients requiring immediate treatment of a type not available in the Pacific Theater, or patients expected to die but whose condition was such that they could be sent home.[22] The Army, always short of what it called "combat effectives," that is, soldiers trained and able to do the fighting as opposed to cooks or clerks or technicians, recycled every combat soldier it could. The 90 day rule was close in my case. I spent 89 days in Army hospitals.

George Sharpe, the Battalion surgeon of our sister regiment, the 20th Infantry, describes how his battalion got many of its soldiers back during this period when they were, like the 63rd, fighting in the wild mountains of Northern Luzon:

> One other phenomenon that was now occurring was the returning of GI's who had been wounded or sent back for other illnesses. Many of these men we never thought we would see again . . . However, much to our chagrin, we would see men being helped out of . . . trucks, Jeeps, and even ambulances with canes . . . crutches, bandages and casts. They had been sent back from general hospitals for "limited duty" or "recuperation." It was like a bad dream, as nobody wanted these men around since there was no such thing as limited duty available in this particular area.[23]

Staff Sergeant Glen Laub of K-Company tells of being sent back to duty still unhealed from shrapnel wounds. He was given the job of training new replacements. Captain Isadore Goldberg, the Regimental surgeon, saw him limping around and had him brought in for examination. Finding his condition to be requiring medical treatment, he sent him back through the Army's chain of hospitals. He ended up on Leyte for the balance of the war.

Another factor that was involved in keeping combat soldiers in the area was that, on June 18, the Joint Chiefs of Staff presented to President Truman their "recommendation that American forces land on Kyushu in November."[24] This was to be followed by a landing on the main island of Honshu on March 1, 1946, a campaign in which my division was scheduled to play a leading role. The need for combat effectives would be tremendous. "With 767,000 men scheduled to participate in the campaign, this would mean 268,000 dead and wounded."[25] A horrible future for those involved.

Paul Fussell, a 21 year old Second Lieutenant, who led a rifle platoon in the European Theater and was on his way to the Pacific to take part in the invasion, wrote some 35 years later: "Although still officially fit for combat . . . I had already been wounded in the back and leg badly enough to be adjudged, after the war, 40 percent disabled. But, even if my leg buckled and I fell to the ground whenever I jumped out of the back of a truck . . . my condition was held to be adequate for the next act."[26]

So the average wounded G.I., like me, developed a sense of hopelessness and despair at the prospect of apparently endless combat duty. That was the harsh reality of being a wounded soldier in the Pacific Theater in July of 1945.

ELEVEN

I Too, Thank God for the Atom Bomb!

. . . we broke down and cried with relief and joy. We were going to live. We were going to grow up to adulthood after all.

—Paul Fussell[1]

T*ime*, the weekly news magazine, called it a "week of decision . . . the true beginning of the Truman Presidency."[2] The *Reader's Digest* later reported the story of two fishermen who had spent this time period deep in the north woods, out of touch with civilization. When they returned, they were astonished by all that had happened in such a short interval of time.[3]

Actually, it was more than a week. It was the period from August 6, 1945 to August 14—nine days that changed our lives completely. It was a veritable watershed in the history of mankind. *It would never be the same again*!!

I spent those historic days, and the four weeks leading up to them, at the 1st Convalescent Hospital on the island of Leyte. This was an Army medical complex on the shore of San Pedro Bay, a mile and a half south of Tolosa, the birthplace of Imelda Marcos.

The 1st Convalescent Hospital was a camp the Army used to house soldiers well enough to be out of a general hospital, but not yet fit enough to return to duty. I had been transferred there from the 133rd General Hospital on the eighth of July. This was about the time that my regiment, the 63rd Infantry, was battling its way into Kiangan, a mining town in Northern Luzon thought to be the headquarters of

General Yamashita. It was also a week before a new, large, experimental bomb was tested at Alamagordo, New Mexico on July 16.

I arrived at the new hospital on an old Army bus. Several soldiers who were waiting to get on the bus helped me get my gear unloaded, since I was having difficulty with my crutches. Surprisingly, one of them turned out to be a man from my platoon. The last time I had seen him was in May when we were conducting mopping-up operations in the mountains west of Clark Field. He had been stricken with hepatitis and sent to the hospital. After two months treatment, he had been restored to health and was now on his way back to duty.

"What happened to you?" he asked, looking at my bandaged leg. I told him about some of the bloody fighting that he had missed. He was a little shocked and confused to hear this because MacArthur had declared the Philippine campaign over on July 5 and my friend didn't know that his buddies, the men of the 63rd Infantry, were still engaged in their toughest campaign of the war. "I feel my hepatitis coming back," he muttered wearily as he boarded the bus that I had just left.

The 1st Convalescent Hospital was a lot different than the 133rd General Hospital. It was sort of like a summer camp, the kind I used to go to when I was a Boy Scout. I was housed with several other patients in a framed squad tent that was, among many, set up in a grove of coconut palm trees, next to the beach. The floor of the tent was concrete and had the usual army cots and mosquito netting. We ate our meals in a central cafeteria and bathed in a common shower and latrine area. There were recreational facilities all over the grounds including a library, a Red Cross canteen and an outdoor theater.

The hospital unit, consisting of 31 officers and 184 enlisted men, had come from Camp Stoneman, California, arriving at Leyte on December 6, 1944 while the battle for the island was still raging. Operations were set up and they received their first patients on December 17. By the end of the month they had admitted 1,241 patients.[4]

The facility was so situated that its long axis ran on a north-south parallel with an expansive 2,800 foot beach frontage. It had a stream, approximately 400 feet from the beach and running in a northerly direction, which bisected the hospital area. This creek offered a natural boundary for the reconditioning companies on the beach side, and the messes and clinical and technical departments located on the inland side.

A quarterly report says that "The location and meteorological conditions are such as to offer cool, restful environment for proper reconditioning of combat troops with limited facilities available for reconditioning during inclement weather."[5] During the month that I was there, it was quite pleasant: I don't recall it raining at all.

This was a unique hospital, the only one of its kind on the island. It received patients from all over the Western Pacific area including Filipino troops and Naval personnel. A total of 2,839 patients were admitted and 4,382 returned to duty during the summer quarter that I was there. It had a capacity to handle about 3,000 at a time.

Except for reporting to the dispensary in the morning at scheduled intervals for examination, change of bandage or the administration of medicines or other treatment, the rest of the time was rather agreeable. We were assigned to groups and had a schedule to follow. A typical day's schedule, as posted on the bulletin board would read:

Group 5

0900 hours	Volleyball
1000 "	Miniature Golf
1100 "	Weight Lifting
1200 "	Lunch
1300 "	Badminton
1400 "	Swimming
1500 "	Discussion Group

We moved as a group of about 15 or more soldiers from one area to another and participated as much as we could. If you were physically unable to do the activity scheduled, you sat and watched. The only pressure the Army exerted was that you had to be with your group and follow the schedule. You couldn't lay around on your cot in the tent while scheduled activities were going on.

The quarterly report says that "sea bathing facilities are excellent." An area had been roped off in the ocean for this purpose. There were several tethered rafts out in the deeper water that I could swim out to, lay on and soak up the tropical sun. The sun and salt water helped the healing process of both body and soul. I really enjoyed it until one day, as we lay on the raft, another soldier pointed out some toilet paper and raw sewage floating by in the water. San Pedro Bay was a busy harbor with many ships that discharged their effluent into the sea. After that I reduced my swimming and when I did, I kept a wary eye out for sewage.

The camp's cadre were clever at making up new recreational games for us and varying the schedule. Time passed quickly. My leg wound, which had been seeping blood when I had arrived, was healing. Soon I was able to get rid of my crutches, first one and then the other. I still limped and my leg swelled up when I exercised it but my mental attitude improved. I had been disappointed and depressed when I arrived because I had expected to be sent home, not back to duty. But, with the resilience of youth, I soon adapted. It actually was a lot better than most of the other places the Army had sent me and the war seemed far away. The whole purpose of the hospital was to recondition men, physically and mentally, for a return to combat. They did their job well.

Not all of the patients had been wounded. Some had broken bones suffered in accidents, some were recovering from tropical diseases, others from some of the infirmities the human body is heir to. Hepatitis was widespread. During the quarterly period that I was there, July 1 to September 30, 1945, 974 admissions for this disease were reported. This compares to a much lower incidence of admissions for malaria, 104, which was attributed to the widespread use of atabrine.[6]

Another patient in my tent had a problem with his tail bone. It hurt him to sit down. The diagnosis was pilonidal cyst, an infection of a congenital cyst at the base of the spine. In the Army it was commonly called "jeep disease" because riding in jeeps or tanks and taking the bumps of basic training seemed to have increased the incidence of this malady. The cure required surgery. One day he was moved to the dispensary and operated on. Several of us tent mates went over to visit him after his surgery.

The dispensary was a mini-hospital ward with four beds. He was the only patient. We found him in considerable pain, lying on a couple of pillows with his bare buttocks raised in the air so that the incision could drain.

"I always figured I'd get shot in the ass," he moaned. "I never expected the Army to cut out a big piece! At least I now have some scars to show for my time in service and all the ass chewing I have had to put up with."

We were visited by several USO entertainers. One day it was Kay Kyser and his Kollege of Musical Knowledge. I had seen him in the movies and heard him on the radio but it was a big thrill to see him in person. There were to be a number of performances and my group was assigned to the afternoon show and I had a front row seat. Kyser's crew was supplemented by a Navy band which entertained the patients before he came on and joined in some of his numbers to make some very rousing music. One of his big hits was "Ac-cen-tchu-ate the Positive,"[7] which went something like this:

You've got to ac-cen-tchu-ate the positive,
E-lim-my-ate the neg-a-tive—
Latch on to the affirmative,
Don't mess with Mister-in-be-tween —

It was a good philosophy and I really enjoyed the show. Afterwards, feeling hot and sweaty after a couple of hours in the tropic sun, I went over to the showers. Several of the band members who were enlisted men in the Navy came in. They noticed the ugly red hole on the front of my leg and stared.

"What happened to you?" one of them finally asked.

"Got hit by a Japanese machine gun, " I answered, trying to be casual about it. Their eyes widened. They wanted to know all about combat and life in the infantry so I gave them a few details.

"That must be exciting," one of them said as we parted. "All we ever do is play music for visiting entertainers." It felt good to be considered something special but I was not anxious to get back to my job of rifleman. If only I had learned to play a musical instrument. . . .

Usually, in the afternoons, a sergeant would read the war news to us and we would then have discussions about world events. In late July, Admiral Halsey and the Third Fleet were bombarding the main islands of Japan with their big guns and airplanes while B-29 Superforts were making daily bombing runs from their bases in the Mariannas.

It was also during this time period, July 16 to August 2 that the Big Three leaders of the Allies, Truman, Churchill and Stalin, met at Potsdam, a suburb of Berlin. Their parley, officially known as the Berlin Conference,[8] was held primarily to settle the issues of the European phase of World War II. Churchill had to leave midway through the meeting as he lost the general election on July 26 and was replaced by the victorious Clement Attlee. In our discussions, we thought that was a poor way to treat a great man who had taken the helm during Britain's darkest hour and had turned things around and led her to victory. But the war was over in Europe and the British electorate was looking for someone to improve their living conditions. The Labor party was thought to have the common man's welfare more at heart.

That same day, Truman released, with the approval of Churchill, Stalin and Chiang Kai Chek, a declaration to the Japanese that they surrender unconditionally or face "prompt and utter destruction" by Allied forces ready "to strike the final blow." It also stated that the Japanese would be limited to their home islands and stripped of the

48. CHURCHILL, TRUMAN AND STALIN at the opening ceremonies of the Potsdam Conference on July 17, 1945. U.S. Army
photo.

power to make war but would not be "enslaved as a race nor destroyed as a nation." Certain parts of Japan though, would be occupied for an indefinite period of time.

The official Japanese radio responded on July 28 with the answer
that Japan "would talk peace only when the whole of East Asia was
free from Anglo-American exploitation." On July 29, Premier Kantaro

Suzuki said that ". . . so far as the Imperial Government of Japan is concerned, it would take no notice of the Allied ultimatum." It should also be noted that the news that day quoted the Australian Prime Minister, Herbert V. Evatt, as saying that the terms of the Allied peace offering were "too lenient." He also complained that Australia had not been consulted on the declaration.

When the Berlin Conference ended on August 2, the final communique broadly outlined Germany's future but there was no mention of Russia and the Pacific War. At the lst Convalescent Hospital we were expecting the war to last another year or two.

On July 30, the cruiser *Indianapolis* was torpedoed in the Philippine Sea as it sailed for Leyte. It went down with the loss of 880 men out of a crew of 1,196. We learned later that the *Indianapolis* had delivered the enriched uranium for the Hiroshima bomb. Had the Japanese been able to sink it before it got to Saipan, instead of afterwards, history might have been a lot different.

On August 6 came the news that a new bomb, said to have the destructive force of 20,000 tons of TNT, was dropped on the Japanese city of Hiroshima.[9] I wasn't too impressed at first because I had heard about bigger and more powerful bombs all through the war. "Block Busters" they called them. They had grown from about 250 pounds early in the war to many tons. What difference did it make anyway? In

The Little Boy.
(*Atomic Energy Commission*)

The *Enola Gay* home from bombing Hiroshima.   (*U.S. Air Force*)

49. THE FIRST ATOMIC BOMB and the airplane that delivered it. Atomic Energy Commission and U.S. Air Force photos.

the infantry we knew that wars were won by foot soldiers, not by bigger or more powerful bombs. The enemy always had to be rooted out of his caves and hiding places after the bombing was over.

However, as the news developed about this new bomb and we learned that it involved new technology, one of the soldiers in our discussion group got quite excited about it. He had spent three years studying science at Purdue University before getting drafted and had an extensive knowledge of physics and chemistry. He immediately recognized the immense potential of this new procedure and talked about splitting atoms—a process called nuclear fission—to yield energy far greater than that released by chemical reaction. According to him, the process could theoretically become self-sustaining through the freeing of neutrons in the nucleus of the atom—a so-called chain reaction. If done rapidly, as in a bomb, it could be very destructive. If controlled, it could be a very cheap source of energy, ushering in a new era for mankind.

As I listened to him talk, I struggled to remember what old Doc Henderson had tried to teach us in Chemistry 101 back at the University of Detroit. I remembered his models of atomic structure—little colored balls held together with lollipop sticks similar to Tinker Toys—and how he rearranged them to change from one element or molecule to another. I didn't remember anything about bombs or electrical energy.

After our discussion group broke up, the Purdue soldier and I went over to the hospital library and found some books which told about the structure of matter and the atomic theories. The soldier from Purdue was especially excited about splitting atoms of lead to change it to gold—the alchemist's dream of old. "The new technology could also lead to the creation of new substances," he said.

My friend with all the atomic knowledge had an ugly red lump on his shinbone (tibia). When I first saw it, I thought it was jungle rot or even worse—cancer. He said it was a bone infection called osteomyelitis and that the doctors were treating it with penicillin. He would laugh nervously and remark that he hoped the treatment would work before the infection got so bad that he had to have his leg amputated. He had been in the hospital for a long time and was getting discouraged.

The man should have been sent back to the United States for treatment, but was another victim of the Army policy of having the medical people patch up every combat soldier they could in order to get them ready for the big invasion of Japan which would finally bring the war to an end. I have often wondered what eventually happened

50. THE MUSHROOM CLOUD over Hiroshima. It changed our lives completely. U.S. Air Force photo.

to him. Like so many others that I met in the Army, when I left the lst Convalescent Hospital our paths never crossed again.

On August 8, the big news was that Russia had declared war on Japan and invaded Manchuria. Ever since Pearl Harbor, American and British leaders had considered the entry of Russia into the Pacific War an important goal. The Soviets had stalled the Allies, making it clear that their battle with Germany was all they could handle. They called this "The Great Patriotic War" and it was a tremendous undertaking. A lot of it was fought on their homeland and they suffered some twenty million fatalities. Finally, at Yalta, Stalin made a promise to enter the Pacific War three months after the victory in Europe. He needed this time to move his armies some 7,000 miles from Central Europe to the Far East. On August 8, three months to the day after V-E Day, he kept his promise.

I Too, Thank God for the Atom Bomb!

At Yalta, the British and Americans had secretly agreed to reward Stalin if he joined them in their Pacific struggle. These incentives included special rights in Manchuria, return to Russia of the southern half of Sakhalin Island, which they had ceded to Japan after their 1904—05 War, and the annexation by Russia of the Kurile Islands. Actually, with the dropping of the atomic bomb, the participation of the Soviets was unnecessary. As subsequent history proved, it put them in a good position to help communize China and the northern part of Korea.

That day, at our discussion group meeting, we were treated to a lengthy talk by one of our cadre who was quite enthusiastic about our Russian Allies. He might have been a Communist Party member. At any rate, he described in detail the Russian system of government, but when he got to equating the Supreme Soviet, the Russian two-house legislature, to our own House and Senate, it was too much for one soldier. He got into a shouting match with the sergeant saying that Hitler had his *Reichstag* and that the Japanese *Diet* was a legislative body that rubber-stamped whatever the ruling militarists wanted, but that didn't make them representative democracies. Most of us considered Communist Russia a totalitarian state like Nazi Germany and an unreliable ally. While their help in beating Japan was a welcome surprise, they had to be watched very closely.

On August 9, a B-29 dropped the second atomic bomb on Nagasaki. It was a more powerful bomb than that used on Hiroshima, but actually killed fewer people. It used plutonium as the fissionable material rather than the enriched uranium that was used in the first bomb. It also had a different triggering method called implosion instead of the gun assembly method. We were being flooded with technical news. A strange new highly sophisticated world was opening up. If two whole Japanese cities were demolished by two bombs in three days, how long could even the fanatical militarists hold out?

We didn't know at the time that the Americans had made only three bombs and that the first one had been exploded at Alamagordo on July 16. The plan was to give the Japanese a one-two punch and knock them out of the war with those two as soon as possible. It would have taken several weeks before we could have assembled some more, taken them to Saipan and then used them.

August 10 brought the marvelous news that Japan had offered to surrender and that the terms of the offer were being studied by the Allies. The Navy and the Air Force announced the withholding of attacks on Japan due to the peace negotiations. When we heard this we started getting excited. Could it actually be possible that the war was

51. THE SECOND ATOMIC
BOMB, known as the Fat Man,
and the destruction at
Nagasaki. Atomic Energy
Commission and
U.S. Army photos.

coming to an end? After all the years of fighting and the expectation
of more to come, it seemed just too good to be true.

The Japanese surrender offer hinged on keeping Emperor Hirohito as the sovereign ruler, but the Allies had consistently demanded
unconditional surrender. As a compromise, the Americans proposed
keeping the Emperor on his throne but subject to the Supreme Commander of the Allied Powers. General MacArthur was soon appointed
to this post. Another sticking point was that the armed forces of the
Allied Powers would remain in Japan until the purposes set forth in
the Potsdam Declaration were achieved.

Then followed three days of suspense while the Japanese leaders argued among themselves. The hard core militarists were for continuing the war with the idea of making it as costly as possible for the Allies to get better peace terms. The peace advocates were concerned about what would happen to the Emperor because one of the provisions of the Allies' reply was that the ultimate form of government was to be established by the freely expressed will of the Japanese people.

August 12 came and went with no progress. The Allies had received no answer from Tokyo to their latest surrender message. Japanese radio broadcasts didn't mention any peace negotiations but stressed unity and loyalty to the Emperor. The Russians continued their attacks, advancing many miles in Manchuria and invading Korea.

The 13th of August brought still no answer from Tokyo so the Third Fleet resumed its attacks, hitting Tokyo with aerial bombing at dawn. The Russians established two beachheads on Sakhalin Island. It was a big letdown for those of us who had hoped for the end of the war.

On the 14th, though, the astounding happened. The news was that Japan had accepted the surrender terms and the Emperor would broadcast a message to his countrymen telling them of his decision and ordering the military to lay down its arms. It was unbelievable! After carrying on a vicious war for over eight years, fighting battles to the bitter end, individually accepting death rather than surrender, all of a sudden the whole country just gave up. Maybe they were ready for it but certainly the atom bombs gave them the needed excuse to surrender or at least a push to make them capitulate.

That night San Pedro harbor was a scene of gigantic celebration. Fireworks and flares were set off, searchlights and tracer bullets swept the skies, big naval guns exploded as the whole Navy and merchant fleet erupted in spontaneous joy. On shore, we sat and watched the spectacle or walked around talking and laughing. We didn't have anything alcoholic to drink so we couldn't get drunk. But we didn't need to, we were already high on peace and deliverance.

In the half-century that has elapsed since, much has been written and said about the morality of using so destructive a weapon as the atomic bomb on a mostly civilian target. It was recognized, right from the start, as being a radically different tool of war. On August 9, as news of the Nagasaki bomb was being published, Japanese radio was protesting the use of the bomb on Hiroshima as an "inhuman weapon." Bishop G. Bromley Oxnam and John Foster Dulles, prominent Protestant leaders, were urging the temporary suspension of the

A-bomb's use on Japan to give the Japanese time to react to the new situation. In London, the *Catholic Herald* criticized the use of the bomb on Japan as an "illegitimate weapon of war" and an "indiscriminate massacre of civilians." The other side was quickly heard from. On August 10 the Inter-American Juridical Commission, meeting in Rio De Janeiro, declared the atom bomb to be a "lawful weapon."[10]

Some of the later arguments get nasty. In an essay entitled "Thank God for the Atom Bomb,"[11] Paul Fussell, who was a 21-year-old infantry lieutenant on his way to the Pacific War at the time, after fighting and being wounded in Europe, takes on critics of its use. One of them is the economist, John Kenneth Galbraith, who was persuaded that the Japanese would have surrendered anyway, even without an invasion. "The A-bombs meant a difference, at most, of two or three weeks," he wrote. Fussell replies that, with Allied casualties running at the rate of 7,000 per week, three weeks would have added 21,000 to the total. He also notes that between the dropping of the Nagasaki bomb and the actual surrender, eight captured American fliers were executed,[12] the 51st United States submarine, *Bonefish*, was sunk with all hands drowned, the destroyer *Callaghan* went down, and the destroyer escort *Underhill* was lost. Then he writes: "That's a bit of what happened in six days of the two or three weeks posited by Galbraith. What did he do in the war? He worked in the Office of Price Administration in Washington. I don't demand that he experience having his ass shot off. I merely note that he didn't."[13]

Even the great Winston Churchill said that people who preferred invasion to A-bombing seemed to have "no intention of proceeding to the Japanese front themselves."[14] He also called the atom bomb "a miracle of deliverance" because it saved thousands of British and Australians, who were not only planning to help invade Honshu in March of 1946, but also had mounted a huge invasion of Malaya and an assault on Singapore. This operation, code named "Zipper" was actually underway at the time of the Japanese surrender. If the war had not ended as it did, the British would have been massacred because the beaches selected were poorly chosen and the landing craft would have foundered, enabling the strong Japanese defenders to annihilate the 256,000 invaders. The atomic bombs came too late for the invasion to be called off—but Emperor Hirohito's command to lay down their arms came in time to prevent the slaughter on the beaches. The Allies landed to surrendering Japanese.

The fact that the A-bomb killed a lot of people in a short time with one great explosion doesn't seem to me to make it any more immoral than lesser bombs. The dead are dead whether they are killed one at a time with rifles or in large numbers simultaneously. A hundred thousand Filipino civilians were killed in the month-long battle for Manila,[15] many of them raped and savagely beaten by Japanese soldiers. Hardly a word is said or written about them as compared to all the hand-wringing statements about the hundred thousand or more who perished at Hiroshima.

I think the Japanese brought it on themselves. Without the sneak attack on Pearl Harbor, the Bataan death march, the rape of Manila, the execution of downed fliers, and all the other atrocities, there would have been no Hiroshima bombing to be sorry for. At the time, most Americans applauded the bombing because it shortened the war. Certainly we, the soldiers and sailors who would have had to invade Japan at a high personal cost, gave a collective sigh of relief. In the long run, more lives were saved, both American and Japanese, military and civilian, than were lost by its use. In addition, demonstrating the true horror of the new technology on actual cities led to its non-use in subsequent hostilities like the Korean and Vietnam wars and the Cuban missile crisis. A demonstration test on an uninhabited Japanese island, as some of its critics have suggested, would not have been anywhere near as effective.

HISTORICAL ADDENDUM

By the middle of 1945, America's top military leaders were in almost unanimous agreement that an invasion of Japan was necessary to end the conflict. Most believed that a naval blockade and heavy aerial bombing could not, by themselves, get the Japanese to surrender *unconditionally* and in the *twelve months* following the defeat of Germany. This artificial time table was determined because our leaders thought that the American public would not support a longer war.[16]

On May 25, 1945 the Joint Chiefs of Staff issued a secret directive to the Pacific commanders, MacArthur and Nimitz, and to Army Air Force Commander Hap Arnold, to proceed with the invasion plans. The first assault would be right after the typhoon season ended later that year. President Truman approved the detailed plans on July 24.

Operation DOWNFALL was its code name. It called for two massive penetrations into the heart of the Japanese Empire with the goal of forcing the Japanese to surrender. In the first, code-named Operation OLYMPIC, 14 American Army and Marine divisions would land on the southernmost Japanese Island of Kyushu on the morning of November 1. The second invasion, code-named Operation CORONET,

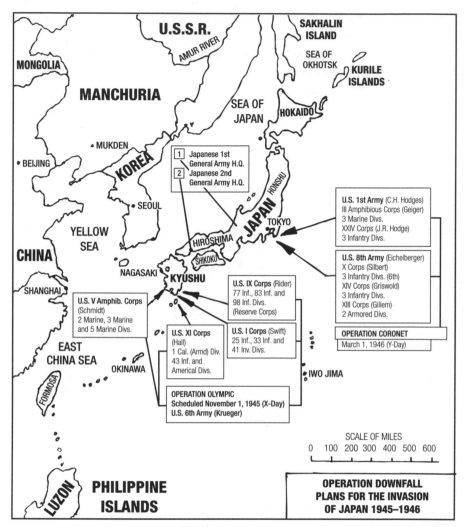

12. OPERATION DOWNFALL. The invasion of Japan was to be in two stages. The 6th Infantry Division was in reserve for Operation Olympic and slated to land near Tokyo with the Eighth Army on March 1, 1946, in the second phase known as Operation Coronet. Map by the author.

would take place on March 1, 1946. There some 28 divisions would be hurled against at least a million Japanese defenders on the Tokyo plain of the main island of Honshu. My own 6th Infantry was to be ready by November 20 as a reserve division for OLYMPIC. If not needed, it was to land on the beach at the head of Sagami Bay and take part in a drive to capture the naval base at Yokosuka in CORO-NET.

Operation DOWNFALL was to have been a mostly American operation with some British help. It called for using the entire Marine Corps, the entire Pacific Navy assisted by the British Pacific Fleet, and most of the Air Force including many units deployed from Europe. All the combat divisions that fought the Pacific War plus many from Europe and in training in the U.S. would also be used. A total of four and a half million men, about 40 percent of all servicemen in uniform in 1945, would be directly involved in the two amphibious landings. Tactical use of the new atomic bomb and possible use of gas warfare against cave defenses were also in the plans.

After the war ended in Europe, a huge transfer of men and materials to the Pacific was begun to get ready for the invasions. By the first week in August, the Marines were making practice landings on the Mariannas Islands, the Air Force was unloading airplanes from Europe, and the islands of Luzon and Okinawa, main jumping-off bases for the invasions, were bustling with men, ships and huge stores of materials and equipment.

The Japanese did not sit idly and wait for the next Allied move. They devised *Ketsu-Go* (Decisive Operation), a plan to defend their sacred homeland. "Causing casualties" was their sole strategic aim. Far from being discouraged by the American victory at Okinawa, they were inspired by the large number of casualties they had inflicted there and were changing their tactics to make the Americans bleed even more. They would try to stop the invasion by hitting the Allied fleet at sea with suicidal boats and airplanes, not let them land unopposed as they had done on Okinawa.

Contrary to American intelligence, the Japanese still had a large number of airplanes. They were hidden in caves and other hiding places and were being saved for the expected invasion. At least half of the 10,500 airplanes were being outfitted for kamikaze missions. Instead of hitting capital ships, as they did at Okinawa, the Japanese were planning on using them primarily against troopships which were lightly armed but heavily loaded with American soldiers.

Japan's top military leaders were able to accurately deduce not only when, but where the United States would land its first invasion forces. They planned their ground defenses accordingly. Much of Kyushu was mountainous, rugged country, the same sort of excellent defensive terrain the Japanese had turned to such good advantage on Luzon and Okinawa. Fifteen divisions and five independent brigades as well as ten battalions of Naval Detachments were deployed there, almost equal to the entire Allied invasion force. American occupation troops counted 216,627 Japanese soldiers in southern Kyushu when they took their surrender in the fall of 1945. Troops planned for the defense of the main island of Honshu were even more numerous.

All along the invasion beaches, the American G.I.s would face mines, coastal batteries, anti-landing obstacles and a network of fortified pillboxes, bunkers and underground fortresses. As the surviving Americans waded ashore, they would face intense artillery and mortar fire as they worked their way through concrete rubble and barbed-wire entanglements arranged to funnel them into the muzzles of Japanese guns. On the beaches would be more mines, booby traps, and suicide units concealed in spider holes.

Beyond the beaches were large artillery pieces set to bring down a carpet of fire from high ground on the invaders. Further back in the mountains were underground networks of caves, bunkers, command posts and hospitals all connected by miles of tunnels with many entrances and exits. Their hope was that the horrific loss of life expended to overcome these defenses would discourage the Americans. They would then accept a peace treaty favorable to Japan, withdraw and go home.

Japanese soldiers defending the home islands would be the home army. Some were elite soldiers, heavily imbued in the warrior *Bushido* code and would fight even more fanatically to defend their homeland than they did in the foreign lands they had overrun. They also were familiar with this terrain, had large stockpiles of arms and ammunition, were backed up by a friendly population and had developed an effective system of transportation and supply which was still functioning despite heavy Allied bombing.

By the end of July, Japan was arming its civilian population, fortifying caves and building underground defenses. All the nation's schools were ordered closed and the children mobilized for military use. Some were trained to be "Sherman Carpets," where they would have explosives attached to their bodies and would roll under American tanks or other vehicles and blow them up. Japanese military officers drew up ambitious plans to recruit up to a million and a half civilians for similar suicidal missions and up to 30 million as a partisan force.

Thus, the Americans had elaborate plans to invade Japan and the men, materials and equipment to do it. The Japanese had plans too, and were ready, willing, even eager to defend themselves against invasion. Two great powers on the verge of Armageddon. The slaughter would have been enormous. Every foot of Japanese soil taken would have been paid for by many Japanese and American lives lost. It could have been the biggest bloodbath in the history of mankind. Admiral William Leahy estimated that there would be 268,000 Americans killed or wounded on Kyushu alone. Others estimated Allied casualties from the entire operation to total over one million by the fall of 1946.[17] Japanese lives lost would have been equally large. Even then, they may not have surrendered unconditionally and the war could have dragged on for many more years.

Fortunately for all of us, Operation DOWNFALL did not take place. Out of the blue came the atomic bombs and the Japanese surrender. The elaborate plans were shelved and can only be found now in the dusty files of the National Archives or in similar places in Japan. It's great material for historical conjecture and argument.

The atomic bomb definitely was a miraculous deliverance for this nineteen-year-old rifleman mending from a wound in a hospital 10,000 miles from home. I certainly would have been on the beaches south of Tokyo the following spring had Operation CORONET been required. The nuclear destruction of Hiroshima and the sudden ending of the war will always be permanently linked in my mind. Its ultimate personal meaning was that I would live, I would go home, resume my college studies, become an engineer, get married, and have children. Hopefully, I would only die of natural causes after a long and useful life, long enough to see my grandchildren and maybe great-grandchildren, as life was meant to be.

However, the Army wasn't done with me yet. I had served less than half my time when the war ended.

TWELVE

The Japanese Surrender

It is in fact the supreme merit of genuine history to show us diversity. By narrating events, naming names, and addressing motives, purposes, and results, history teaches us what life beyond our immediate experience is like.

—Jacques Barzun and Henry F. Graff[1]

With the war officially over, rumors spread like wildfire among the patients at the 1st Convalescent Hospital. "They are going to close this place and send us all home on a hospital ship" was the most often heard and my favorite. To be home-bound was a pleasant thought, resurrecting all the hopes I had in June and early July. Maybe I would make it home for the fall semester at the University of Detroit.

When I reported to the dispensary for my first routine examination after VJ Day, the doctor asked me how I was getting along: "Any problems with this leg?"

"Yes, sir," I answered. "It swells up when I do any exercise."

"How's that?"

"This depression where the bullet came out swells up and becomes a bump." I pointed to a round hole about an inch and a half in diameter.

"Hmm. Tell you what. Take a hike around the compound and report back to me when the swelling is at a maximum."

I did as I was told, walking as fast as I could and giving the leg a strenuous workout. When I returned, hot and winded, the red depressed area had changed into a red mound.

"Hmm, hmm," said the doctor, assuming the inscrutable look that

270

medical practitioners use when they are called upon to diagnose. "We are going to have to do something about that. Pack your gear and report to the transportation office. I am sending you back to the General Hospital."

This was great news. I wanted to ask him what was wrong with my leg but he had already moved on to another patient. I went back to my tent and packed my gear in my duffel bag. My tentmates were playing miniature golf so I stopped and said goodbye. They wished me well and immediately resumed their game as men do to hide their emotions. I knew the feeling. When someone else got lucky and had their lives suddenly changed for the better by an omnipotent Army, I had felt the same pangs of envy. This time I was the lucky one. I had arrived at the lst Convalescent Hospital on crutches, depressed and bleeding, not looking forward to a return to duty and an endless war. Now, in a little over a month, the war was over, my wound had healed and I was walking again. The swelling didn't hurt but I expected it would get me on a plane or boat going home.

The 133rd General Hospital seemed different the second time around. Maybe it was because I was in a different ward. A lot of personnel had changed, although I recognized some of the nurses. There weren't as many patients and the sense of urgency that had been evident during my first stay there in late June and early July was missing. In fact the ward I was in had many empty beds. Across the aisle from me, the bed was occupied by a Philippine Scout named Federico. He was frail, thin and brown-skinned and spoke in a low soft voice about his 30 years in the Army. I never did find out why he was in the hospital. I got the impression that the Army had parked him there until it could figure out what to do with him next.

A couple of empty beds away from me was a soldier who had a lot of shrapnel in his legs. He had been returned to duty but had found his way back to the hospital when the tiny pieces of metal began working their way to the surface. He had hundreds of them and the doctors were going to take some of the bigger pieces out surgically. There weren't any fresh battle casualties as there had been in June and July. The war was indeed over.

In the bed next to me was a young soldier who was being treated for intestinal worms. He had been there several weeks while the doctors tried different medications trying to rid his system of these parasites. This led to a lot of sickening bull sessions on worms as other patients told stories, real or fancied, about various kinds of worms that they had seen or heard about.

The soldier with the shrapnel in his legs had been a meat cutter in civilian life and told about how in cutting meat he sometimes would hit a hard spot in the flesh. This was caused by a calcium encrusted cyst that contained the larvae of the trichina worm. Anyone who ate meat that was not thoroughly cooked could be infected as that was nature's way of transmitting the worm from one host to another. He also told of German prisoners of war complaining about getting trichinosis in America because of the lower standards in the American meat industry. Apparently trichinosis was rare in the Third Reich.

Other soldiers had horrible tales of beef worms and tape worms that attached themselves to the wall of people's intestines and grew over 20 feet in length while the hosts practically starved to death no matter how much they ate. They said that you got them from eating meat or fish. This got everyone to examining their food very carefully when our meals were brought around.

Still another soldier brought out pictures he had picked up in New Guinea that showed natives suffering from filariasis. This parasitical disease is caused by tiny, thread-like worms that live in lymphatic tissue. The worms block the lymph channels, resulting in fluid build-up and tremendous enlargement of parts of the body, especially the lower extremities. The condition is known as elephantiasis. Some of his pictures showed victims with one huge arm or leg but the worst was an unfortunate man who had a huge penis and testicles about the size of a basketball! Apparently someone had made a business of selling copies of these photographs as I saw the same pictures several times in later years in various places.

All that talk of worms made me nervous because I had passed some worms in my stool after living in the filth and slime of the *Shimbu* Line back in April. That had been a temporary condition apparently, as I had been checked for parasites when I first arrived at the 133rd General Hospital in June and found to be free of them. Still, I was glad to see the soldier with the worms discharged from the hospital about a week later.

My doctor turned out to be a surgeon; the Marine surgeon apparently had been transferred. Captain John J. Feehan, M.D., had me repeat the exercise that I had done for the doctor at the Convalescent Hospital.

"You have what is called a muscular herniation," he said when I returned from walking around the hospital grounds with a large lump on my leg. "The tibialis anterior is affected."

"What does that mean?"

"Well, it is similar to a regular hernia. Your leg muscle fascia has been torn by the bullet and when you exercise, gravity pulls it down into the cavity where the flesh is missing. It is very similar to a rupture where the wall of the groin is weak or split and the intestines push into the scrotum."

I could understand that. The Army was always checking us for hernia by having a medic stick his finger up your scrotum on each side of your penis and having you cough.

"We will take care of it by surgery, opening up the area and suturing the ruptured muscle sacs."

I asked if this meant I would be going back to the States for the operation. Foolish question to ask a surgeon, especially someone who needed some work to do!

"Oh no. I will be doing the surgery. We will schedule it for Saturday at 8:30 A.M. You will be back on your feet in a short time."

That was a letdown. I would not be going back home; I would be returning to duty. Somehow, I wasn't really too surprised or disappointed. A few months more of Army life and then I would be home for sure. After all, I had been drafted for the duration of the war plus six months. The war was over. We were working on the six months, I thought.[2]

On the day of the surgery, August 18, I was wheeled into the operating room and climbed onto the operating table under my own power. A local anesthesia was injected into my leg so I was able to follow the procedure although I couldn't see much since I was lying flat on my back. The masked surgeon sat on a stool next to the operating table. He rested his arms on the table as he did the delicate work. There wasn't much pain. I could feel warm blood running around my leg after he made the incision and tugging and pulling as he made the delicate sutures repairing the torn muscles. Not much else. The whole procedure lasted about an hour.

The next day when the bandage was removed, I could see that the ugly red hole had been replaced by a neat line where the skin had been pulled together and held with black silk stitches. I counted them. There were six. These were the first stitches that I had ever had.

"There's a lot more," the doctor said. "I probably used another twenty or so internally. We will take them out in about a week or ten days."

"How do you take out the internal stitches?" I asked, anticipating another operation. "We don't take them out, only the silk stitches," he assured me. "The others will dissolve in time. Stay off that leg for at least a week or so: we don't want those stitches to pop until they have done their job."

52. THE JAPANESE SURRENDER aboard the battleship *Missouri* on September 2, 1945. The long war is officially over. U.S. Army photo.

I spent the next ten days in bed reading and getting caught up on the news. There was plenty of it. By late in August it had been two weeks since the Japanese had given up. Their capitulation had been so sudden and unexpected that it had taken a couple of weeks to organize the surrender ceremonies. The most prominent of these took place on the battleship *Missouri* in Tokyo Bay on September 2, with Supreme Commander MacArthur conducting the formal ceremonies ending the hostilities that began at Pearl Harbor. After the signing ceremonies, MacArthur went ashore and took over the job of ruling the Japanese. The long war was officially over as of this date.

The American llth Airborne Division parachuted into Atsugi Airport near Tokyo and the 4th Marine Division made an amphibious landing at Yokosuku, and no one knew for sure what to expect. But the Japanese surprised everyone by surrendering in vast numbers—to the Americans in Japan; to the Russians in Manchuria; to the British in Hong Kong, Maylaya and Singapore; to the Chinese at Nanking and Shanghai; and to the Australians in New Guinea and the Solomon Islands. Except for a few isolated incidents, the surrenders

53. GENERAL TOMOYUKI YAMASHITA, Commander of the Japanese Army in the Philippines, as he lead his men out of the mountains of Northern Luzon near Kiangan on Sept. 2, 1945. The official surrender ceremony was held the next day at Baguio. U.S. Army photo.

all went peacefully. There wasn't much fight left in the enemy. When their emperor said the war was over and to surrender, most of them did as they were told.

In the Philippines, General Yamashita met representatives of the

32nd Division on a rugged mountain trail three miles from Kiangan. After hiking into Kiangan, his party of twelve, including four generals and several admirals, were taken by air to Baguio, the summer capital. There formal ceremonies were delayed to allow for the arrival of Lieutenant General Jonathan Wainwright and British Lieutenant General Arthur E. Percival. Both men had known the agony of defeat, Wainwright at the fall of Corregidor in May of 1942 and Percival at the hands of Yamashita when he surrendered Singapore earlier in the same year. Wainwright had spent the rest of the war in a prison camp in Manchuria until rescued on August 19, 1945. Both men had taken part in the ceremonies on the battleship *Missouri* at Tokyo and then flown to Baguio via Manila.

The Philippine ceremony began in a brilliantly lighted room a few seconds after noon on September 3. General Yamashita signed a document similar to that which the Japanese surrender envoys signed before General MacArthur.

"They have surrendered," Wainwright remarked. "They are the last. The war in the Philippines is now over."[3] Yamashita, in a faded and patched uniform, surrendered his 700 year old ancestral sword and was quoted as saying he would not commit *hari-kiri*. The G.I.s gave him a new nickname, "The Gopher of Luzon." He was arrested immediately after the ceremonies and subsequently charged with the responsibility for the atrocities committed by some of the men under his command. Wainwright was promoted to four-star general, awarded the Congressional Medal of Honor, addressed a joint session of Congress, and was given a hero's ticker-tape parade in New York City.

Lieutenant General Shizuo Yokoyama, the commander of the forces defending the *Shimbu* Line surrendered to the 38th Division on September 10. There were still several thousand Japanese troops in the remote Sierra Madre mountains and it was expected to take several days to round them up.[4]

On the neighboring island of Cebu, almost 10,000 officers and men, including female nurses, surrendered to the Americal Division. They were all neatly dressed and armed with rifles, mortars, grenades and machine guns.[5] It was surprising how many Japanese were still left in the Philippines when the war ended. American intelligence had consistently underestimated the strength of the enemy.

However, they all didn't surrender right away. Some hid out for years and only came out of the jungle very reluctantly. A few diehards were still being found as long as 25 years afterwards.

Back in America, people were trying to make up for four years of

54 and 55. SURRENDERING JAPAN-
ESE ON THE ISLAND OF CEBU, August 28, 1945. On the left, soldiers at
ease awaiting the formal ceremonies. at
the right, young female medical personnel. Some 10,000 neatly dressed and
well armed enemy soldiers were still on the island after months of fighting.
From: Robert C. McGiffert, "Surrender on Cebu," *American Legion Magazine*,
Sept. 1981. Used with permission of the author.

deprivation.[6] They celebrated the end of gas rationing and the lifting
of the 35 miles per hour speed limit. The *New York Times* reported
that the weather was good, gas plentiful, and people enjoying the
Labor Day holiday by leaving the city in record numbers. Some food
items were no longer rationed; whipping cream, for instance, was
taken off the restricted list. On September 6, President Truman gave
Congress a program for the peacetime conversion of the wartime

economy. I was anxious to get back to civilian life and enjoy some of those pleasures.

In the meantime, plans for the further occupation of Japan were announced by MacArthur's headquarters on September 10. Last on the list was the 6th Infantry Division. My division was scheduled to occupy the Osaka-Kyoto-Nagoya area starting October 23.[7] The meat cutter soldier said that it would be good duty in Kyoto because the city had been spared the heavy bombing that the other major Japanese cities had suffered. The reason for this was that it had been the center of Japanese culture and government for over a thousand years, up until Tokyo became the capital in the nineteenth century. Kyoto contained many magnificent temples, gardens and ancient shrines and was considered to be sacred by many of the Japanese.

Plans were announced to cut the strength of the Army from 8,050,000 men to 2,500,000 by July of 1946. This would be done by stepping up discharges from 250,000 a month in September to a peak of 672,000 in January. Six new separation centers, bringing the total to twenty-six, would be opened to handle these men returning to civilian life.[8] The drafting of 18 to 25-year-old men would continue, however, until it was clear that the Army got enough volunteers to sustain its planned strength level.

A new date, September 2, had been set for calculating the points necessary for discharge. "Eighty" was the new magic number to get out in September but the score would be lowered in stages over the next few months. I now had 39 points based on my service, battle stars and medals, so I hoped to get out in time to make the spring semester at college.

On September 17, I was finally discharged from the hospital, 89 days after I was wounded. A truck took me to a replacement depot. It wasn't too far from the hospital because I visited the hospital several times while I was awaiting my travel orders. This camp was another compound of Army tents and corrugated sheet metal buildings. It may even have been the same replacement depot that I was in when I arrived on Leyte in March but I did not recognize it as such.

All these Army camps had a sameness about them. I was housed in a tent with other soldiers awaiting travel orders to their outfits. The Army calls them "casuals" which I always thought was a peculiar label since casual means informal and relaxed. We were anything but relaxed and informal. We were uptight and anxious to get moving and back to our regular outfits.

The hospital clerk had given me my personnel records when I was discharged. They were in a large brown envelope. I was instructed to take these with me and give them to the company clerk when I had rejoined my unit. I opened the envelope after I had gotten settled in and was looking at the papers. One of my new tentmates noticed them and asked to see them.

"You've got your complete records here," he said. "Why, you could take off with these and the Army wouldn't even know you existed! I'm surprised that they gave you them." Apparently all the other casuals only had travel orders. It was a tempting idea but not too practical. I would not have known where to start to go home on my own.

I had the rude shock of returning to regular Army duty when I was assigned to K.P. in the enlisted men's mess. It started the next morning about 5:00 when I was awakened by a surly sergeant telling me to get a move on to the kitchen where I spent a long hot day peeling innumerable potatoes and scrubbing unending numbers of greasy aluminum pots and pans. My nice hospital vacation, like the war, was officially over!

The next day I was assigned to work in the officer's mess hall. This was better. There were considerably fewer officers than there were enlisted men so there was a lot less work to do. Also the food was superior. Where the enlisted men's mess tended to serve large batches of stews and casseroles, the officers ate steaks and chops and the food was prepared in smaller quantities. It was still served cafeteria style and I was surprised to see some white civilians, men, women and children, coming through the chow line as I handed out the pork chops. When I asked about them later on, the mess sergeant told me that they had been prisoners of war and were, like the rest of the casuals, waiting for transportation to somewhere, probably home. Most of them were missionaries or business people who had been captured by the Japanese when they overran the Philippines early in the war.

It must have been quite a job for the Army to sort out all these people and arrange transportation to get them back where they belonged. In my case, my regiment had been in action near Kiangan when the war ended. They got the first news of the Japanese surrender on August 16. According to the official history, "Forward elements held their ground, taking no offensive action. On August 18, the entire regiment went into garrison training, with emphasis on discipline, ceremonies and interior guard duty. All training was directed toward future occupational duty."[9]

On August 30, the 63rd Infantry Regiment moved by motor truck from Bagabag to San Fernando, La Union on the west coast of Luzon. This was a port and capital city of mountainous La Union province in northwest Luzon. A staging area was set up along the beach, south of the town of some 24,000 people, to prepare for movement to Japan. San Fernando was a good 500 miles as the crow flies from where I was on Leyte and I had a long wait for a boat to take me to Luzon. No airplane rides this time. They were too busy ferrying soldiers and supplies to the occupation areas of Japan.

When I finally got my orders and rode by truck to the harbor at Tacloban, the boat turned out to be an LCI (landing craft infantry). This is a rather small ship running about 160 feet from bow to stern and was designed to carry 200 infantry soldiers in amphibious operations. There were two catwalks, one on each side of the bow of the ship so it could be driven into a beach, the catwalks lowered and a company of soldiers hurriedly emptied out on the beach down the catwalks.

We entered the ship, since it was docked, via a gangplank onto the lower deck. There were about 30 of us passengers berthed in the bow of the ship where there were bunks along both bulkheads. The rest of the furnishings were spare—a toilet and some ship's equipment which we could sit on. Since it was rather narrow and confining there we spent most of the voyage on the upper deck at the bow. The weather was warm and sunny and the seas calm.

Our route took us northwest through the narrow straits between the islands of Leyte and Samar, across the Samar Sea, past Masbate Island and into the Sibuayan Sea. We left the busy harbor in the early afternoon so we had a good view of the islands, watching a procession of palm trees, thatched huts, villages, beaches and green hills pass by on both sides. We were close enough to shore to wave back at the people as they waved to us. For supper, cases of C-rations were opened up and we sat around the decks eating and watching the scenery go by. No cafeteria or dining hall on this boat, at least not for the soldier passengers. It was enjoyable traveling even though the amenities were primitive.

When we awoke the next morning, our ship was working its way through the Verde Island passage between Mindoro and Luzon and by noon we had turned north and made our way to the opening of Manila Bay. We entered through the South Passage between Corregidor Island and the Luzon mainland. It was late afternoon when we had crossed the bay to the city and put out anchor.

Manila harbor was full of ships of all sizes and shapes. When I first entered this harbor in April, most of the ships were sunk and resting on the bottom of the bay with their masts sticking forlornly out of the water. Now it was a very busy port with much of the war's

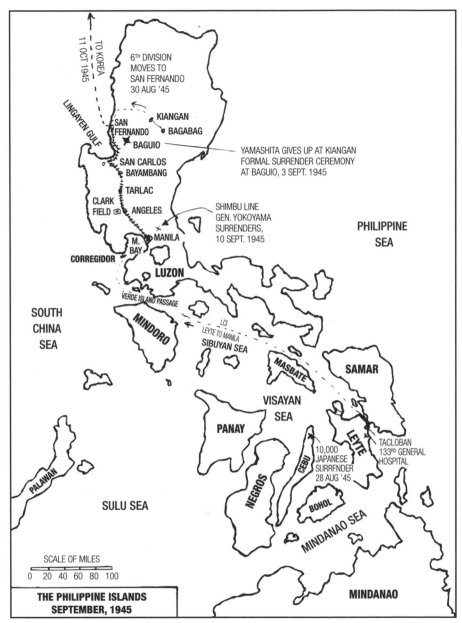

6TH DIVISION
MOVES TO
SAN FERNANDO
30 AUG '45

TO KOREA
11 OCT 1945

KIANGAN
SAN
FERNANDO
BAGABAG
BAGUIO
LINGAYEN GULF
SAN CARLOS
BAYAMBANG
TARLAC
CLARK
FIELD
ANGELES
M.
BAY
MANILA
CORREGIDOR

YAMASHITA GIVES UP AT KIANGAN
FORMAL SURRENDER CEREMONY
AT BAGUIO, 3 SEPT. 1945

SHIMBU LINE
GEN. YOKOYAMA
SURRENDERS,
10 SEPT. 1945

PHILIPPINE
SEA

LUZON

VERDE ISLAND PASSAGE

SOUTH
CHINA
SEA

MINDORO

LCI
LEYTE TO MANILA
SIBUYAN SEA

MASBATE

SAMAR

VISAYAN
SEA

PANAY

LEYTE

TACLOBAN
133RD GENERAL
HOSPITAL

CEBU

10,000
JAPANESE
SURRENDER
28 AUG '45

NEGROS

BOHOL

MINDANAO SEA

SULU SEA

PALAWAN

SCALE OF MILES
0 20 40 60 80 100

THE PHILIPPINE ISLANDS
SEPTEMBER, 1945

MINDANAO

13. THE PHILIPPINE ISLANDS, SEPTEMBER, 1945. It was a long trip back to
my outfit from the hospital on Leyte to the 6th Infantry Division on the beach at
San Fernando. Map by the author.

destruction cleaned up. Our little LCI anchored right next to a British aircraft carrier. It was huge, tall and painted white. I was fascinated by the rows of Hawker Hurricane fighter planes, the air of professionalism and the many messages that came over their loud speaker that always ended with: "This is the *King's*, Ny—vee!" It was like looking into a whole different world. I learned much later that this was the H.M.S. *Implacable*, Britain's largest wartime carrier. Launched in 1944, it displaced some 32,000 tons and had a speed of 32 knots. It saw service against Japan in 1945.[10]

Early the next morning our ship moved to shore and we were unloaded at a pier and told that transportation had been arranged. The LCI sailed away so another ship could use the wharf. We sat around and waited and waited. It was about 5:00 in the evening before some trucks arrived to take us to the replacement depot. I believe that was the only time that the Army ever left me stranded. We didn't even get lunch. Through some foul-up they hadn't been informed that we had arrived. We might still be there had not some M.P.s come along and asked us what we were doing on the dock, made some calls and arranged transportation for us.

At the replacement depot I met an older soldier from the lst Infantry. He had been hospitalized in Manila and was awaiting transportation to San Fernando. I told him that it had taken me almost three weeks to get this far. He said we would be going north by train and that we would not have to wait long. In the meantime, he said, "How about going into Manila to do some sightseeing and buy some souvenirs?" He wanted to get some jewelry for his wife as he was a high point veteran and expected to go home soon. It was good to have someone who knew his way around so I went with him.

The city appeared to have recovered somewhat from the war- inflicted damage I had seen in April. The shops were open, throngs of people were buying, and traffic was bumper to bumper. Many soldiers were wearing European Theater ribbons indicating that they had been moved here after the war ended in Europe. Manila was a staging area for the expected invasion of Japan and we passed many warehouses and fenced-off areas filled with materiel gathered to supply this expedition. I was impressed by the stacks and stacks of cases of beer in one complex. It looked like they had enough beer to supply the whole Army for years!

At one point I mentioned to my 6th Division compatriot that I was looking forward to our occupation of Kyoto, the ancient capital of Japan.

"We are not going there. Our orders have been changed," he said.

This was news to me. "But I read it in the newspaper."

"Now we are going to Korea."

"Korea! Where the hell's Korea?"

I had never heard of the place but I soon learned that it was an ancient and little-known oriental country on the Asiatic mainland. It was a peninsula south of Manchuria and east of China. Lying only 110 miles west of the Japanese island of Kyushu, it pointed "like a dagger" at Japan. Japan and Korea had fought many wars over the centuries and in 1910 the Japanese had formally annexed its smaller and weaker neighbor and changed its name to Chosen.

Korea had been in the news but I hadn't paid any attention. In August, when the Russians had joined the war, they had invaded Korea to cut off any Japanese Kwangtung Army forces retreating south from Manchuria. On August 27 MacArthur disclosed that the U.S. was to occupy Korea south of the 38th parallel while the Russians would occupy the country north of this latitude. The Japanese forces in Korea would surrender to the commanding general of the XXIV Corps, which would transfer from Okinawa to Korea.[11]

On September 8, amphibious forces led by the 7th Infantry Division poured ashore at Jinsen (Inchon) in full battle array. They were greeted enthusiastically by the natives as liberators. The Japanese had been ordered to stay 12 miles away from the port. Marching to the capital, Seoul, the Americans took over the Imperial Governor's Palace where a formal surrender ceremony took place. The Koreans cheered as the hated Japanese flag was taken down and the stars and stripes went up.

Lieutenant General John R. Hodge, commander of the Army's XXIV Corps, then made the mistake of announcing that the Japanese would be used to administer the country until suitable Korean leaders could be located and installed in office. The Koreans were furious at this announcement. They organized protest marches and even sent telegrams to President Truman. They had had 35 years of cruel Japanese domination and didn't want a day more. The State Department disclaimed any part of this military order of leaving the Japanese in office temporarily. MacArthur had to issue a proclamation telling the Koreans that their rights would be protected and that American troops were in southern Korea only to ". . . enforce the instrument of surrender."[12] The occupation of Korea had gotten off to a shaky start.

I enjoyed my stay in Manila, probably because I don't remember having to do K.P. or guard duty. There was a lot of gambling being done in the camp. It was like a huge outdoor casino. Nobody had to squat down to roll the dice on the ground like most crap games were played in the Army. Some enterprising soldiers had built crap tables out of packing case lumber, lining the surfaces with Army blankets to simulate the green felt. I had spent what little money I had on souvenirs so I was only able to watch. Some of the games went on all night and the stakes were high.

One night we went to the open air theater where a magic show was being held to entertain the troops. The magician was a mysterious oriental, the Great something or other, who was touted as being famous throughout the Pacific region for his marvelous powers. He looked Filipino to me but he was said to have performed in Singapore, Bangkok, Saigon and other Asiatic capitals.

Many standard magic tricks were performed. A woman was sawed in half. Another was put in a basket and the basket run through with swords from all directions, the magician yelling and stabbing with great force. Of course the victim emerged after the swords were removed, unhurt. He levitated a few people and made them disappear but the feat that impressed me the most was called The Indian Rope Trick. The magician came out dressed in only a loincloth and headdress like a Hindu swami would wear. He carried a short length of rope and a musical instrument.

Asking for volunteers from the soldier audience, he had them examine the rope and they pronounced it a regular piece of rope. The "swami" then coiled the rope like a snake on the floor of the stage, sat down cross-legged a short distance behind it and started playing the musical instrument. It was a horn that gave out a weird monophonic oriental sound that most Westerners found grating to the ears.

As he played, the end of the rope suddenly twitched like the head of a snake and then slowly began to uncoil and rise slowly upward. It undulated from side to side until it reached a height of about 12 feet. It then stiffened like a pole. One of his assistants, a pretty Filipino woman then proceeded to shinny up the rope as the swami continued playing his weird music.

When the rope climber got near the top, she did horizontal handstands and other exercises on the vertical rope which remained as rigid as a steel rod. After she came down and took her bows, the magician abruptly stopped the music and the rope immediately became limp and fell to the stage as the audience roared its approval. Afterwards, there were many explanations of some of his other tricks but nobody had an adequate explanation for the Indian Rope Trick.

The next day we were given our travel orders and were taken by truck to the Paco railroad station in Manila. The train's engine was small. It reminded me of the train that is used at the Detroit Zoo to haul people around to the animal exhibits. My friend from the 1st Infantry said it was the "Toonerville Trolley." He was referring to a ramshackle vehicle in the comic "Toonerville Folks" which delighted readers during the '20s and '30s. Toy trains, made to its image, were also very popular.[13]

It was long after sunset when the engineers, an Army sergeant and his Filipino assistant, finally showed and cranked up the engine. We chugged northward through the darkened countryside. It was not a fun ride. The passenger cars were open on both sides in the Filipino manner of eliminating windows so we were quite windblown when the train got up to speed. The painted, hardwood seats had nearly vertical backs which made for uncomfortable sitting and the narrow seats were too small to lie on and sleep. There were no toilets and only a swinging Lister bag at one end of the coach which dispensed warm, rubbery-tasting water.

Our route took us to Angeles and Clark Field near the foothills of the Cabusilian Mountains where I had spent the month of May and part of June patrolling around Mount Pinatubo. Then it was north through Tarlac, Bayambang, San Carlos, and on to the shores of Lingayen Gulf where the great invasion took place in January. The train made many stops to let passengers on and off. It was dawn now. Hugging the shoreline of the Gulf, we made our way to the end of the line, Bauang. A few miles north lay San Fernando, temporary home of the 6th Infantry Division.

It had taken us all night to go about 208 miles.[14] I was mighty glad to get off that train about 8:00 in the morning. At 6th Division Headquarters I learned that I couldn't rejoin Company K, 63rd Infantry, because the Third Battalion was already loaded on ships in the harbor and were about to depart for Korea. "Don't worry," the sergeant said, "there are still elements of the 63rd Infantry here. We are putting the strays that show up with Cannon Company. You will go to Korea with them when they sail in about a week." Cannon Company was bivouacked on the beach between Bauang and San Fernando.

These were the soldiers with the M7 mounted 105's that I had first seen on Hill A in April when they were brought up to blast the Japanese on Mount Pacawagan. They were housed in tents along the seashore so I, with several other casuals, reported for duty there. We were well-received. They needed extra hands to get everything ready for the move to Korea as they had lost a lot of high point men who had been sent home for discharge.

For the next few days we worked at taking the encampment apart and packing up the gear for shipment. In the hot afternoons after work, I would swim in the ocean. An older soldier warned me that there was an undertow and said that two soldiers had drowned there. The sparkling waters of the South China Sea looked too inviting for me to worry about an undertow and I really didn't believe the story about the soldiers drowning. Every day the older man would come with me and sit on the beach and watch while I enjoyed myself swimming in the azure sea.

Later we would take showers. The shower was one of those primitive wood contraptions that had a raised wood platform for standing on and an overhead tank. To bathe, you had to carry five gallon cans of water up a ladder and fill the tank. Because the camp was being dismantled, the modesty fence was gone.

I was in the middle of taking my shower when a jeep came down the road to the beach which passed right by the open air shower. On the passenger side rode a young woman. My companion, who had completed his shower and was dressing, got a big charge out of telling everybody about it. "You should have seen that WACs eyeballs pop out when she saw Russ as naked as a jaybird!" he would say. As I recall it, she turned her head as the jeep went by. Anyway, I had been in the Army too long to worry much about who saw me without my clothes on.

One day we walked up the beach to explore some old ruins. I thought they were the remains of a fortress or castle from the time that the Spanish ruled the Philippines but we never found anybody who knew much about it. According to some travel guides there were ancient Chinese settlements in this area.

Another thing we did was listen to re-broadcasts of the World Series baseball games. These came over the Armed Services Radio Network and were condensed so that there was no waiting between innings. Sometimes we knew who had won the game beforehand. I was especially interested because Detroit had clinched the American League pennant on September 30 when they beat the St. Louis Browns, 6 to 3. Hank Greenberg, newly discharged from the Army, hit a grand slam homer in the ninth inning to win that game.

The Chicago Cubs were victors in the National League and the two teams took turns winning games until the World Series was tied at three games each. In the last and deciding game on October 10, the first three Tigers up to bat hit singles and when the mighty Greenberg took his turn, he hit a sacrifice bunt. This was unheard of for a slugger of his caliber. A home run king never bunted. It was years later that I found out that he had seriously hurt his hand in the sixth game and didn't expect to play in the seventh game. The severity of his injury had apparently been kept secret. Manager Steve O'Neil sent him in anyway saying, "It'll look bad otherwise." Fortunately, Greenberg didn't have any fielding to do because he couldn't throw with his sore hand either. Despite this handicap, Detroit went on to win 9 to 3 to become the World Champions for 1945.[15]

On the last morning, we had steak and fresh eggs for breakfast. This was a new treat for me. "We ought to eat like this more often," was the general consensus. *It's eating like officers do*, I thought, remembering my K.P. duty in the officer's mess on Leyte.

After breakfast, we dismantled the last of the camp, struck our tents and loaded the remaining trucks. A large hole was gouged in the beach with a bulldozer and all the remaining debris thrown in. This was doused with gasoline and set on fire. After the flames died down the hole was filled with sand and smoothed over. We left our camping area with little evidence that we had been there.

Cannon Company's transportation to Korea was a fleet of LSTs

56. 6TH INFANTRY DIVISION LOADS FOR KOREA. M7s being driven through the open doors of the LST on a sand roadway built out to the beached ship. From: Tom and Ray Fallen, *The First Infantry Regiment in World War II*, (Chicago: Adams Press, 1990), p. 75

which were embedded in the beach south of our camp. We spent the greater part of the day loading the ship. Trucks, jeeps, and mounted 105s were placed all over the ship, from the top deck to the inside cargo space, using every available space. When the last vehicle was loaded, the entrance ramp was raised and the bow doors closed. The engines were started and run full speed astern. Nothing happened. The ship wouldn't budge from the shore.

"We're overloaded," I said to a sailor but he wasn't worried.

"Sometimes we have to get pulled off the shore by another vessel," he said.

In the meantime there was a lot of activity with men and shovels digging in the sand around the front of the ship. I don't think that they did much good but eventually, after an hour or so of struggle, the ship gave a mighty shudder and backed off the beach. We were off to the Hermit Kingdom. It had been an eventful seven months in the Philippine Islands from the middle-of-the-night landing on the shore at Leyte under wartime security conditions to the departure from the sun-blanketed beaches in broad daylight in peacetime. Life had indeed changed in a very short time and further adventures beckoned.

THIRTEEN

Occupying the Hermit Kingdom

*Happy are those who can tie together in their thoughts
the past, the present and the future.*
—Alexis de Tocqueville[1]

The way to Korea was by plowing through the waters of the South China Sea in a northward direction, with the coast of Luzon on the starboard side, then veering northeasterly past Formosa on the port side, through the Ryukyu Islands into the East China Sea, and then north into the Yellow Sea where the Korean peninsula would be on our starboard side. Our ship didn't have a name, only a number, LST-XXX. It was one of many in a convoy so progress was determined by the slowest boat. To complicate matters, it was the typhoon season.

This is the time of the year, July through October, when violent tropical cyclones sweep over the western Pacific ocean from the Philippine Islands to Japan and the coast of China. Similar storms are called hurricanes in the Caribbean Islands and eastern United States. Typhoons begin in the low latitudes, move northwest and then northeast in a storm path from 50 to 100 miles wide. They travel slowly and their violent, gusty winds often cause great destruction.[2] A particularly bad one hit Okinawa while we were en route. Although we were never in the path of a typhoon, we did have rough water most of the way to Korea.

Everybody got seasick, even some of the sailors. One told me that he got seasick every time the ship pulled out to sea. I remember

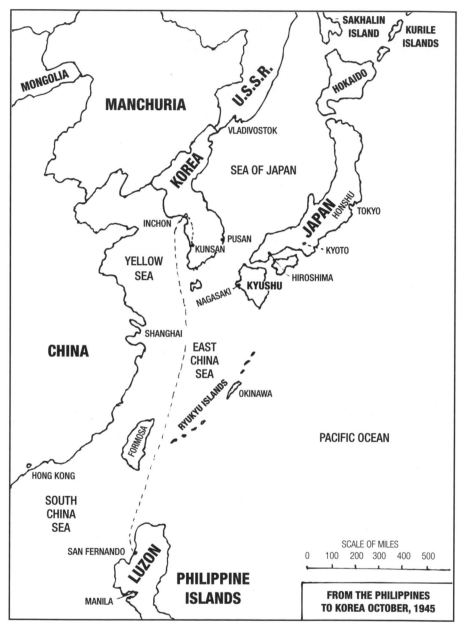

14. FROM LUZON TO KOREA, OCTOBER 1945. It was a long and rough ride from the Philippine Islands to our new duty station in Korea. Map by the author.

standing on the deck the second night out, still feeling wretched but actually on the mend, when the soldier next to me, vomiting over the railing said, "I'm so miserable, I'm tempted to jump overboard. The only thing that keeps me from doing it is that the next boat coming along would surely rescue me!"

The LST was long and slim. It reminded me of the ore boats I used to see plying the Detroit River. It didn't go up and down much in the heavy seas but rolled along its axis unmercifully. The ship's galley was to the stern and had a passage we entered on the port side to get our meals. We passed along a counter to pick up the components of the meal as we moved to the starboard side where there was another opening. I often watched this opening when I started in line at meal-times. When the ship reached the end of its roll in the starboard direction, all I could see through the opening was inky dark sea. When it reversed and rolled in the other direction, all I could see through the opening was clouds or pale blue sky. This went on for what seemed like forever.

The ship also shuddered when it hit a particularly high wave head on and the stern end would kind of whip side to side. I wondered if the ship would hold together with this awful beating but the sailors assured me that the ship was sound and that they had been through a lot worse pounding. Unlike the troopships I had been on where the Army and the Navy were kept separate, we were bunked in with the enlisted crew along the sides of the ship. We shared their quarters and ate our meals with them. It was a higher standard of living than I was accustomed to in the Army. The officers, of course, had separate quarters and a dining room with a black Navy steward to wait on them.

There were nearly 200 people aboard the LST, half Army and half Navy. The reason I know this is because I was assigned to work in the bakery. While I didn't do much the first night or two because of seasickness, after I got my sea legs we settled into a regular routine. I would report to the galley about 7:00 in the evening after the kitchen was cleared of the supper dishes. The first order of business was to get rid of the previous day's bread. Usually it was a few loaves—although when there was a lot of seasickness, there was plenty of left over bread.

"Throw it *all* overboard!" the Navy baker would say, not wanting any day-old bread contaminating his fresh bread locker. He was a slim, blonde haired, youthful looking sailor from Ohio who had been a baker in civilian life so was quite expert in the culinary arts. There was also an Army baker. A big southerner, he was not as skilled, having learned the trade at the Army's Cooks and Bakers School and was also at a disadvantage because it was the Navy baker's kitchen. He was an Army man in the position of having to go along with the Navy way of doing things.

My job was to do the grub work. Besides throwing yesterday's bread overboard, we used the ocean to dispose of any trash or garbage we generated. I fetched the flour, sugar and butter, opened cans, washed the pans and mixing bowls and any other thing that needed cleaning. After awhile they let me do some of the more important work like spreading frosting on gigantic sheet cakes or painting equally large pies with condensed milk so they came out of the ovens with that glistening golden coloration that made them so appetizing. I used a regular two inch paint brush to do this. We always made a desert or two every night and sometimes cinnamon rolls for breakfast.

However, the most important job was baking the bread. The Navy baker fussed and fumed and worried about *his bread.* I think the desserts, which I found fascinating to make and much more satisfying to eat, were only a sideline to the baker. His formula for the staff of life was a half a loaf of bread per man per day. Since there was something like 194 men aboard the ship that meant baking 100 loaves every night. It was the first thing he started early in the evening and the last thing out of the oven. He began by mixing up a huge mass of flour, water, sugar, salt, shortening and yeast. The sponge, as it was called, was then placed in the warmest part of the galley and covered with moist towels while we turned our attention to the dessert making. The fermentation process, over time, would cause the leavened dough to rise and expand until it resembled a huge mushroom head.

The baker would check it periodically, muttering about its progress and how difficult it was to make good bread when the ship rolled in the high seas. When the sponge rose to its peak, he would uncover it, roll it, knead it and pound it down to a smaller size by forcing out the carbon dioxide from the fermentation. He would then re-cover it with moist towels and allow it to rise again. He did this three times in the course of the evening. It was often close to midnight before he was satisfied that the dough was ready for baking. This was too much for the Army baker who thought some of these steps were unnecessary and said so. It went unheeded, kind of like a daughter telling her mother to throw out the old family recipe and buy a commercial product instead.

When the dough was declared ready, we would cut it up into one pound pieces. They had to be carefully weighed and modified to insure uniformity before they were placed in the baking tins. These were multi-cavity, holding eight loaves each. Baking took about a half hour so by the time the bread was finished, the loaves put away and the pans washed it was usually about 2:00 in the morning when we left the galley with the aroma of freshly baked bread still hanging in the air. I can still remember it. Is there anything else that smells as sweet?

The black steward was allotted half a dozen loaves for the officers' use. However, one day I noticed him opening up a can of commercial bread. It had the distinctive markings, multi-colored circles on its waxed paper wrapping, of Wonder Bread, a local Detroit product. I mentioned this to the baker that night as we labored on yet another hundred loaves. He gave me a pained look and muttered, "Because some of them are assholes who would rather eat junk than good, freshly baked bread!" I was sorry I mentioned it as it seemed to upset him quite a bit.

I usually went right to bed after my stint in the bakery and slept until 10:00 or 11:00, skipping breakfast since I could eat anything I wanted when I worked in the bakery. After lunch I would wander around the ship, watch the endless ocean going by, talk to the sailors, or lay in my bunk and read. One of the books that I read was *Yankee from Olympus* by Catherine Drinker Bowen. It was a biography of Supreme Court Justice Oliver Wendell Holmes who was famous for his liberal views and even his dissents helped shape American law. His major contribution was in convincing men that the law should develop along with the society it serves. I was especially impressed with the fact that he was wounded three times[3] in the Civil War and still managed to live to the ripe old age of 94.

Three weeks and over 2,000 loaves of bread later, we finally chugged into the island-studded port of Inchon. The sailors called it by its Japanese name—Jinsen. This caused some confusion but we gradually learned to use the Korean names for places as the long Japanese rule of Korea came to an end. Inchon definitely looked Asiatic with the classical Chinese junks anchored around the bay. The word "junk" comes from the Portuguese "junko" adapted from the Javanese word for ship, "dyong." Junk is the name applied to a variety of Far Eastern sailing vessels characterized by flat bottoms, square bows, and high sterns. The typical junk sail is essentially a lugsail stiffened with horizontal battens. The ship also has a dragon's head on the prow.[4] Another thing that gave the port a different look than Manila were the oriental signs with their ideographic characters on the buildings. It was the end of October and cold as compared to the Philippines.

We had been given an Army pamphlet which gave some elementary facts and history of this strange country we were about to enter, as well as some rudimentary language phrases we might need. We learned that the Korean peninsula had many mountains and small valleys, so beautiful that it was sometimes called the "Switzerland of Asia." Its ancient and proud people, who were neither Chinese nor Japanese, traced their national history back some 3,000 years. As early as 1000 B.C. they had a national flag and called their country "Chosun" which means "morning calm."

The Koreans perfected the use of movable type 100 years before Gutenberg. That, and the invention of an alphabet that was easy to learn, made reading and learning widespread. The first encyclopedia was developed in 1405, preceding the Encyclopedia Britannica by several hundred years. Other early inventions were the mariner's compass and suspension bridge.

While the Koreans learned much from the Chinese and improved upon it, they were much further ahead of the Japanese, whose history farther back than 1500 years is lost in legends. The Koreans, since they were closer to Japan than the Chinese, passed on much of their learning and culture to their backward neighbors. It took a long time to take hold because the Japanese samurai considered learning to be beneath his dignity. The only arts and sciences he honored were those of war. In Korea, war was considered an evil, if sometimes necessary activity. It interfered with the true purpose of man, the advancement of civilization.[5]

The first Japanese invasion of Korea was in 1592 at Pusan. For the next six years Japanese armies ravaged Korea but in the end they were defeated. Part of the reason for their defeat was the development, by the Koreans, of an exploding shell which was new in this part of the world. Another was the use of an iron- clad navy which inflicted great damage on the larger Japanese fleet which was attempting to come to the relief of the troops already there. This was a good 270 years before the *Monitor* and the *Merrimac*.

The Japanese withdrew but they left a wrecked country. Cities were ruined, monasteries were burned, libraries destroyed, and scholars put to death. Six years of holocaust impoverished the people.[6] For the next three hundred years Korea refused entry to all foreigners and came to be called the "Hermit Kingdom." This period of isolation ended in 1876 when Japan forced Korea to open several ports to trade. The United States made a commercial treaty with

57. KOREAN MEN IN TRADITIONAL COSTUME. The one on the left is wearing the traditional white robe which was a symbol of resistance to the Japanese occupation. Both are wearing hats made of horse hair. Corbis-Bettmann photo.

Korea in 1882 and other countries soon followed. The Americans built the country's first trolley line, railroad and waterworks, and missionaries arrived to spread not only Christianity but Western technology, education and medical advances.

The Japanese, after defeating China in their war of 1894—95 and Russia in their war of 1904–05, made Korea their colony by poisoning the Korean king and deposing his dynasty. In 1910, after bitter and prolonged resistance by Korean insurgents, Korea was formally annexed. It ceased to exist as a country and became known as Chosen, an integral part of the Japanese Empire. For the next 35 years, Japan developed the Korean economy mainly to exploit it for themselves. They gave the country modern transport, developed its mines, exploited its farms and opened Shinto shrines. The Japanese also kept the Koreans in virtual economic and political slavery, tarring the Korean's traditional white clothing, and jailing them for "thought crime."

The Koreans fought back periodically and there were major massacres in 1919, 1923 and 1942. In 1919, in a remarkable display of passive patriotism, Koreans declared their independence. The Japanese retaliated with executions and the flogging of 11,000 demonstrators. Many Koreans fled the country. The largest group, some 300,000, found refuge in Siberia. Another 100,000 or so ended up in China and smaller groups settled in other parts of the world.

In 1919 some of the exiles organized a Provisional Government at Shanghai. They eventually won financial support and de facto recognition from Generalissimo Chiang Kai-shek. The government in exile did not include the 300,000 Koreans in Siberia who were inaccessible. The Russians claimed them to be Soviet citizens. At least 30,000 of them were said to be organized in a Red Army unit.[7]

During World War II, the Korean's hopes were revived considerably as the tide of battle turned in favor of the Allies. At the Cairo Conference of December 1943, Roosevelt, Churchill, and Chiang Kai-Shek took up the liberation of peoples enslaved by the Japanese. The final declaration at the close of the conference said that "in due course" Korea was to be free and independent.

At the Yalta Conference in February 1945, with the Allies pressuring Russia and offering concessions to join in the war against Japan, no agreement was reached on the post-war status of Korea except that it would be initially occupied by both the United States and the Soviet Union. The 38th parallel was noted to be in about the middle of the peninsula so it was agreed that the Russians would move into and occupy the territory north of this line. The Americans would occupy the land to the south. They would each disarm the Japanese troops in their zones, send them home, and then get together to set up a single government for the whole country. Then, presumably, they would both depart and the Koreans would become an independent country once again.

When the atomic bombs ended the war so abruptly, the Americans had to move fast. The Russians, who had entered the war in its last week, overran their assigned part of the Korean Peninsula in short order, even pushing south of the 38th Parallel in places. The Army's XXIV Corps was given the job of occupying the American half because it was on Okinawa, closest to Korea. The XXIV Corps consisted of the 7th Infantry Division, which landed at Inchon on September 9, and the 40th Infantry Division which landed at Pusan on September 19. Somewhere along the line it was decided to add a third division, the 6th Infantry. Since we were much farther away on Luzon, our first troops didn't get there until October 18.

According to Operation Black List,[8] Field Order No. 1 which is

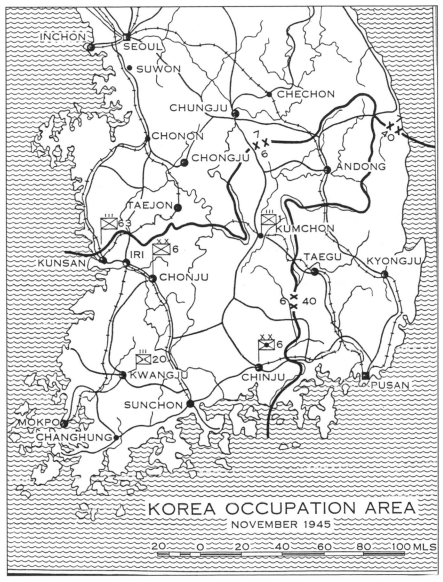

15. THE OCCUPATION OF KOREA. The 63rd Infantry was assigned to the Cholla-Puckto Province which is in the area of Kunsan, Iri and Chonju. From: *The 6th Infantry Division in World War II: 1939-1945*, (Nashville: The Battery Press, 1983), p. 153.

dated 3 October 1945, the three divisions were to occupy the part of Korea south of the 38th parallel as follows: the 7th Infantry would occupy the provinces in the northern portion, the 40th Infantry provinces in the southeast and the 6th Infantry Division provinces in the southwest. They were all to exercise control over all adjacent islands in their zones.

The 63rd Infantry Regiment had the following (much abridged) specific orders to follow:

1. Occupy initially Kunsan and Chonju.
2. Occupy as rapidly as possible the remainder of Cholla-Pukto province and establish control over all adjacent islands.
3. In this zone of responsibility we would:
    a. Supervise the disarmament of the Japanese armed forces and maintain control of Japanese Army Forces moving to the south for evacuation to Japan.
    b. Assist in the establishment of military government and later post-war civil government.
    c. Suppress activities of individuals and organizations which were inimical to the operations of the occupation forces.
    d. Insure the maintenance of law and order among the civilian population.
    e. Recover and repatriate any Allied prisoners of war.

There were other orders that had to do with facilitating peaceful commerce, securing and safeguarding intelligence information, seizing and securing Japanese records, and insuring the uninterrupted use of existing communication facilities. Unit commanders had the additional responsibilities, among others, of

"indoctrinating their men in the realization that, as representatives of the United States, exemplary conduct and appearance would reflect great credit to their Army and to their country, and that by such action the respect and obedience of both the defeated Japanese and the liberated Koreans [would] be insured."

Of course, as a lowly private, I didn't know all this detail at that time but I think that most of us had a general sense of what we were there for—to kick the Japanese out, get the Koreans back in the business of running their own country and then go home. Nice theory. Too bad it didn't quite work out that way. We and the Russians laid the groundwork for another horrible war and extreme tragedy for the long-suffering Korean people.

We were in the harbor at Inchon for a couple of days waiting our turn to use the pier to unload. Some of the sailors got liberty and went ashore in a launch. We were attracted to the deck by the commotion they made when they returned, uproariously drunk. The Navy has a little ceremony that the sailors all go through when they board a ship. As they are about to step on the deck they stop, salute the Officer of the Deck and request permission to board the vessel. The O.D. returns the salute and grants permission, whereupon they can then step aboard. The drunken sailors had a hard time scrambling up the ladder. When they got to the top, they gave a very unsteady and swaying salute. Only the frantic clutches of their companions and the men on deck prevented some of them from tumbling into the sea.

We got off the boat late in the evening and were trucked to a deserted factory building to spend the night. It was a forge shop that made heavy railroad equipment. We set up our Army cots next to some drop hammers. Since there was no production going on, the forges were unfired. It was early November and bitter cold so we slept with our clothes on.

The next day, after the ship was completely unloaded, we moved to the Chosen Christian College which was somewhere in Seoul. That night we were billeted in a classroom in the dental department. The walls were lined with dental charts and huge pictures of teeth and various gum diseases. I set up my cot between a couple of dental chairs and slept fitfully, dreaming of toothy Japanese trying to kill me with gigantic dental drills.

We left early the next morning, a long convoy of trucks heading southward. The road was rough and bumpy and the country hilly so the going was slow. We stopped periodically to relieve ourselves and then would find that we were surrounded by curious Koreans. We weren't the first Americans that they had seen because the occupation was several weeks old when I got there. However, their curiosity was still intense. I remember mostly a sea of oriental eyes looking at me, especially the young children who had a special unblinking, direct stare. The young women would glance bashfully and if we ventured a step in their direction would run away giggling. There were old men dressed in long white coats and black stovepipe hats who would stare solemnly. The Koreans didn't appear to be hostile or frightened, only inquisitive. What was going through their minds? Hope for a better future, or were they thinking, *We are exchanging one set of invaders for another*? Probably a little of each.

The villages we passed through had narrow crooked streets, densely covered with small houses and courtyards. Many of the com-

58. KOREAN CHILDREN. Like children everywhere, the younger Koreans were cute. Unlike their white-clad parents, the children wore colored clothes. If they went to school, they wore dark blue uniforms. This boy lacks pockets, so he has tied his packet of papers in his kimono strings. From: Willard Price, "Jap Rule in the Hermit Nation", *The National Geographic Magazine*, Oct. 1945, p. 443.

mercial shops occupied the fronts of the houses. There was usually a large hand-painted sign or banner at the entrance to the town which said in English: "Welcome to the United States Army" although sometimes the words were misspelled as in "Welcom to the Uneted Stats Armi."

It took all day to make the trip from Seoul to Kunsan, some 130 miles. It was dark when we arrived at the Japanese Air Base near Kunsan where the third battalion was billeted in wooden barracks. I reported to a young First Lieutenant who had taken over command of K-Company when Captain Fleming went home on points right after the war ended. He was new to me and it was said that he was Regular Army and had come from the European theater. He asked me what platoon I had been in and when I answered, "The first, sir," he told me where they were located in the building.

I caused quite a stir when I rejoined my former mates. These were mostly the younger soldiers who had survived the vicious battles along Highway 4 to Kiangan. They were astounded when I showed up after being gone some four and a half months. Most couldn't believe that the Army would send a man back to duty after being severely wounded and especially after the war had ended. I assured them that I wasn't the only one. The Army had a policy of patching up the wounded and sending them back to duty, especially infantrymen. The ending of the war didn't change the policy a bit.

"Captain Fleming said you had a million dollar wound when they hauled your ass off that hill!" said one.

"Well, Dick was wrong," I answered. "Captains don't know everything. By the way, where is he?"

"Gone home on points."

Most of the older men were gone. When I asked about various individuals like Sergeants Shaw or Gibson, I was also told, "Gone home on points." I had just missed Lieutenant Tom Atchley. He had come to Korea with the company, stayed a week or so and then been sent home on points. Others weren't so fortunate. Sad answers abounded. "He got hit at Bolog or Lane's Ridge," or worst of all, "Killed by the Japs." They were especially saddened by the death of Staff Sergeant Edward Mauer of Chicago, Illinois, who was killed near Kiangan on July 13. Ed was a quiet, thoughtful man who was well-liked by his men. The fact that he had served long and faithfully, accumulated a lot of points and would have been eligible for discharge soon made his death especially unreasonable. July had been a very bad month for K-Company. Of the Regiment's 24 men killed in action during the month of July, fully a third (eight), had been in K-Company.[9]

There were a lot of new and strange faces. The few that I knew were mostly the replacements who had joined the company when I did or when we were in the hills west of Clark Field. We had spent a lot of time together dodging shells on Hill A, manning that machine gun emplacement near Clark Field, on patrol in the hills around Mount Pinatubo and in attacking the retreating Japanese along Highway 4 in Northern Luzon. Most of them had moved into positions of authority as the older men had left. They were now the sergeants and squad leaders. One had even taken on the job of mess sergeant. They told me that the only old-timers left were Lieutenant Colonel Mueller, who still commanded the 3rd Battalion, and Dave Darnell who had advanced from private first class to staff sergeant. He had taken the promotion in lieu of going home. The rest of the platoon couldn't understand that, and Dave was a quiet, highly intelligent man who wouldn't say much about it. Some soldiers said that he was Regular Army and that he had found a home in it.

Colonel Mueller was Regular Army too but he at least had gotten a 30-day furlough to go home right after the war ended and had just gotten back to lead the 3rd Battalion in Korea. We all wanted to go home too, but when we got there we were going to stay and forget about the Army, the war, and everything else about this strange, exotic part of the world with all its problems. We felt that we had done our share of duty and should go home soon.

Doc Horne, the platoon medic was also gone. He had been wounded, late in the war, by a Japanese booby trap[10] and one of my former squad-mates had taken over his job. (It was worth an extra stripe to corporal.) He didn't have much of a medical job to do since we weren't in combat and was anxious to be of help. I also think that he was curious to see my wound. He said that he had some salve that was good for relieving pain so I let him rub some on my leg so he could think he was doing something beneficial. Actually, I hadn't experienced any pain in my leg since the operation in September.

Sergeant Hile had gone home from Luzon so I reported to a new supply sergeant the next morning for some winter clothes, field equipment and an M1 rifle. When I asked about my duffel bag, he said that when they were packing up for the move to Korea, they went through all the bags of the soldiers who were in the hospital, mailed their personal things home and returned the Army's stuff to general stores.

"We really didn't expect you to come back from the hospital," the new supply sergeant said which didn't make me feel too welcome. It was like, "You shouldn't even be here." I don't know for sure whether he was telling me the truth or not because no personal effects were ever received at my home in Detroit. They might have been lost, stolen or destroyed. I missed mostly my camera, family pictures, old letters, books and the educational materials for the correspondence course I was taking from the University of Wisconsin. I had expected to have some mail waiting for me too, but was told that it had all been forwarded to the hospital. I had been in four hospitals on Luzon and two on Leyte so who knows where it all ended up?

Then there was the matter of money. I hadn't been paid since June 1 except for a couple of partial payments of five or ten dollars that I had received in the hospital. I also had just missed the November 1 payroll and was told I would have to wait until December. There wasn't much opportunity to shop so not having money wasn't a real hardship.

I was back into the routine of an infantry rifle company: close order drill, long marches, calisthenics, training and guard duty. One day we even went down to the town and practiced village fighting maneuvers, much to the consternation of the villagers. The Army was doing its thing to keep us in "fighting trim." I never did any disarming of the Japanese, most of them having been rounded up and shipped out just before I got there. There were some left but I didn't see any of them.

It was rice harvesting time in that part of Korea. I spent many cold nights pulling guard duty in the fields. We would be trucked out to the rice paddies for four-hour stints of standing or sitting by the piles of harvested grain. I was appalled when I saw soldiers burning the rice to keep themselves warm. I suspected that it was a wasteful and inefficient way to ward off the cold and that what they burned would feed a lot of Koreans. There wasn't much I could do about it except make myself unpopular by denouncing the practice, which I didn't.

At that time, more than three-quarters of the Koreans depended on farming for their living. Over the years, the Japanese had taken over most of the good farms and made tenants out of the Korean owners. Half of the year's produce had to be delivered to the Japanese landlord. Much of the remainder went for taxes and the expenses of planting. The tenant-farmer was left with about one-sixth of the harvest to feed himself and his family until the next crop was ready. During the spring, when the storage jars were empty, many families lived on bark, grass, roots, rice hulls and weeds. The Koreans had a name for this annual, unhappy experience, "the spring suffering."[11] I don't think they appreciated us burning the rice to keep warm, but then, we did get rid of the Japanese overlords so their standard of living had to improve. The rice would now be kept in Korea and not shipped to Japan, as it had been.

The barracks we lived in were very long and constructed of wood. The interior walls were made of paper-thin plywood. A long, narrow, central hallway ran the length of the barracks some 250 or 300 feet. There were small rooms on both sides of the hallway housing offices and sleeping quarters of the men, six or eight to a room. They were unheated and veritable fire traps.

Apparently the Japanese military were hardy souls who could live in that climate without heating the barracks. We Americans, who had just arrived from a tropical island, were always cold. We had available for our use small portable kerosene stoves. They were about six inches in diameter and eighteen inches high, about the size of a kerosene lantern, with a single burner on top. We used these little stoves mostly to keep warm, but also to make tea or coffee or to boil fresh eggs which we obtained from the local Koreans.

The eggs came wrapped in rice straw, a long package of ten tied at intervals to provide pockets for each egg. We always asked the Koreans where the other two eggs were but apparently their "dozen" was ten. One of the men in my platoon never bothered to cook his eggs but would crack one open on his teeth and eat it raw right out of the shell, much to the disgust of some of his fellow soldiers. The burners could also be used to heat *sake*, but I don't remember any enlisted men getting any of this Japanese wine made from rice at that time. The officers did.

According to Ervan Rose, 3rd Platoon sergeant, the big fire started in his room when one of his men accidently knocked over one of these little stoves, instantly igniting everything. Kind of like Mrs. O'Leary's cow starting the great Chicago fire of 1871 by kicking over a lantern. It happened late at night. I had returned from a stint of guard duty at one of the supply depots, crawled into bed and fallen into a deep sleep. Before long, I was rudely awakened with cries of "Fire! Fire!" and "Wake up, everybody outa' here." It was all so sudden and confusing. There was a loud roaring noise and smoke was everywhere. Someone shouted not to go out into the hallway but to go out the window, so that's what we did. It was an easy drop to the ground because this was a one story building.

I stood in my underwear some distance from the burning barracks, astounded by the size of the fire. Flames rose in the darkened sky as high as 30 or 40 feet. The heat was intense, forcing us to back up even further. Small arms fire went off occasionally, adding to the excitement, danger and the need to keep a safe distance. The mess sergeant had managed to get his foot locker out and had left it on the ground near the burning building. The intense heat started it on fire as he stood some distance away, watching helplessly. Somebody handed me a blanket to wrap up in. The flames died down almost as fast as they had gone up. Soon all that was left of the barracks was a long rectangle of smoldering ashes and the blackened remnants of our shelter, possessions and equipment.

We moved to another barracks and slept on the floor for the rest of the night. In the morning we were issued new clothes and equipment. The local Red Cross unit sent over some toilet articles and writing materials as most of us had lost everything. I came out of the burning barracks with only the underwear that I was sleeping in. The next morning, searching through the ashes, I salvaged a very scorched and blackened set of dog tags, the only thing that wasn't obliterated. I had lost everything that I had accumulated in the hospital and on my journey back to my unit, including some nice souvenirs that I had bought in Manila.

At the time of the fire, I was reading *The Robe* by Lloyd C. Douglas[12] and had gotten about halfway through the book when it was lost in the fire. I have never gotten another copy and finished reading it. When I see the movie occasionally on late-night T.V., my mind goes back to that cold night in Korea when the barracks burned up and most of us miraculously escaped death or serious injury. It was said that the only one burned was the soldier who started the fire by knocking over the kerosene stove. We soon settled back into our regular routine in another barracks, as there were plenty of them left on the airbase.

On November 20, Colonel Everett Yon went home to a well-earned retirement. The regimental commander returned to Gainesville, Florida where he had a wife and two sons aged eight and ten. He retired from the Army and was appointed executive secretary of the University of Florida Alumni Association. There he resumed his studies that were interrupted in 1916. He graduated with a Bachelor of Science degree in 1949. Upon his death in 1965, he was Director of Public Relations for the University Athletic Association and Director of Gator Boosters. Because of his many achievements and contributions to University athletics, Yon Hall, a building on the campus, was named in his honor. Both of his sons followed in their father's footsteps and had distinguished Army careers.[13]

Colonel Bruce Palmer, Jr., took over as commanding officer of the 63rd Infantry Regiment. Palmer had been a staff officer with the 6th Division, joining it in Hawaii. A new commander is always of some concern to the men in the ranks. They wonder if he will be "chicken shit" and make a lot of changes. We spent many hours cleaning up the barracks and getting everything in good military shape for his review. His visit lasted about five minutes and we didn't hear any bad reports so we must have passed his inspection. In later years, he was one of the leading generals in the Vietnam war.

When we were not occupied with military duties, we spent time looking around the place. There were hangers and Japanese airplanes to look at. Also a complete machine shop and maintenance stores. One building, which must have been officers' quarters, had a mini-swimming pool in it which turned out to be a communal bath tub. It had a ledge half way down in the water that ran completely around its perimeter. The story was that the Japanese all bathed together and sat around on the ledge. They cranked the heat way up and the last one to get out was considered to be the toughest. We used it as a reservoir of hot water and dipped buckets out of the pool to bathe.

The Yellow Sea was within walking distance and we often walked down to the shore. The tides in this part of the world are enormous, sometimes running as high as 30 feet. When it was at low tide we could stand on the beach and look out over miles and miles of mud flats with the ocean barely discernible on the horizon.

We could also catch a ride to town, which was a congested, smelly place of mud houses with thatched roofs. The shops were full of junk that we weren't interested in buying. Hair pomades, for instance. There seemed to be hundreds of jars of the stuff in every other shop. They were also overstocked with incense and equipment to burn it. Some soldiers bought some but got a lot of complaints when they tried burning it in the barracks.

We were forbidden to eat or drink any of the native foods because they didn't have much and needed what little they did have to keep from starving, and their standards of public health were much lower and the prevalence of communicable intestinal diseases, principally typhoid fever and cholera, was very high. This was because they used human excrement as a fertilizer on their farms.

The ban didn't bother me any because the food the natives had to offer was very unappetizing. One was sea cucumber a mass of green, gelatinous slime that looked similar to a slice of cucumber if it was cut longitudinally from one end to the other and laid with its flat side down on a board with the rounded, green, prickly side up. The natives bought it by the slice and ate it with great relish. To me it looked and smelled awful. It came out of the bottom of the Yellow Sea and should have been left there. Another popular dish was *kimchi* which consisted of highly spiced and pickled cabbage, peppers, onions and garlic, none of which I liked to eat. I think it was the combination of *kimchi* and human fecal matter which made the town smell so rank.

Actually, Kunsan was a fairly large city of some 40,000 people at that time. It was Korea's sixth largest port and could accommodate ships of 4000 tons. However, a ship drawing more than eight feet of water could reach the harbor only at high tide. Kunsan was being used to ship out the Japanese and bring in the repatriated Koreans. I heard some medics talking once about how they had to meet the incoming ships, mostly LCIs and LSTs, and spray delousing powder on the Koreans before they were allowed to board trains for their home towns.

I was at the Kunsan harbor early on Thanksgiving Day that year. Normally a holiday, it was a work day for about a dozen other soldiers and me who were assigned to the ammo disposition detail that day. Because of the tide, we had to get up about 2:00 A.M. for a truck ride from the air base to a dock in Kunsan where we boarded a good-sized wooden barge filled with cases of Japanese hand grenades, mortar shells, and rifle and machine gun bullets. A young lieutenant was in command of this detail. He got on the tug boat that was pulling the barge with a large cable. We sat on the small mountain of wooden boxes of ammo as we chugged in the darkness down the Kumgang River and out into the Yellow Sea. It was windy and cold. The cases of ammo made for uncomfortable seating and the barge bobbed up and down when we got out into the rough, open ocean.

The sun was just coming up over the far distant Korean coastline when the command was given to start throwing the cases overboard. By this time several soldiers had gotten seasick from the rocking of the flat-bottomed barge. At first the work wasn't too strenuous. The cases of ammo were piled high and all we had to do was heave them sideways into the ocean. However, as we worked our way down the pile we had to start lifting them up over the gunwale. More soldiers got sick as the barge rocked and pitched. Some threw up on the ammo. The looie got impatient with the slow progress we were making and kept shouting and cursing from the deck of the tug.

"If you bastards don't get this goddam job done pretty soon we will all be stuck out here for twenty-four-fucking-hours until the next goddam high tide allows us to bring the fuckin' boat back to harbor!!" is what he said, but I think I might have left out some of the swear words. We cursed him back under our breath and also the seasick soldiers who vomited on the ammo or were too sick to work. By keeping my mind on the job at hand, I managed to keep from getting sick. Also, I hadn't eaten for about 12 hours, which helped. By the time we got the last cases overboard we were lifting them six or seven feet to heave over the side. The tug made a wide arc and headed back for port as we lay on the bottom of the barge gasping for breath from our hard labor.

We arrived back at the barracks about noon, famished for lunch. There would be no special Thanksgiving turkey dinner waiting for us, the kind the Army's public relations people love to publicize with pictures and stories of smiling soldiers stuffing themselves with turkey, mashed potatoes, pumpkin pie and all the trimmings. It seems that in Korea that year we were at the far end of the supply line and the ingredients for our holiday feast were still in transit. We did have it though, a week or so later.

I never had to work the ammo disposition detail again because on

November 30, there was a huge explosion at the dump. I was in the barracks when it happened. I heard a loud noise, like distant thunder, which rattled the window panes. Rushing outside with the others, we saw a plume of black smoke rising in the distance. Later that day, we heard that it had been a serious blast and that people had been killed, including American soldiers.

Strangely, there is nothing in the Unit History about this tragedy. (Or about the K-Company fire either.) However, the *New York Times* reported on December 1, 1945, that there was a ". . . large Japanese Army ammunition dump explosion in Korea . . . an American officer and one civilian were killed . . . and 25 soldiers and 300 Koreans injured." It also reported that this was a second explosion, the first one being on November 9 when a United States Army bomb disposal squad went to work to deactivate 300,000 tons of Japanese ammunition near Kunson [sic] and two American soldiers lost their lives.[14]

I sent a copy of the *New York Times* story to Colonel Arndt Mueller, who wrote me as follows:

> As regards the ammo dump explosion . . . I don't remember two explosions. I do not recall 25 soldiers being injured. We did not have that many around the dump that morning for obvious reasons. Capt. [Henry R.] Hillenmeyer, our S3 Operations Staff Officer, and Lt. (or Capt.) Connor or O'Connor were killed.[15] At least one and maybe a few more soldiers at the entrance were injured.
>
> There were numerous Korean casualties. Some were the brave firemen . . . the rest were in the neighboring village. Most of the houses were flattened. A fierce fire broke out. The figure of 300 Korean casualties is not out of line and may even be a low figure.
>
> This was a tragedy waiting to happen. Every time I went into that dump, my skin would crawl . . . Ammo, black powder, picric acid explosives, fuses and blasting caps were all mixed up. Black powder had been spilled on the ground. The Japs did not observe the strict ammo storage procedures that we did. . . .
>
> My first act was to request higher Hq to allow me to use the Jap Regiment under my command to dump the stuff at sea . . . But higher Hq (Division, as I recall) was apprehensive that the Japs might set it off—not an unreasonable fear in view of the Jap reputation for treachery . . . Division sent us an explosives expert who was to supervise the job of reducing the dump . . . An engineer Lt. in charge of repair of a nearby bridge said that the last he saw of the expert, (just before the explosion), he was standing on top of a pile of explosives directing the Korean firemen in their attempt to put out a fire in the rice stubble inside the dump.

GENERAL HEADQUARTERS
UNITED STATES ARMY FORCES, PACIFIC
OFFICE OF THE COMMANDER-IN-CHIEF

A.P.O. 500,

December 21, 1945.

Mrs. Lucy R. Hillenmeyer,

229 Highland Street,

Winchester, Kentucky.

My dear Mrs. Hillenmeyer:

The report has just reached me that your husband, Captain Henry R. Hillenmeyer has laid down his life for his country. I am immeasurably distressed by his untimely death and extend my deepes sympathy to you, his wife. May God in his infinite wisdom comfort you in this hour of trial.

Faithfully yours,

Douglas MacArthur

59. COPY OF A CONDOLENCE LETTER received by Mrs. Lucy R. Hillenmeyer, widow of Captain Henry R. Hillenmeyer who was killed in the Kunsan ammo dump explosion. General MacArthur was said to spend two or three hours every day on matters of "personal concern" and personally signed all such letters. From the files of Henry R. Hillenmeyer, Jr. Used with permission.

The morning of the explosion, the Asst Div Commander, a Colonel, came to inspect us. So, I accompanied him. Otherwise, I would have been at the dump along with the two officers who died. When the explosion shook the town and broke windows the Colonel said that he could see that I was going to have a lot to do so he discontinued his inspection.

After the explosion, Division said it was OK to use the Japs to dispose the ammo at sea. They did it without incident . . . gave me no trouble—followed all of the rules I laid down to the letter. I even took my guards off their compound.[16]

As for me, I am glad to hear after all these years that the Japanese got to finish that nasty job. I never enjoyed my one experience with it. But I soon had other things to think about as my life changed abruptly.

There had been posted on the Company bulletin board a notice saying that a clerk was needed in the Personnel Section at Headquarters Company. "Must be able to type 30 words a minute," it read. I had taken a year of typing in high school and could type. Maybe not 30 words per minute but I could put out a decent letter or term paper. At least I could before the Army made a rifleman out of me. However, I was leery of putting my name in because I had heard many old Army stories about sergeants asking for volunteers who knew how to type and when the unsuspecting recruits had eagerly responded, they soon found themselves digging latrines or doing other nasty jobs totally unrelated to office work.

Still, when I thought about the long hours of boring guard duty and the experience of dumping Japanese ammo into the Yellow Sea, the job became very appealing. I submitted my name to the first sergeant not really expecting to hear any more about it. In the early evening of the day after the ammo dump explosion, I was called into the captain's office.

"You applied for the job of personnel clerk at Headquarters Company?" he asked.

"Yes, sir," I replied, not knowing what to expect. I hadn't spoken to him since the night I returned from the hospital, about a month earlier.

"You've been accepted. Pack your gear and be ready to go in 20 minutes."

Just like that. No interviews, no typing test. It didn't take me long to pack as I didn't have much stuff after the fire except a few Army clothes in a duffel bag. The next thing I knew, I was in a jeep heading for Chonju through the dark and cold Korean countryside. I had not even had time to say goodbye.

Regimental Headquarters had moved from Kunsan to Chonju on November 24. With the regiment spread out over Cholla Pukto province, it afforded a more central location. Chonju, population 47,230, was the provincial capital and like Kunsan was a crowded mass of houses and unpaved roads. The only significant industries were a hemp textile mill and a large tobacco factory and warehouse.

My new quarters were in a cluster of stone buildings, somewhere near the edge of town, with a magnificent view of the mountains. This was much better housing than the wood firetraps we lived in at Kunsan. The Personnel Record Section was in a crowded office building jammed with desks, typewriters and file cabinets.

It was a time of transition for the Regiment. Confusion abounded because the regiment had suffered a massive decrease of 715 men in November (70 officers and 645 enlisted men).[17] Apparently a fourth of the regiment had arrived in Korea, served a few weeks and then gone home on points. They were the oldest and most experienced soldiers left after the large group had gone in September. Everyone was new on the job and I don't remember getting much direction.

I was assigned to the 3rd Battalion's records and remember spending a lot of time shuffling through the files. It was interesting reading. There were records of court martial proceedings against men who were absent from their posts during combat for as little as half an hour. There were also many records of soldiers being awarded medals for heroism above and beyond the call of duty. We had several requests from men who were already home for copies of their citations. Since the Xerox machine hadn't been invented yet and the mimeograph masters had been destroyed, I would rummage through copies of the General orders, find the man's award, and type up an abstracted and certified duplicate to send him. This had to be an exact copy including any typos or misspelled words on the original. It was easy and interesting work. It was still the Army though. We had to leave our desks every day while a sergeant put us through an hour or so of close order drill and calisthenics.

We also had rifles and ammunition. One of the men was an avid hunter. One day he brought in a large goose he had shot, saying it was wild when the rest of us accused him of getting it in some Korean farmer's back yard. He was after pheasants which were quite numerous in that part of the country. I went with him one day lugging my M1 rifle while he carried a shotgun he had obtained somewhere. Pheasants were scarce that day and it started snowing and getting dark early so we turned around and headed back. Along the way back a red fox ran across our path. We fired our guns with great enthusiasm but the fox was lucky and got away.

I got along well with my new buddies, most of whom were my age with similar backgrounds but who had arrived after the war ended. They hadn't been in combat and liked to hear stories about life on the *Shimbu* Line and what it felt like to get a machine gun bullet through your leg. They were, like me, anxious to get home and resume their education.

From where we were situated we could see a large mountain. It stood out from the rest and didn't seem to be too far away. We often talked about climbing it and one Sunday, when there was nothing else to do, another soldier and I set out for it. It turned out to be a long, long way. On our way to the mountain we passed through farms and clusters of houses. We stopped to examine a Buddhist crematorium. It was like a small church with openings on all sides. Towards the front was an altar upon which the Buddhist priest could cleanse a dead body while prayers were chanted. A furnace was adjacent to the altar so the body could be slid right into the fires of purification without lifting it. The walls of the shrine were decorated with oriental pictures which were smoke-blackened. It was a spooky and forlorn place reminding us of our own mortality and the need to confront, on a psychological plane, death and the disposal of lifeless bodies. I had seen a lot of that in the past year. We didn't stay long.

Farther on we stopped to watch a family portrait being taken. The family consisted of a middle-aged father, seven daughters lined up like a stepladder with the tallest, a teenager, next to the father, down to a three-year-old tyke next to the mother. They were all dressed in the traditional Korean white and were having their picture taken in front of their house. Our appearance on the scene caused the teenagers to giggle, the younger ones to point and the littlest one to squirm around behind the mother. The photographer popped out from under a black cloth hood to see what was disturbing the picture. We backed up some distance away from this odd but strangely homey scene. The father stood there impassively, and his sad solemn face did not indicate any emotion or the fact that we were there. The photographer, with much chattering, got everyone back in line and gave us a look which indicated we had better leave, which we did. I've often wondered how that father felt having seven daughters and no sons in a land where daughters are considered somewhat of a liability. Maybe that's why he appeared so somber.

We eventually reached the mountain and began the climb to the top. The farther we climbed, the steeper it got. Towards the summit, we were pulling ourselves up by grabbing onto small trees which grew on the close to vertical slope. "I'll bet we are the first ones to ever climb this mountain," my companion said, over and over again, as we labored to make the pinnacle. When we finally got to the top and were looking out over a gorgeous view of the valley and the other mountains in the distance, we found out that we definitely were not the first. Sitting under a tree, reading a book, was a young Korean. We recognized him as a student from his blue uniform and visored cap. He apparently used the top of the mountain as a quiet place for undisturbed study. We tried to carry on a conversation with him but his knowledge of English was very limited. When it was time to leave, he showed us a path down the mountain. We had ascended up the steepest face.

The Unit History says that the "Regiment participated in Christmas programs and activities" that year. I don't remember any. I was assigned the duty of "Charge of Quarters." This meant that I reported to the office at noon on Christmas Eve and stayed there until noon of Christmas Day. The main duty was to be there to answer the phone, which didn't ring. I had a cot to sleep on and the sergeant relieved me at mealtimes. I also had visitors, buddies who didn't want me to be alone on Christmas, so it wasn't too bad.

Some enterprising soldier had printed Christmas cards for our use. Besides a Nativity scene it also had pictures of shrines and Korean people on the front and a map of Korea on the inside page. Unfortunately, it had a verse that said something like, "From this oriental isthmus,/ We wish you a very merry Christh-mus" Coming from the great two-peninsula state of Michigan, I knew that Korea was not an isthmus. When I pointed out this error, however, everybody said I was being too technical. I sent many of these cards out to friends and relatives in Michigan. They thought it was kind of odd too.

The Unit History also says that by December 31, 1945, the 63rd Infantry had accomplished the following (abridged) missions in Korea:

a. Completed the occupation of Cholla-Pukto Province.
b. Completed the disarmament and evacuation of 3,751 Japanese Army troops to Japan.
c. Military Government in Cholla-Pukto Province down to all 14 Guns (Counties) totaling 1,700,000 in population.
d. Completed the evacuation of 22,095 Jap civilians to Japan.
e. Established a processing station at the port of Kunsan. A total of 33,845 Koreans from Japan were unloaded and dispatched by rail

to relocation centers in Korea. A total of 251 Chinese were dispatched by LST to China.

f. Approximately 600 tons of Japanese ammunition and explosives were destroyed.[18]

I had made my small contribution to the group's effort.

A few days after Christmas, the commanding officer called me into his office. He said that they needed a man in the Regimental Supply Office and that he really had too many clerks at Headquarters Company, which was true. The Regimental supply officer was a friend of his and he had selected me because I had done good work. However, it meant transferring to Service Company which was located in the town of Iri. I didn't want to make the change: I liked it where I was. But when you are an enlisted man, you can't argue with an officer: he knows what's good for you better than you do. So as the eventful year of 1945 drew to a close, the boy soldier found himself in a jeep going to a new assignment in a new town. Would it ever end?

FOURTEEN

Bring The Boys Home!

*In writing a book one cannot always ask, "How will this
be interpreted?" You have to think, "What actually
happened?" My duty was to describe things as they
happened.*

—Alexander Solzhenitsyn[1]

The year 1945 had been one of tremendous world events and contrasts. The death of the beloved President Roosevelt had been followed by the violent deaths of the hated tyrants Mussolini and Hitler. Some of the longest and fiercest battles of the war were succeeded by the exhilaration of a sudden peace. The development of the atomic bomb and its beneficial use to end the war was sharply contrasted against its potential for world destruction. The horrors of the Holocaust became public knowledge and were being weighed in the trials that were beginning at Nuremburg, and the great satisfaction of victory was tempered by a tense new international rivalry already underway between the United States and Russia.[2]

In far-off Korea, we were out of touch with the rest of the world during the last part of this epochal year. We received only snippets of news and, while many things happened which affected us one way or the other, the news wasn't quite as exciting as the bulletins we had received during the first three-quarters of the year. Because I didn't pay much attention to it at the time, I was in for some surprises when I reviewed it some 40 years later.

The occupation of Japan was successful beyond all expectations. Supreme Commander MacArthur swiftly established a firm, authoritarian control over all the country and had become, in spite of critics in our own State Department, something of a hero to the Japanese

315

people. Foreign conqueror though he was, they paid him unlimited respect. It bordered on adulation. Everywhere he went, he drew crowds of admiring Japanese. This was turning out to be the first military occupation in history that met with the expressed approval of the vanquished. It was almost as if the Americans were liberators instead of conquerors.

This was not quite what the average, battle-hardened occupation soldier had expected. Many had a bitter hatred for the Japanese they had recently been fighting and expected to get knives in the back from this treacherous foe. Instead, most were, more often then not, at first puzzled and then charmed by the essentially well-mannered and law-abiding Japanese civilians; these were the same people who had lost loved ones and all their possessions to American air raids. The answer to this strange turn-about lies somewhere in the defeated Japanese psyche and to the tight ship that MacArthur ran. American troops were well- disciplined, showed good will and did not pillage and rape in the traditional manner of conquering armies.

The Korean occupation, however, was a different matter entirely. While the Koreans were grateful to get rid of the hated Japanese, they were frustrated to find their country split into two zones, with the Americans busily establishing military government in the south and the Russians setting up a "puppet" Communist regime in the north. The Koreans had expected to be freed and to be allowed to run their own show.

It is said that the 38th parallel, as a dividing line, was suggested by a junior officer near the end of the proceedings at Yalta—when the hour was late and everyone was weary and anxious to come to an agreement and return home. The Allies were keen to get Russia into the Pacific War and the 38th parallel division, in their eyes, was only a temporary line until they disarmed the Japanese and turned the country over to the Koreans. In light of the great power rivalry, it did have the two-fold virtues of being approximately in the middle of the Korean peninsula and, more importantly, the Russians were agreeable.

Otherwise, the division made no sense. It divided the country into two unequal parts. The larger northern zone was about the size of Louisiana, some 48,000 square miles. The smaller southern zone, about the size of Indiana, was 36,000 square miles. The line cut across cities, towns, villages and farms; it split up 3 of Korea's 13 provinces and it sliced across more than 85 rivers and streams. On the western side of Korea, it cut off some 375 square miles of the Oshin Peninsula, placing the southern part in the American zone. To supply troops garrisoned there, American trucks had to drive through the Russian zone. This created many problems because the Russians set up arbitrary rules and times for passing through their road-blocks.

The geographic problems were small compared to the economic problems, however. The Russian zone contained virtually all of Korea's hydroelectric power and much of its heavy industry, while the southern zone was largely agricultural and light manufacturing. The economy of the country had been established by the Japanese over the period of their 35 year rule and was functioning efficiently until it was chopped in two.

The Koreans were quick to protest this unnatural division of their land. The *New York Times* on September 21 quotes unnamed Korean leaders asserting "the crime of the occupation set-up" was that the Allies had "broken faith" with small countries in the Far East. They could not see how bisecting the country could do anything but hinder Korean independence. They also argued, very prophetically, that "when the Russians and the Americans leave—if you do leave—Korea will have two governments. It's like drawing a line down the center of the United States with the western half a Communist government and the eastern half a democracy."[3]

On October 20, it was reported that Kim Koo, the chairman of the Korean Provisional Government at Chungking, China, was planning to return to his native land after 26 years of exile. Kim Koo, also known as Kim Ku, was born in Hwanghae province in 1876. From the age of 16, he was active in Korea's anti-foreign movements. In 1896, he killed a Japanese officer and was jailed. He escaped two years later but was again apprehended for complicity in the attempted assassination of the Japanese resident-general in 1909. Paroled in 1914, he was involved in nationalist organizations until the failed uprising of 1919 forced him to flee to Shanghai. There he headed the police bureau of the Korean Provisional Government in Exile and later became its president. He masterminded a grenade attack on the Japanese emperor's state procession in 1932, the bombing of Japanese dignitaries in Shanghai and a second unsuccessful attempt to assassinate Hirohito. Beginning in 1931, he received financial support from Chiang Kai-Shek and organized military units out of fellow Korean expatriates who fought the Japanese along with the Chinese army. Koo himself survived an assassination attempt by a political rival in 1938. He recovered and resumed his leadership of the Provisional Government which took on new life as the tide turned against the Japanese during World War II. He headed the most conservative faction in Korean politics.[4]

Koo said that the Allies' occupation troops should be withdrawn as soon as possible. He thought that the U.S. would leave but was "not so sure of Russia." Mr. Koo was highly critical of the occupation plan that divided Korea into two zones. "From every point of view, economically and politically, the division is not satisfactory," he said. "Politically, the party people cannot go from one area to the another. Economically, most of the Korean electricity is in the north while industry is in the south. Southern Korea supplies the foodstuffs for the country, and again, it is difficult to send rice north."[5]

This was followed the next day by a report that Dr. Syngman Rhee, Koo's rival, had returned to Korea. Rhee was also born in Hwanghae Province in 1875. A distant relative of the Korean royal family, he was given a Confucian education and also learned English at an American Methodist mission school. As a young man he was imprisoned in 1897 for political activities seeking to reform the Korean government. There he converted to Christianity. Released in 1904 he came to the United States to further his education and received a bachelor's degree from George Washington University, a master's from Harvard and a doctorate from Princeton where he came under the influence of Woodrow Wilson. In 1911, he returned to Korea as a YMCA teacher-evangelist but was forced by the Japanese to flee back to the U.S. two years later. After the Korean revolt of 1919, he directed the activities of the Korean Commission in Washington and concurrently served as president of the Provisional Government in Exile in China until succeeded by Kim Koo. In his youth, Rhee had a traditional arranged marriage: his wife gave birth to a son who died. In 1933, while trying to present the Korean case to the League of Nations in Geneva, he met and later married Francesca Donner, an Austrian.[6]

At a celebration staged by the Koreans for the United States military forces, he was introduced by Lieutenant General John R. Hodge, the American commander, who said, "I want to introduce to you a great man who has given his entire life to the freedom of Korea . . . a man driven from his home by oppressors who has done great work for his country. He has worked without personal ambition to get Korea back into the family of nations."

Although not scheduled as a speaker, the spunky 70-year old Rhee had plenty to say that might have burned the ears of the American guests: "We remained unconquered and undivided through all the years under Japanese oppression; we shall remain so. We shall fight to remain so at the cost of our very life. The Allied powers might as well know this now." Declaring, "Someone must know the answer to this question," Dr. Rhee asked, "Is one part of Korea to be slave and the other master? What program is the 38th parallel part of? Is the United States Government cooperating with the army that occupies the northern half of Korea? Is the military government cooperating with that army? Is it intended to divide Korea half and half? Is that army in the north going to remain there permanently?"[7] These were tough questions and the Americans didn't have satisfactory answers.

During November, Rhee, as elder statesman, presided over a meeting of Korean political groups. The result was a resolution supported by 43 political parties that called upon the United Nations to end the division and to grant Koreans "an opportunity to organize our national life as a unified whole to meet the requirements set forth in the Cairo declaration." It further declared that "we now are all united . . . we want our independence . . . we ask for an opportunity to prove ourselves capable of working out our own destiny." The Koreans said that they could "set their house in order" within a year with the help of the Allies, would hold democratic elections and cooperate with the United Nations. "We resent being treated like a conquered enemy," they added.[8]

On November 16th, the State Department issued a statement saying that it "hoped" that as a result of conversations that had been in progress for some time with the Soviet Union, that communications, free trade and free passage of individuals would be resumed "soon" between the north and south parts of Korea. This would facilitate the ultimate establishment of an independent and unified country. The statement went on to review the conditions in Korea since the landings in September. The 38th parallel was intended only as a dividing line for the surrender of Japanese forces because of the distribution of Allied forces at the end of hostilities. The United States commander received complete authority to settle with the Soviet commander any local problems caused by this unnatural division of the country. Because "practical difficulties" have been encountered locally, the United States government had taken the subject up with the Soviet government in Moscow with the suggestion that they be solved by negotiation.[9] It wasn't much comfort for the Koreans to be told that problems of communication, economics and free travel in their own country would be negotiated by the two foreign occupying powers who caused the problems in the first place.

As the year ended, news came that the Big Three foreign ministers, meeting in Moscow to settle on peace treaties and other postwar issues, had discussed the Korean problem and decided that a joint U.S.-Soviet Control Commission would administer Korea under a "trusteeship" for up to five years while preparing the Koreans for self-rule. Problems brought about by the 38th parallel would be worked out in the meantime by further talks between the military commanders in Korea. General Hodge was ordered to meet with his Soviet counterpart within two weeks.

The word "trusteeship" was an unfortunate choice of words. When the Japanese first took over Korea on August 29, 1910, it was under the guise of establishing a trusteeship. The Koreans understood trusteeship to mean government by foreign armies and an inability to manage their own affairs. They were enraged and insulted. Then followed three days of riots and disorders in Seoul and incidents of stoning Americans. Military personnel in some cities were restricted to their barracks. The *New York Times* reported that all of General Hodge's Korean servants quit in protest, forcing officers on his staff to perform menial tasks. Examples included a captain and a lieutenant shoveling coal to keep the general warm in the severe Korean winter and also performing other domestic duties.[10] Under the Army's caste system, the enlisted men ordinarily do the grub work, so this was different and newsworthy.

In meetings with Kim Koo, Syngman Rhee and the other Korean leaders, General Hodge strove to make the Koreans understand they weren't being abandoned, that our program was still to get rid of the Japanese and train the Koreans for self-rule. He was handicapped by the lack of experienced Koreans able to take over key jobs vacated by the departing Japanese and by the multiple parties all claiming to be the real Korean government. Hodge estimated that it would not take the five years cited by the Moscow communique. Somewhat mollified, the Koreans called off their demonstrations and the general's servants returned to work. Meetings with the Russian commander were scheduled for mid-January.

Another subject of great interest, about which we also didn't hear the complete story while in Korea, was demobilization. Since almost everybody wanted out as soon as the war ended (opinion surveys showed that only two percent of the soldiers polled planned to make the Army a career),[11] those in charge of reducing the Army to peacetime size had a huge problem to solve.

They had devised a point system as the fair way to demobilize. Points were awarded for time in service, for months overseas, for battles and campaigns fought, and for medals and decorations awarded. Thus, it was designed to favor those who had served the longest and done the most heroic work. However, points were also given for children—12 for each child up to a maximum of 36. This was done to help reunite families but was actually out of line with the rest of the program. It caused some resentment among single men or those fatherless married men who couldn't conceive children when they were thousands of miles away from their spouses. There was also griping about the 12 points awarded for begetting a baby as compared to 5 points for a long-fought campaign or a Purple Heart medal for a severe but non-disabling wound. Most soldiers however, recognized the social good in returning fathers home to their children sooner than others without progeny.

Because the point system provided for the discharge of individuals instead of units, as had been done after previous wars, there was a massive shuffling of personnel. High point men would leave and be replaced by new draftees or lower point transferees. There was a constant turnover in some units as the number of points required for discharge was lowered. The Army did this in stages. The 80 points required in September became 70 points in October, 60 in November and by the end of December the requirement was 50 points. Those scores were for enlisted men. For officers it was somewhat higher. Women Army Corps veterans were discharged on a lower scoring value and the Navy and Marines also had different scores for discharge.

In addition, there were too many exceptions. Enlisted men over 35 years of age could get immediate discharges, regardless of point scores, as could those deemed to be of no further use to the Army, which became a notorious source of abuse. However, some who had essential jobs, medical doctors or language experts for example, were temporarily frozen on the job until a replacement could be found even though they might have very high scores.

Added to this complicated system were the practical problems of arranging transportation home for millions of men and women scattered all over the world. It had taken several years to get them all overseas, now they all wanted to come home at once. There weren't enough ships or other modes of transportation available. Some American soldiers thought that returning Japanese soldiers home from the areas they had overrun was using up boat capacity that should have been employed taking our boys home. The Army's explanation was that the Japanese were being transported on ships unsuited as to health and hygienic standards for Americans and pointed out that the sooner they were back in Japan, the less need there would be for American soldiers to guard them in far distant places.[12]

Naturally, everybody didn't get out when they thought they should. Congress was considered the remedy and its members were deluged with mail as the American public let its senators and representatives know how they felt. Some received hundreds of pairs of baby shoes with the message: "Please send my Daddy home!" In a campaign started by Pacific veterans who were tired of waiting for transportation, many letters were stamped: "No Boats, No Votes. Get Us Home".

By the end of the year and with strenuous efforts, the Army had reduced its size from the 8,300,000 men and women it had in its ranks on May 8, 1945 to about half that size.[13] Thus, over four million made it home for Christmas. This was an excellent job but it didn't satisfy those still in. Then the top brass realized that at this rapid rate of demobilization, versus the slow pace that replacements in the form of enlistments and the draft were coming in, it would empty the Army of most of its ranks by the spring of 1946. This would leave the Army dangerously short of sufficient personnel to effectively perform its main tasks of occupying enemy countries and returning or disposing of the huge stocks of war materials scattered around the world. A slowdown was ordered.

Upon news of this, the complaints grew even louder. Many soldiers and their families, were not agreeable to staying in the Army. They deluged the newspapers with indignant letters pointing out all kinds of perceived unfairness. Even the conservative *Wall Street Journal* got in on the act with an editorial denouncing the War Department's demobilization procedure as ". . . a policy which is perfectly idiotic . . . We wonder if anyone in Washington has any idea of the resentment that is being built up in this country."[14]

A "Bring the Boys Home" movement sprang up and there were demonstrations, rallies, petitions, and peaceful protests by soldiers at Army installations all over the world. Money was collected for full page ads in major newspapers to protest their delay in getting home and also to cable their congressmen. The movement, which one historian called "the Army mutiny of 1946", was very active in the Philippines where, at the end of the year, the Army still had over 300,000 troops and much government property accumulated. This was a result of the huge build-up in anticipation of the invasion of Japan. One of the leaders of the Philippine protesters was Sergeant Emil Mazey of Detroit, pre-war president of Local 212, United Auto Workers.

The participants could have been court-martialed under the Articles of War for mutiny or sedition but, since the men were war heroes (Sergeant Mazey had earned a Bronze Star medal) and had the general public's overwhelming support, Army commanders wavered between the carrot of concessions and the stick of punishment. They attempted a variety of approaches in their efforts to stop the spread of

Bring the Boys Home!

60. AMERICAN SOLDIERS DEMONSTRATING IN MANILA. American soldiers organized demonstrations against the slow pace of demobilization during the winter of 1945 –46. The demonstrations were spontaneous and occurred all over the world. The soldiers were largely supported by the public. AP/WIDE WORLD PHOTOS.

the movement. Some generals made speeches to the troops stressing patriotism and the need to impress the defeated enemy with their discipline. Others took a harsher position. When 4,000 soldiers marched in a Christmas Day demonstration in Manila, their commander, Colonel J.C. Campbell, ordered them back to their barracks with a reprimand: "You men forget you're not working for General Motors: you're still in the Army."

He was alluding to the many industrial strikes that took place in the United States during this period, especially a strike by 225,000 G.M. workers. The strikers had accepted wage freezes for patriotic reasons during the war years and now wanted large increases to make up for the lost wages. The cost of living had increased about 30 percent during that period.[15]

The Army's chief psychiatrist, Brigadier General William C. Menninger, following a tour of the Pacific Theater, stated that neuropsychiatric problems among American troops indicated the need for an orientation program to reconcile the soldiers to their duty and convince them of the necessity of occupation service. While pointing out their morale problems, he also said their general health was good although they were stationed in the most disease-ridden areas on earth.[16]

By mid-January 1946, participants in the movement could see the tide turning in their favor. The War Department decreased the number of points again. Army Chief of Staff, General Dwight D. Eisenhower announced that the new scores would reduce Army strength to 1.5 million in six months, almost halving previous projected

CITIZEN SOLDIER

LET'S NOT BE OVER CONFIDENT! The War Department has just begun to fight back. By lowering the point score two points and the service length by four months, they have flatly ignored our demands to speed up demobilization.

WHO AND WHAT are responsible for this deliberate slow down in demobilization? Is it typical army "snafu?" Do the "brass" want to protect their authority? Is it simply confusion in the War Department? No! That's part but not all of the story. It is rapidly becoming obvious to all of us that the responsibility for the slowdown rests with those who make our foreign policy.

WHAT EVIDENCE DO WE HAVE to show that there is a connection between retarded demobilization and our own present foreign policy? Maury Maverick, President Trumans special adviser after a tour of the Far East, himself admitted this connection when he said: "After establishing a firm diplomatic and economic policy we have got to have a military policy--which we can't have unless we stop rapid demobilization."

HERE IS FUTHER PROOF THAT AMERICAN TROOPS AND EQUIPMENT HAVE BEEN AND ARE BEING USED TO CARRY OUT AN IMPERIALIST FOREIGN POLICY.

In China US men and material have been used to bolster one of two warring factions. A large American military force in the Far East will make China safe for American Big Business.

In The Friendly Philippines now preparing for independence, the US is (1) Recruiting an army of 50,000 Filipino Scouts for service in the US Army; (2) Maintaining a force of over 200,000 GIs; (3) Reactivizing the 86th Division along "battlelines"; (4) Planning a permanent garrison of 70,000 Americans. Since no "critical need" could justify such a huge force, it is clear that the plan is to guarantee the predominance of American prewar vested interests in the Philippines. Nor will such a force reassure our allies in the Pacific of our peaceful intentions.

In Indonesia American equipment is being used with or without labels. The next step will be American troops to protect our surplus property in Java.

THE MUZZLING OF GI NEWSPAPERS IS AN ATTEMPT TO KEEP US FROM LEARNING THE TRUTH!

WE WERE TALKING ABOUT GOING HOME! TO GET THERE WE MUST CONTINUE OUR CAMPAIGN!

DEMAND AN END TO AMERICAN INTERVENTION IN THE FAR EAST!

DEMAND THE WITHDRAWAL OF ALL US TROOPS FROM CHINA AND THE PHILIPPINES!

PUBLICIZE AND PROTEST THE GAGGING OF THE DAILY PACIFICAN!

DEMAND THE IMMEDIATE DISCHARGE OF ALL TROOPS EXCEPT THOSE NEEDED FOR OCCUPATION OF JAPAN AND GERMANY!

NO LET-UP IN THE CABLES HOME TO CONGRESS; THE PRESS, AND TO OUR DISCHARGED BUDDIES!

61. SAMPLE OF A HANDBILL that was circulated among soldiers in the Philippines to get them to demonstrate against the slow pace of demobilization in January 1946. Courtesy of John W. Campbell, Jr., who served in the 86th Infantry Division mentioned in the sixth paragraph.

strength levels. He promised that all 45 pointers would be on their way home by April 30 and all 40 pointers, or those with two years service, would be home by June 30. That was the absolute best he could do if the Army was to fulfill the missions assigned to it to meet national goals.

Eisenhower stuck to his point system plan even though he was subjected to unusual pressures from the wives of servicemen. A delegation representing various local branches of the "Bring Back Daddy Association," the "Fathers' Release Association" and the "Servicemen's Wives' and Children's Association" intercepted him as he was going in to testify before the House Military Affairs Committee on his plans for demobilization. They had him backed into a corner answering questions until he was rescued by the committee chairman. Eisenhower told the committee that he had been "emotionally upset" by the incident and that if he could discharge all fathers at once, "two thirds of my troubles would be over."[17]

To accomplish this, Eisenhower reduced basic training from 17 weeks to 8 weeks to speed the new replacements overseas. Further training would be received on the job at their occupation posts. To further encourage enlistments, he provided free transportation to Europe for families of soldiers who agreed to stay for two years. He also promised transportation for families to Pacific posts when housing became available. To tap into a pool of 1,250,000 4-Fs who were nonfathers, the Army reduced its physical standards saying that it would now accept inductees with crooked spines, moderate psychoneurosis, mild mental deficiencies, and stuttering or stammering problems.[18]

Eisenhower also banned any further demonstrations saying the soldiers had made their point and it was now time to get back to doing their duty. Inspector-generals would be available to listen to personal complaints. Commander-in-Chief Harry Truman also came out in support of the Army. In a statement to the American people he indicated that it was a wonder that so many soldiers had already been released, but that the slowdown was inescapable in order to carry out our obligations during this difficult post-war period. "The future of our country now is at much at stake as it was in the days of the war," he declared.[19]

In the Pacific, Lieutenant General Robert C. Richardson Jr., Mid-Pacific commander, ordered court-martials for soldiers in his command who continued agitation for faster demobilization, as did General Joseph McNarney, head of the occupation forces in Europe. The "Bring the Boys Home" movement faded into history.[20]

In the "Land of the Morning Calm," we seemed to have been immune to much of the unrest that affected our comrades around the rest of the globe, although the *New York Times* reported that there was a demonstration in Seoul that General Hodge had to deal with. Soldiers were said to have raised $2,100 to buy advertisements in the *Washington Post* demanding congressional action. They were being led by the 7th Infantry's Sergeant Alexander Roberts, a combat photographer who won a Bronze Star medal for leading litter bearers, under fire, to the body of Ernie Pyle on Ie Jima, the previous April.[21]

I don't remember hearing about this, or any other demonstration, down in rural Iri where I was stationed when most of this was going on. What I do remember is 6th Division soldiers performing their military duties and patiently waiting for the point system to get down to the score they had earned so that they could go home. I also remember the Army making a strenuous effort to get soldiers to sign up for more service. There were inducements such as an immediate 30-day furlough home to the United States and your choice of job and duty station. I don't remember any takers among my teenage cohorts. We wanted to go home, but stay there. I had reconciled myself to missing the spring semester at college and thought I would easily make it home in time to enroll for the fall semester.

In the meantime, I kept busy during my off-duty hours by taking correspondence courses from the Armed Forces Institute to make up for the deficits I lacked in my college qualifications as a result of my vocational school education. I remember completing the solid geometry course with the first sergeant giving me the exam. He looked at my answer sheet with all its computations, scratched his head and said, "I'm impressed. I never was any good at math." But I had studied hard and was motivated to do well.

A couple of soldiers from the Boston area told me about the Massachusetts Institute of Technology. They described it in such glowing terms that I wrote for a catalog and an application. I received a fat package of materials in the return mail but the tuition was higher than what the G.I. Bill would pay and their math entrance requirements were tough. They started their engineering freshmen with calculus. I decided that I would be more than happy to get back to the University of Detroit.

In the Philippines, aside from the slowness of demobilization, the big news was the trial of General Yamashita. The Americans didn't lose any time bringing the defeated Japanese Commander to trial. He was formally arraigned on October 8, 1945 on charges that he ". . . unlawfully disregarded and failed to discharge his duty as commander, to control the operations of members of his command, permitting them to commit brutal atrocities and other high crimes. . . ."[22] Any horrible event that happened in the Philippines between October 9, 1944 and September 2, 1945 while Yamashita was in charge was allowed to be introduced as evidence. He, of course, pleaded "not guilty" and the trial was set to begin October 29 in the shell-scarred, high-ceiling ballroom of the Philippine High Commissioner's residence, a large building facing Manila Bay.

The court was an Army Military Commission, set up under the authority of an order issued by General MacArthur as supreme commander. The trial of Yamashita stemmed from a Sept. 12 directive of President Truman which instructed MacArthur as supreme commander to proceed with trials before appropriate military tribunals. They were to include all Japanese war criminals "as have been or may be apprehended."[23]

It was the first U.S. war crimes trial of the Pacific War. Five American generals, none of whom were lawyers, sat as judges and six lesser officers with law degrees were given the unhappy job of defending the Japanese commander. Most of those involved in the trial devoutly hoped to see Yamashita convicted and executed, so the proceedings tended to favor the prosecutors, who were all district attorneys in their prior civilian lives.

The object of their wrath was a frog-like, 60-year-old man with a shaven head and sleepy eyes. He sat in a green uniform, almost motionless and sometimes puzzled looking, at the end of a long table while one witness after another testified to the most horrible crimes that occurred while he was in command.

There were 64 charges of wholesale atrocities in the original indictment, which was subsequently amended to add 59 more, for a total of 123. They involved the deaths of 57,000 Americans, Filipinos and other Allied nationals, both civilian and military. The prosecution was expected to take about three weeks to present its case with some of its witnesses brought in on litters. The trial was open to the public, who scrambled for the 250 seats available. Chief judge General R.B. Reynolds was from Dundee, Michigan.

The lead-off witness was a pretty, 26-year-old Filipino film actress who described in graphic detail how her ten-month old baby was killed by four Japanese sailors in a Red Cross emergency hospital where she had taken refuge during the battle for Manila. The baby was bayoneted three times. She herself had been shot in the elbow and stabbed nine times, but somehow had survived. As she spoke, her bandaged, withered arm hung limply from her shoulder.

62. GENERAL TOMOYUKI YAMASHITA ON TRIAL IN MANILA. Behind him stands an interpreter while to the left, an Army photographer adjusts his camera. U.S. Army photo.

A parade of widows followed, telling variations of stories involving drunken Japanese soldiers leading their husbands and sons away to be killed. Witness after witness described Japanese military men bayoneting and shooting civilians, indiscriminately throwing hand grenades, defiling bodies and deliberately starving prisoners even though food was available. On one Manila street, a 15-year-old girl was held up by the hair and hacked at her neck with a sword as she prayed for mercy.

Japanese soldiers put candy and whiskey in the center of the dining hall of St. Paul's College where some 800 civilians were imprisoned. When the half-starved prisoners crowded around the strange offering, explosives mounted to the ceiling were set off, killing hundreds. Japanese troops rounded up hundreds of women and girls as young as 12, chose the prettiest, and led them off to Manila hotels to be raped. Many returned to testify.

One typically sensational witness for the prosecution was 11-year-old Rosalinda Andoy whose parents were both murdered by Japanese soldiers during the battle for Intramuros where the family had lived. They had taken refuge in a crowded cathedral, but Japanese soldiers came and hauled her father and the other males off to Fort Santiago, the dreaded interrogation center. There they were tortured and then killed. In the meantime, soldiers herded Rosalinda, her mother, and the other women and children into a nearby church. There they lobbed grenades into their midst and then bayoneted the survivors.

The little girl had been wounded 38 times. As tears ran down her cheeks and stained her pink dress, she turned toward the five judges and showed them the evidence. There were 10 scars on her left arm, 4 more on her right arm, 18 scars on her chest and stomach, one on her back, and 5 on her legs.

Rosalinda had stayed with her dying mother on the bloody church floor until dawn. Her mother's last words to her had been, "Always be good, Rosalinda." The little one then crawled away—slowly because her intestines were coming out of one of her stomach wounds. She made her way to Santa Rosa College where she was taken in by the nuns.[24]

While all this gruesome testimony was being heard, some of which would be considered improper or hearsay in a regular court of law, Yamashita, for the most part, sat quietly staring at the table in front of him. When his turn came to defend himself, he neither cringed or swaggered. He bowed politely to the five judges and, seating himself in the witness chair, calmly denied that he had ever known of the Philippine atrocities, let alone ordered or condoned them. During the battles inside Manila, which took place against his specific orders, he was far to the north, at Baguio directing the *Shobu* group's defense of northern Luzon.

His statement was followed by many hours of cross-examination. Even during long periods of elaborate sarcasm by some of the prosecutors, he was never trapped into contradiction. He simply waited, seemingly without anger and answered the questions directly in unhesitant Japanese. His defense was simple. He had arrived in the Philippines only nine days before the American landings on Leyte, had been unfamiliar with the country, the people and even his own officers. He was not the supreme commander, Count Terauchi was. The

4th Air Army, the Maritime Command and some other units were outside his jurisdiction. When the Americans attacked soon after his arrival, he had been involved, from then on, in the nerve-wracking confusion of losing battles. "I was under constant attack by superior American forces," he said, asking for understanding. "I . . . put forth my maximum effort to control my troops . . . I feel that I did my best."[25]

Character witnesses were flown in from Tokyo. They testified that Yamashita was a good soldier and family man, a humanitarian and not one of the militarists that had started the war. Because of his political beliefs, they testified, Tojo had banished Yamashita to an isolated post in Manchuria. This was right after Yamashita's brilliant victory in Malaya, when he should have received a hero's welcome home to Tokyo.

Just before the verdict was to be rendered, his interpreter read a statement that Yamashita had prepared: "I wish to state that I stand here today with [a] clear conscience. I want to thank the United States of America for a fair trial. I swear before my Creator that I am innocent of the charges brought against me."[26] The General's spirited defense emphasized the lack of precedent for war crimes trials, the vagueness of the rules of war and the exact responsibility of a military commander whose subordinates disobey his orders.

Nevertheless, at the end of the 32 day trial, he was found guilty and sentenced to be hanged. Only a majority of the five judges, voting in secret, was needed. His case was appealed to the U. S. Supreme Court where he lost by a vote of six to two. The majority's opinion, written by Chief Justice Harlan Stone, merely held that the Manila military court had been legally set up under our Articles of War and that it did not violate any military rules, laws or the Constitution. Furthermore, wrote Stone for the majority, "If military tribunals have lawful authority to hear, decide and condemn, their action is not subject to judicial review merely because they have made a wrong decision on disputed facts. Correction of their errors of decision is not for the courts but for the military authorities."[27]

However, a dissent by Michigan's Justice Frank Murphy revealed some deeper reservations. He wrote: "[Yamashita] was rushed to trial under an improper charge, given insufficient time to prepare an adequate defense . . . and summarily sentenced to be hanged. In all this needless and unseemly haste there was no serious attempt to charge him with a recognized violation of the laws of war . . . to subject an enemy belligerent to an unfair trial, to charge him with an unrecognized crime, or to vent on him our retributive emotions . . . hinders the reconciliation necessary to a peaceful world."[28]

A second, longer dissent by Justice Wiley Rutledge attacked the legal basis and the procedure of the military commission and its admission of improper evidence and hearsay. He also was concerned about the trial being unprecedented in our history saying, ". . . mass guilt we do not impute to individuals . . . certainly in none where the person is not shown to have participated . . . ."[29]

The wheels of justice turned mercilessly. MacArthur reviewed the proceedings and could find no "mitigating circumstances" that would allow him to show mercy to his defeated adversary. In fact, because Yamashita "profaned the sacred trust" of the "military cult," he ordered that the sentence be carried out with the Japanese general stripped of his uniform, decorations and other appurtenances signifying membership in the military profession. Petitions for clemency were signed by the Japanese people who considered the stripping and hanging order unnecessarily brutal. They expected the Americans to kill Yamashita but felt that a defeated warrior, raised in the code of *Bushido*, should be executed by a firing squad in full uniform. MacArthur ordered further news of the Yamashita story censored in Japan. Secretary of War Patterson ordered a stay of execution while a clemency plea was made to President Truman. It was lifted when Truman sent his secretary to tell newsmen that he was taking no action on the petition for clemency.

The execution order traveled down the Army chain of command to the Commandant of Luzon Prisoner Camp Number 1 near Los Banos where Yamashita was being held along with some 10,000 other Japanese soldiers and civilians, to the Officer of the Day, then to the Corporal of the Guard. The enlisted man marched down a fenced street between rows of tents housing sleeping Japanese to the inner compound and summoned Yamashita, who had been watched day and night by military police. It was after midnight on Friday, February 23, 1946. The unlucky general was hung at 3:02 A.M. under the glare of three floodlights from a rude scaffold in a Philippine cane field along with two other Japanese war criminals who had been tried separately. The condemned general was wearing U.S. Army fatigues—the symbol of military disgrace ordered by his conqueror, General Douglas MacArthur. Yet these were the same clothes that most of us common soldiers wore everyday.

In his final written statement, the Tiger of Malaya seemed to hold no grudge: ". . . I know that all you Americans . . . have tolerance and rightful judgment. I don't blame my executioners. I thank you."[30] His grave was marked by a waist-high, white post with no name or rank. It was indistinguishable from some 5,000 other posts that marked the graves of his men who had died in the camp of dysentery and malaria after their surrender.

The trial of Yamashita was only the beginning of the war crimes trials. Even before he was hanged, the trial of General Masaharu Homma, the Japanese commander during the infamous Bataan death march, had been completed in Manila. The trial judges considered marching him to death but reconsidered and had him executed by a firing squad. Other trials of Japanese who committed atrocities were held at various places all over the Pacific Theater and in Tokyo the major militarists were brought to justice, American style. All ended with similar results.

While all this was going on, I had reported to my new assignment around the 29th of December. The Regimental Supply office was part of Service Company, 63rd Infantry, and was located in a wooden office building in Iri, a small town midway between Kunsan and Chonju. It appeared to be like the other two Korean towns in which I had been stationed, with its crowded, muddy streets and its pungent odors. I was billeted in another wooden building that wasn't as nice as the stone building I had lived in at Chonju.

The work in the Regimental Supply Office was rather simple. The main job for me was to type lists of supply items that were being shipped that day. There was a flurry of activity in the morning when it was decided what supplies were available to be distributed and to which companies. These were mostly food items. They came to Iri by train or truck and were kept in a big warehouse. The manual labor of loading and unloading was done by a crew of Korean civilians.

I was directed by two sergeants. Staff Sergeant "Smith" was the Regimental supply sergeant and Sergeant "Jones" was his assistant. (These are not their real names. I can't remember them, which is just as well.) Sergeant Jones normally gave me the work assignments. "When you run out of things to do," he said, "Staff Sergeant Smith has a fill-in job for you to do." He pointed to a table in the corner of the room where there were piles of Army regulations. "Those all have to be filed," he said. I don't think many had been filed since the invasion of Luzon, the previous January. And more came in all the time.

When I ran out of work to do one day, I asked Sergeant Jones to show me how to file them. "You'll like this job," he said. "You get a chance to look at Bebe." Bebe was a girlfriend of Sergeant Smith's brother, who was a soldier in Italy. An Italian native with long blonde hair and a voluptuous body, she had posed for an 8 x 12 glossy photo which was mounted on the inside back cover of the book of Army regulations. The book was one of those hardcover, loose leaf affairs that had to be taken apart when old regulations were removed and new or revised regulations put in.

This was 20 years before *Playboy* popularized full frontal nudity, but here was Bebe in all her naked glory, from her bulging breasts to her hairy crotch. She was half-sitting, half-standing against an Army desk in a similar Army office somewhere in Italy, smiling through pouty lips. The picture had been inscribed with a pen: "I will love you always! Bebe." Staff Sergeant Smith had put the picture there thinking it would spice up the otherwise dull job of reading dense Army regulations and trying to find their proper place in a complicated filing system. However, it could also have been the reason why so many were not filed or even misfiled.

I remember New Year's Eve as being rather quiet without much celebrating. On New Year's Day, I took a walk around the countryside since we didn't have to work on a holiday. It was cold, the sky was a grey overcast and there was about an inch of snow on the ground. Iri was said to be in one of the most fertile rice growing regions in southern Korea, producing two crops a year. This day, however, the rice paddies had a thin layer of ice on them and the whole landscape exhibited a curious, barren, austere beauty.

Down by the river, several Korean women were washing their clothes in the frigid waters, using the ancient time-honored way of beating them with a wooden paddle against the rocks to get them clean. They were dressed in white and blended well with the grey and white landscape to form an unforgettable tableau. A statistician once figured Korean women spent three billion hours a year laundering their white clothes.[31]

Most of the Koreans still wore white. It was originally the color used for mourning. In their early history, whenever a member of Korean royalty died, the entire population was required to wear white for the following three years. During one period, royalty died off so fast that the people were continually in white for a long period of time and became used to wearing it. It became the normal, traditional color. To get more work out of their vassal population, however, the Japanese occupiers ordered the Koreans to be practical and wear dark clothes, but the Koreans refused. Wearing white then became a badge of honor in their 35 years of resistance to the Japanese oppressors.

January 1 also brought payday, my first in seven months. My sudden move to Chonju had prevented me from getting paid on Decem-

63. KOREAN WOMEN. While they spent many hours washing their white clothes in the river, they also spent many hours removing wrinkles by beating them with wooden bats on cold stones. It imparted a fine satiny sheen to the fabric. From: Willard Price, "Jap Rule in the Hermit Nation", *The National Geographic Magazine*, Oct. 1945, p. 438.

ber lst. We were paid in Bank of Chosen yen. After deductions for insurance, war bonds and the few partial payments that I had received along the way, it came to about 4,500 yen or $300.00. It was the most money that I had ever had at one time in my young life. Our local P.X. didn't have much to sell me because of supply problems but I did buy a beautiful 17-jewel Hamilton watch for about $50.00, the first wrist watch that I ever owned.

About a week later, I learned that Grandpa had died. I sent most of the rest of the money home to Grandma to help with the funeral expenses as I knew that he didn't have any insurance. That was one of Grandma's main worries which she had vocalized many times. It seems that Grandpa had canceled or cashed in all of his insurance during the Depression, saying that the equity in his house would take care of his last expenses. This left Grandma with the vision that she would be put out on the street after he died. His monthly pension stopped and he didn't qualify for Social Security.

According to what I have been told by my sister Rosemary, Grandpa fell out of bed on Saturday morning, December 29, 1945.

When my grandmother called my brothers to help get him back into bed, he was dead. He had not been sick but he had been failing, getting weaker as time went on. He was just short of his 83rd birthday. Because it was his expressed wish, Grandpa was laid out in the living room of the house on Dakota Avenue and many people came to call. Rosemary remembers stepmother Nettie in the kitchen making spaghetti and three-year-old Patrick being bratty. She also remembers Aunt Margaret as the loudest of the mourners at the funeral which took place at St. Benedict Church on January 2, 1946. He is buried in an unmarked grave in Mount Elliot Cemetery in Detroit.

The news of his death hit me pretty hard. He had been like a surrogate father to me after my mother died and he had agreed to take us six motherless children into his home. I remembered the many good times that we had together. The last time I had seen him was when I was home on furlough the previous January. He had surprised me with his knowledge of Texas and his tales of delivering seed packets by horseback in rural Texas and Arkansas at the turn of the century. He was a quiet, gentle man and after all the violence I had seen in the past year and a half, it was good to remember and grieve for a man who rarely even raised his voice.

Other news from home was happier. Aunt Helen, whose Christmas package to me arrived sometime in January, announced that she was expecting a baby. On February 8, 1946, she gave birth to Mary Louise Shubnell, named after my mother.

After several months in Korea and not taking the atabrine drug, I began to suffer from malaria, mostly chills, fever and vomiting. The disease is caused by a one-celled animal called a protozoan. They spend part of their lives in the red blood cells of infected humans and the other part in the female *anopheles* mosquito, which spreads them from one of the infected humans to others. The purpose of the atabrine is to work as a prophylaxis, keeping the symptoms in check by destroying some of the parasite. It doesn't cure the disease and has some unwanted side effects such as giving your skin a yellow color. Most of us who had served in the Philippines had been infected.

There was a slit trench latrine outside the Regimental supply office, since it didn't have indoor toilet facilities. When the need arose, I would dash out of the office and throw up into the snow-covered trench, meanwhile shivering uncontrollably. The local medic told me to resume taking the atabrine tablets even though there were no mosquitoes in wintry Korea. This I did until the malaria symptoms disappeared. Then I would quit again as I didn't like the yellow discoloration.

There was a Quartermaster Corps baking company nearby that supplied bread to the regiment through Service Company. In our segregated Army, the baking company consisted of all-black soldiers. They were always having equipment breakdowns and there would then be no white bread for the white troops. (Rather symbolic, isn't it?) The local mess sergeants would then make biscuits. They didn't taste very good and we soon grew tired of eating them morning, noon and night.

Sergeant Jones was the liaison between the supply office and the baking company. He was always reporting back to Staff Sergeant Smith how undisciplined the black bakers were. I remember hearing him tell that when he made a personal inspection to find out why there was again no bread being baked, he found their first sergeant still in his bunk in the middle of the afternoon. He stayed in bed while talking to the supply sergeant. In bed with him was a Korean woman. After spelling out, very politely, his usual litany of how the equipment didn't work properly and what he was doing to get it going again, the black baker said, "You gentlemen will just have to excuse me now, I have some fuckin' to do!"

Jones also made the mistake of referring to the black soldiers as "those goddam nigger bakers" in a phone conversation with some irate company mess sergeant who had called to complain about the lack of bread. Our phone system was rather primitive and he was overheard by one of the black soldiers. They promptly went on strike for a week and Sergeant Jones had to make several abject apologies to their officer, one of which I heard when he called the Regimental supply office. I remember this incident quite well because it was the first time that I had ever heard that the word "nigger" was so offensive to black people. It seemed to be a word that was quite commonly used when I was growing up in pre-war Detroit. In fact, when we had to make up our minds or choose between two other kids for a team, we would recite a rhyme that went: "Eenie, meanie, minie, moe, Catch a nigger by the toe. If he hollers, let him go. Eenie, meanie, minie, moe." I had also heard them refer to each other by that name.

It is always a revelation to find out things like that. Nowadays it is called "political correctness" to refer to black people by names they approve of, like "African-Americans." Back then, we were either insensitive or ignorant. Maybe both. We lived in our own "whites only" world, had very little contact with black people and didn't really know much about them.

Around this time we were issued the new Eisenhower jacket that replaced the old style Army blouse. Typical of Army clothes, it didn't

64. THE BOY SOLDIER IN HIS NEW EISENHOWER JACKET. This picture was taken in a Korean photographer's studio in the town of Iri, sometime in February, 1946.

fit very well. A group of us went to a Korean tailor and had them modified. Mine had to be shortened considerably. Then we went to a photographic studio and had our pictures taken. There is nothing like new clothes to brighten up an otherwise dull existence.

It was also around this time that American soldiers burned up a Korean school building that was just down the street from the Regimental supply office. They were billeted in part of it and through carelessness had started the fire. It happened during the daytime when school was in session and I remember hundreds of blue-uniformed Korean kids forming bucket brigades in a futile effort to save their school. But, just like the fire we had in the Japanese barracks at the Kunsan Air Base, huge flames soon rose high up in the air and in a short time the whole building was gone. The American soldiers were soon re-quartered in another building. I don't know what the Koreans did to continue their children's education.

The building that I lived in didn't have any centralized heat. We had individual room heaters which burned oil. You opened a petcock and let a small amount of heavy fuel oil into the bottom of an enclosed pan and lit it with a match. The heat generated was regulated by the amount of oil that was dispensed into the pan and you turned it off by closing the valve and shutting a vent. To conserve oil, we turned it off when we went to work in the morning. One day, when we came back in the evening, the oil valve had not been turned completely off and had dripped a large amount of oil into the pan.

"We are going to have to siphon most of that oil out of there," I said to one of my roommates.

"Nah, we'll just burn it up," he replied.

Before I could object, he had tossed a lighted match into the oil. We instantly had a roaring fire. Then followed some extremely anxious moments as we watched the heater get hotter and hotter. The whole furnace, which fortunately sat in a large box of sand, and the exhaust pipe eventually glowed a fiery red. Most of the building was toasty warm before the oil was used up. We were fortunate that we didn't have an explosion, hot oil spewed about, and another Korean building turned to ashes.

In the spring of the year, the company commander called me into his office. Because of the constant turnover in personnel, he was reorganizing things and thought the supply office could operate with one less clerk. He needed more truck drivers but I didn't have a driver's license. I had grown up in the Motor City in a family without an automobile and had never had the opportunity to learn to drive a family car, let alone a truck. This was long before schools took on the job of driver's education. The officer didn't have the time or the facilities to train me for truck driving, he said, but he also needed another telephone switchboard operator. I would rather have tried the truck driving but I ended up the new switchboard operator.

It was a 24-hour-a-day job, but there were two other 18-year-olds, newly arrived replacements to share the load. We rotated four-hour shifts during the busy daytime hours. At night, since there were very few calls, one of us slept on a cot in the telephone room from 10:00 P.M. to 6:00 A.M. The switchboard night alarm would wake us if a call came in that needed to be connected.

The equipment was a small, desk-mounted, rectangular apparatus that had about 30 stations on the face of it. There were a few long distance lines but most of the stations were local: the supply office, the motor pool, the mess hall, et cetera. It was primitive and well worn. It had been through the New Guinea and Philippine campaigns and was ready for the junk pile.

We sat in front of it with headphones over our ears with the switchboard in front of us showing the various telephone stations with hand-lettered identification. When a call came in, a little metal flap would open up and a buzzer would ring. We would identify ourselves by saying "Guard Service." (Guard was the code name for the 63rd Infantry.) Whoever was calling would identify themselves and tell us who they wanted to speak to. We would then make the connection by plugging in the right wires. A simple job, but it sometimes got hectic when everybody called at once or we had to deal with impatient officers who liked to pull rank and interrupt someone else's call.

I was working the switchboard one day when a call came in from XXIV Corps Headquarters in Seoul. It was a major on General John R. Hodge's staff who wanted to know if Syngman Rhee had arrived yet. I had heard that the Korean leader was coming to Iri on a political swing through the area but, as far as I knew, he hadn't gotten here. I offered to connect the major to our company commander's office but he declined, telling me to forward a message to the effect that Rhee was to call General Hodge as soon as he arrived. He also gave me instructions on how to patch the call through.

Several hours later, when Rhee finally got on the phone and I had him connected to the top military man in Korea, I listened to their conversation. We weren't supposed to do this, except to make sure of the connection, but we often stayed on the line when there was something interesting to hear. Hodge was unhappy because Rhee had been advocating that southern Korea form its own government and go its own way, regardless of what the northern half did. Rhee had grown tired of the long-stalled joint American-Russian talks on uniting the two halves of Korea and had begun talking about the south becoming an independent nation. Hodge pleaded with the veteran politico to stop such advocacy as it was making the Russians unhappy. He also spoke of the pressure he was getting from the State Department to keep pushing for a united Korea. They would never get there if Rhee didn't stick to the program. I got the impression that the wily Rhee knew that a united Korea was already a lost cause, but he did reluctantly agree to soft pedal the idea of a separate government, at least for a while. Later that evening I saw him, a wizened and wispy-looking oriental gentleman strolling around the officer's compound with his younger, Austrian wife. We would hear a lot about him in years to come.

This was about the time that Winston Churchill made his famous "Iron Curtain" speech in Fulton, Missouri. He had said, "From Stettin in the Baltic to Trieste in the Adriatic, an *iron curtain* has descended across the Continent. Behind that line lie all the capitals of the ancient states of Central and Eastern Europe . . . all are subject to Soviet influence . . . and . . . increasing control from Moscow." He might just as well have included Korea north of the 38th parallel from the Yellow Sea to the Sea of Japan.

On February 9, 1946, Premier Joseph Stalin, in a rare public address in Moscow, had declared that communism and capitalism were incompatible and that another war was inevitable. Confrontation with the capitalist West would come in the 1950s, when America would be in the depths of another depression, he predicted. This was soon followed by the news of a spy ring in Canada. They had been busy stealing secrets of the atom bomb for the Russians. Churchill's speech, delivered after an introduction by President Truman, was in answer to these developments. It caused a sensation due to the already difficult relations between the United States and Russia.[32]

In Korea the cold war was well under way. *Time*, in a report on the Seoul conference, called it ". . . a thorough failure. No accord was reached on the critical matter of exchange of raw materials and food between the U.S. and Russian zones, nor in establishing a unified currency, or telephone and telegraph communications. Colonel General Terenty Shtykov, the Soviet negotiator, had scowlingly refused to even discuss the issue of removal of machinery . . . ."[33] The Russians were suspected of systematically stripping the northern zone of industrial equipment and shipping it back to Russia. The naive Americans also thought they had an agreement with him to allow the Kore-

65. AMERICAN COMMANDER LIEUTENANT GENERAL JOHN R. HODGE confers with Russian Commander, Colonel General Terenty Shtikov, in Seoul. The man in the middle is an unidentified interpreter. Intended to arrange for the unification of Korea, the talks went on from January 1946 to May 6. No agreement was ever reached on any of the vital issues. From: General John R. Hodge, "With the U.S. Army in Korea," *The National Geographic Magazine*, June 1947: p. 830. U.S. Army photo.

ans to cross the 38th parallel for family reasons, but even this modest concession was suddenly canceled without explanation. Prospects for a united Korea dimmed as the reports of a communist people's government under Kim Il Sung for the northern zone filtered in.

Around this time, the Regimental dentist, Captain Sol Koch, came to Iri to checkup on the dental health of every soldier. This was something new. I don't remember anybody checking my teeth since I had been inducted. I guess this dentist was new and wanted the business. He marked me down for an appointment to have a cavity filled. His office was in Chonju so on the appointed day I found myself the only passenger in an Army truck bound for that city. On our way, we came upon a Korean walking along the side of the road, carrying a load of fresh eggs. The driver stopped the truck and offered him a ride. He made the Korean sit in the back with the cargo. When we got to where the Korean wanted to get off, the driver, over the Korean's loud protests, relieved him of some of his eggs.

When we were on our way again, the driver muttered, "Goddam gooks. You give them a ride and they don't even appreciate it." He even offered me some of the loot but I said something about not liking eggs. The whole incident left me feeling uneasy. That was bad enough, but while I was sitting in the anteroom waiting for the dentist, another truck driver came in looking for medical personnel. The dental office adjoined the aid station.

"I hit a gook!" he said.

"Where is he?" asked a medic, coming out.

"In the back of the truck!"

Then followed an argument about whether to treat him there or transport him to a Korean hospital. They finally gave him some first aid before sending him on. He was unconscious and appeared to me to be seriously hurt.

Having my tooth filled was a traumatic experience. There was no anesthesia and the dentist's drill was a treadle-operated apparatus powered like my grandma's sewing machine. Dr. Koch had an assistant, a soldier whose feet provided the power as he handed the dentist his tools. There was no high speed, painless dentistry in Korea at that time.

The Regimental chaplain came to Iri from Chonju on Mondays to say Mass for the Catholic soldiers in the area since the regiment was spread out all over Cholla-Pukto Province and he was limited in the number of Masses he could say on Sunday. On Easter Sunday, a soldier I will call "Walter" asked me to go with him to the native Catholic church in Iri. I reminded him that the Army priest was coming the next day but Walter wanted to celebrate the Lord's Resurrection on the appropriate day. He said he knew where the native church was located when I told him that I had never been there. We put on our dress uniforms and took off on a cool, overcast morning.

As we walked along, Walter told me that he came from Chicago and was of Polish descent but his Catholic family was not very religious when he was growing up. They seldom even went to church. He had married a very pious Catholic woman and had gotten a lot more interested in spiritual things through her example. In fact, the chaplain was preparing him for the sacrament of Confirmation. Would I be his sponsor? I said that I would.

After wandering for an hour or so through a maze of deserted

66. TRAIN DEPOT IN IRI, KOREA circa 1946. Note white garments on adults waiting for train. Photo courtesy of E.R. "Sammy Simpson.

streets where all the houses looked the same to me, we still hadn't found the Catholic church. It seems Walter only "thought" he knew where it was. We finally gave up looking. On our way back, we passed a building that had a sign on it reading "Off limits by order of the 6th Military Police." Walter got excited, forgetting all about going to church.

"This must be a whorehouse!!" he exclaimed, peering in. Entrance to the building was barred by a stone fence with broken glass embedded in its concrete top and a wrought iron, grille type gate. The warning sign was enough to keep me moving but Walter was a suddenly changed man. He was determined to get in. He rattled the gate, pounded on the wall and yelled for quite some time, to no avail. If it really was a whorehouse, the girls were probably enjoying their day off and not about to answer some crazy American's call for sex on Easter Sunday morning. I remember that on the walk home, after Walter finally gave up, he was rather subdued, not friendly and talkative like he was on the way out. He never brought up the subject of me being his sponsor for Confirmation again, either.

The married draftees and the Regular Army soldiers were more likely to use the services of a prostitute in Korea. The virginal 18 and 19-year-old draftees mostly avoided them. We found the whole idea repugnant. Better yet, we concentrated on the idea that we would be going home soon—to America where the real beauties were.

One story that made the rounds concerned a Regular Army man who visited a Korean prostitute. While he was busily engaged with the woman, the M.P.s raided the place. As they came busting in, the panicked soldier disengaged, grabbed his clothes and ran out the back door. In the darkened back yard he tripped and fell into a pit that the Koreans used to collect human feces for fertilizer. Up to his

67. SQUATTING KOREAN CHILDREN are relieving themselves in the streets. Some adults did that too but most fecal matter was carefully collected and used by farmers as fertilizer. Photo courtesy of E.R. "Sammy" Simpson.

neck in the foul stuff, and unable to climb the slippery sides to get out, he could only shout for help until the M.P.s found him. He stunk so bad, they didn't even bother to arrest him.

Sometime in May we moved to new quarters. The Army had taken over an abandoned Japanese Shinto shrine on top of a hill outside of town. The shrine building itself was large and had been remodeled on the inside to house the Service Company offices and switchboard room. Modern plumbing was also installed with a shower room. Quonset huts were built for sleeping quarters on terraces descending down from the top of the hill. It was quite an improvement over where we had been billeted. With permanent housing, it looked like the occupation of Korea was going to last for a long time.

In July, I suffered a severe attack of malaria and was sent to the Army hospital in Chonju. Burning up with fever and shaking with chills, I remember sitting through a movie that first night in the hospital. It was *The Two Mrs. Carrolls*[34] starring Humphrey Bogart as an insane, homicidal artist who secretly paints a horrible portrait of his wife when he feels that her inspiration has run dry. He then murders her and looks for a new source of artistic motivation. Barbara Stanwyck played the part of the unsuspecting second wife who slowly finds this out. Alexsis Smith played the part of the next potential victim.

Somehow, the combination of the malarial fever and the movie made me feel that I was going insane myself and I had several sleepless nights in that hospital in Chonju. When I returned to duty a week later, I was feeling weak and depressed. I had missed the Regimental Day ceremonies where Lieutenant Colonel Arndt Mueller had accepted the Presidential Unit Citation on behalf of the 3rd Battalion, 63rd Infantry for its heroic action at Hill 400 the previous year.

There were very few of us left who had been anywhere near the *Shimbu* Line. From a regiment of fighting liberators, we had been reduced to a motley collection of unwanted occupiers of a strange, foreign land. I don't know how it was in the rifle companies, but in Service Company it didn't seem to be very military anymore. We wore uniforms but our daily duties were like civilian jobs. It had been a long time since we had had any inspections, close order drill or calisthenics. We didn't stand guard duty. If the belligerent Russians had decided to sweep down the Korean peninsula, we would have had a hard time defending ourselves. Besides being out of shape physically and mentally, we had no weapons. They had long since been taken away from us.

I needed a rest or change of scenery. In June, the Army had announced a limited number of three-day passes, with transportation provided, to cross the Yellow Sea and visit Shanghai, China. I applied for one but was turned down on the grounds that I was too close to going home. The passes were awarded to Regular Army men. When I got out of the hospital one of them had already returned with glowing tales of exotic Shanghai, its Chinese prostitutes, opium dens and unlimited supplies of alcohol. This was before the communists took over and put an end to that city's vice.

Part of the problem with Service Company was its leadership. In the spring, the first sergeant had gone home. He was replaced by the Mess Sergeant (of all people!), a Regular Army man who had arrived sometime in the winter. The promotion was too much for his limited abilities. When the officers weren't around, which was most of the time in Korea as they were billeted in separate quarters, the first sergeant set the tone for the enlisted men. This one had his cot at the front end of our quonset hut. We younger soldiers had ours at the other end of the long building.

Late one night, near the end of July, there was a commotion at the

68. VIEW OF SERVICE COMPANY'S MOTOR POOL. Heavy rains in July 1946 turned it into a quagmire. The rains came after the Koreans beat drums continuously for three days and nights because planting time had come and the paddies were dry. The rain gods answered their prayers with the heaviest rain and worst flooding in memory. Photo courtesy of E.R. "Sammy" Simpson.

front of the building. A Korean pimp had brought a prostitute around and was pedalling her services like a door-to-door salesman. We all went to the front of the building to see her. She looked like most of the Korean women I had seen washing clothes in the river, squatting by the side of the road or working in the fields. They all looked prematurely old and wrinkly and had a uniformity of appearance—small bodies, straight black hair severely combed back and done up in a bun at the back, flat faces with not much of a nose and narrow, dark eyes. The first sergeant was negotiating a price with the pimp, who might have been the woman's husband. "You guys can have her after me," he said, turning to us.

"No thanks, Sarge!" we answered, almost in unison, and went back to bed.

Because my induction notice said that my service would be for a period that included the "duration plus six months," I understood that to mean that I would be home within six months of the war's end. By that reckoning I would have been home before March 2, 1946, since the Pacific war officially ended September 2, 1945 when MacArthur signed the surrender document on the Missouri in Tokyo Bay.

If the Army had stuck to the point system, I might have made it. After the "Bring the boys home" movement subsided, it abandoned the point system at 40 points. I had 39. One of the complaints of the Manila demonstrators was that no points were added for service after September 2, 1945. Secretary of War Patterson said he would do something about this but no action was ever taken. The Navy discharged sailors with point scores as low as 30 on April 2 and 28 on May 2. The Army insisted that all inductees, whether they had any combat experience or not, serve a minimum of two years.

Hugh Diamond, who was drafted with me, was discharged by the Navy in the spring of 1946. My brother Bob was also in and out of the Navy while I was serving in Korea. He was discharged early because the Navy was going to an all-volunteer force. This proved to be a problem for him during the Korean War when the government drafted anyone who hadn't served at least a year during the World War II era. He had served in the Navy about ten months. When he graduated from Michigan State College in 1951, he then put in two more years in the Army, one of them in Korea.

I had just about abandoned all hope of ever getting home when orders finally came through in August. I packed up my few belongings and went down to the railroad station in Iri to begin the long trek home. After more than a year of false hopes, the boy soldier was finally going home.

FIFTEEN

Long Journey Home

. . . memory becomes an actor on its own. You try to
make it tell the truth, and that's the best you can do.
—Tobias Wolff[1]

The train ride from Iri to Seoul took a good part of the day. Besides myself and a few other American soldiers, there were hundreds of Koreans jam-packed into every seat and standing in the aisles of the rail coaches as we chugged north through the Korean countryside. The train stopped occasionally to let some Koreans off and others would rapidly fill their places. The whole memory of the train ride has a certain surreal quality to it as I was still in disbelief that I was actually going home.

We arrived in Seoul in the middle of the afternoon. While waiting for trucks to take us to an Army depot in Inchon, another soldier and I decided we needed to use the bathroom. We asked an old Korean gentleman who was waiting nearby—using a process of animated gestures and the few Korean phrases that we knew—where the restroom was. He indicated we needed to go up the steps of the railroad station and then to the right. When we did as he told us, we found a restroom. However, it had a clear plate glass door at the entrance through which we could see two young Korean women combing their hair and putting on cosmetics. Thinking this was the women's restroom, we looked around for the men's room but could find none.

We then went back down the steps and asked the Korean to repeat his directions. He again gave us the same instructions. When we argued with him, he led us up the steps and to the right and then almost pushed us through the same glass door. The girls were still in there primping. They smiled at us, but we waited until they went out before relieving ourselves. It was a unisex facility. There were stalls with no doors on them and no seats either, only slots in the tiled floor to be used by both genders, either squatting or standing. I had been in Korea for almost ten months and had never seen anything like this before.

The replacement depot in Inchon, where we were housed for a few days while waiting for transportation home, was similar to the ones in the Philippines in which I had spent so much time. Crowds of soldiers were assembled into large, industrial type buildings. Sleeping was done in double-deck Army beds set up on the cement warehouse floor and meals were served in a huge cafeteria. This depot processed most of the incoming and outgoing Korean occupation soldiers. It was quite full when I arrived.

Since enlisted casuals were used for work details here, per the usual Army custom in replacement depots, I soon found my name on a roster to pull guard duty. I ended up on one of the gates to the compound. It was boring work. I was alone and there was very little traffic, only an occasional officer coming in or heading out in a jeep. It was also late in the afternoon of a hot August day. I was tired and still feeling the effects of that last malaria attack. My eyes wanted to close. I sat down in the little guard station. . . . The next thing I remembered was a voice booming out, "Hey soldier, you can still be shot for sleeping on guard duty!" Fortunately it was an enlisted man passing through the gate and not some officer or the sergeant of the guard. I became instantly alert. This was no time to screw up. Why, I could end up dead or the Army could keep me in Korea forever!

The next day, August 17, 1946, we boarded a ship, carrying all our belongings in duffel bags. We seemed to be taking a lot less back home. The difference was that all the combat gear -helmet, gas mask, entrenching tool, et cetera—that we brought over with us to fight a war was no longer carried in peacetime.

Our ship, the U.S.S. *Sea Star*, was fairly new. It was built in 1943 by the Ingalls Shipbuilding Corporation at Pascagoula, Mississippi and was operated by the Matson Navigation Company during World War II and afterwards, carrying troops all over the globe. The *Sea Star* was a Victory C3 type cargo ship that had been completed as a troopship. About 500 feet long and 70 feet wide, it had a top speed of 16 knots and carried up to 2,108 passengers who were housed in three large cargo holds labeled A, B and C.[2] I was assigned to the C hold with about 700 other soldiers, all jammed into a cavernous space, six and eight bunks high.

A voice on the ship's loudspeaker, as we got underway, an-

69. U.S.S. SEA STAR, the vessel that carried me from Inchon, Korea to Oakland, California in sixteen days. It was a much better voyage than when I went the other way. U.S. Navy photo.

nounced that our destination was Seattle, Washington and that it would take two weeks to get us there. It was about 5,200 nautical miles by the great circle route across the North Pacific Ocean, taking us almost to the Aleutian Islands. The crew were civilian Merchant Marines and the atmosphere was much more relaxed than the wartime regimen that we endured going over. Since there were no Japanese submarines to worry about, there were no guns, no calls to general quarters, no dousing the smoking lamp at sunset and no armed Marine guard keeping order among the troops.

The first night out, we were again in the typhoon zone as we passed between the Ryukyu Islands and the Japanese island of Kyushu. We had missed the most recent typhoon but the seas were still very rough and a lot of soldiers were already seasick, including me. I was assigned to K.P. that night in the enlisted men's mess and couldn't keep anything down as I washed pots and pans under the baleful glare of a grumpy mess sergeant. He had cooked a lot of food for the troops but not many soldiers were able to eat it.

We eventually reached calmer waters, got our sea legs and settled into the routine of a troopship at sea: reading, playing cards, shooting craps, shooting the bull and watching the endless dark blue waters go by. It was the latter part of summer, quite warm and pleasant even as far north as we were, so we spent most of the time on the crowded main deck. One enterprising soldier set up his barbering equipment and spent the voyage cutting soldier's hair at a dollar a head. His price was a little high—we were used to paying fifty cents—but he did a lot of business because everyone wanted to look good when they arrived home.

A highlight of the trip was watching some seagulls who had followed the ship out to sea when we left Inchon harbor. They flew along behind and would feed when the garbage was dumped overboard. They followed us all the way across the ocean. Maybe, similar to illegal aliens, they were migrating to a better land. I hadn't noticed any birds following us on our westward voyages, but then we were heading into a war zone. The birds might have known that.

Another highlight was meeting Verne Mattson on board. The last time that I had seen him was when we were both at Killer's Kollege at Camp Hood, Texas. We were tentmates and he had gotten pneumonia, spent a month or so in the hospital and then was placed in another battalion to complete his training. He came overseas later than I did and was assigned to the 7th Infantry Division on Okinawa and then had gone to Korea. We talked about various people we had trained with and compared notes. All had survived the war, as far as we knew.

There were outdoor movies every night on the rear deck just after dark. The movies were well attended with soldiers crowding every available space, sitting on the deck, the railing or any other available equipment. A Protestant chaplain scheduled his evening services just prior to the time the movie was to be shown. We Catholics soon realized that in order to get a decent seat for the movie, we had to get there early and sit through the Protestant service. This made the chaplain happy. As the sun set in the ocean behind the ship, he preached to a huge congregation of believers and those just there to see the movie.

We crossed the International Date Line again. This time we had two days that were the same calendar date. This was so that we could return from tomorrow back to today. We had lost a day 18 months before going the opposite way. It didn't seem as odd to be living the same date over again, as it did losing a day out of our lives. At sea, one day is pretty much the same as any other.

About two-thirds of the way across the ocean, our destination was changed to San Francisco. This added a couple of days to our voyage and we finally made port 16 days after leaving Inchon. This we did at night so I missed sailing under the San Francisco bridge. It had been one year, 6 months and 23 days since I had passed through the Golden Gate going out.

When I got up on deck on that morning of September 1, we were docked at a pier in Oakland. It was exciting to be back in America. The California sun was shining, the sky was blue. Even the buildings, actually only warehouses from what I could see, looked good. Soldiers were crowded at the pier-side rail, shouting and whistling at a pretty, blonde-haired woman standing on the dock. She was trying to find out if a certain soldier was aboard. I don't think she ever located her man but lots of soldiers said they would be willing to fill in for him.

There were no welcoming crowds or band, only the blond woman and a few port officials. We were at the Oakland Army Base so it was a short hike, when we disembarked, to one of the warehouses where we were billeted while awaiting further transportation. It was the usual Army accommodations, hundreds of soldiers packed into a large warehouse filled with double decker bunks and a loudspeaker blaring out announcements from time to time.

One of the first things we had to endure, besides the usual medical exam, was a thorough inspection of our baggage. Contraband and weapons were confiscated. A lot of soldiers had their souvenirs taken away from them. I had been forewarned that this would happen so I had mailed home a Japanese rifle and bayonet that I had obtained at the Kunsan air base. Soldiers with large amounts of cash were also detained for further questioning although some of them had come by their cache legitimately in the shipboard gambling games or by cutting hair.

It was the morning of the following day before we were given an opportunity to telephone home. After what seemed like an eternity, I got through to Grandma. It was Labor Day and she said that it was no holiday for her as she was washing clothes. She had three kids to get ready to go back to school the next day. Mary Lou was a senior in high school, George was a sophomore and Kenny was a freshman. But then, she always did do her laundry on Mondays. It was a vivid reminder that other people's lives and all their routines go on without you when you are away for a long time. Some things do change but many remain the same.

Grandma was as tough as ever. Grandpa's death hadn't slowed her down one bit. At age 76, she was dealing with life's problems with her usual verve. When she didn't like the crowd that Mary Lou was running with at St. Benedict School, she yanked her out and sent her to an all-girls Catholic high school in Royal Oak. She also said that she was sending George to U of D High School as she felt he needed the guidance of the Jesuit teachers there. Unmentioned at the time was a serious problem with my Uncle Russ that she was also trying to handle herself.

Grandma reported that everyone was healthy. Rosemary was still working and Bob was already home, discharged from the Navy. He was planning on enrolling at Michigan State College. Hugh Diamond, who had been drafted the same day that I was had been home for some time. What was holding me up? "Only the Army's reluctance to let loose of a valuable man like me," I told her. What we both didn't know at the time was that it would be two more months before I would be officially discharged.

We were offered passes for the rest of the day. I went to San Francisco with several other young soldiers on an electric train that ran on one deck of the Oakland Bay bridge. At that time, the train ran on one deck and two-way auto traffic ran on the other. When I returned to the Bay Area in 1958, I was surprised to see that the train had been eliminated and each deck carried one-way auto traffic. Subsequently, a very expensive train system called BART was built to supplement the ever-growing traffic between San Francisco and Oakland.

Because we were all underage, we couldn't get into a bar so we ate dinner at a restaurant on Market Street. Vast quantities of fresh milk and ice cream, food that we hadn't eaten for more than a year and a half, were consumed. We then went to the movies. I was disappointed my companions didn't want to see some of the city's other attractions. This was my second visit to the city by the bay and I still hadn't seen much of it. It would be 12 years before I would be back.

On the train returning to the base we met a couple of soldiers who had some disquieting news. They said that civilian life was tough. There weren't many jobs and the low pay of the few available made for a very frugal existence. They had tried it themselves for about six months and had then returned to the Army. They advised us to re-enlist. When we protested that we would never go back in the Army, they said, "You will see things differently after you are out a while. You'll see!"

We left the Oakland Army Base late in the afternoon of the next day, the train noisily straining to make it up the grade as it rose to get over the coastal range. I was struck by the straw color of the grassy hills which, in September, were burned out from lack of rain. The California hills had been a brilliant emerald green when I last saw them—in February of the previous year.

Our train coach was not a Pullman or a sitting coach. It was a freight car that had been modified to carry troops. Not the famous "forty and eight" of World War I which transported forty soldiers and eight horses in rather primitive conditions. Ours had regular seats which were quite comfortable. They made up into double deck bunks at night. The converted car still had the center freight doors on one side. While they had to be closed at night when the beds were made up, during the day we left them open as we traveled across the vast western states. We took turns sitting in the door openings, our feet dangling out of the freight car like hoboes.

At stops along the way, I bought copies of *Time* magazine and several newspapers. The price of *Time* had increased from 15 to 20 cents a copy while I was gone.[3] Pauline Betz, the foremost woman tennis player of that era, was on the cover of one of them.[4] She won the women's national championship for the fourth time that week at Forrest Hills. Also in sports, Ben Hogan won the National Pro Golf championship and Paul Mantz won the Bendix Air Race from California to Cleveland. He flew a P-51 at 435.6 mph, 135 miles per hour faster than the last race which was held in 1939. Milestones reported that Fielding Yost, as coach and athletic director for 40 years the grand old man of University of Michigan football, had died in Ann Arbor at age 75.

It felt good to get caught up on what was happening. President Truman was back from an 18-day vacation, cruising the North Atlantic on the presidential yacht, the *Williamsburg*. It was said that he was able to vacation for the first time in his presidency because Congress was in recess, his desk was cleared and he had no major emergency facing him. He took the cruise even though he didn't like fishing and he got seasick in the rough waters. He felt a lot better after they pulled into port at Bermuda.[5]

In foreign relations, the State Department was busy. Acting Secretary Dean Acheson was demanding indemnity payments for five fliers and two planes shot down by Yugoslavia in August. The planes were unarmed and had strayed into Yugoslavian air space. Marshall Tito formally apologized.[6] Notes were also sent to Poland, protesting that the communist dominated government was not living up to its agreement to hold free and fair elections there, and to Russia, rejecting its bid to share control of the strategic Dardanelle Straits with Turkey. Also in the Mediterranean Sea, Admiral Halsey was quoted as saying that his fleet will go ". . . anywhere we please." Movement of the aircraft carrier, the U.S.S. *Franklin D. Roosevelt*, to Greece to support a Greek election had been criticized by the Communists as "Gangster Diplomacy." The Greeks voted to bring back King George II.[7]

In Germany, the Nuremburg war crimes trials were finally over after 284 days. They had produced a 15,000 page, five million word record and death sentences for most of the convicted Nazis. From Japan came a report from MacArthur on the first 12 months of occupation. Japan's war potential had been destroyed and her Army of five million soldiers disarmed and repatriated. Thousands of Japanese civilians had also been brought back from overseas and resettled. The emperor had renounced his divinity and the Shinto religion was separated from government sanction and barred from being taught in schools. Under a new constitution, women had been liberated and an election held in which 27 million Japanese voted. The chief problems remaining were rebuilding the war-shattered economy and feeding the people. Food had to be imported, mostly from the U.S.[8] In Korea, the U.S. State Department reaffirmed all of its original pledges made to the Koreans at Cairo and Potsdam. It blamed the Russians for the present chaos and said that U.S. troops would stay until Korea had democracy.

In Vietnam, the big question seemed to be "Who was Ho Chi Minh?" The answer, according to *Time*: "Ho was a self-styled president who demanded Vietnam's right to manage its own affairs and annex neighboring Cochin China (Laos). He walked out of the peace conference when the French, who were negotiating to maintain their presence in an all Indo-China Federation, said 'no.'"[9]

The Army continued to have manpower problems. After a two month summer draft holiday, the local Selective Service boards had prepared notices for 25,000 men to enter the Army during September. They weren't drafting 18-year-olds anymore and were limited to conscripting men from 19 to 29 with many exceptions. Exempt were fathers, essential agricultural, production, transportation and home construction workers, college and university professors and veterans who had served overseas or for at least six months in the United States. Temporarily deferred from military duty were medical, dental, and veterinary students and certain researchers in physical sciences and engineering. The Selective Service planned on inducting 200,000 men into the Army before the current draft law extension expired in April of 1947.[10]

The Navy announced that it had closed 29 separation centers. It had met most of its manpower needs through voluntary enlistments. Over 3,070,581 officers and enlisted men had been discharged out of a VJ-Day total of 3,400,000. The only non-regulars still on duty were a few essential doctors and corpsmen and some reservists who had volunteered to stay on until the following July.

In the business section of *Time* the news concerned the drop in the stock market. The Dow-Jones industrials had dropped 8.56 points in a week, the worst weekly drop since the last bull market in 1937. The writer didn't seem to know what this presaged. The Price Decontrol Board ordered a restoration of ceiling prices on meat. When hog and cattle producers heard this, they held back from bringing their animals to market. When the effective date was reset to September 1, there was a thunderous stampede of animals to the slaughtering houses. Prices hit an all time high.[11]

The 1946 harvest was huge but there was a lack of rail transport to get the produce to market. Potatoes were especially plentiful. Secretary of Agriculture Clinton Anderson had set a goal of 378 million bushels. However, near perfect weather and the use of DDT had resulted in a bumper crop of 455 million bushels. With people starving in war-ravaged Europe and Japan, it would seem logical to send them the extra potatoes, but they wanted grain. Most of the excess would rot in the fields. My Irish ancestors were probably spinning in their graves. They might have been heartened a little by the news that some of the spuds were bought up, at bargain prices, by distillers and would be used to make alcohol.[12]

Radio was still a major entertainment; commercial television hadn't arrived yet. Arthur Godfrey, who had been on the air since 1930 with an early morning radio show, was moving his *Talent Scouts* to Tuesday evening at 10:00 P.M. on CBS. "If I am successful," he said, "I won't have to get up early anymore." He was going against Bob Hope on another network.[13]

Time's program listing noted that Frank "The Voice" Sinatra was beginning his winter series of programs that week at 9:00 P.M. Wednesday evenings on CBS. George Burns and Gracie Allen were returning for their fifteenth year and Edgar Bergen could be heard on Sundays at 8:00 P.M. on NBC.

The music writer thought he detected a movement away from swing music. Big bands were going out after being king for 12 years. Charlie Barnet was cutting down from his 21 piece, 6 trumpet band, and at Chicago's College Inn, teenagers were dancing to Claude Thornhill's sedate, glossy arrangements of *Warsaw Concerto*, the *Nutcracker Suite*, and *Yours Is My Heart Alone*. Sweet music was in, loud music out. Maestro Benny Goodman, the daddy of big band swing, summed up the plight of his fellow noisemakers: "The trouble is that they just play too damn loud. A guy who is good doesn't have to worry about trends."[14] The idea of teenagers schmoozing to softly played music seems kind of quaint now to a fellow who lived through the advent of amplified rock 'n' roll and had to constantly wrestle with his teenagers over the volume control, during the tumultuous 60s nd 70s.

Movies were still the major entertainment. *Time* was listing as Current and Choice, *The Killers*, an adaptation of the Hemingway short story with Burt Lancaster and Ava Gardiner, *The Big Sleep*, with Humphrey Bogart and Lauren Bacall, and *Notorious*, with Ingrid Bergman and Cary Grant. There were no war movies listed although Alfred Hitchcock's *Notorious* was about post-war Nazis plotting and spying in South American capitals.[15] The public had had enough of battle scenes, at least for awhile.

In the books section, *Mr. Roberts* (Houghton Mifflin, 221 pages, $2.50), Thomas Heggen's report of life aboard the good ship, U.S.S. *Reluctant* was said to be an accurate and humorous portrayal of Navy duty for many of its sailors during World War II.[16] It later became a very successful Broadway play and movie.

It took more than three days to get across country during which I soaked up the news and watched the panoramic mountain and prairie scenery go by. It was similar to Rip Van Winkle returning after his 20 year sleep. I had only been gone a year and a half but everything seemed different in peacetime America compared to what it had been like when I left during wartime.

I remember waking up in Dubuque, Iowa, early Friday morning and crossing the Mississippi River into Illinois soon afterwards. "A few hours more and we will be pulling into Fort Sheridan," I told everyone. However, the train turned south and entered the Chicago area from the southwest. The whole afternoon was wasted as we sat on one siding after another in the stockyards section of this great city, waiting for clearance to proceed. A trainload of human cargo sitting next to trainloads of cattle and other animals destined for slaughter.

Eventually, long after dark, we passed through Chicago and were headed north through the Lake Michigan suburbs. Almost to our destination, we were again shunted to a siding to allow a fast passenger train which ran from Chicago to the Twin Cities to pass. Our troop train seemed to have the lowest priority of all the trains. We finally shuffled into Fort Sheridan about 10:30 P.M. As the crow flies, the distance between Dubuque and Fort Sheridan is about 155 miles but our round-about trip had taken over 13 hours.

At the Fort we were greeted with the news that, with the heavy flow of veterans to be separated and the lack of staff, it was taking about ten days to process soldiers for discharge. The sergeant-in-charge said that we would not have to spend it all at Fort Sheridan. If we volunteered for work details the next day, he would give us three-day passes to go home. The German POWs, who did a lot of the grub work when I had been at the Fort in 1944, had long since been repatriated home.

Some of the veterans said they didn't want to go home until they could stay there. They had long distances to travel and it would be too hard for them to return. They would wait out the Army and wouldn't volunteer for work either. The idea of volunteering for work was distasteful to me too, as I had had enough of K.P. and guard duty to last me a lifetime. But, I also wasn't going to hang around the Fort waiting. The next morning I applied for a pass but didn't sign up for any work details. The day was spent resting and getting ready to go home. When the passes became available late in the afternoon, I picked mine up and was out of there before they could check up on me. There is still a certain amount of satisfaction in this memory because it was the only time I ever got away with anything during my entire Army service.

It took about ten hours of train and streetcar riding and walking to get from Fort Sheridan, Illinois, to my home in Detroit. I arrived there in the wee hours of Sunday morning, noticing that a new grocery store had been built where a used car lot had been on the corner of Woodward and Six Mile Road. No one had told me about that news. When you are thousands of miles away from home you like to know what is happening in the old neighborhood. Why hadn't they written me about that?

Since my trip was rather hurried, I hadn't called ahead. I had to ring the doorbell and wake everyone up. There were welcoming hugs and kisses, smiles and tears, everybody talking at once and awkward silences. The boy soldier was home from the war at last, looking pretty much the same as when he left. At least that is what they told me. From my point of view, everyone looked strange and yet familiar at the same time. The younger ones had grown quite a bit and changed the most. Grandma decided that I needed nourishment and cooked a pork chop dinner for me. I ate it at three o'clock in the morning although I wasn't hungry.

It was great to be back, even temporarily. But I was still in the Army and I had to go back after three days.

SIXTEEN

You Know You're Home When. . .

Sometimes I stopped and looked about me with disbelief.
It really was true. I was out of the Army. . . . I was very
nearly twenty-one years old. I was free! Free!
                                                    —A. N. Wilson[1]

On the train going back to Fort Sheridan, I met a soldier who had gone to the Ford Trade School with me. Corporal Charles MacLachlan (June '44) was in the Finance Corps at the Separation Center and told me all about the monetary benefits I would be getting. There was three hundred dollars mustering out pay, spread out over three months, as well as the money for first-class transportation from the Fort to my home. I would also receive pay for all the unused leave time which soldiers earn at a rate of 30 days a year. Since I had had only a one-week furlough in the two years that I had served, I had 53 days leave coming. This was welcome news.

When the conductor came through announcing that the dining car was now serving dinner, my classmate got up to go while I hesitated. In all my train travels, I had always been fed by the Army or had eaten snacks or lunches prepared by Grandma. "Come on," he said, "you can afford it." He was right—with all that Army money I had coming, I could eat first class. I followed him into the dining car where we enjoyed a sumptuous meal served by attentive, white uniformed stewards on fine china with elegant table linens and silverware while the beautiful Michigan scenery raced by. Everything looked so green after the miles and miles of the arid western states

I had recently traveled through. This is how officers eat, I thought to myself.

I only fumbled once. I showed my ignorance of Pullman dining cars when I tried to give my order orally to the black waiter. I was directed to write down my choices on a little pad at the right side of my place setting. I have always thought that was a strange custom, but then it put the responsibility on the diner. It also helped the chef if the waiter couldn't read or write, which was common.

Charles also reported that big changes were taking place at our alma mater. Superintendent F.E. Searle had retired and there had been a large shuffle in school personnel. The academic department had moved out of the Rouge plant. Camp Legion, its new site, was the name of an encampment on a 521 acre piece of land that Henry Ford owned in Dearborn. In the spring of 1939, he had set up a group of tents for the sons of disabled veterans of World War I. The boys worked the land eight hours a day and in return received room, board, agricultural training, and two dollars a day pay. The crops, mostly garden vegetables, were sold and the money divided among the boys. After a couple of years, the tents were replaced by wooden barracks. In early 1945, this project was discontinued, more buildings were built and the site was used for World War II veterans' rehabilitation. That program was also discontinued in 1946 and the academic division of the Henry Ford Trade School moved there on September 3, 1946.[2]

My friend also reported that the Michigan Superintendent of Public Instruction was going to allow the school to issue high school diplomas as the curricula was being revised to eliminate deficiencies. New entering students would be required to have completed the ninth grade. This meant no more going to night school to complete college entrance requirements. I had been born six years too soon!

Other changes had been revisions of the scholarship payments, elimination of the Thrift Fund and the installation of automatic time clocks to speed up the entrance and exiting of the 1,000 students. This was about two-thirds of what the enrollment had been during the war. It would be harder for new boys to get in but their education would be much improved. We fantasized the eventual enrollment of girls into the school which would have been exciting. For that time, it would have been revolutionary.

All this was a reflection of the new, vigorous management at the Ford Motor Company under the leadership of Henry Ford II, who had taken over completely the previous year. The school's founder, the original Henry Ford, was said to have declined in mental and physical abilities and was living out his last days in virtual seclusion at Fairlane, his vast estate in Dearborn.

Henry Ford died of a cerebral hemorrhage the following April. He had expected to live to be one hundred years old because he took care of his health and watched his diet. However, he suffered a series of minor strokes in 1938 and in the early 40s. After Edsel's death in 1943, he seemed to Harry Bennett his closest associate, ". . . a tired old man who just wanted to live in peace." Just before the auto pioneer died, severe rains caused the Rouge River to overflow its banks, flooding his private powerhouse and disrupting his telephone service. He left the world lit by candles and warmed by log fires, just as he had entered it 83 years previously. His final ride to the cemetery was in a Packard. But that was appropriate: the cars he manufactured were for ordinary people, not grandiose enough for hearse work.[3]

Back at Fort Sheridan it took the better part of the following week to go through the process of separating from the Army. They didn't just hand you your discharge and money and show you the door. We had to go through another complete physical examination and listen to lectures on what the separation process consisted of, what to expect in changing from the military to civilian life and options we had to consider in regard to our serviceman's life insurance and other matters.

Each soldier was interviewed individually and given an opportunity to re-enlist in the regular Army or sign up for the Army Reserves. The incentive for joining the reserves was that in the event of another war, you would hold your rank or occupational specialty. I declined, saying that if there was another war and I had to go, I hoped to be in the Navy. That wasn't received too well by the regular Army sergeant trying to get me to re-enlist.

We also were given the option of choosing the unit and occupational specialty we wanted printed on our discharge form from all the units we had served in and the jobs we had performed. I had been trained and served mostly as a rifleman, but my record also showed time spent as a medical orderly, clerk typist and telephone switchboard operator. The corporal interviewing me advised putting "clerk typist" on the discharge, saying it would help to get a job in civilian life. We both agreed that there were not many employers looking for riflemen. However, in subsequent years, I never applied for a clerk-typist job and regretted having it put on my discharge.

We were also given an opportunity to apply for disability compensation if we had suffered wounds, injuries or illnesses. The Army didn't do this but there were representatives from the various veterans organizations at the Fort who would act as your agent if you joined their ranks. The much vilified Red Cross was also performing this service. Since I wasn't ready to choose a veteran's organization at that time, I went to the Red Cross. A female Red Cross volunteer took down all the information and filled out the necessary forms for me. She must have done a good job because I wasn't home very long when I received a letter from the Veterans Administration awarding me 30 percent disability compensation for my gunshot wound and ten percent for the malaria I was suffering from.

The malaria faded away over time, as is the case if you move away from an area where you are being constantly reinfected. The Veterans Administration rescinded the award after three years. The only long term problem I had was that I could never donate blood. Any mention of a history of malaria was a cause for rejection. The Veterans Administration called me in for a physical examination of my gunshot wound after five years and renewed the award at 30 percent. I haven't been examined since. My leg aches if I drive a car for long distances, and more so the older I get, but otherwise it hasn't been much of a problem.

There were other salesmen at Fort Sheridan who were trying to sell us everything from unit history books that hadn't even been published yet to used cars and insurance. I declined all offers.

At one of the stages of separation, the Army was supposed to issue all the medals we had earned and had not received. Besides the Sharpshooter's Medal that I had earned at Camp Hood, I had received only my Purple Heart Medal. I had quite a few more medals coming. Ribbons, representing the medals and worn on one's uniform, were sold at Post Exchanges and Army and Navy stores. The medals themselves had to be issued by lawful authority.

When I passed through Fort Sheridan, all that they had on hand was a huge hamper of Good Conduct Medals, which no one really wanted. The Good Conduct Medal was given for an unblemished record of three years service, which was the normal enlistment period. During the war, this was reduced to one year. Most soldiers weren't eager to get one since this meant you were some kind of a goody two-shoes. However, the Army was determined to issue the medal. When I was in Korea, it issued a General Order awarding the medal to several hundred of us who had passed the one-year mark without getting into trouble. I wish now that I had kept my copy since it had a lot of names of my buddies whose names I have long forgotten. The private manning that station stamped my name on one, placed it in a box, handed it to me and said, "You will have to write to the War Department for the rest of your medals. We are out of everything else."

I finally got most of the rest of my medals in 1963 when I wrote to the Department of Defense. They sent me the Bronze Star Medal, the Asiatic-Pacific Theater Medal with two bronze battle stars, the Victory Medal, and the Army of Occupation Medal. I also wrote to the Philippine government several times for a Philippine Liberation Medal. It took six years to get one.

When I went to collect my pay, I learned that I wouldn't get all my money then; I would have to serve out my time at home on terminal leave. My discharge date would be November 2, 1946. The Army would pay me as I used up my leave by sending me pay checks on October 1 and November 1. I wouldn't have to come back for any ceremony; they would mail my discharge certificate to me after November 2.

Terminal leave had been a bone of contention during 1946. Officers got it as a matter of course but the vast majority of enlisted veterans passed through separation centers during the first wave of demobilization without receiving it. Realization of this inequity resulted in letters to congressmen and to the editors of leading publications. The Army belatedly began giving it out in the summer of 1946. In far-off Korea, I hadn't heard about it so it was news to me. The government actually saved money in my case because my Army pay was less than the veteran's benefits—disability compensation and student allowance, that I couldn't collect while still on the Army payroll.

One of the last things we did was to turn in all our extra clothes. We were allowed one set each of summer and winter uniforms to go home in. Still in the Army, I went home to stay.

While I was in the service, my brothers had worn out all my clothes, believing that they wouldn't fit me when I got back home. Actually, I had checked out of the Army at 141 pounds compared to the 140 I weighed in at. I had to wear my uniforms until I could buy some civilian clothes. Suits took about a week to buy and get altered to fit so I was in my dress uniform for a while, at least whenever I went somewhere that I was expected to look nice. Since they were still giving servicemen free rides on the busses and streetcars and lower admission prices at places of amusement, being in uniform had some advantages, although I was usually greeted with the question "What are you doing still in uniform?" It was no longer fashionable.

I visited a lot of friends and relatives during my three-day pass and the first week or so that I was home for good. There had been many articles in the newspapers and in popular publications on how returning combat veterans would behave. People worried about the psychological effects of war on their loved ones. Post-traumatic stress disorder as a medical condition hadn't been recognized yet, but combat soldiers of World War II were suspected of possibly suffering psychoneuroses from their ordeal. Many writers offered suggestions on how returning veterans should be treated. As a result, I got the impression that I was under surveillance until they realized that I had come home quite normal.

However, for a long time afterwards I had a recurring dream that bothered me. In it, I was attacking a superior Japanese position. I couldn't seem to find sufficient cover as I advanced. I would wake up shaking with fear as I lay exposed and shot at. It varied from time to time. In one manifestation, I was in a classroom at the Ford Trade School. The Japanese were set up at the teacher's desk and I was trying to find cover behind one of the seats in the back row. I leave it to psychologists to figure out what that connection means.

My father, whom I caught staring at me at our first dinner together, said that he had a hard time getting used to seeing me smoke cigarettes. Grandma expressed relief that I hadn't taken up drinking. She also had read or heard too many stories about the sexual activities of servicemen overseas.

"I hope I don't answer the door someday and find a Chinese woman with a papoose looking for you, Russell," she said. While she made a joke of it, I knew she was serious because she repeated it on several occasions. I patiently explained that the Army had kept me too busy to get in trouble and they were Koreans where I was stationed, not Chinese, and they didn't call their babies "papooses," but *agi* or *yua*. I was glad my conscience was clear, although it was more a result of lack of opportunity than virtue on my part.

My uncle Bill is the only one who asked me about combat. The others all observed the rule that a veteran was not to be quizzed about his battle experiences. We were alone, smoking cigarettes in his den after one of Aunt Katherine's big dinners. As was the custom then, she was in the kitchen cleaning up after preparing the meal while we men were taking our ease. She had a full-time teaching job, too.

Uncle Bill grew up on a farm and hunting was part of his life experience. He had a whole gun case full of rifles and shotguns in his den. However, in his later years when he went deer hunting every fall, he never shot a deer. He just liked to see deer in their natural setting and it bothered him to kill one.

He prefaced his question by saying that he knew he shouldn't be asking this and if I really didn't want to answer it, he would understand. "What," he asked, "did it feel like to shoot at people?" I told him that I had been given long and intensive training and that when the situation arose, I just reacted instinctively. Most of the feeling was fear and excitement. Since I had no control over what I had to do and believed that what we were doing was necessary, I really didn't experience guilt. Anyway, combat was only a small part of my total Army experience. It seemed to satisfy him. He never brought up the subject again.

Other people showed no interest at all. I called up the girl who had sat next to me in Chemistry 101 at U of D and had written me such nice letters while I was overseas. We arranged a date to go to the Cass Theater. *Cyrano de Bergerac*, with Jose Ferrar in the title role, was playing. When I arrived at her house, she wasn't quite ready to go so I had to sit in the living room with her father. I was in my dress uniform. After a perfunctory introduction, he went back to reading his paper leaving me to stare at the ceiling. Now if I had a young man, fresh from overseas and displaying a Combat Infantryman's Badge, a Purple Heart Medal and several other ribbons and citations on his uniform, about to take my daughter out, you can be damned sure that I would be asking him some penetrating questions. I had been anxious to make a good impression. He ignored me completely.

My friend was now a senior at U of D while I was returning as a second-semester freshman. She didn't ask me much about my Army experiences either, preferring to talk about the impending school semester. She invited me to the Freshman Welcome Dance that was to take place on Friday night following the football game. The senior women were sponsoring this dance for the freshmen and she was on the committee. She needed to be there early. "Look for me," she said as we parted. "I will be there."

On the way home from the date, I took the McGraw-Davison bus that ran from the Ford Rouge plant to Highland Park. I had ridden it regularly when I had worked the afternoon shift before being drafted. Some of the passengers who were going home from work recognized me and showed a lot of interest.

"You making a career of the Army?" they asked.

"Hell, no!" I answered, somewhat irritated. "I just got home and haven't been able to get some new clothes yet."

"When you coming back to work at Ford's?"

"Not for a long time, maybe never. Uncle Sam is going to pay me to go to college."

"Some people have all the luck," one said. Others wished me well, saying that they wished they had gone to college. They wouldn't be working for Ford's.

I had written to the university while I was in Korea and told them I expected to get back in time for the fall semester. They had acknowledged it by sending me an admissions card.

I had made it home just in time. Registration was the first week that I was home for good. It was chaotic. When I had entered the university in January of 1944 there were only 27 incoming freshmen in the College of Engineering so it had been quite pleasant. The college officials had been very welcoming and we had all been personally interviewed by the Dean of Engineering.

Registration in the fall of 1946 was another story entirely. The freshman engineering class numbered over one thousand with the upper classes equally crowded. All this was because of the vast wave of returning veterans who were taking advantage of the G.I. Bill and the opportunity for a free education. The lines were interminably long, the school officials tired and cross. Before I was completely registered, they called a halt to the proceedings and told us we had to come back at the end of the week. They had some serious problems with the scheduling of classes for so many students. To their credit, they solved all the problems and we completed the registration process at the end of the week.

I went to the football game with Eddie Greiner, a classmate from Ford Trade School who was also attending the university at night. He worked during the day at the Detroit Edison Company and had not been in the service. He was driving his mother's business coupe[4] and had his girlfriend with him. The three of us squeezed in for the short ride to the stadium. I was wearing my new suit.

The Titans romped to an easy victory over their opponents. Their new head coach was in his second season. Charles "Chuck" Baer was assistant coach at the University of Illinois when he was hired by the University of Detroit to be their head coach in February 1944. He had his work cut out for him as U of D had been out of competition for two years because of the war. He fielded his first team in the fall of 1945 after much recruiting around the country. Many of the players had returned from the military where they had honed their skills playing for service teams instead of fighting the enemy. U of D football was very successful during Baer's tenure, 1944-1951. The revenue from the football games was said to have funded the whole athletic program.

The dance was held afterwards in the gym. It was supposed to be limited to the college's women and the men of the freshmen class. However, it looked like the whole student body had moved from the stadium over to the gym and crowded in. The men outnumbered the women ten to one. It reminded me of some of the USO dances that I had attended, except that all the men were in civilian clothes.

I searched a long time before I found my friend from the senior class. She was sitting in the stands with a man I didn't recognize. He looked like an upperclassman who hadn't been in the service. The stranger held her hand tightly but he was turned facing several other people that he was talking to. The band was big, loud and brassy. The trend toward smaller bands playing softer music had definitely not reached U of D.

"You look nice in your new suit," she said, trying to be heard above the din. She hadn't said anything about having a steady boyfriend. He let go of her long enough to shake my hand when she finally introduced us but immediately resumed his possessive hold. After some more small talk, they moved on to the crowded dance floor. I made an attempt to find my friend Eddie in the mob but couldn't locate him. I figured he was probably in his mother's car trying to make out with his girlfriend.

I decided to walk home. It was a mild September night and the distance was about two-and-a-half miles, not much for an infantryman. I had done it many times going to my Aunt Margaret's house, which was nearby, or going home from classes prior to being drafted. I was soon marching east on McNichols Road counting cadence. Hup, tew, ter-ee, forp, hup, tew, ter-ee, forp! I was still in the Army and acting military.

But then it struck me. Technically, I would still be in the Army for another five or six weeks, but in reality I was home to stay forever. The new suit had done it. I had regained the place in life that I had been forced to leave to serve my country. There was a sense of closure.

At Fort Sheridan, an officer had lectured about some veterans being "disoriented" and not fitting into a "changed society." It was probably another Army trick to get soldiers to re-enlist. I was a free

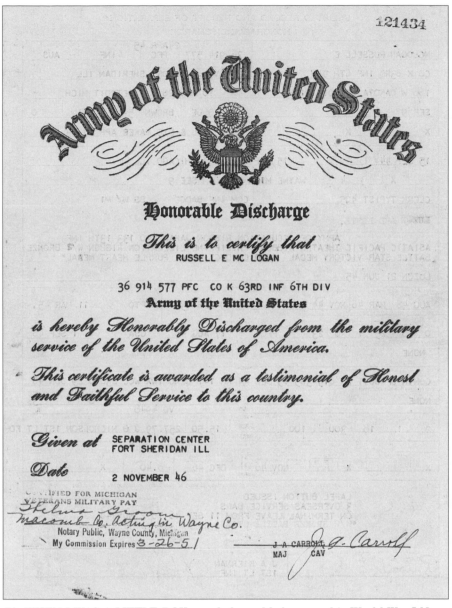

121434

Army of the United States

Honorable Discharge

This is to certify that

RUSSELL E MC LOGAN

36 914 577 PFC   CO K 63RD INF 6TH DIV

Army of the United States

is hereby Honorably Discharged from the military service of the United States of America.

This certificate is awarded as a testimonial of Honest and Faithful Service to this country.

Given at   SEPARATION CENTER
FORT SHERIDAN ILL

Date   2 NOVEMBER 46

CERTIFIED FOR MICHIGAN
VETERANS MILITARY PAY

*Thelma Groom
Macomb Co. acting in Wayne Co.*
Notary Public, Wayne County, Michigan
My Commission Expires 3-26-51

J A CARROLL   *J. J. Carroll*
MAJ   CAV

70. WHEN I WAS A LITTLE BOY, my dad would show me his World War I Navy discharge and tell me that it was worth a million dollars. What he meant was that you couldn't buy one for any amount of money; you had to earn it. I felt that I had earned mine.

RUSSELL E MC LOGAN

To you who answered the call of your country and served in its Armed Forces to bring about the total defeat of the enemy, I extend the heartfelt thanks of a grateful Nation. As one of the Nation's finest, you undertook the most severe task one can be called upon to perform. Because you demonstrated the fortitude, resourcefulness and calm judgment necessary to carry out that task, we now look to you for leadership and example in further exalting our country in peace.

Harry Truman

THE WHITE HOUSE

71. ALONG WITH THE DISCHARGE CERTIFICATE, we were given this personalized copy of a letter from President Truman thanking us for our efforts.

THE UNITED STATES OF AMERICA

TO ALL WHO SHALL SEE THESE PRESENTS, GREETING:

THIS IS TO CERTIFY THAT
THE PRESIDENT OF THE UNITED STATES OF AMERICA
AUTHORIZED BY EXECUTIVE ORDER, FEBRUARY 4, 1944
HAS AWARDED

THE BRONZE STAR MEDAL

TO

Private First Class Russell E. McLogan, 36 914 577, Infantry

FOR
MERITORIOUS ACHIEVEMENT
IN GROUND OPERATIONS AGAINST THE ENEMY
Pacific Theater of Operations, during the Luzon Campaign

GIVEN UNDER MY HAND IN THE CITY OF WASHINGTON
THIS   8th   DAY OF   January   19 63

MAJOR GENERAL, USA
THE ADJUTANT GENERAL.

SECRETARY OF THE ARMY

72. AFTER THE WAR, the Army announced that any soldier who had earned a Combat Infantryman Badge was entitled to a Bronze Star Medal. When I received mine in 1963, it was signed by Cyrus Vance who later became the Secretary of State in the Carter administration.

man now, one with a purpose. I could handle things on my own, no matter how changed they were. No more boy soldier!

I was eager to start my new classes on Monday morning. Who would be my new lab partner in Chemistry 102? My friend had moved on but there were other girls that I was interested in. Maybe I would call one tomorrow. I slowed down to a saunter and kicked a pop bottle, sending it bouncing down the sidewalk. The noise re-echoed up and down McNichols Road. It felt good.

The best was yet to come!

THE END

Endnotes

Preface and Acknowledgements

1. I found this quote in a publication of the Department of Michigan, Military Order of the Purple Heart. The author wishes to remain anonymous.

2. Studs Terkel, *"The Good War": An Oral History of World War Two*, (New York: Pantheon Books, 1984), pp. 3, 16.

Chapter One
The Boy Becomes a Soldier

1. Robert Goralski, *World War II Almanac 1931–1945*, (New York: G.P. Putnam's Sons, 1981), p. 422.

2. William A. Mann, "Color Blindness", *World Book Encyclopedia*, Vol. 4, (Chicago: Field Enterprises, 1971), p. 667.

3. Herman J. Miller, S.J., *The University of Detroit 1877–1977: A Centennial History*, (Detroit: University of Detroit Press, 1976), p. 216.

4. Lorretta Chyba, "ASTP Leaves University", *The Varsity News*, 23 Feb. 1944, p. 1.

5. Martha E. Sorenson and Douglas A. Martz, *View From the Tower: A History of Fort Sheridan, Illinois*, (Highwood, Ill.: Tower Enterprises, 1985), pp. 5–10.

6. Sorenson and Martz, p. 36.

7. Sorenson and Martz, p. 35.

Chapter Two
Killers Kollege

1. "Joy and Hate", *Time*, 23 Nov. 1942, p. 21. McNair was in charge of training for all U.S. Army Ground Forces. He was killed while on an inspection tour in Normandy when American bombers accidently hit his observation post near St. Lo.

2. Population figure of 63,500 is from the *AAA TourBook for Texas*, 1992 Edition. The 1946 *Encyclopedia Britannica* shows a population of 1,263, which is the census figure for 1940.

3. These figures are from information furnished by the Fort's Public Affairs Office entitled "III Corps and Fort Hood, Home of the Mobile Armored Corps, Facts as of 30 Sep 1991."

4. Most of the historic information that I have cited can be found in: Odie B. Faulk and Laura Faulk, *Fort Hood: The First Fifty Years*, (Temple, Texas: The Frank W. Mayborn Foundation, 1990), chapters 1 through 4.

5. Odie and Laura Faulk, p. 38.

6. Odie and Laura Faulk, p. 43.

7. Odie and Laura Faulk, p. 81.

8. Odie and Laura Faulk, p. 56.

9. Odie and Laura Faulk, p. 85.

10. Odie and Laura Faulk, p. 187.

11. Odie and Laura Faulk, pp. 3–9.

12. Odie and Laura Faulk, p. 49.

13. Frank Loesser, *The Frank Loesser Songbook*, (New York: Simon & Schuster, 1971). "What Do We Do in the Infantry?" was introduced by Bing Crosby and was a popular hit in 1943.

14. Directed by Frank Capra, they were made by the U.S. Army Signal Corps in 1943 and 44 using newsreel footage and Hollywood stars as narrators.

15. Kent Roberts Greenfield, general editor, *The United States Army in World War II, Volume I: The War Against Germany*, (New York: Artabras Publishers, 1990), p. 262.

Chapter Three
Fort Ord and a Long Voyage

1. "Buy a Bomber Campaign Successful", *The Craftsman*, January, 1945, p. 3.

2. "Hollywood Canteen", *New York Times*, 16 Dec. 1944, p. 19, Col. 2.

3. The information on Fort Ord is from *Welcome to Fort Ord: Home of the World's Greatest Fighters*, (San Diego: Marcoa Publishing, Inc., 1987), 44–58.

4. General Stilwell, known as "Vinegar Joe" for his forthright manner, went on to become commander of all the United States Forces in the China-Burma—India Theater. He later commanded the Tenth Army on Okinawa after Lieutenant General Simon Bolivar Buckner was killed in June of 1945.

5. Lee Kennett, *G.I.: The American Soldier in World War II*, (New York: Warner Books, 1989), p. 94.

6. Kennett, p. 111.

7. Written in 1944 by Bud Green, Les Brown and Ben Homer, "Sentimental Journey" was a very popular hit tune in 1945, running second in record sales and fifth on the Hit Parade. It was the first major record success for Doris Day. Les Brown made it the theme song for his band.

8. His report understated our losses. By the time the war ended seven months later, total casualties were 1,103,641, of which 292,131 were killed. In addition, there were 115,187 deaths of servicemen from non-battle causes and 6,000 civilian deaths, mostly in the Merchant Marine. Figures are from:

"World War II," *Encyclopedia Britannica*, Vol. 29, (Chicago: Encyclopedia Britannica, Inc., 1991), p. 1,023.

9. Kitty Kelley, *His Way: The Unauthorized Biography of Frank Sinatra*, (New York: Bantam Books, 1986), p. 104.

10. Susan R. Pollack, "Sea Sickness Can't Be Waved Away", *The Detroit News*, Sept. 10, 1989, Section J, pp. 1–3.

11. Roland W. Charles, *Troopships of World War II*, (Washington, D.C: The Army Transportation Association, 1947), p. 169.

12. Roland W. Charles, p. 169.

13. *Hasenpfeffer* is a variation of euchre and played with 25 cards. It was invented by the Pennsylvania Dutch and the name translates to "jugged hare with pepper"—one of their favorite dishes.

14. Kennett, p. 117. The *Dorchester* was famous for the four chaplains who gave up their life belts so that other soldiers could live.

15. Samuel Taylor Coleridge, "The Rime of the Ancient Mariner", Part II, lines 121, 2.

16. Ronald H. Spector, *Eagle Against the Sun*, (New York: MacMillan, 1985), p. 502.

17. John Costello, *The Pacific War*, (New York: William Morrow & Co., 1982), p. 547.

18. Justus M. van der Kroef, "New Guinea", *World Book Encyclopedia*, Vol. 14, (Chicago: Field Enterprises, 1977), p. 178.

Chapter Four
On The Trail of MacArthur

1. Lance Morrow, "Folklore in a Box", *Time*, 21 Sept. 1992, p. 50.

2. "Murphy, Frank", *Encyclopedia Britannica*, Vol.15, (Chicago: University of Chicago, 1947), p. 977.

3. James A. Robertson and Charles S. Lobingier, "Philippine Islands", *Encyclopedia Britannica*, Vol. 17, (Chicago: University of Chicago, 1947), pp. 725–33.

4. Robertson and Lobingier, p. 727.

5. H. de la Costa, S.J., *Readings in Philippine History*, (Manila: The Bookmark, Inc., 1965), pp. 278–9.

6. "MacArthur's Legend", *Time*, 2 March 1942, p. 23.

7. William B. Breuer, *Retaking the Philippines*, (New York, St. Martins Press, 1986), pp. 7–8.

8. Most of the facts of the Leyte campaign that I have used can be found in books like William B. Breuer's *Retaking the Philippines* and Rafael Steinberg, et al, *Return to the Philippines*, (Alexandria, Va.: Time-Life Books, 1980).

9. To make it more difficult to break the American code, most messages were padded at either end with meaningless gibberish. In this case, Nimitz's encoding officers had added the phrase "the world wonders" as extra bag-

gage. For unknown reasons, Halsey's decoders failed to discard the extra words as they normally would. Thus Halsey got what he considered a sarcastic and insulting message.

10. Breuer, p. 77.

11. Breuer, pp. 50–51.

12. In February 1945, Suzuki with Yamashita's approval, started to evacuate the best of his troops to other islands where he hoped to hold out indefinitely. It ended in dismal failure as Allied aircraft and PT boats prevented any large scale movement, although about 1,000 Japanese, including Suzuki himself, made it to Cebu by the middle of March. In April, he lost his life in a vain attempt to sail on to eastern Mindanao. See: Robert Ross Smith, *Triumph in the Philippines*, (Washington, D.C.: Government Printing Office, 1963), p. 587.

13. Steinberg, p. 91.

14. National Archives, *History, 21st Replacement Depot*, 10 Oct 1944–Jan 1946, REDE-21-0.2 Box 22959.

15. Bill Mauldin, *Up Front*, (New York: Henry Holt & Co., 1945) pp. 125–7.

16. National Archives, *Military History, 4th Replacement Depot*, Period: February and March, 1945, p. 8.

17. Oliver Stone, Writer/Director, *Platoon*, Helmdale Film Corp., 1986. An Orion Pictures release.

18. Lee Kennett, *G.I.: The American Soldier in World War II*, (New York: Warner Books, 1989), p. 73.

19. "City's Leading Airman is U.D. Grad", *Varsity News*, March 21, 1945, p. 1.

20. Kennett, p. 141.

21. Michael Curtiz, Director, *This is the Army*, Warner Brothers, 1943. The film had all the soldier entertainers of the road show plus a galaxy of Hollywood stars including George Murphy, Joan Leslie and Ronald Reagan. The future President, listed as Lieutenant Ronald Reagan in the credits, played George Murphy's son. The movie was nominated for three Academy Awards and won one for Best Scoring of a Musical Picture.

22. Susan Sackett, *The Hollywood Reporter Book of Box Office Hits*, (New York: Billboard Books, 1990), p. 42.

23. The Americal Division had no number like all the other infantry divisions. It had been formed in New Caledonia in the early days of the war from regiments of other divisions when the Army changed from having four regiments to three per division. The Americal Division saw action on Guadalcanal and Bougainville before coming to the Philippines.

Chapter Five
The Day the President Died

1. During a presidential campaign speech in New York, Nov. 3, 1932. It was also used by Woodrow Wilson in his 1912 campaign. Wendell Wilkie

hammered on that theme to no avail during the 1940 campaign but a sizable majority of the electorate thought Roosevelt was indispensable and elected him to an unprecedented third term. In the 1944 election, the majority again felt that he was indeed indispensable to the war effort. See: Bergen Evans, *Dictionary of Quotations*, (New York: Delacorte, 1968), p. 345.

2. Truman said this to newsman the day after Roosevelt died. See: "The 32nd", *Time*, 23 April 1945, p. 22.

3. J.P. McCarthy was a local radio personality who broadcast a morning talk show over Detroit AM station WJR for many years. In 1992 he was inducted into the Radio Hall of Fame at the Museum of Broadcast Communications in Chicago.

4. Ray Tucker, "Roosevelt, Franklin Delano", *1946 Britannica Book of the Year*, (Chicago: Encyclopedia Britannica, Inc., 1946), p. 647.

5. James Roosevelt and Sydney Shalett, *Affectionately, F.D.R.: A Son's Story of a Lonely Man*, (New York: Harcourt Brace & Co., 1959), pp. 361–65.

6. Charles S. Lobingier, "Manila", *Encyclopedia Britannica*, Vol. 14, (Chicago: Encyclopedia Britannica, Inc., 1947), p. 806.

7. There are many accounts of the liberation of Manila. I have drawn heavily from Robert Ross Smith, *Triumph In the Philippines*, (Washington, D.C.: Government Printing Office, 1963), chapters XII through XVI. This is the official Army version. Also used is a more vernacular account which is not as accurate: Laurence Cortesi, *The Battle for Manila*, (New York: Kensington Publishing Corp., 1984).

8. William B. Breuer, *Retaking the Philippines*, (New York: St. Martin's Press, 1986), pp. 125–6.

9. Raphael Sternberg, et al,, "Deliverance at Santo Tomas," *Return to the Philippines*, (Alexandria, VA: Time-Life Books, 1980), pp. 123–133.

10. *Mabuhay* means "victory" in Tagalog, the main dialect of the more than 70 languages and dialects spoken in the Philippine Islands. I was surprised that most of the Filipinos I met spoke English, although with a few peculiarities. It is hard for them to pronounce the "F" sound since it is missing from their native tongue. Even the word Filipino comes across as "Pilipino."

11. Bill Underwood, "Freeing Camp Santo Tomas", *The American Legion Magazine*, March 1995, p. 36.

12. Breuer, p. 260.

13. Roosevelt and Shalett, p. 366.

14. Anonymous, *The 6th Infantry Division in World War II— 1939–1945*, (Nashville: The Battery Press, 1983), p. 160.

15. Anonymous, p. 161.

16. Wilson A. Heefner, *Twentieth Century Warrior*, (Shippensburg, Penn.: White Mane Publishing Co., 1995), p. 151.

17. For biographical information on Colonel Yon, I am indebted to R. Wayne McDaniel, Alumni Director, University of Florida, Gainesville, Florida, who sent me a packet of information on their alumnus from their files.

18. Jennifer St. John, *Sixth Infantry Division History*, (Paducah, Ky.: Turner Publishing Co., 1989), p. 68–9.

19. The Presidential Unit Citation was approved and finally awarded more than a year later. At a ceremony at Camp Hillenmeyer, Korea on July 20, 1946, Lieutenant Colonel Arndt Mueller, (still 3rd Battalion Commander), accepted the honor for his men.

20. Bandoleers were cloth bands which had pockets for the eight-round clips of bullets. With two of them criss-crossed over our shoulders and down our chests, we carried about 160 rounds of ammunition. Our cartridge belts also had pockets for clips, but they weren't used as much because they were harder to get at in an emergency.

Chapter Six
On the Shimbu Line

1. Bill Mauldin, *Up Front*, (New York: Henry Holt and Co., 1945), p. 5.

2. Ronald H. Spector, *Eagle Against the Sun*, (New York: MacMillan, 1985), pp. 518–19.

3. Arndt L. Mueller, *Objective: New York–New York*, (Unpublished monograph, 1994), p. 29.

4. They socialized together and Edison had written a letter to Henry Ford about the evils of tobacco which was also on display at Greenfield Village.

5. General Order 37, Headquarters 6th Infantry Division, A.P.O. #6, 28 March 1945, p. 1. There seems to be an error of date or place in the General Order. It gives the location as Cauringan and the date as February 4. However, Company K had moved from Cauringan by Feb. 4, to Abar #2 between Munoz and San Jose. I have given the location as Abar #2, as the day-to-day history shows a 47mm gun knocked out there. Confusing the names of Philippine places is very common in the records.

6. General Order 120, Headquarters 6th Infantry Division, A.P.O. #6, 26 June 1945, p. 2.

7. Arndt L. Mueller, *A, B & X: An Agonizing Enigma*, (Unpublished monograph.) Much of the narrative on the taking of Hill A, B and X is excerpted from Colonel Mueller's writing.

8. Mueller, p. 1.

9. Mueller, p. 5.

10. Captain Isadore E. Goldberg, Assistant Regimental Surgeon.

11. Arndt L. Mueller, *Objective: New York, New York*, pp. 28–9.

12. Glen P. Laub to Russell McLogan, Nov. 20, 1991.

13. Both men were evacuated to hospitals and returned to duty as the war ended, in time to go home on points. Laub says he enjoyed the Army and would do it again. Highlights of his Army service were meeting his wife, Elsie, at a watermelon party while taking basic training at Camp Wheeler, Georgia, and learning to pick cotton in Tennessee. The yankee boy was paid 80 cents for working all day.

14. The proximity fuze, VT(Proximity) relied upon the completing of an electrical circuit to detonate the shell when its own radio waves responded to an object in its lethal area. They could provide air-bursts above the heads of enemy infantry. Unfortunately, the Japanese usually hid in their caves and only came out when the shelling stopped.

15. Mueller, *A, B & X: An Agonizing Enigma*, p. 9.

16. John Munschauer, *War and Remembrance*, (Unpublished monograph.) p. 17. Munschauer joined the company about a month before I did as a replacement for an officer who was injured.

17. William Shakespeare, *The Life of King Henry the Fifth*, Act IV, Prologue, lines 1–9. This play was made into a four star movie with Sir Laurence Olivier reciting those immortal lines on the eve of the battle of Agincourt. Filmed in wartime England, the movie was released through United Artists to American audiences in 1946. The depiction of medieval England's triumph on the Continent was appropriate for the time and the movie was well received as the British celebrated their victory over Nazi Germany. Olivier was awarded a special Academy "Oscar" for outstanding achievement since he was the movie's producer, director and principal actor.

18. Munschauer, p. 17.

19. The carabao is a species of water buffalo that was the principal beast of burden in the Philippines at that time. They had been domesticated and used to draw carts, carry loads and cultivate the rice paddies. When the Japanese fled into the hills, they took a lot of the Filipino's carabaos with them to carry their equipment. Many were killed in the ensuing battles.

20. Charles Ford was still 17 when he lost his life in a training accident. According to his brother, John Ford, in a letter to me dated October 30, 1992, Chuck was in a formation of VT 10 torpedo bombers, when two of them collided and spun into the ocean off Martha's Vineyard on October 4, 1944. Chuck's position was radio-gunner in the bottom rear of the plane. No bodies were ever recovered. When the crash took place, they were in the final phases of their flight training prior to assignment to carriers in the Pacific Theater. He is remembered in a memorial stone at the National Cemetery in Fort Custer near Battle Creek, Michigan.

21. Boblo is a Canadian island located at the mouth of the Detroit River where it empties into Lake Erie. It had an amusement park and other recreational facilities but the best part of going there, in those days, was often the hour and a half boat ride from Detroit. The boats don't run anymore and the island is being developed for upper income housing.

22. The gecko is a small lizard that inhabits warm, tropical climates and has the ability to climb on smooth surfaces such as rock. It comes out at night and feeds on insects. The loud call that these reptiles make gives them their name. With variations in the sound, it is a short step from GEHK'-O to the "F-word".

23. Sergeant John McLeod, "The Heavyweight", *Yank, The Army Weekly*, Sept. 21, 1945, p. 4.

24. After the war ended, the War Department decided that anyone who earned a Combat Infantryman's Badge was also entitled to a Bronze Star Medal. It differed from the regular Bronze Star Medal that was given for heroic actions. In the inscription, it says "For meritorious achievement in ground operations against the enemy" and is based on having shown exemplary conduct in action. Those who got the medal for a specific heroic action had their feat written up in a General Order.

25. Rafael Steinberg, et al, *Return to the Philippines*, (Alexandria, Vir.: Time-Life Books, 1980), chapter 6.

26. Steinberg, p. 178.

27. Steinberg, p. 179.

28. Robert Ross Smith, *Triumph in the Philippines*, (Washington, D.C.: Government Printing office, 1963), p. 398.

Chapter Seven
In Kembu *Country*

1. As quoted in an interview for the *Jackson [Mich.] Citizen Patriot.* Faye Moskowitz is an author who was born in Detroit and raised in Jackson, Michigan. A professor of writing at George Washington University, Washington, D.C., she has won rave reviews for several autobiographical books and poems. See Linda Braun-Hass, "Bridges to the Past", *Jackson Citizen Patriot*, November 20, 1991, P. 4.

2. The reason for the seeming confusion appears to be in Change Order 1 to Field Order No. 8, 63rd Inf 22 April 1945. On the original order, the 2nd Battalion was ordered to follow the 3rd Battalion to the Clark Field area on May 5. The change order redirected the 2nd Bn. to the Mount Natib area on April 30 and to use the trucks that were to take us to Clark Field. While we were waiting for new transportation, we were under the control of the 38th Division. Switching 15,000-man divisions around is a massive logistics problem and bound to have a few glitches.

3. Arndt L. Mueller to Russell McLogan, July 15, 1993.

4. Arndt L. Mueller to Russell McLogan, July 15, 1993.

5. The hand-out was marked "approved for mailing" so I don't know why it was butchered by the censor. However, censorship was a subjective thing and I found a lot of ludicrous examples in my research.

6. Anonymous, "Operations on Luzon, P I For Period 9 January 30 June 1945", *Unit History—63rd Infantry Regiment*, File 306 Inf (63) 0.3 (Washington, D.C.: National Archives), p. 31.

7. The material on the battle for Clark Field and the surrounding hills is drawn from: Robert Ross Smith, *Triumph in the Philippines*, (Washington, D.C.: Government Printing Office, 1963), chapters X & XI.

8. Smith, p. 186.

9. Smith, p. 207.

10. I had a similar experience when we were patrolling in the 6th Division

rear areas near Noviliches. We came upon a battery of heavy artillery and stopped to rest. The artillerymen went out of their way to be hospitable to us, offering food, cigarettes and candy. They spent most of their war far behind the front and rarely saw the enemy that they were constantly shelling. They said that they had a lot of respect for the infantryman who had to deal directly with the Japanese.

11. George Cukor, Director, Metro Goldwyn Mayer, 1944. At the time, I didn't realize that this was a five star movie in which both Charles Boyer and Ingrid Bergman were nominated for top Academy Awards. Bergman got hers for Best Actress but Boyer was edged out by Bing Crosby for *Going My Way*. *Gaslight* also saw the movie debut of Angela Lansbury as a flirtatious maid. She was a 17-year-old clerk at Bullock's Department Store without any acting experience before she made the movie, but did so well that she was nominated for Best Supporting Player.

12. Anna Rothe and Helen Demaret, *Current Biography: Who's News and Why, 1945*, (New York: H.W. Wilson Co., 1946).

13. "Screen Comedian Who Turned Serious," *New York Times*, December 23, 1945, P. 15.

14. S-2 Periodic Reports, *Unit History—63rd Infantry Regiment*, File 306 Inf (63) 0.3 (Washington, D.C.: National Archives), shows Japanese being killed approaching the K-Company outpost on 24 May 1945 and also on 1 June 1945. It must have been the one killed on June 1 that I helped to bury since I was on patrol May 24–26.

15. The 38th Division had killed about 8,000 more of the *Kembu* by the time it was relieved by the 6th Division on May 3. See Smith, p. 207. Our Division historians credit the 6th Division with 1,320 killed and 269 captured during our stay here. See *The 6th Infantry Division In World War II: 1939–1945*, (Nashville: The Battery Press, 1947), p. 125.

16. S-2 Periodic Reports, *Unit History—63rd Infantry Regiment*, File 306 Inf (63) 0.3 (Washington, D.C.: National Archives).

17. S-2 Periodic Reports, 3 June 1945 says that this prisoner, who ". . . surrendered to K Co. at 910 this morning . . . led a patrol to the area near [the] 345 Bomber Gr 3 1/2 miles NE of STOTSENBURG, where one Jap body was found apparently killed by guerrillas. PW forwarded to Division."

18. S-2 Periodic Reports, 25 May 1945.

19. "Brrr! What Global Warming", *Time*, 20 July 1992 p. 19.

20. Arndt Mueller, *Objective: New York, New York?*, (Unpublished monograph, 1993), p. 29.

Chapter Eight
Up Against the Shobu

1. Emil Swiatek, S.T.L., "War", Hi-Time (Elm Grove, WI) Vol. 15, Issue 7, 12 Feb. 1971, p. 4. The author gave no reference for this quote and I have been unable to verify it. Frank Magill in his book, *Magill's Quotations in*

Context, (New York: Salem Press: 1965), p. 1095, acknowledges that the statement "War is hell!" was ascribed to Sherman before his death in 1891 but says that in a search of newspapers and his speeches, he could not find the exact words. The closest he could come was in a speech that Sherman made to some fellow veterans at Columbus, Ohio on August 11 , 1880 in which he said: ". . . There is many a boy here today who looks on war as all glory, but boys, it *is all hell*. You can hear this warning voice to generations to come. I look upon war with horror, but if it has to come I am here."

2. Anonymous, "The Case for War," *Time*, 9 March 1970, p. 46. The famous World War II General seemed to glory in it.

3. Anonymous, "Two Steaks for the General", *Time*, 4 June 1945, p. 46.

4. Anonymous, "Half War, Half Peace", *Time*, 4 June 1945, p. 19.

5. Anonymous, "Balloon Bombs", *Time*, 11 June 1945, p. 56. Also see: "Picnickers Beware", *Time*, 4 June 1945, p. 22.

6. Anonymous, "The People Agree", *Time*, 4 June 1945, p. 23.

7. The material on the Okinawa campaign is mostly drawn from John Keegan, *The Second World War*, (New York: Penguin Books, 1989), chapter 31. Another good short account that I used is: Ronald H. Spector, *Eagle Against the Sun*, (New York: MacMillan, 1985), pp. 532–40.

8. Anonymous, "The Vortex", *Time*, 28 May 1945, p. 26.

9. Anonymous, "Hero of Hen Hill", *Time*, 25 June 1945, p. 31.

10. Keegan, pp. 568, 573.

11. Anonymous, "Plans for Punishment", *Time*, 25 June 1945, p. 31.

12. Anonymous, "Twilight in Tokyo", *Time*, 11 June 1945, p. 29.

13. "Plans for Punishment", p. 31.

14. Material on the Mindanao Campaign is from Robert Ross Smith, *Triumph in the Philippines*, (Washington, D.C.: Government Printing Office, 1963), chapter XXXI, and from Rafael Steinberg, *Return to the Philippines*, (Alexandria, VA: Time-Life Books, 1980), chapter 5.

15. Smith, pp. 403–415.

16. Anonymous, "Shootin' Texan", *Time*, 11 June 1945, p. 33.

17. Material on the *Shobu* Group is from Smith, Part Six, "The Conquest of Northern Luzon", pp. 449–572.

18. Smith, pp. 509–10.

19. Smith, p. 539.

20. Arndt Mueller to Russ McLogan dated May 3, 1991.

21. Herb Fowle, *The Men of the Terrible Green Cross*, (Hillsdale, MI: Herb Fowle, 1991).

22. Anonymous, "Operations on Luzon, P.I. For Period 9 January–30 June 1945", *Unit History—63rd Infantry Regiment*, File 306 INF (63) 0.3 (Washington, D.C.: National Archives), p. 34.

23. Smith, p. 561.

24. The official Army history uses the word "route" for these roads. The 6th Division history calls them "highways". I use the term "highway" because that is what we called it at the time.

25. Smith, pp. 563–568.

26. Anonymous, "Operations on Luzon, P.I. For Period 9 January–30 June 1945", pp. 34–35. I quoted only what the unidentified historian wrote about the 3rd Battalion since we were in the lead. The other two battalions were engaged in guarding the rear areas during this first week of the campaign. The periods covered are from 1700 hours (5:00 P.M.) one day to 1700 hours the following day.

27. Konon was not the first regimental fatality. I Company lost a man, Private First Class Henry A. Hopper, on the 15th.

28. Anonymous, "Operations At Kiangan, Mountain Province, Luzon, P.I., 1 July–21 August 1945", *Unit History—63rd Infantry Regiment*, File 306 Inf (63) 0.3 (Washington, D.C.: National Archives), p. 1.

29. The MlAl Thompson submachine gun fired a .45 caliber bullet from a 20 round box magazine. It had a regular rifle stock. Another version, the M3 had a telescopic tubular butt and was known as a "Grease Gun."

30. Casualty Report For the month of June [1945], National Archives, File 306 Inf (63).

31. Enemy casualties are drawn from the S-2 Periodic Reports. They started a new count when we moved north, although they continued to accrue the totals from the landing on January 9. By then they were showing a total of 3,836 killed and 115 captured.

32. Much of this can be found in a pamphlet published by The Christophers. See Joseph J. Fahey, *Peace, War and the Christian Conscience*, (New York: The Christophers, 1970). A shorter version can be found in Richard N. Ostling, "The Moral Debate: A Just Conflict, or Just a Conflict?", *Time*, 11 Feb 1991, pp. 42–51.

33. Studs Terkel, *"The Good War"*, (New York: Pantheon Books, 1984). He says in a note at the front of the book that the quotation marks had been added, not as a matter of caprice or editorial comment, but simply because the adjective "good" mated to the noun "war" is so incongruous. It was also good marketing because there is a natural inclination to compare World War II, the good war, with Vietnam, the bad war.

34. Lee Kennett, *G.I.: The American Soldier in World War II*, (New York: Warner Books, 1987), p. 12.

Chapter Nine
The Million Dollar Wound

1. N. Wilson, Incline Our Hearts, (New York: Viking, 1989), p. 20.

2. Anonymous, "Kiangan Operation", *Unit History—63rd Infantry Regiment*, File 306 Inf (63) 0.3, (Washington, D.C.: National Archives), p. 35.

3. Lee Kennett, *GI: The American Soldier in World War II*, (New York: Warner Books, 1989), pp. 176–7.

4. Raphael Steinberg, *Return to the Philippines*, (Alexandria, VA: Time-Life Books, 1980), p. 190.

5. Form 52 C, Medical Dept., U.S. Army as filled out by 6th Med Bn, Coll. Co. C.

6. Anonymous, *Unit History—6th Medical Battalion*, File 306 Med 0.7, (Washington, D.C.: National Archives), p. 33.

7. The 55th Portable Surgical Hospital was attached to the 63rd Infantry Regiment on the 13th of June and the 6th Medical Battalion Unit History says that they were set up south of Bagabag adjoining their headquarters. *Unit History—6th Medical Battalion*, File 306 Med 0.7, p. 32. However, they don't appear on any of my medical records.

8. CBS Television Network, *M*A*S*H*, 1972–1983. This popular program, combining medicine and war, gave its viewers some realistic insights into the treatment of the wounded in the Korean Conflict.

9. Kiangan Operation, p. 35.

10. Kennett, pp. 175–176.

11. Robert Ross Smith, *Triumph in the Philippines*, (Washington, D.C.: Government Printing office, 1963), pp. 235–236.

12. Tom A.E. Atchley to Russ McLogan, August 18, 1991.

13. Sergeant William Fuller is among those listed as wounded in action on 21 June 1945, on the regimental Casualty Report for Month of June. Other veterans have told me that they visited him in the hospital in Manila and that the medics were unable to save his leg.

14. Videotape of veterans of Company K, 63rd Infantry Regiment at the 6th Infantry Division Association Reunion, Peoria, Illinois, August 6, 1988.

15. Mexico, *1946 Britannica Book of the Year*, (Chicago: Encyclopedia Britannica, 1946), p. 477. Also, James P. Gallagher, "El Jarro Mejicano", *Air Classics*, April 1977, pp. 44–48. Pilots who spoke to them at Lingayan said that their English wasn't very good and that errors of understanding, especially over a static-filled radio transmission, were readily understandable. They also were of the opinion that the Mexicans weren't very good pilots and shouldn't have been given brand-new airplanes to fly.

16. Anthony J. Kupferer, *The Story of the 58th Fighter Group of World War II*, (Dallas: Taylor Publishing Co., 1989), p. 258.

17. Kupferer, p. 262.

18. William G. Tudor to Russ McLogan, June 6, 1996.

19. Tom A.E. Atchley to Russ McLogan, August 18, 1991.

20. Arndt L. Mueller, Colonel U.S.A. (Ret.) to J.H. Childs of Brownwood, Texas, no date. First Lieutenant Childs had been commander of the M-Company mortar platoon until he was severely wounded during the battle for Hill 400 on 24 Feb. 1945.

21. 6th Division Public Relations Section, *The 6th Infantry Division in World War II: 1939-1945*, (Nashville: The Battery Press, 1947).

22. Casualty Report For Month of June (1945), *Unit History—63rd Infantry Regiment*, File 306 Inf (63). Apparently four soldiers suffered from injuries other than bullet wounds that were caused by the air attack.

23. Captain Ralph M. Finnerty, the 3rd Battalion S-3 officer.

24. I have been unable to identify anyone by this name in the Regimental rosters.

25. The 6th Medical Battalion Unit History says that starting around June 19, the Clearing Platoons "were swamped by malaria cases from the Philippine Army troops attached to the Division. For a four day period, 25 to 50 per day were evacuated." The epidemic was attributed to the Filipinos not taking their atabrine tablets. Malaria was relatively rare among American troops who did take the preventive medicine.

26. Anonymous, *Quarterly Report of 91st Field Hospital*, 8 July 1945, SWPA Box 593, (Washington, D.C.: National Archives), p. 1.

27. Catherine Bell Palmer, "Flying Our Wounded Veterans Home", *The National Geographic Magazine*, Sept. 1945, p. 379.

28. Palmer, p. 372.

Chapter Ten
Life In Army Hospitals

1. Jay Cocks, "Throwing In the Crying Towel," *Time*, 1 May 1989, p. 64.

2. Robert Ross Smith, *Triumph in the Philippines*, (Washington, D.C.: Government Printing Office, 1963), p. 160–164.

3. Annual Report of 7th Evacuation Hospital for the year 1944, National Archives File HD319.1-2.

4. Quarterly Report of 7th Evacuation Hospital, 31 March 1945. National Archives File HD319.1-2.

5. James Jones, *WWII–A Chronicle of Soldiering*, (New York: Ballantine Books, 1975), p. 6.

6. The material on the Aparri operation is based on Robert Ross Smith, *Triumph in the Philippines*, p. 569–71.

7. Smith, p. 562n.

8. Smith, pp. 565–6.

9. Smith, p. 571.

10. Smith, p. 569.

11. The material on the Corregidor campaign is based on Robert Ross Smith, *Triumph in the Philippines*, pp. 338–45.

12. James H. and William M. Belote, *Corregidor*, (New York: Jove Books, 1984), 256.

13. Anonymous, *Historical Record of the 133rd General Hospital*, File MDGH–133–0.1, National Archives, Washington, D.C.

14. Quarterly Report, Jan.–Mar., 1945, 133rd Gen. Hosp. File MDGH–0.1.

15. Quarterly Report, July–Sept., 1945, 133rd Gen. Hosp. File MDGH–0.1.

16. There seems to be some confusion in the number of battle casualties treated. The 283 figure is from the Quarterly Report For History of Medical Activities, p. 3. There is also a quarterly report of the Activities of the Surgical Services which says that 1,009 cases of war injuries were disposed of during this same period. Of these, 385 were fractures, 59 were burns and 565

were wounds other than fractures and burns. See: 133rd General Hospital, Quarterly Report of the Activities of the Surgical Services, 30 Sept. 1945, p. 1. File MDGH–0.1.

17. Ann Landers, *Hillsdale [Mich.] Daily News*, 11 March 1989, p. 6a.

18. Lionel Hampton, *Steppin' Out, 1942–1945*, MCA 1315.

19. Smith, p. 577.

20. R. L. Lapica, editor, *Facts on File Yearbook–1945*, (New York: Persons Index, 1946).

21. Glenn Miller, "I've Got a Gal In Kalamazoo", RCA CPS20693.

22. Catherine Bell Palmer, "Flying Our Wounded Veterans Home", *The National Geographic Magazine*, Sept. 1945, p. 366.

23. George Sharpe, M.D., *Brothers Beyond Blood*, (Austin, Texas: Diamond Books, 1989), p. 226. He sent most of them back to the hospital.

24. Ronald H. Spector, *Eagle Against the Sun*, (New York: MacMillan, 1985), p. 543.

25. Spector, p. 543.

26. Paul Fussell, *Thank God for the Atom Bomb and Other Essays*, (New York: Ballantine Books, 1988), p. 14.

Chapter Eleven
I Too, Thank God for the Atom Bomb!

1. Paul Fussell, *Thank God for the Atom Bomb and Other Essays*, (New York: Ballantine Books, 1988), p. 18.

2. "The Presidency—Week of Decision", *Time*, 27 Aug. 1945, p. 19.

3. "Life in these United States", *Readers' Digest*, Nov. 1945, p. 64.

4. Medical Monthly Summary Report, 4 January 1945, lst Convalescent Hospital, National Archives, File MDCH-1-0.9: 1.

5. Quarterly Report for History of Medical Activities for Period Ending 30 September 1945, lst Convalescent Hospital, National Archives, File MDCH-1-0.9: 1.

6. Quarterly Report, p. 4.

7. Harold Arlen and Johnny Mercer, "Ac-cen-tchu-ate the Positive," Decca Records, 1944.

8. For a thorough report on this historic meeting see: Charles L. Mee, Jr., *Meeting at Pottsdam (New York: Dell Publishing*, 1975).

9. R.L. Lapica, editor, assisted by Barbara Brilliant, *Facts on File Yearbook 1945*, (New York: Person's Index, 1946), pp. 243–253. This source was the most used for what happened during that fateful nine days.

10. Lapica, p. 254.

11. Fussell, p. 5.

12. For a graphic description of this atrocity see: William Craig, *The Fall of Japan*, (New York: Dell Publishing, 1967), pp. 123–125.

13. Fussell, p. 5–6.

14. Stephen Harper, *Miracle of Deliverance*, (Briarcliff Manor, N.Y.: Stein and Day, 1985), pp. 61–108.

15. Laurence Cortesi, *The Battle for Manila*, (New York: Kensington, 1984), p. 278.

16. The material in the Historical Addendum is from Lee Enderlin, "Greatest of All Invasions" *Military History Magazine*, Nov., 1988, pp. 13–17, and John Ray Skates, *The Invasion of Japan: Alternative to the Bomb*, (Columbia, S.C.: University of South Carolina Press, 1994).

17. Ronald H. Spector, *Eagle Against the Sun*, (New York: MacMillan, 1985), p. 543.

Chapter Twelve
The Japanese Surrender

1. Jacques Barzun & Henry F. Graff, *The Modern Researcher: Fourth Edition*, (New York: Harcourt Brace Jovanovich, 1985), p. 267.

2. On September 17th, MacArthur declared that all draftees in the Japanese Theater would be released within six months and the occupation would be entrusted to 200,000 regulars. See "M'Arthur Sees Cut of Force to 200,000 Within Six Months," *New York Times*, 18 Sept. 1945, p. 1. This was followed quickly with a denial by State Department spokesman, Dean Acheson, who said that MacArthur had issued his occupation estimate without consultation with Washington and that American policy is fixed by a committee of top War-State-Navy officials. See "Acheson Sets Path", *New York Times*, 20 Sept. 1945, p. 1.

3. "Yamashita Yields in Philippines; Wainwright Takes the Surrender," *New York Times*, 3 Sept. 1945, p. 1.

4. "Foe Near Manila Yields," *New York Times*, 11 Sept. 1945: p. 3.

5. Robert C. McGiffert, "Surrender on Cebu," *American Legion Magazine*, Sept. 1981, p. 18.

6. "Holiday Traffic Near 1941 Level; 'Gas' is Plentiful," *New York Times*, 2 Sept. 1945, p. 1.

7. "American Forces Slated to occupy More Japanese Cities," *New York Times*, 11 Sept. 1945, p. 2.

8. "Army Will Be Cut to 2,500,000 By July, House Group is Told," *New York Times*, 29 Aug. 1945, p. 1.

9. "Operations at Kiangan, 1 July–21 Aug. 1945," *Unit History—63rd Infantry Regiment*, File 306 Inf (63) 0.3 (Washington, D.C.: National Archives), p. 16.

10. Gino Galuppini, *Warships of the World*, (New York: Random House, 1983), p. 113.

11. Frank L. Kluckhorn, "Yanks to Land in Korea," *New York Times*, 27 Aug. 1945, p. 2.

12. "Koreans March in Protest Against Keeping Japanese," *New York Times*, 11 Sept. 1945, p. 1.

13. Ron Goulart, editor, *The Encyclopedia of American Comics*, (New York: Promised Land Productions, 1990), p. 367.

14. Even modern travel guides have their doubts about this train, which is still running. After describing how to take a bus from Manila to San Fernando, La Union, Jens Peters notes: "You can also travel to San Fernando by train which takes a little longer than the bus. [And there is some risk.] 'God knows how it stays on the tracks' reported one traveler." See Jens Peters, *The Philippines: A Travel Survival Kit*, (Victoria, Australia: Lonely Planet Pub., 1981), p. 121.

15. Hal Bock, "Remember '45 World Series," *Hillsdale [Mich.] Daily News*, 20 Sept. 1984, p. 12.

Chapter Thirteen
Occupying the Hermit Kingdom

1. As quoted in *Time*, 1 May 1989, p. 50.

2. James E. Miller, "Typhoon", *World Book Encyclopedia*, 1977, vol. 18, p. 444.

3. The first wound, a bullet in the chest, was received at the battle of Balls Bluff, Virginia; the second, a bullet through the neck, was at Antietam; and the third was shrapnel in the foot at the battle of Chancellorsville. See Catherine Drinker Bowen, *Yankee From Olympus*, (Boston: Little, Brown, 1944), pp. 154–8, 167–179, 184–9.

4. Graham Blackburn, *The Illustrated Encyclopedia of Ships, Boats, Vessels and Other Water-Borne Craft*, (Woodstock, N.Y.: Overlook Press, 1978), p. 183.

5. Willard Price, "Jap Rule in the Hermit Nation", *The National Geographic*, Oct. 1945, p. 441.

6. Price, p. 448.

7. "Korea: Kim Koo and Kim Kun," *Time*, 10 Sept. 1945, p. 42.

8   8. "Black List Operation Field order No. 1", *Unit History—63rd Infantry Regiment*, File 306 Inf (63) 3.9,, (Washington, D.C.: National Archives).

9. "Casualty Report for Month of July", *Unit History—63rd Infantry Regiment*, File 306 Inf (63) 3.9, (Washington, D.C.: National Archives), p. 1.

10. In a letter to me dated August 18, 1991, Lieutenant Tom Atchley says that ". . . [Horne] was a good one, always there when we needed him. Somewhere along the way, he was wounded, he and several others . . . Melvin picked up something off the ground that the Japs had left laying. There were several [others] looking at the object. Melvin then pitched it back on the ground, and when it hit, it exploded. I was almost hit, too. I had just turned and walked off a few steps." He didn't think that any of them were seriously hurt.

11. Price, p. 450.

12. This bestseller of the forties was a novel about the garment that

Roman soldiers cast lots for at the crucifixion of Jesus. See: Lloyd C. Douglas, *The Robe*, (Boston: Houghton Mifflin, 1942).

13. Information on Colonel Yon's post-Army career was based on information furnished by the University of Florida Alumni Office.

14. "Blast In Korea Kills 2", *New York Times*, Dec. 1, 1945, p. 3. A thorough search of November and December issues turned up no stories about a first explosion of November 9 or any follow up stories on the November 30 blast. I remember only one blast.

15. He is identified as Second Lieutenant Thomas F. Connors of Yonkers, New York. He may have been the Lieutenant who led the groups out to sea on the dumping expedition that I was with on Thanksgiving day. Both he and Captain Hillenmeyer were awarded the Soldier's Medal (posthumously) for heroism combatting the grass fire that led to the explosion. See General Order 10 (12 March 1946) Headquarters 6th Infantry Division. Section I–Award of Soldier's Medal–Posthumously. Four enlisted men were also listed as receiving the medal.

16. Arndt L. Mueller, Colonel U.S.A. (Ret.) to Russ McLogan, May 3, 1991.

17. History of the Regt. (21 Aug. 45–31 Dec 45), *Unit History—63rd Infantry Regiment*, File 306 Inf (63) 0.1 (Washington, D.C.: National Archives), p. 1.

18. History of the Regiment (21 Aug. 45 -31 Dec 45), p. 2.

Chapter Fourteen
Bring the Boys Home!

1. David Aikman, "Russia's Prophet In Exile", *Time*, 24 July 1989, p. 58.

2. Ray Hoopes, "A Year in History", *American History Illustrated*, June, 1985, p. 19.

3. "Koreans Protest Two-Zone Control", *New York Times*, 21 Sept. 1945, p. 4.

4. Ainslie T. Embree, editor in chief, *Encyclopedia of Asian History*, Vol. II, (New York: Charles Scribner's Sons, 1988), pp. 313–14.

5. "Rebel Chief Maps Return to Korea", *New York Times*, 20 Oct. 1945, p. 6.

6. Embree, Vol. III, pp. 339–40.

7. Richard J. H. Johnston, "Rhee Calls Korea to Resist Division", *New York Times*, 21 Oct. 1945, p. 30.

8. Richard J. H. Johnston, "Koreans Demand to be Free Now", *New York Times*, 3 Nov. 1945, p. 3.

9. "U.S. and Soviet Eye Problem in Korea", *New York Times*, 17 Nov. 1945, p. 2.

10. Richard J. H. Johnston, "Hope For Freedom Brings Korean Calm", *New York Times*, 2 Jan. 1946, p. 2.

11. Lee Kennett, *GI: The American Soldier in World War II*, (New York: Charles Scribner's Sons, 1987), p. 223.

12. "Crude Ships used to Haul Japanese", *New York Times*, 27 Dec. 1945: p. 2.

13. Kennett, p. 224.

14. Hedda Garza, "Bring the Boys Home!", *American History Illustrated*, June, 1985, p. 37.

15. Garza, p. 38.

16. "Psychiatry Urged on Troops Abroad", *New York Times*, 13 Jan. 1946, p. 16.

17. "Wives of Soldiers Query Eisenhower", *New York Times*, 23 Jan. 1946, p. 1.

18. "Physical Standards Lowered For Army", *New York Times*, 15 Feb. 1946, p. 11.

19. "Truman Says Need of Troops Overseas Slows Discharges", *New York Times*, 9 Jan. 1946, p. 1.

20. Garza, p. 41.

21. "Patterson Visits Korea", *New York Times*, 13 January 1946, p. 18.

22. "Army Law to Rule in Yamashita's Case", *New York Times*, 7 Oct. 1945, p. 29, The sources that I used for the Yamashita trial narrative were the almost-daily dispatches in the *New York Times* and several stories in *Time* magazine.

23. "Yamashita's Appeal is Denied, 6–2", *New York Times*, 5 Feb. 1946, p. 12.

24. "The General and Rosalinda", *Time*, 19 Nov. 1945, p. 22.

25. "Yamashita Takes Stand in Defense", *New York Times*, 28 Nov. 1945, p. 5.

26. "Attention!", *Time*, 17 Dec. 1945, p. 18.

27. "Yamashita Appeal, Denied", *New York Times*, 5 Feb. 1945, p. 12.

28. "Supreme Court: A Word for Yamashita", *Time*, 11 Feb. 1946, p. 21.

29. Yamashita Appeal Denied", *New York Times*, 5 Feb. 1945, p. 12.

30. "Yamashita Hanged for War Crimes", *New York Times*, 23 Feb. 1946, p. 4.

31. Willard Price, "Jap Rule in the Hermit Nation", *The National Geographic*, Oct. 1945, pp. 437, 444.

32. David McCullough, *Truman*, (New York: Simon & Schuster, 1992), p. 486–490.

33. "Korea: Complete Miss", *Time*, 18 Mar. 1946, p. 30.

34. *The Two Mrs. Carrolls*, Warner Brothers, 1945. This odd movie was made in 1945 but was not commercially released to the public until 1947. In the meantime, it was tried out in a few limited places like Army posts in Korea. The *New York Times* review of April 7, 1947 said it was: ". . . an incredible monstrosity, as wretched a stew of picture making as has been dished out in many a moon."

Chapter Fifteen
Long Journey Home

1. John Skow, "Memory, Too, Is An Actor", *Time*, 19 April 1993, p. 62–3. He is talking about his 1989 memoir, *This Boy's Life*. The book was critically well-received and subsequently made into a movie of the same name starring Robert De Niro and Ellen Barkin.

2. Roland W. Charles, *Troopships of World War II*, (Washington, D.C.: The Army Transportation Association, 1947), p. 272.

3. The "Pony Editions" that we received overseas were only five cents per copy and often free.

4. "Sport: The Way of a Champ", *Time*, 2 Sept. 1946, p. 57.

5. "The Presidency: Back to Work", *Time*, 9 Sept. 1946, pp. 21–22.

6. "Foreign Relations: Hard Words", *Time*, 2 Sept. 1946, p. 15.

7. "Foreign Relations: 'We Will Go Anywhere . . .'" , *Time*, 9 Sept. 1946, p. 21.

8. "Japan: Strategic Springboard", *Time*, 2 Sept. 1946, p. 27.

9. "Vietnam: Who is Ho?", *Time*, 9 Sept. 1946, p. 34.

10. "Army & Navy: Citizens Only", *Time*, 2 Sept. 1946, p. 27.

11. "Prices: Wild Week", *Time*, 2 Sept. 1946, p. 77.

12. "Food: Spuds, Spuds, Spuds", *Time*, 2 Sept. 1946, p. 77.

13. "Radio: Early Bird", *Time*, 2 Sept. 1946, p. 87.

14. "Music: The Swing From Swing", *Time*, 9 Sept. 1946, p. 94.

15. "Cinema: The New Pictures", *Time*, 9 Sept. 1946, p. 100.

16. "Books: From Tedium to Apathy", *Time*, 2 Sept. 1946, p. 100.

Chapter Sixteen
You Know You're Home When. . .

1. A.N. Wilson, *Incline Our Hearts*, (New York: Viking, 1989), p. 228. Wilson's hero, a callow 20-year-old returning Army veteran, meets a prostitute on his journey home and ends up in a hotel with her. Only in fiction, not in real life.

2. "Camp Legion Was Garden Project Site", *The Craftsman*, October, 1946, p. 5.

3. Robert Lacey, *Ford: The Men and the Machine*, (Boston: Little Brown & Co., 1986), pp. 441–449.

4. A business coupe was a two-door that had only a front seat and an unusually large trunk. They were sold mostly to salesmen who needed a lot of trunk space for their samples and catalogs. It was not a very practical car to go double-dating in.

References & Bibliography

Official Records

Annual Report of the 7th Evacuation Hospital for the Year 1944. Washington: National Archives, File HD319.1-2.

"Black List operation Field order No. 1." *Unit History—63rd Infantry Regiment.* Washington: National Archives, File 306

4th & 5th Replacement Depot Military History. Washington: National Archives, File 98-USF1-RPC-0.2.

General Order 10 (12 March 1946) Headquarters 6th Infantry Division. Section I Award of Soldier's Medal to Captain Henry R. Hillenmeyer (from the files of his son, Henry R. Hillenmeyer Jr.).

General Order 37 (28 March 1945) Headquarters 6th Infantry Division, Section I Award of Bronze Star Medal to Technical Sergeant Tom A.E. Atchley (from his personal files).

General Order 120 (26 June 1945) Headquarters 6th Infantry Division, Section II Award of Silver Star Medal to Lieutenant Tom A.E. Atchley (from his personal files).

Historical Record of the 1st Convalescent Hospital. Washington: National Archives, File MDCH-1-0.9.

Historical Record of the 133rd General Hospital. Washington: National Archives, File MDGH—0.1.

"History of the Regiment 21 Aug 45–Dec 45." *Unit History—63rd Infantry Regiment.* Washington: National Archives, File 306 Inf (63) 0.1.

III Corps and Fort Hood, Home of the Mobile Armored Corps, Facts as of 30 Sep 1991. A publication of the Fort Hood, Texas Public Affairs Office, 1991.

"Operations at Kiangan, Mountain Province, Luzon, P.I., 1 July–21 August 1945." *Unit History—63rd Infantry Regiment*, Washington: National Archives, File 306 Inf(63) 0.3.

"Operations on Luzon, P.I. for Period 9 January–30 June 1945." *Unit History—63rd Infantry Regiment*, Washington: National Archives, File 306 Inf (63) 0.3.

Quarterly Report of 91st Field Hospital, 8 July 1945, Washington: National Archives, SWPA Box 593.

"S-2 Periodic Reports." *Unit History—63rd Infantry Regiment*, Washington: National Archives, File 306 Inf (63) 0.3.

6th Medical Battalion Unit History. Washington: National Archives, File 306 Med 0.7.

21st Replacement Depot Unit History. File REDE-21-0.2 Box 22959, National Archives, Washington, D.C.

Letters and Personal Papers

Letter, Tom A.E. Atchley to Russell E. McLogan August 18, 1991.

Letter, Arndt L. Mueller to J.H. Childs, no date.

Letter, Arndt L. Mueller to Russell E. McLogan, May 3, 1991.

Letter, Arndt L. Mueller to Russell E. McLogan, July 15, 1993.

Letter, William G. Tudor to Russell E. McLogan, June 6, 1996.

Mueller, Arndt L. *A, B & X: An Agonizing Enigma.* Naples, Fla.: Unpublished monograph, 1992.

Mueller, Arndt L. *Objective: New York, New York.* Naples, Fla.: Unpublished Monograph, 1994.

Munschauer, John. *War and Remembrance.* Ithaca, N.Y.: Unpublished monograph, 1991.

Magazines and Newspaper Articles

"Acheson Sets Path." *New York Times*, 20 Sept. 1945, p. 1.

Aikman, David. "Russia's Prophet in Exile." *Time*, 24 July 1989, p. 58.

"American Forces Slated to Occupy More Japanese Cities." *New York Times*, 11 Sept. 1945, p. 1.

"Army & Navy: Citizens Only?" *Time*, 2 Sep. 1946, p. 27.

"Army Law to Rule in Yamashita's Case." *New York Times*, 7 Oct. 1945, p. 29.

"Army Will Be Cut to 2,500,000 By July, House Group is Told." *New York Times*, 29 Aug. 1945, p. 1.

"Attention." *Time*, 17 Dec. 1945, p. 18.

"Balloon Bombs." *Time*, 11 Jun. 1945, p. 56. Inf (63) 3.9.

"Blast in Korea Kills 2." *New York Times*, 1 Dec. 1945, p. 3.

Bock, Hal. "Remember '45 World Series." *Hillsdale [Mich.] Daily News*, 20 Sept. 1984, p. 8.

"Books: From Tedium to Apathy." *Time*, 2 Sep. 1946, p. 100.

Braun-Hass, Linda. "Bridges to the Past." *Jackson [Mich.] Citizen Patriot*, 20 Nov. 1991, p. 4.

"Brrr! What Global Warming?" *Time*, 20 July 1992, p. 19.

"Buy a Bomber Campaign Successful." *The Craftsman* (Monthly publication of the Henry Ford Trade School). Dearborn, Mich., Jan. 1945, p. 3.

"Camp Legion Was Garden Project Site." *The Craftsman*. Dearborn, Mich., Oct. 1946, p. 5.

"Cinema: The New Pictures." *Time*, 9 Sep. 1946, p. 100.

"City's Leading Airman is U.D. Grad." *Varsity News* (publication of the University of Detroit). 21 March 1945, p. 1.

Cocks, Jay. "Throwing In the Crying Towel." *Time*, 1 May 1989, p. 64.

References

"Crude Ships Used to Haul Japanese." *New York Times*, 27 Dec. 1945, p. 2.

Enderlin, Lee. "Greatest of All Invasions." *Military History Magazine*, Nov. 1988, p. 13.

"Foe Near Manila Yields." *New York Times*, 11 Sept. 1945, p. 1.

"Food: Spuds, Spuds, Spuds." *Time*, 2 Sep. 1946, p. 15.

Foreign Relations: "Hard Words." *Time*, 2 Sep. 1946, p. 15.

Foreign Relations: "We Will Go Anywhere." *Time*, 9 Sep. 1946 p. 21.

Gallagher, James P. "El Jarro Mejicano." *Air Classics*, April 1977, p. 44.

Garza, Hedda. "Bring the Boys Home!" *American History Illustrated*, June 1985, p. 37.

"Half War, Half Peace." *Time*, 4 Jun. 1945, p. 19.

"Hero of Hen Hill." *Time*, 25 Jun. 1945, p. 31.

Hodge, John R., "With the U.S. Army in Korea," *The National Geographic Magazine*, June 1947, p. 830.

"Holiday Traffic Near 1941 Level; 'Gas' is Plentiful," *New York Times*, 2 Sept. 1945, p. 1.

Hoopes, Ray. "A Year in History." *American History Illustrated*. June 1985, p. 19.

"Japan: Strategic Springboard." *Time*, 2 Sep. 1946 p. 27.

Johnston, Richard J.H. "Hope For Freedom Brings Korean Calm." *New York Times*, 2 Jan. 1946, p. 2.

Johnston, Richard J.H. "Koreans Demand to be Free Now." *New York Times*, 3 Nov. 1945, p. 3.

Johnston, Richard J.H. "Rhee Calls Korea to Resist Division." *New York Times*, 21 Oct. 1945, p. 30.

"Joy and Hate." *Time*, 23 Nov. 1942, p. 21.

Kluckhorn, Frank L. "Yanks to Land in Korea." *New York Times*, 27 Aug. 1945, p. 2.

"Korea: Complete Miss." *Time*, 18 Mar. 1946, p. 30.

"Korea: Kim Koo & Kim Kun." *Time*, 10 Sept. 1945, p. 42.

"Koreans March in Protest Against Keeping Japanese." *New York Times*, 11 Sept. 1945, p. 2.

"Koreans Protest Two-Zone Control." *New York Times*, 21 Sept. 1945, p. 4.

Landers, Ann. *Hillsdale [Mich.] Daily News*, 11 Mar. 1989, p. 6A.

"Life in these United States." *Readers' Digest*, Nov. 1945, p. 64.

"MacArthur's Legend." *Time*, 2 Mar. 1942, p. 23.

"M'Arthur Sees Cut of Force to 200,000 Within Six Months." *New York Times*, 20 Sept. 1945, p. 1.

McGiffert, Robert C. "Surrender on Cebu." *The American Legion Magazine*, Sept. 1981, p. 18.

McLeod, John. "The Heavyweight." *Yank, the Army Weekly*, 21 Sept. 1945, p. 4.

Morrow, Lance. "Folklore in a Box." *Time*, 21 Sept. 1991, p. 50.

"Music: The Swing from Swing." *Time*, 9 Sep. 1946, p. 94.

Nimitz, Chester. "Your Navy As Peace Insurance." *The National Geographic Magazine*, June 1946, p. 708.

Ostling, Richard N. "The Moral Debate: A Just Conflict, or Just a Conflict?" *Time*, 11 Feb. 1991, p. 42.

Palmer, Catherine Bell, "Flying Our Wounded Veterans Home." *The National Geographic Magazine*, Sept. 1945, pp. 363–84.

"Patterson Visits Korea." *New York Times*, 13 Jan.1946, p. 18.

"Physical Standards Lowered For Army." *New York Times*, 15 Feb 1946, p. 1.

"Picnickers Beware." *Time*, 4 Jun. 1945, p. 22.

Pino, Gabriel. "3rd Bn Gets Pres. Citation." *The Sightseer*, (a publication of the 6th Infantry Division). 22 July 1946, p. 2.

"Plans for Punishment." *Time*, 25 Jun. 1945, p. 31.

Pollack, Susan R. "Seasickness Can't Be Waved Away." *The Detroit News*, 10 Sep. 1989, p. Jl.

"Prices: Wild Week." *Time*, 2 Sep. 1946, p. 77.

Price, Willard. "Jap Rule in the Hermit Nation." *The National Geographic Magazine*. Oct. 1945, p. 429.

"Psychiatry Urged on Troops Abroad." *New York Times*, 13 Jan 1945, p. 16.

"Radio: Early Bird." *Time*, 2 Sep. 1946, p. 87.

"Rebel Chief Maps Return to Korea." *New York Times*, 20 Oct. 1945, p. 6.

"Rhee Calls Korea to Resist Division." *New York Times* 21 Oct. 1945, p. 30.

"Screen Comedian Who Turned Serious." *New York Times*, 23 Dec. 1945, p. 15.

"Shootin' Texan." *Time*, 11 Jun. 1945, p. 33.

Skow, John. "Memory, Too, is an Actor." *Time*, 19 Apr. 1993, p. 62.

"Sport: The Way of a Champ." *Time*, 2 Sep. 1946, p. 57.

"Supreme Court: A Word for Yamashita." *New York Times*, 11 Feb. 1946, p. 21.

"The General and Rosalinda." *Time*, 19 Nov. 1945, p. 22.

"The Case for War." *Time*, 9 Mar. 1970, p. 46.

"The People Agree." *Time*, 4 Jun. 1945, p. 23.

"The Presidency: Back to Work." *Time*, 9 Sep. 1946, p. 21.

"The Presidency: Week of Decision." *Time*, 27 Aug. 1945, p. 19.

"The 32nd." *Time*, 23 Apr. 1945, p. 22.

"The Vortex." *Time*, 28 May 1945, p. 26.

"Truman Says Need of Troops Overseas Slows Discharges." *New York Times*, 9 Jan. 1946, p. 1.

"Twilight in Tokyo." *Time*, 11 June. 1945, p. 29.

"Two Steaks for the General." *Time*, 4 June. 1945, p. 46.

Underwood, Bill. "Freeing Camp Santo Tomas." *The American Legion Magazine*, March 1995, p. 36.

"U.S. and Soviet Eye Problem in Korea." *New York Times*, 17 Nov. 1945, p. 2.

"Vietnam: Who is Ho?" *Time*, 9 Sep. 1946, p. 34.

"Wives of Soldiers Query Eisenhower." *New York Times*, 23 Jan. 1946 p. 1.

"Yamashita Hanged for War Crimes." *New York Times*, 23 Feb. 1946, p. 4.

References

"Yamashita's Appeal is Denied, 6–2." *New York Times*, 5 Feb. 1946, p. 1.

"Yamashita Takes Stand in Defense." *New York Times*, 28 Nov. 1945, p. 5.

"Yamashita Yields in Philippines; Wainwright Takes the Surrender." *New York Times*, 3 Sept. 1945, p. 1.

Books and Pamphlets

Barzun, Jacques and Henry F. Graff. *The Modern Researcher: Fourth Edition*, New York: Harcourt Brace Jovanovich, 1985.

Belote, James H. and William M. *Corregidor*. New York: Harper & Row, 1967.

Blackburn, Graham. *The Illustrated Encyclopedia of Ships, Boats, Vessels and Other Water-Borne Craft*. Woodstock, N.Y.: Overlook Press, 1978.

Bowen, Catherine Drinker. *Yankee From Olympus*. Boston: Little Brown & Co., 1944.

Breuer, William B. *Retaking the Philippines*. New York: St. Martin's Press, 1986.

Charles, Roland W. *Troopships of World War II*. Washington: The Army Transportation Association, 1947.

Cortesi, Lawrence. *The Battle for Manila*. New York: Kensington Publishing Co., 1984.

Costello, John. *The Pacific War*. New York: Rawson, Wade, 1981.

Craig, William. *The Fall of Japan*. New York: Dell Publishing, 1967.

de la Costa, S.J., H. *Readings in Philippine History*. Manila: The Bookmark, Inc., 1965.

Douglas, LLoyd C. *The Robe*. Boston: Houghton Mifflin, 1942. Embree, Ainslie T. editor. *Encyclopedia of Asian History*. New York: Charles Scribner's Sons, 1988.

Evans, Bergen. *Dictionary of Quotations*. New York: Delacorte, 1968.

Fahey, Joseph J. *Peace, War and the Christian Conscience.* New York: The Christophers, 1970.

Faulk, Odie B. and Laura E. *Fort Hood: The First Fifty Years*. Temple, Tex.: The Frank W. Mayborn Foundation, 1991.

Fowle, Herb. *The Men of the Terrible Green Cross*. Hillsdale, Mich.: Herb Fowle, 1991.

Fuld, James J. *The Book of World Famous Music*. New York: Crown Publishers, 1966.

Fussell, Paul. *Thank God for the Atom Bomb and Other Essays*. New York: Ballantine Books, 1988.

Galuppini, Gino. *Warships of the World*. New York: Random House, 1983.

Goralski, Robert. *World War II Almanac 1931–1945*. New York: G.P. Putnam's Sons, 1981.

Goulart, Ron, editor. *The Encyclopedia of American Comics*. New York: Promised Land Productions, 1990.

Guthrie, Chester L., "Mexico." *Britannica Book of the Year 1946*. Chicago: Encyclopedia Britannica, 1946.

Harper, Stephen. *Miracle of Deliverance*. Briarcliff Manor, N.Y.: Stein and Day, 1985.

Heefer, Wilson A., *Twentieth Century Warrior: The Life and Service of Major General Edwin D. Patrick.*, Shippensburg, Pa.: White Mane Publishing Co., 1995.

Jones, James. *WWII—A Chronicle of Soldiering*. New York: Ballantine Books, 1975.

Keagan, John. *The Second World War*. New York: MacMillan, 1985.

Kelley, Kitty. *His Way: The Unauthorized Biography of Frank Sinatra*. New York: Bantam Books, 1986.

Kennett, Lee. *G.I.: The American Soldier in World War II*. New York: Warner Books, 1989.

Kupferer, Anthony J., *No Glamour . . . No Glory! The Story of the 58th Fighter Group in World War II*. Dallas: Taylor Publishing Co., 1989

Lacey, Robert. *Ford: The Men and the Machines*. Boston: Little, Brown & Co., 1986.

Lapica, R.L., editor. *Facts on File Yearbook: 1945*. New York: Person's Index, 1946.

Loesser, Frank. *The Frank Loesser Songbook*. New York: Simon and Schuster, 1971.

Longbingier, Charles Sumner. "Manila." *Encyclopedia Britannica*. Chicago: Encyclopedia Britannica, Inc., 1947.

Magill, Frank. *Magill's Quotations in Context*. New York: Salem Press, 1965.

Mauldin, Bill. *Up Front*. New York: Henry Holt & Co., 1945.

Mauldin, Bill. *Back Home*. New York: William Sloan Associates, 1947.

McCullough, David. *Truman*. New York: Simon & Schuster, 1992.

Mee, Charles L. *Meeting at Potsdam*. New York: Dell Publishing, 1971.

Miller, James E. "Typhoon." *World Book Encyclopedia*. Chicago: Field Enterprises Educational Corp., 1977.

Munschauer, John. *World War II Cavalcade: An Offer I Couldn't Refuse*. Manhattan, Kansas: Sunflower University Press, 1996.

Peters, Jens. *The Philippines: A Travel Survival Kit*. Victoria, Australia: Lonely Planet Pub., 1981.

Roosevelt, James and Sydney Shalett. *Affectionately, F.D.R.: A Son's Story of a Lonely Man*. New York: Harcourt, Brace & Co., 1959.

Rothe, Anna and Helen Demaret. *Current Biography: Who's News and Why, 1945*. New York: H. W. Wilson Co., 1946.

Sackett, Susan. *The Hollywood Reporter Book of Box Office Hits*. New York: Billboard Books, 1990.

Skates, John Ray. *The Invasion of Japan: Alternative to the Bomb*. Columbia, S.C.: University of South Carolina Press, 1994.

Sharpe, M.D., George. *Brothers Beyond Blood*. Austin, Tex.: Diamond Books, 1989.

6th Infantry Division Public Relations Section. *The 6th Infantry Division in World War II, 1939–1945*. Nashville: The Battery Press, 1983.

References

Smith, Robert Ross. *Triumph in the Philippines*. Washington: Government Printing office, 1963.

Sorenson, Martha E. and Douglas A. Martz. *A View From the Tower: A History of Fort Sheridan, Illinois*. Highwood, Ill.: Tower Enterprises, 1985.

Spector, Ronald H. *Eagle Against the Sun*. New York: MacMillan, 1985.

Steinberg, Rafael, editor. *Return to the Philippines, World War II*. Alexandria, Va.: Time-Life Books, 1980.

Swiatek, Emil. "War." *Hi-Time* (Elm Grove, Wis.) Vol. 15, Issue 7, 12 Feb. 1971.

Terkel, Studs. *"The Good War": An Oral History of World War Two*. New York: Pantheon Books, 1984.

Tucker, Ray, "Roosevelt, Franklin Delano." *Britannica Book of the Year 1946*. Chicago: Encyclopedia Britannica, 1946.

van der Kroef, Justus M. "New Guinea." *World Book Encyclopedia*. Chicago: Field Enterprises, 1977.

Welcome to Fort Ord: Home of the World's Greatest Fighters. San Diego: Marcoa Publishing, Inc., 1987.

Willoughby, Charles A. and John Chamberlain. *MacArthur: 1941–1951*. New York: McGraw-Hill, 1954.

Wilson, A.N. *Incline Our Hearts*. New York: Viking, 1989.

"World War II." *Encyclopedia Britannica* Vol. 29. Chicago: Encyclopedia Britannica, 1991.

Young, Peter, editor. *Atlas of the Second World War*. New York: G.P. Putnam's Sons, 1974.

Miscellaneous

Videotape of veterans of Company K, 63rd Infantry Regiment, at the 6th Infantry Division Association Reunion, Peoria, Illinois, August 6, 1988.

Index

Index

Mueller, Colonel Arndt L., xvi, xviii,
120–22, 131, 133–36, 155–57, 167, 181,
192, 221–25, 301–02, 308–09, 345,
378–79, 380, 384, 389
Munschauer, John, 137, 379
Murashi (battleship), 81
Murphy, Frank, 74, 330, 375
Murphy, George, 376
Mussolini, Benito, 141
Mydans, Carl, 108

N
Nagasaki, 261–64
Nagle, Harry, xviii
Nail, Jim, 177
National Archives, xv-v, 90, 128, 138, 156,
181, 199, 238, 269, 376, 380–89,
National Geographic Magazine, iv, 59, 67,
228, 300, 334, 341, 386, 388
National Maritime Museum, 60
National Personnel Records Center, xv
National Velvet (movie), 54
NBC, 357
Negrito, 163, 171
Neilson Field, 233
New Guinea, ix, xiv, xvii, 8, 58, 60, 67–70,
89–90, 98, 115–17, 171, 177, 190, 272,
274, 339, 375
New Jersey (battleship), 83
New Year's Day, 40, 333
New York *Times*, 48, 277, 308, 317, 320,
326, 387, 389–90
Nimitz, Admiral Chester, 76–78, 83, 98, 265,
375
Ninth Air Force, 218
Nisei, 16, 21
Nishimura, Vice Admiral Shoji, 81
91st Field Hospital, 217, 226, 385
93rd Infantry Division, 119
96th Infantry Division, 87, 186
Notorious (movie), 357
Nuremburg, 315, 355

O
Oakland Army Base, 352–354
O'Brien, Jack, 67
O'Connor, S.J., Rev. Edward, 148
O'Neil, Steve, 287
Okinawa, 84, 141, 150, 185–87, 220–21, 246,
267, 283, 289, 296, 351, 382
Oldendorf, Admiral Jesse B., 82
Oliver, Private First Class Charles R., 189
Olivier, Laurence, 379
100th Japanese Division, 188

105th Japanese Division, 201
123rd Infantry Regiment, 233
129th Infantry Regiment, 160, 196
133rd General Hospital, 238–39, 241, 245,
252–53, 271–72, 385
145th Infantry Regiment, 144
149th Infantry Regiment, 160, 189
150mm mortar (Japanese), 134, 137, 152
173rd Infantry Replacement Training
Battalion, 21
187th Glider Infantry Regiment, 88
Operation Black List, 296–98, 388
Operation CORONET, 265–69
Operation DOWNFALL, 265–69
Operation Mike II, 106
Operation OLYMPIC, 265–66
Operation *Wa*, 87–88,
Operation Zipper, 264
Ord, Major General Edward Otho Cresap,
50
"Oscar", 379
Osmena, Sergio, 75, 98–99
Owen Stanley Mountains, 69
Oxnam, Bishop G. Bromley, 263
Ozawa, Vice Admiral Jisaburo, 81, 83

P
Pace, John, 19
Pacific Ocean, 49, 51, 65, 67, 289, 351–2
Pacific Theater of Operations, 8, 33, 54, 95,
117, 157, 162, 183, 187, 244, 247,
250–51, 323, 332, 364
Palawan massacre, 98
Palmer, Catherine Bell, 228, 385–86
Palmer,Jr., Colonel Bruce, 305
Pangasinan Regiment, 225
Papua, New Guinea
Paratrooper, 62, 70, 87–88, 227, 232–38, 274
Patrick, Major General Edwin, 117
Patrolling, 37, 148–49, 153–54, 157, 175–80,
203, 205, 285, 301
Patton, General George C., 10, 17, 79, 183,
200, 242, 382
Paul Hamilton (Troopship), 63
Payawan, Luzon, 98
Payday, 95–96, 149, 333
Peace, War and the Christian Conscience
(pamphlet), 383
Pearl Harbor, 2, 18, 73, 115, 126, 186, 260,
265, 274
Peckham, Linda, xviii
P-38 Lightning (airplane), xviii, 129, 143,
144, 223–24

Index

409

RUSSIA

MONGOLIA

MANCHURIA

SAKHALIN
ISLAND

KAMCHATKA
PEN.

KOREA

SEOUL
KUNSAN

JAPAN

TOKYO

CHINA

SHANGHAI

NAGASAKI

HIROSHIMA

OKINAWA

IWO JIMA

FORMOSA

BURMA

HONG
KONG

INDO-CHINA

SIAM

MANILA

PHILIPPINE
ISLANDS

LEYTE

MARIANAS
ISLANDS

TINIAN

SAIPAN

GUAM

SAIGON

MALAYA

PALAU ISLANDS

SINGAPORE

SUMATRA

BORNEO

HOLLANDIA

NEW GUINEA

SOLOMON
ISLANDS

FINSCHHAFEN

JAVA

PORT
MORESBY

GUADA-
CANAL

DARWIN

INDIAN OCEAN

CORAL SEA

NEW

AUSTRALIA

BRISBANE

SYDNEY